COPING WITH MINORITY STATUS

Responses to Exclusion and Inclusion

Society consists of numerous interconnected, interacting, and interdependent groups, which differ in power and status. The consequences of belonging to a more powerful, higher status "majority" versus a less powerful, lower status "minority" can be profound, and the tensions that arise between these groups are the root of society's most difficult problems. To understand the origins of these problems and develop solutions for them, it is necessary to understand the dynamics of majority–minority relations. This volume brings together leading scholars in the fields of stigma, prejudice and discrimination, minority influence, and intergroup relations to provide diverse theoretical and methodological perspectives on what it means to be a minority. The volume, which focuses on the strategies that minorities use in coping with majorities, is organized into three parts: "Coping with exclusion: Being excluded for who you are"; "Coping with exclusion: Being excluded for what you think and do"; and "Coping with inclusion."

Fabrizio Butera is Professor of Social Psychology at the University of Lausanne, Switzerland, as well as director of the Social Psychology Laboratory. His research interests focus on social influence processes, conflict, and social comparison. He currently is a member of the Executive Committee of the European Association of Social Psychology and recently served as Associate Editor of the *European Journal of Social Psychology*. Professor Butera has published extensively in leading journals in social psychology and has coedited several volumes, including *Toward a Clarification of the Effects of Achievement Goals* (with C. Darnon and J. Harackiewicz), *Learning at the University* (with R. Johnson, D. Johnson, and G. Mugny), and *Social Influence in Social Reality* (with G. Mugny).

John M. Levine is Professor of Psychology and Senior Scientist in the Learning Research and Development Center at the University of Pittsburgh. His research focuses on small group processes, including innovation in work teams, group reaction to deviance and disloyalty, majority and minority influence, and group socialization. He is a Fellow of the American Psychological Association and the American Psychological Society and served as Executive Committee Chair of the Society of Experimental Social Psychology and as Editor of the *Journal of Experimental Social Psychology*. Professor Levine has published papers on a wide range of small group phenomena ⌐⌐⌐⌐⌐⌐⌐⌐⌐⌐⌐ ⌐⌐⌐ *Teacher and Student Perceptions: Implications for Learning* (with M⌐⌐⌐⌐⌐⌐⌐⌐⌐⌐⌐⌐⌐⌐⌐⌐⌐⌐⌐⌐⌐⌐⌐⌐⌐⌐⌐⌐ *Cognition* (with L. Resnick and S. Teasley⌐⌐⌐⌐⌐⌐⌐⌐⌐⌐⌐⌐⌐⌐⌐⌐⌐⌐⌐⌐⌐⌐ *ations: The Management of Knowledge* (with

Coping with Minority Status

RESPONSES TO EXCLUSION AND INCLUSION

Edited by

Fabrizio Butera

University of Lausanne

John M. Levine

University of Pittsburgh

CAMBRIDGE
UNIVERSITY PRESS

CAMBRIDGE UNIVERSITY PRESS
Cambridge, New York, Melbourne, Madrid, Cape Town, Singapore, São Paulo, Delhi

Cambridge University Press
32 Avenue of the Americas, New York, NY 10013–2473, USA

www.cambridge.org
Information on this title: www.cambridge.org/9780521671156

First published 2009

Printed in the United States of America

A catalog record for this publication is available from the British Library.

Library of Congress Cataloging in Publication data
Coping with minority status : responses to exclusion and inclusion / edited by Fabrizio Butera,
John M. Levine.
p.   cm.
Includes bibliographical references and index.
ISBN 978-0-521-85499-3 (hardback) – ISBN 978-0-521-67115-6 (pbk.)
1. Marginality, Social–United States.   2. Prejudices–United States.   3. Minorities–United
States.   4. Discrimination.   I. Butera, Fabrizio, 1965–   II. Levine, John M.   III. Title.
HN90.S6.C67 2010
305.5′6–dc22   2009007772

ISBN 978-0-521-85499-3 hardback
ISBN 978-0-521-67115-6 paperback

CONTENTS

CONTRIBUTORS

JOSHUA ARONSON, New York University, USA

MANUELA BARRETO, Centro de Investigação e Intervenção Social, Portugal

KATHLEEN M. BLEE, University of Pittsburgh, USA

NYLA R. BRANSCOMBE, University of Kansas, USA

FABRIZIO BUTERA, Université de Lausanne, Switzerland

ADRIENNE R. CARTER-SOWELL, Purdue University, USA

ANNALISA CASINI, Université Libre de Bruxelles, Belgium

ARMAND CHATARD, Université de Genève, Switzerland

XIAOYAN CHEN, University of Maryland, USA

P. NIELS CHRISTENSEN, Radford University, USA

NAOMI ELLEMERS, Universiteit Leiden, The Netherlands

NICHOLAS EMLER, University of Surrey, UK

JUAN MANUEL FALOMIR-PICHASTOR, Université de Genève, Switzerland

SARAH J. GERVAIS, Pennsylvania State University, USA

MICHAEL INZLICHT, University of Toronto, Canada

JOLANDA JETTEN, University of Queensland, Australia/University of Exeter, UK

ARIE W. KRUGLANSKI, University of Maryland, USA

JOHN M. LEVINE, University of Pittsburgh, USA

RODOLFO MENDOZA-DENTON, University of California, Berkeley, USA

SERGE MOSCOVICI, Ecole des Hautes Etudes en Sciences Sociales, Paris, France

ANGELICA MUCCHI-FAINA, Università di Perugia, Italy

GABRIEL MUGNY, Université de Genève, Switzerland

NICHOLAS PEARSON, Pennsylvania State University, USA

JUAN A. PÉREZ, Universitat de València, Spain

RADMILA PRISLIN, San Diego State University, USA

ALAIN QUIAMZADE, Universités de Genève et Fribourg, Formation Universitaire à Distance, Switzerland

MARGARITA SANCHEZ-MAZAS, Université de Genève, Switzerland

FABIO SANI, Univerisity of Dundee, UK

CHARLES STANGOR, University of Maryland, USA

JANET K. SWIM, Pennsylvania State University, USA

JEAN-PIERRE VERNET, Instituto Superior de Ciências do Trabalho e da Empresa, Portugal

KIPLING D. WILLIAMS, Purdue University, USA

Introduction

FABRIZIO BUTERA AND JOHN M. LEVINE

Society consists of numerous interconnected, interacting, and interdependent groups. Of the many dimensions that differentiate these groups, perhaps the most important are power and status. The consequences of belonging to a larger, more powerful "majority" group versus a smaller, less powerful "minority" group can be profound, and the tensions that arise between these two kinds of groups are the root of society's most difficult problems. To understand the origins of these problems and to develop solutions for them, it is critical to understand the dynamics of majority–minority relations.

Social psychological research on intergroup relations has tended to assume (either explicitly or implicitly) that (a) majorities have more impact on minorities than vice versa, and (b) it is more important, for both theoretical and applied reasons, to understand the cognitive, affective, and behavioral responses of majorities than of minorities. In recent years, however, these two assumptions have been challenged, with the result that increasing

---

Many of the chapters in this volume are based on presentations given at an international conference entitled "Hoping and Coping: How Minorities Manage Their Social Environments" that was held in Grenoble, France, in 2003. The goal of the conference was to stimulate intellectual exchange among a diverse set of researchers with shared interests in how minorities cope with their social environments. The success of the conference motivated us to invite participants and other scholars to contribute to the current volume.

We wish to thank the following institutions for their support of the Grenoble conference: Université Pierre Mendès France, Université de Savoie, Conseil Général de l'Isère, Grenoble-Alpes Metropole, Ville de Grenoble, and the American Embassy in Paris. We also wish to thank the Région Rhône-Alpes for its contribution to the production costs of this volume. Finally, the Swiss National Science Foundation sponsored F. Butera's work during the preparation of the book.

attention is being devoted to how minorities influence majorities and how minorities respond to majorities' (often negative) reactions toward them. For example, research indicates that numerical minorities can exert influence when they adopt particular behavioral styles (e.g., Moscovici, Lage, & Naffrechoux, 1969) and that members of stigmatized minorities, such as African-Americans, perform worse on standardized intellectual tests when negative stereotypes of their group are made salient (e.g., Steele & Aronson, 1995).

Although research of this sort is quite valuable in enriching our understanding of majority–minority relations, it nevertheless fails to reflect the broad range of strategies that minorities can use to cope with their (typically) low power and status. For example, whereas minority-influence researchers have done numerous studies on how majority members react to variations in minority members' behavioral style, they have shown little if any interest in the factors that lead minority members to adopt one style versus another. In addition, whereas stigma researchers have devoted substantial attention to minority members' intrapersonal responses to perceived prejudice and discrimination (e.g., emotional reactions, cognitive coping strategies), they have been less interested in minority members' interpersonal and intergroup responses (e.g., assertiveness, collective action).

AIM OF THIS VOLUME

This volume focuses on how groups with low power and status respond to their social environments. Of course, low power and status are often associated with other group characteristics. These include small group size; limited access to resources; recent entry into society (i.e., immigrants); ethnic and religious distinctiveness; and a history of discrimination (see Seyranian, Atuel, & Crano, 2008). But these associations do not always occur. For example, in the case of women, low power and status are associated with large group size. For this reason, we will use the term "minority" to refer to low-status, low-power groups, irrespective of their numerical size. Finally, it is worth noting that the causal relationships between various group characteristics are often difficult to specify (e.g., small group size might lead to low status and power, or low status and power might stimulate member defection, thereby reducing group size).

For this volume, we assembled a set of leading scholars in the fields of stigma, prejudice and discrimination, minority influence, and intergroup relations, who provide diverse theoretical and methodological perspectives on what it means to be a minority. We believe that this diversity is a major strength of the book, because it underscores the complexity and richness of the phenomena under consideration. Notwithstanding their diversity, however, all of the authors address the core issue of the volume, namely how minorities cope with their social environments. In so doing, they clarify coping strategies at different levels of analysis – intrapersonal, interpersonal, and intergroup.

STRUCTURE AND CONTENT OF THE VOLUME

The volume is organized into three parts. The first two deal with how minorities cope with *exclusion* by majorities. This emphasis on exclusion is appropriate in light of the ubiquity of prejudice and discrimination toward minorities and the difficulties they create for minorities (see Levine & Kerr, 2007). Given the large amount of work on how minorities cope with exclusion and the various kinds of minorities that have been studied from this perspective, we divided the relevant chapters on the basis of the underlying reason for the exclusion. Part 1, "Coping with exclusion: Being excluded for who you are," examines how minorities defined by uncontrollable personal characteristics (e.g., race, gender, ethnicity) cope with exclusion. Membership in such minorities is involuntary, in the sense that members have no choice about their affiliation. Part 2, "Coping with exclusion: Being excluded for what you think and do," examines how minorities defined by controllable characteristics (e.g., beliefs, behaviors) cope with exclusion. Membership in such minorities is voluntary, in the sense that members have substantial choice about their affiliation. Finally, Part 3, "Coping with inclusion," examines an interesting, but relatively neglected, type of coping – namely coping with *inclusion* by majorities. Although it might be assumed that inclusion is so desirable and pleasant that "coping" involves simply embracing it, inclusion often has unpleasant features that elicit more complex forms of coping. Several of these forms of coping are discussed in Part 3.

Part 1: Coping with exclusion: Being excluded for who you are

This part, which is concerned with exclusion on the basis of uncontrollable characteristics, begins with the chapter, "On being the target of prejudice: Educational implications," by Michael Inzlicht, Joshua Aronson, and Rodolfo Mendoza-Denton. These authors are interested in how being the target of prejudice on the basis of one's race, ethnicity, or gender affects students' thoughts, feelings, and behaviors in academic settings. They review evidence indicating that membership in a stigmatized group (e.g., African-Americans) often undermines students' performance on standardized tests, academic engagement, academic self-concept, institutional trust, and overall achievement. Their analysis is informed by a theoretical model of threatening academic environments that highlights the importance of stereotype threat, attributional ambiguity, and race-based rejection sensitivity. In a concluding section, the authors adopt a more optimistic tone, arguing that motivational and performance decrements produced by social identity threat can be overcome with careful attention to how tasks are framed and what students are taught.

The second chapter, "To climb or not to climb? When minorities stick to the floor," by Margarita Sanchez-Mazas and Annalisa Casini, focuses on how women adapt to the workplace. Despite the removal of formal barriers to gender equality and increased opportunities for upward mobility, women are underrepresented at the top levels of most organizations. This state of affairs suggests that there are invisible impediments that prevent women from ascending the corporate ladder, a phenomenon known as "the glass ceiling effect." This chapter addresses some possible social-psychological antecedents of women's reluctance to search for or accept promotion in work settings (i.e., the self-selection hypothesis). Experimental studies are presented testing the hypothesis that willingness to climb the social ladder depends on the degree of fit between gender-related variables (e.g., participants' psychological orientation toward instrumentality vs. relatedness) and work-setting variables (e.g., organizational norms regarding instrumentality vs. human relations).

Although members of stigmatized minorities often respond rather passively to their social environments, this is not always the case. In some cases, minority members (e.g., African-Americans, women, gays) actively challenge the status quo. In the third chapter, "Managing the message: Using social influence and attitude change strategies to confront interpersonal discrimination," Janet K. Swim, Sarah J. Gervais, Nicholas Pearson, and Charles Stangor discuss minority members' use of confrontation to reduce prejudice and discrimination. These authors define confrontation as "any behavior or verbalization that indicates disagreement with another's behavior or comments." Swim and her colleagues review their own and others' work on this topic using the classic message-learning framework developed by attitude-change researchers. According to this framework, attitude change depends on message attention, comprehension, and acceptance. In addition, translating attitudes into behaviors requires retaining the message and applying it to later action. The authors first examine confronters' goals vis-à-vis perpetrators of discrimination and bystanders. They then consider the ways that confronters can use messages to manage their impressions on others. Finally, they examine features of audiences that influence the success of confrontations.

Different minority groups use different strategies for confronting majorities. This thesis is developed by Serge Moscovici and Juan A. Pérez in the fourth chapter, "A new representation of minorities as victims." The authors point out that theoretical and empirical work on minority influence has traditionally focused on "active minorities," which provoke conflict and reject the norms and beliefs of the majority with the goal of converting the majority to a new set of beliefs or an alternative lifestyle. Moscovici and Pérez argue that more attention should be given to how victimized minorities produce change by arousing social culpability in majorities. Such culpability is based on majorities' recognition of a contradiction between their basic principles and their behavior toward minorities. In a series of studies portraying Gypsies as either an active or a victimized minority, the authors provide evidence that a victimized minority (which seeks recognition for its suffering) elicits more compensation from a majority than does an active minority (which seeks change in how the majority feels about the minority). These findings suggest that the "ethical" relationship elicited by a victimized minority is different from the "antagonistic" relationship elicited by an active minority.

Various strategies that stigmatized minorities might use for coping with rejection are discussed in the last chapter in this part, "Marginalization through social ostracism: Effects of being ignored and excluded," by Kipling D. Williams and Adrienne Carter-Sowell. Although their discussion of how people respond to being ignored and excluded does not focus explicitly on those who are ostracized because of uncontrollable personal characteristics, victims of ostracism often assume that their treatment is based on who they are rather than what they think and do. Williams and Carter-Sowell argue that ostracism elicits both reflexive and reflective responses. The former responses involve psychological pain and distress, which occur immediately in the wake of ostracism and are not moderated by individual differences, situational forces, or causal attributions. The latter responses include pro-social actions (meant to fortify needs for belonging and self-esteem) and anti-social actions (meant to fortify needs for control and meaningful existence). Pro-social actions include attending carefully to social information, conforming to others' views, and working hard on collective tasks. Anti-social actions include direct and indirect aggression.

Part 2: Coping with exclusion: Being excluded for
what you think and do

This part, which is concerned with exclusion on the basis of controllable
characteristics, begins with chapter 6, "Delinquents as a minority group:
Accidental tourists in forbidden territory or voluntary emigrées?," by
Nicholas Emler. In analyzing why young people join and remain in delinquent groups, Emler criticizes several conventional analyses of deviance
(e.g., negative group influence, inadequate socialization, labeling theory),
arguing instead that delinquency is a self-chosen rather than an externally
imposed status. According to his analysis, young people enter and stay in
delinquent groups because they desire certain goals, such as protection from
victimization and fair treatment, but have little confidence that they can
attain these goals through compliance with conventional norms. By adopting a delinquent identity, young people perceive themselves as tougher and
braver, and hence less likely to be victimized. Once adopted, a delinquent
identity is reinforced in several ways – by selective association with delinquent peers, by polarization of shared norms within the delinquent group,
by "intergroup" encounters with authorities, and by the reinforcing effect of
negative societal reactions on delinquents' self-perceptions and affiliations
with like-minded peers.

A complementary view of why some people join and maintain loyalty to
devalued groups is proposed by Jolanda Jetten and Nyla R. Branscombe in
chapter 7, "Minority group identification: Responses to discrimination when
group membership is controllable." Basing their analysis on social identity
and self-categorization theory, these authors suggest that people sometimes
join devalued groups (e.g., counter-culture youth groups, radical political
organizations, terrorist groups) "precisely because they are devalued by the
powers that be." They argue that affiliation with and loyalty to such groups
occurs because ingroup identification allows members of devalued groups
to differentiate their ingroup from outgroups that discriminate against it.
Jetten and Branscombe identify three bases of identification with devalued
groups that are relevant to the interplay between intragroup and intergroup
self-categorization: (1) politicized identity, which is associated with efforts
to gain acceptance for "being different"; (2) rebel identity, which is associated with efforts to demonstrate the uniqueness of one's group; and (3) identity as resource, which is associated with efforts to obtain psychological
support to counteract discrimination. The first two identities derive from
intergroup processes, whereas the third identity derives from intragroup
processes.

Members of stigmatized groups based on controllable characteristics are often targets of persuasion efforts designed to change their thoughts and behaviors, with the ultimate goal of "liberating" them from their stigmatized identity. A salient example in contemporary society is smokers, whose responses to persuasion efforts are analyzed in chapter 8, "Coping with stigmatization: Smokers' reactions to antismoking campaigns," by Juan Manuel Falomir-Pichastor, Armand Chatard, Gabriel Mugny, and Alain Quiamzade. These authors point out that, although smokers recognize their stigmatized status and smoking prevention campaigns use expert persuasion sources, smokers often resist the messages in these campaigns and continue to smoke. Why is this the case? The authors argue that antismoking campaigns often threaten the social identity and self-esteem of smokers, which causes them to resist injunctions to quit smoking. In documenting their claim, they present the results of several studies investigating the impact of smokers' acknowledgment of their social stigmatization and the threat that expert sources pose to smokers' identity and freedom.

In addition to identifying with a stigmatized group and resisting majority pressure to leave it, other minority coping strategies involve active efforts to change the majority. In extreme cases, these strategies involve horrific acts of violence. Such acts are the hallmark of terrorist organizations, which are discussed in chapter 9, "Terrorism as a tactic of minority influence," by Xiaoyan Chen and Arie W. Kruglanski. These authors note that research in social psychology has focused on minorities that use nonviolent and socially sanctioned means in an effort to influence majorities. But in the last several decades, the world has seen a dramatic increase in minorities that attempt to exert influence through the use of terrorism, defined as "the deliberate targeting of civilians by non-state actors, aimed to advance political objectives through the induction of fear." In analyzing terrorism as a tactic of minority influence, Chen and Kruglanski argue that this strategy appeals to minorities for several reasons. These include terrorism's ability to gain observers' attention and convince them of the minority's commitment, to equalize the minority's power vis-à-vis the majority, and to create cognitive conflict in the majority. The authors further suggest that the efficacy of terrorism is influenced by several factors, including its persistence and tenacity, conformance to the Zeitgeist, and leadership. These and related issues (e.g., the perceived morality of terrorism, the proximal vs. distal effects of terrorism) are discussed in reference to contemporary terrorist movements.

White supremacist/anti-Semitic groups that seek to marginalize, expel, or physically destroy Blacks, Jews, Asians, and other "non-Aryans" also sometimes use violence to attain their goals. In chapter 10, "The stigma of racist activism," Kathleen M. Blee focuses on how members of such groups cope with the stigmatization they face for their views. Blee reports narratives from extensive life history interviews with women racist activists, who represent an increasingly important component of White supremacist groups. These women regard themselves as unfairly stigmatized by mainstream society and hold deep and wide-ranging conspiratorial beliefs about the power of their "enemies," particularly Jews. They respond to their perceived stigmatization in several ways, for example by disengaging from people they see as hostile to White supremacism, attempting to blend into mainstream society, drawing distinctions between acceptable and unacceptable racist activities, arguing for the victimized status of White Aryans, and flaunting their racial beliefs in public situations. These responses are shaped by racists' perceptions of their external environment as well as the internal dynamics of racist groups.

Yet another coping strategy available to minorities is leaving the group to form a competing group or to join another existing group. This strategy is discussed by Fabio Sani in chapter 11, "Why groups fall apart: A social psychological model of the schismatic process." Sani presents a model of schisms based on data from the Italian Communist Party and the Church of England. The model postulates that schismatic intentions are caused by the perception that the identity of the group is being subverted by a new norm. This occurs because perceived identity subversion reduces group identification and increases dejection- and agitation-related emotions, both of which affect schismatic intentions. Finally, the impact of these variables on schismatic intentions is moderated by the extent to which the people who oppose the new norm feel that they have "voice" (i.e., will not be discriminated against if they state their views). More specifically, voice reduces the impact of group identification and dejection/agitation on schismatic intentions.

Part 3: Coping with inclusion.

As noted above, it seems obvious that minorities desire inclusion and hence embrace it with "no questions asked." Why, after all, look a gift horse in the mouth? In fact, the reality of majority–minority relations is not so simple. In some cases, inclusion has unpleasant connotations for minorities and hence elicits more complex forms of coping. The first chapter in this part, Chapter 12, "Multiple identities and the paradox of social inclusion," by Manuela Barreto and Naomi Ellemers, examines how social inclusion of minorities can paradoxically contribute to feelings of social exclusion. The authors' central argument is that assimilative (i.e., inclusionary) pressures on members of minority groups are problematical for three reasons: they constitute a threat to the distinctiveness of the minority's subgroup identity, they imply a lack of respect for that identity, and they threaten minority members' self-definition by imposing an external definition of the self in place of the person's preferred identity. Barreto and Ellemers review research documenting these effects of assimilative pressures and demonstrating their negative impact on social cohesion and the inclusion of all groups in a superordinate category.

In chapter 13, "Prominority policies and cultural change: A dilemma for minorities," Angelica Mucchi-Faina argues that certain well-intentioned inclusionary policies, namely "hard" affirmative action and language reform, can have paradoxical effects on members of the groups they are designed to help. In support of this contention, she reviews evidence documenting the negative consequences of these two policies. For example, hard affirmative action has been found to reduce the self-esteem, motivation, and performance of the beneficiaries of this policy and to create negative attitudes toward these beneficiaries. Mucchi-Faina suggests that work needs to be done to identify when minorities should shift from collective protest and demands for equal treatment to efforts to institutionalize newly-gained rights.

The last two chapters in this part also examine paradoxical effects of minority "success." In these chapters, success is defined as moving from minority to majority status by convincing other group members to adopt one's position. In chapter 14, "Influence without credit: How successful minorities respond to social cyptomnesia," Fabrizio Butera, John M. Levine, and Jean-Pierre Vernet examine how minorities respond when they succeed in producing influence but fail to get credit for doing so (i.e., social cryptomnesia). The authors argue that successful "nomic" minorities, which are motivated to produce social change, are upset by failure to gain recognition for the influence they produce. As a result, they become more homogeneous in their beliefs, more committed to their position, and more resistant to majority influence. Research confirming these hypotheses is presented.

Finally, in chapter 15, "Influence and its aftermath: Motives for agreement among minorities and majorities," Radmila Prislin and P. Niels Christensen discuss how members of minority and majority factions respond to changes in their relative status within the group (i.e., promotion to majority status in the case of initial minorities vs. demotion to minority status in the case of initial majorities). They present research relevant to their theory, which postulates that loss of majority status elicits a strong negative reaction, whereas gain of majority status elicits a weak positive reaction. As a result, the immediate effect of social change is a reduction in members' overall identification with the group. Their research indicates that an initial minority's motives (social validation, social acceptance, social control) have a substantial impact on its reaction to becoming a majority. For example, when minorities are motivated to attain social validation and acceptance, gaining numerical dominance leads to identification with the group only when majority members' conversion seems genuine.

REFERENCES

Levine, J. M., & Kerr, N. L. (2007). Inclusion and exclusion: Implications for group processes. In A. E. Kruglanski & E. T. Higgins (Eds.), *Social psychology: Handbook of basic principles* (2nd ed., pp. 759–784). New York: Guilford.

Moscovici, S., Lage, E., & Naffrechoux, M. (1969). Influence of a consistent minority on the responses of a majority in a color perception task. *Sociometry, 32,* 365–380.

Seyranian, V., Atuel, H., & Crano, W. D. (2008). Dimensions of majority and minority groups. *Group Processes and Intergroup Relations, 11,* 21–37.

Steele, C. M., & Aronson, J. (1995). Stereotype threat and the intellectual test performance of African Americans. *Journal of Personality and Social Psychology, 69,* 797–811.

PART I

COPING WITH EXCLUSION: BEING EXCLUDED FOR WHO YOU ARE

1

On Being the Target of Prejudice: Educational Implications

MICHAEL INZLICHT, JOSHUA ARONSON,
AND RODOLFO MENDOZA-DENTON

Jews rule the world by proxy. Or so says the former prime minister of Malaysia, Dr. Mahathir Mohamad. In October 2003, in a speech to the 57-nation Islamic Summit in Malaysia, the then-prime minister lashed out at world Jewry. "The Europeans killed 6 million Jews out of 12 million," stated Mohamad, "but today the Jews rule this world by proxy and get others to fight and die for them." However disturbing and offensive Dr. Mohamad's words, they were not surprising to at least one of us who had spent a summer vacationing in Malaysia. Upon his arrival into Kuala Lumpur International Airport, Inzlicht noticed thousands of copies of *The protocols of the learned elders of Zion* on prominent display. Seeing this "classic" book – which is a fraudulent document purporting to describe a plan to achieve Jewish global domination – shocked and affronted Inzlicht, who happens to be Jewish. When he later entered the country, Inzlicht could not help but ask how his social identity was impacting the way others saw and interacted with him: He was mistrustful of others, watchful of what he said and did, and vigilant for the way others interacted with him. Having to enter a land that so vilifies and demonizes his Jewish identity was, in short, threatening.

This chapter is concerned with the psychological effects of entering threatening environments, focusing not on the relatively clear case above, but on the more subtle and commonplace phenomenon of individuals entering environments where their cultural identity is devalued and stigmatized. How do academic performance, motivation, and self-concept suffer when people feel excluded, discriminated against, or exposed to negative

This chapter was written in part with the support of a National Academy of Education/ Spencer Foundation Post-Doctoral Fellowship and a Canadian Social Sciences and Humanities Research Council grant to Michael Inzlicht. We thank Catherine Good, Linda McKay, Michael Johns, Alison Chasteen, and Naomi Sarah Ball for valuable insights.

stereotypes? For example, how would a Jewish student perform and feel in a Malaysian classroom knowing what the former prime minister believes? And what can educators and policy makers do to help people overcome the obstacles posed by discrimination? These questions are important because our world is increasingly becoming a tapestry of different cultures, races, and religions, and with these changes the importance of harmonious inter-group relations is increased.

For the past few years we have been trying to find answers to these questions and in so doing understand what it means to belong to a group with a stigmatized social identity (Goffman, 1963). Although social psychologists have long been interested in the roots of stereotyping, prejudice, and discrimination among those who hold prejudiced beliefs, only recently have they focused significant attention on the psychological effects of these processes among the targets of prejudice (Major & O'Brien, 2005; Swim & Stangor, 1998). This emerging research has demonstrated that stigma – an attribute that, in a particular context, marks individuals as different and leads them to be devalued and marginalized in the eyes of others – has far-ranging effects on its targets (Crocker, Major, & Steele 1998). Stigmatized individuals are judged not on the content of their character but on the basis of their group membership. As a result, these individuals experience more negative outcomes than their nonstigmatized counterparts. African-Americans, for example, suffer from academic underachievement, have more stress-related illnesses, face higher risks of physical attack, and have reduced access to housing, employment, and education (see Allison, 1998, for a review). The possibility that one can be the target of prejudice and discrimination is therefore the defining feature of stigmatization (Crocker et al., 1998).

We focus here on a model that draws on research from social psychology to help us understand how being the target of prejudice affects people. Although prejudice can affect many different aspects of people's lives, we concentrate on how it undermines such outcomes as standardized test performance, academic engagement, academic self-concept, and institutional trust. We begin by reviewing research showing how environmental cues that on the surface appear benign and innocuous can communicate to people that they could be devalued, stigmatized, or discriminated against because of their particular social identity. We describe, for example, how being in the minority can activate negative race stereotypes and undermine African-Americans' standardized test performance through a phenomenon known as *stereotype threat* (Steele & Aronson, 1995). We next explore the specific processes through which stereotypes can influence the targets of prejudice. We focus specifically on the affective, cognitive, and motivational consequences of negative stereotypes. We also consider individual risk factors for prejudice effects and discuss a particular vulnerability – *race-based rejection sensitivity* (RS-race) (Mendoza-Denton, Downey, Purdie, Davis, & Pietrzak, 2002). Third, we examine how coping with prejudice can shape a person's identity and self-concept. By drawing on the concept of *attributional ambiguity* (Crocker & Major, 1989), we illustrate how negative stereotypes can lead people to devalue and disidentify from important domains in their lives and foster unclear and inaccurate self-concepts. We end with a hopeful note, showing that the consequences of stigma are not inevitable, but rather situationally determined and open to remediation. Rather than offering a comprehensive analysis of stigma research (see Major, Quinton, & McCoy, 2002; Steele, Spencer, & Aronson, 2002), this chapter presents a working model of prejudice effects and provides a selective review of key components of this model. We begin by describing our working model.

HOW PREJUDICE AFFECTS TARGETS: A MODEL

Figure 1.1 presents a model we've adapted from Cohen, Garcia, Masters, and Apfel (2005), describing how prejudice can hurt the targets of stigma. While Cohen et al.'s (2005) framework focuses on social-identity threat more generally, our model focuses specifically on academic outcomes. This model begins with the targets of prejudice being aware of their group's stigmatized social identity, including the awareness that their group has lower status, compares unfavorably to other groups, and is negatively stereotyped (Steele et al., 2002). Negative stereotypes about members of chronically stigmatized groups, for instance, are well known and widespread in our society, even among individuals who do not personally believe or endorse those stereotypes and among members of stigmatized groups themselves (Devine, 1989; Vorauer, Main, O'Connell, 1998). Awareness of their stigmatized status then leads people to become vigilant and to question whether negative stereotypes will be used as a lens through which their actions and behaviors will be judged. The awareness of stigma, in other words, creates suspicions of bias and discrimination, and causes people to be cautious and uncertain about whether they are being treated unfairly because of their social identity.

In their landmark paper on stigma, Crocker and Major (1989) called this state of uncertainty *attributional ambiguity* and defined it as the doubt that people have about whether they are being judged because of personal deservingness or because of the prejudices held against their group. For

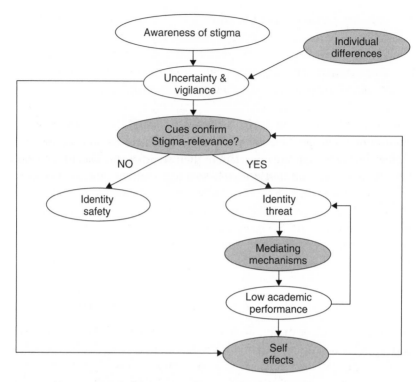

FIGURE 1.1. A model of threatening academic environments.

example, after receiving a failing grade, an African-American student may question whether her poor grade reflects her own performance or her professor's racism. By blaming discrimination rather than the quality of her work, this uncertainty allows her to maintain positive self-regard (Crocker, Voelkl, Testa, & Major, 1991). When she discounts the instructor's feedback, however, she also rob herself of opportunities to gain self-knowledge and to develop a stable self-concept (Aronson & Inzlicht, 2004). Attributions unrelated to one's efforts (i.e., to discrimination) can also lead people to feel that they have little control over their outcomes and destinies. We will return to these self-relevant effects later. For now, let's focus on people's vigilance.

Vigilance means that people survey their surroundings to determine whether they are in a potentially threatening environment. People become vigilant for, and sensitive to, the cues communicating that their group's stigmatized social status may be relevant in the immediate situation (Kaiser, Vick, & Major, 2006). Some settings provide few cues that stereotypes and prejudice are relevant, and thus result in individuals experiencing little or no threat to their social identities. These "identity-safe" environments assure individuals that their stigmatized social identities pose no barrier (Davies, Spencer, & Steele, 2005). Other situations, however, are less hospitable and can become identity threatening by dint of cues within them. Scanning the titles in a bookstore and noticing that one of the bestsellers is, say, an anti-Semitic tract, sends a not-so-subtle message that Jews are devalued in that environment and perhaps not welcome (see Inzlicht & Good, 2006, for a review). When people are uncertain of their standing, are watchful for stigma-relevant cues, and find themselves in just such an inhospitable environment, a process is set off that can hurt environmental trust, self-concept, and intellectual performance. Steele and colleagues (2002) have called this phenomenon *social identity threat*.

Social-identity threat is the discomfort individuals feel when they suspect that their social identity can put them at risk for social devaluation, exclusion, and biased treatment. It is a situational predicament that occurs when individuals become fearful of being treated not as an individual, but as a member of their devalued social category. One of the more pervasive forms of social-identity threat, and the one we focus on here, is stereotype threat – being at risk of confirming a negative stereotype about one's group (Steele & Aronson, 1995). Consider the example of an African-American or Latino student trying to solve a difficult question written on the blackboard. As with his White classmates, this student faces performance pressures – he wants to look smart, wants to get the correct answer, and wants to avoid looking dumb. He also, however, faces an additional pressure not faced by his White classmates, the pressure stemming from the desire to disconfirm stereotypes alleging African-American or Latino intellectual inferiority (see Aronson, 2002).

This second pressure, arising from a devalued social identity, can increase anxiety and arousal (Ben-Zeev, Fein, & Inzlicht, 2005; Blascovich, Spencer, Quinn, & Steele, 2001; Mendoza-Denton et al., 2002; O'Brien & Crandall, 2003), tax the cognitive resources of self-regulation and working memory (Inzlicht, McKay, & Aronson, 2006; Schmader & Johns, 2003), and negatively tilt the motivational frame with which people view situations (Seibt & Förster, 2004). Returning to our aforementioned example, anything our African-American or Latino student does or says can be interpreted along stereotypical lines, and this possibility is stressful; it diverts his cognitive resources away from the task at hand, and changes the way he approaches and views the problem. Instead of thinking about the question posed to him, he may become concerned with his group's and his own reputation; and to the extent that he values his social standing, this can be unnerving. The likely result, as numerous studies have now shown, is that he underperforms. And to the extent that he repeatedly finds himself immersed in such threatening environments, he may even change the way he views himself and the way he values academics. In other words, not only does prejudice affect the way the stigmatized perform in threatening environments, it can affect the way they perceive and relate to the environment in the future and the way they conceive of themselves and their prospects in that environment.

But who is most likely to be affected by negative stereotypes? The series of steps outlined in Figure 1.1 delineating the psychological course targets take when confronted with prejudice and stigma is not uniform. Important individual differences make some people more susceptible and others more resilient to the kinds of effects we have outlined so far. Our model illustrates two junctions that can lead to either identity safety or identity threat. One type of risk factor influences whether people expect and readily perceive cues confirming stigma relevance. Some individuals, for example, have a long history of experiencing discrimination and therefore come to anxiously expect and readily perceive it in the future (Kaiser et al., 2006; Mendoza-Denton et al., 2002; Pinel, 1999). These individuals feel chronic uncertainty about whether they are being viewed equitably or stereotypically and are therefore chronically vigilant and reactive toward cues confirming this latter possibility. The other type of risk factor affects how people respond to stereotypes once they're "in the air" (Steele, 1997). Some people, for example, may assess themselves as capable of disproving the stereotype and feel able to handle the pressure (Lazarus & Folkman, 1984), as is the case, say, when someone feels challenged and not threatened by negative stereotypes (Inzlicht, Aronson, Good, & McKay, 2006). Thus, individual differences may exist not only in whether a threat is activated in the first place, but also in how well people can regulate an activated threat.

This model has recursive elements. Initial low performance on a test, for example, can feed into threat perception and further lower performance, thereby creating a positive feedback loop. Similarly, self-effects, such as an unclear self-concept, can render people less certain about themselves and the outcomes they receive, thereby exacerbating the effects of stigma. In the remainder of the chapter, we use this framework to discuss key elements (shaded areas in Figure 1.1) of our model. We start by exploring those situations that communicate stigma relevance.

THREATENING ENVIRONMENTS

Threatening environments can be thought of as settings where people come to suspect that they could be devalued, stigmatized, or discriminated against because of a particular social identity. When they find themselves in a new setting, targets of stereotypes form a hypothesis about the setting and evaluate a broad set of cues to determine whether discrimination is in fact occurring. Any cues that signal that one's group is excluded from certain functions, is not valued socially, or is marginalized in any way, should foster mistrust and create a threatening environment (Steele et al., 2002). These environments need not directly arouse stigma relevance, but may do so indirectly through more subtle, seemingly innocuous cues. A casual chat in one's dorm room may become threatening when a student, who was once proud to say that he is the first in his family to complete high school and attend college, realizes that all his roommates' parents are college graduates and highly paid professionals (e.g., Croizet & Claire, 1998).

Settings where people find that their social group is in the numerical minority – literally outnumbered – may be particularly threatening. According to distinctiveness theory (McGuire, McGuire, Child, & Fujioka, 1978), we are selective self-perceivers and attend to those aspects of ourselves that are distinct and peculiar in our immediate social context. Thus, an African-American medical student who finds herself outnumbered by her White classmates will tend to notice and think about her "Blackness" in her White classroom, but in a different setting, say a class full of men, her race loses salience and she will become more conscious of being a woman. When people ruminate about their distinct social identity, they may also think about the stereotypes associated with and prejudices held against that identity.

Inzlicht et al. (2006), for example, found that Black participants were more likely to think about stereotypes about their race when Whites outnumbered them. In their study, Black participants took a test with two other people – two other Blacks, two Whites, or one Black and one White. Before taking the test, participants completed an implicit measure of stereotype activation. In accordance with the distinctiveness theory (McGuire et al., 1978), stereotypes should be more active for the Black participants the less their race was represented in the group (i.e., the more distinct they were). Results confirmed predictions. The more participants were racially outnumbered, the more often they ruminated on the stereotypes about their group. Our point here is that being outnumbered can increase awareness of one's distinct social identity and of the stereotypes associated with that identity, and, ultimately, create a threatening environment where people expect stereotypes to be used in evaluating them.

And as outlined in our model mentioned earlier, this can trigger a chain of psychological events leading to underperformance. For some of the Black participants, being outnumbered by Whites and thinking about the stereotypes about their group led to lower standardized verbal test performance, presumably as an outgrowth of stereotype threat (Inzlicht et al., 2006). In another study, this time manipulating the sex composition of three-person groups, women who were outnumbered by men did worse on a math test – a domain for which women are stereotyped as inferior (Spencer, Steele, & Quinn, 1999) – than women in a same-sex group (Inzlicht & Ben-Zeev, 2000). Thus, a seemingly innocuous contextual cue – the number of Whites or men in a room – can create a threatening intellectual environment and undermine performance (see also Sekaquaptewa & Thompson, 2002).

Organizational philosophies – statements about social-identity ideology – can also increase the relevance of stereotypes in a setting. Working for a business that, say, has a strict colorblind policy can be reassuring to a new Latina employee who is welcomed by a rainbow coalition of diverse employees on her first day on the job. However, the message sent by this policy is quite different if she is greeted by a phalanx of White males. Purdie-Vaughns and colleagues (2008) examined this exact scenario when she handed African-American business people a brochure of a Silicon Valley company that claimed either a multicultural or a colorblind philosophy of fairness and then portrayed either a diverse or a homogeneous White workforce. As expected, contextual cues communicating social-identity ideology went beyond simple minority effects: Although everyone felt they would be less comfortable working for a predominantly White company, this was particularly true when the context failed to convey a commitment to diversity. Environments sending cues indicating that one's social identity is not of value can therefore be threatening.

Far from being an exhaustive list, our point here is to highlight how indirect, seemingly innocuous cues can send powerful messages about who does and does not belong in a situation. These situations can foster mistrust, evoke stereotype threat, and, through a number of mechanisms, lead to low intellectual performance. We next discuss some of these mechanisms.

MEDIATING MECHANISMS

Stereotype threat is best thought of as a predicament faced by a person in a situation. Given the range of possible situations, groups of people, and types of stereotypes, it should come as no surprise that stereotypes can threaten people through multiple, possibly interacting, routes. We focus here on the affective, cognitive, and motivational mechanisms.

Arousal

As described earlier, when a Black or Latino college student takes a test, he faces an additional pressure not faced by his White classmates, a pressure related to the stereotypes about his group. This additional social-identity pressure, because it threatens central goals – feeling competent and appearing competent to others – can be nerve-wracking. Indeed it appears to be sufficiently unsettling to temporarily raise blood pressure (Blascovich et al., 2001). However, can this hypertension explain the lower intellectual performance found in this and other studies?

Although stereotypes increase blood pressure, this may not directly contribute to lower performance (Steele et al., 2002). It is more likely that high blood pressure is a reflection of the state of arousal and anxiety produced by stereotype pressure, and it is this arousal that does the mediating. Using the classic misattribution paradigm (e.g., Zanna & Cooper, 1974), Ben-Zeev and colleagues (2005) examined this proposition. As with the Inzlicht and Ben-Zeev (2000) study described earlier, women took a math test with either two men or two women. This time, however, half of the participants were also given the opportunity to attribute the negative arousal presumably triggered by threat to a benign source – in this case, a "silent" subliminal tone. As expected, when misattribution to the tone was not elicited, women in the minority environment performed worse on the math test than women in the same-sex environment. However, when given the opportunity to misattribute their arousal, women in the minority group performed as well as those in the same-sex group. That is, when participants were told that a subliminal noise might make them feel anxious, they no longer underperformed when they were in the minority, presumably because the arousal was attributed to the tone, rather than the more unsettling cause of low ability. Contending with negative stereotypes, therefore, can increase arousal, and the manner in which this arousal is attributed can play an important role in mediating minority underperformance. In other words, threatening environments may increase feelings of apprehension and stoke the fires of arousal, and it is this arousal that can contribute to intellectual underperformance (see also O'Brien & Crandall, 2003).

Cognitive Disruption

Coping with the negative stereotypes about her math ability may not only increase a woman's arousal, it can also leave her preoccupied with distracting thoughts and worries. When asked to answer a difficult question, she may begin focusing on task-irrelevant thoughts – worrying, say, about making her gender group look bad or about how much she hates math. And ultimately, these negative thoughts can contribute to her lower performance. Recently, a team of researchers looked at the types of thoughts women had when taking a math test under either threatening or nonthreatening environments (Cadinu, Maass, Rosabianca, & Kiesner, 2005). When women suspected that stereotypes were situationally relevant, they began thinking that math was too difficult for them or that they were no good at math. When stereotypes were not situationally relevant, however, they were unlikely to have these thoughts. Importantly, negative task-related thoughts interfered with test performance later on, and resulted in the former group of women performing worse than the latter group. Stereotypes, therefore, trigger a wave of intrusive domain-specific thoughts that are capable of inhibiting performance.

But how does this happen exactly? How do negative thoughts about math inhibit a woman's performance? Given the limits of cognition, it's possible that these negative thoughts divert her attention and reduce her cognitive capacity for the task at hand – answering the difficult question. More specifically, when worried about confirming a stereotype, these intrusive, negative thoughts can reduce working-memory capacity.

Working memory refers to that type of memory used to focus attention on temporarily activated information while keeping task-irrelevant thoughts at bay (Engle, 2002). It is also a key component of the higher-order cognitive operations underlying problem solving. Therefore, if working-memory capacity is occupied with disruptive thoughts, it will be less capable of handling a central task. Schmader and Johns (2003) examined this possibility in a series of elegant studies. In one study, female college students completed an operation-span task – an index of working memory – under either stereotype-threatening or -nonthreatening situations. In this dual-processing task, participants evaluated mathematical equations while memorizing words for later recall (e.g., Turner & Engle, 1989). As expected, when women suspected that their stigmatized social identity was situationally relevant, they showed less cognitive capacity than their nonthreatened counterparts, as measured by the number of words they recalled within the task. In a second study, Schmader and Johns not only replicated this effect, but also found that this impaired capacity directly disrupted intellectual performance on a standardized test. Working-memory disruptions, therefore, can contribute to threat-induced intellectual underperformance.

Coping with stereotypes is hard; it leads people to have intrusive thoughts that drain the limited capacity of working memory. And the extent to which this happens determines the extent of intellectual impairment.

Motivational Mechanisms

New research shows that threatening environments not only limit working-memory capacity, but also self-regulatory capacity, which is analogous to the common-sense concept of willpower (Baumeister, Heatherton, & Tice, 1994). Getting out of bed in the morning, eating or drinking in moderation, and persisting on a difficult reading assignment are all examples of actions that require the self-regulatory capacity to inhibit one set of behaviors (e.g., pulling the covers over one's head, getting drunk, quitting), and replace them with more adaptive behaviors. Self-regulation is not always easy, however. Research is now beginning to reveal that people have only a limited supply of self-regulatory strength, and that any task requiring controlled, willful action quickly depletes this central resource. Factors that consume a person's strength, say coping with a stressful event, should contribute to self-regulation failure – a process known as "ego depletion" (Muraven & Baumeister, 2000; Muraven, Tice, & Baumeister, 1998).

Given this limited capacity, it should follow that dealing with the prospect of confirming a negative stereotype – a situation rife with arousal and disruptive thoughts – depletes self-regulatory capacity and leaves people less able to self-regulate in other domains. Inzlicht and colleagues explored this possibility. In one study (Inzlicht & Hickman, 2005), men and women were placed in either a minority-sex or same-sex "math focus group" and then asked to work for as long as they wished on an ostensibly unrelated anagram task. Results indicated that women in the minority, who were dealing with stereotype pressures, gave up more quickly on the anagram task than all other students. Other studies revealed that, compared to non-threatened Black students and women, respectively, stereotype-threatened Black students were less able to attentionally self-regulate, as measured by the color naming Stroop task, and threatened women were less able to physically self-regulate, as indexed by the amount of time they could hold on to a hand exerciser, a difficult and sometimes painful exercise (Inzlicht, McKay, et al., 2006). Stigma, therefore, is ego depleting.

Stereotypes can affect motivation a second way, by affecting the motivational frame with which people view situations. Recently, Seibt and Förster (2004) found that stereotype threat could change the regulatory focus of targets of negative stereotypes. That is, it could induce a motivational style characterized by prevention, avoidance, and risk aversion (Higgins, 1997). When dealing with potential prejudice, as is the case, say, for the Latino trying to solve a difficult question on the chalkboard, the negative stereotype is the reference point and avoiding it is the goal. Such a situation can induce a prevention focus state of vigilance and of wanting to avoid failures at all costs, and not a focus on promotion of desired goals (see also Keller & Dauenheimer, 2003). Although being vigilant for failure does not always reduce performance, it can lower engagement and intrinsic liking for a topic (Elliot & McGregor, 2001). These separate lines of research suggest that stigma leads not only to a qualitative change in motivational mind-set in which individuals interact with a situation – by, for example, inducing a prevention or performance avoidance focus – but also to a quantitative change in the amount of self-control people have at their disposal (e.g., Inzlicht, McKay et al., 2006).

Being the target of prejudice is a messy affair. It leads people to become anxious, introduces disruptive thoughts, and affects the quantity and quality of self-regulatory resources available. Stereotype threat, however, is most likely not mediated by one of these psychological processes operating alone, but rather through a complex interplay between them. We thus agree with the position offered by Steele and colleagues (2002) that being the target of stereotypes is a multifaceted phenomenon that varies from situation to situation, and person to person. We now turn to the variability found from person to person, by focusing on an important individual difference variable known as RS-race.

INDIVIDUAL DIFFERENCES

Although much of the research discussed earlier focuses on between-group differences in performance situations and performance outcomes, it is important to recognize that not all members of stigmatized groups experience anxiety or cognitive disruption in contexts where their identity may be threatened. One mechanism through which within-group variability may occur is through individual differences in how well a particular protective mechanism can be enacted in the face of threat (e.g., Inzlicht, Aronson et al., 2006). Another possibility, however, is that some people within a stigmatized group may not be as reactive to the identity-threat cues in the environment to begin with.

How might such individual differences come about? Drawing on models emphasizing the importance of prior experiences in shaping future expectations (e.g., Bowlby, 1988; Downey & Feldman, 1996), Mendoza-Denton and colleagues (Mendoza-Denton et al., 2002; Mendoza-Denton, Page-Gould, and Pietrzak, 2005) have proposed that prior experiences of mistreatment, prejudice, and discrimination can make the possibility of future rejection on the basis of a stigmatized characteristic more chronically accessible to a person (Higgins, 1997). In other words, the more one has experienced discrimination in the past, either personally or vicariously, the more likely one is to fear being discriminated against in the future (see also Pinel, 1999). Individual differences in RS-race have been found to be important in explaining within-group variability in educational outcomes and, importantly, to begin to shed light on yet another mechanism through which stigmatization can lead to performance decrements.

Mendoza-Denton et al. (2002) conducted a longitudinal study of incoming African-American students within a university setting. The researchers measured RS-race before students' first day of classes at the university. Over the first 3 weeks of college, students who scored high on RS-race felt less a part of the university community, less liking for their majority peers, and less trust in professors relative to their low RS-race counterparts. At the end of the first year of college, high RS-race students accorded less legitimacy toward (i.e., felt less trust in and obligation to) the university, an effect that was mediated by students' initial feelings of belonging during the first few weeks of school (Mendoza-Denton, 2003). By students' second and third years in college, RS-race was negatively predictive of attendance at review sessions and use of professors' office hours, as well as grade point average (GPA).

These findings highlight that in addition to arousal, cognitive disruption, and motivational depletion – which can affect performance in specific evaluative situations – concerns about stigmatization can lead to longer-term performance decrements through an alternative pathway. As the work with RS-race shows, when students feel unwelcome and devalued, they may be less likely to trust representatives of the university (e.g., professors, university officials), and feel a reduced sense of obligation to the university. As a coping strategy, students may then decide to avoid office hours, study sessions, and other institutionalized opportunities to help overcome the academic difficulties all students experience (see also Aronson & Inzlicht, 2004).

Individual Differences in Context

Two clear messages emerge from our discussion so far: The first is that stigma-related threat processes are best understood as a situational predicament, such that altering the elements of context or environment should increase or reduce such threat. The second message is that within stigmatized groups, people differ in the chronic accessibility of discrimination expectations. Recognizing a common focus on process, the question becomes not "person or situation?" but rather "which person and when situation?"

Recent research has begun to clarify the conditions under which we might expect to see "the power of the situation" (Ross and Nisbett, 1991) versus individual differences emerge as the primary determinant of behavior in stereotype-threat situations. Going back to an earlier example, seeing thousands of copies of anti-Jewish literature prominently on display at an airport is a situation that is likely to elicit belonging (and safety) concerns among most of the people against whom the hate is directed. The majority of stigma-relevant situations, however, are likely to be much less clear, particularly in modern times when overt discrimination has gone underground, at least in the United States (McConahay, 1986). It is precisely in such ambiguous situations that one might expect chronic individual differences to emerge as predictors of behavior.

To test this idea, Mendoza-Denton, Shaw-Taylor, Chen and Chang (2009) asked female college students to participate in a graduate-school interview with a male graduate student. The décor of the graduate student's room was experimentally manipulated: In one condition, posters of bikini models and books with sexist themes strongly suggested the man was chauvinist, while in the other condition, the décor of his office was innocuous. The findings were clear: Whereas all women expected to be negatively stereotyped in the chauvinist décor condition, only women who were high on gender-based rejection sensitivity (RS-gender) (London, Downey, Rattan, & Velilla, 2003) experienced such expectations in the innocuous-décor condition. In other words, although the evaluative nature of an interview created the potential for negative evaluation in both conditions, the condition in which the graduate student was not overtly chauvinist was ambiguous with respect to whether gender might play a role in any such evaluation – thus allowing an individual a difference variable (RS-gender) to affect behavior.

Does this mean that individuals for whom discrimination is chronically accessible – for example, women high on RS-gender or minority individuals

high on RS-race – are likely to perceive rejection across all contexts, seeing
the world through "stigma-colored glasses?" Evidence suggests that this is
not the case. As research both on stereotype threat and status-based rejection sensitivity shows, threat is activated only in the presence of an applicable discrimination-relevant cue in the situation. In the *absence* of such
cues, people will not react with anxiety, cognitive disruption, or mistrust.
Brown and Pinel (2003), for example, find that when a math test is framed
as completely free of gender bias, all women – regardless of their chronic
accessibility of gender stigmatization (stigma consciousness) (Pinel, 1999) –
performed well on the exam. Taken together, then, the aforementioned
findings suggest that rather than focusing on whether stigma-related threat
is a situational predicament or a personal disposition, both the *applicability*
and *strength* of stereotype-/discrimination-related cues in a given context
are critical in understanding whether the dynamic illustrated in Figure 1.1 is
activated, and in whom it is activated.

COPING WITH THREAT: EFFECTS ON THE SELF

Although less researched than performance effects of prejudice, identity-
coping strategies have been documented among students when their devalued social identities are challenged by cultural stereotypes, mistrust, or
other threats to belonging.

Disengagement and Disidentification

The most extreme and costly of these strategies are disengagement and disidentification, in which individuals reduce the degree to which they invest
self-esteem into a particular domain (Steele, 1997; Crocker et al., 1998).
These adaptations reflect a strong desire for self-esteem in the face of a situation where one's prospects for full acceptance or belonging are seen as
either unattainable or simply not worth the effort. By disengaging, we refer
to the early disconnecting of esteem from a particular threatening domain.
This way one can maintain physical presence in a domain where positive
outcomes are unlikely or tenuous, in essence, by reformulating one's priorities. In contrast, we use the term disidentification to mean the more chronic
coping strategy of dropping a domain from personal identity or as a foundation for self-esteem (Crocker et al., 1998). Individuals who disidentify,
in essence, no longer care about the threatened domain. The research suggests that individuals are quite adept at employing the Jamesian calculus:
maintaining global self-esteem by dropping or reducing the importance of

certain problematic "pretensions," in this case, academic achievement (see also Crocker & Knight, 2005).

One would reasonably expect that groups that are most severely under-represented and most acutely stereotyped would also come to be the least academically identified. The literature on African-American males who fit this description strongly suggests this linkage. For example, numerous studies find a lower correlation between self-esteem and academic achievement for Black males (e.g., Demo & Parker, 1987) despite finding that Black males do not differ from other groups in overall self-esteem. In a cross national study employing the National Educational Longitudinal Survey (NELS), Osborne (1995, 1997) found that despite being enrolled and physically present in high school, African-American boys reduced their identification with academic achievement steadily between the 8th and 12th grades, a trend remarkably more pronounced than for Black females, whose identification with achievement more closely resembled that of Whites. Indeed, by the 12th grade, Black males in the sample were completely disidentified; in fact, there was a negative correlation between self-esteem and academics. This finding offers some support for the cultural inversion hypothesis, which holds that African-Americans cope with their marginalized status by defining themselves in opposition to the prevailing White culture (e.g., Fordham & Ogbu, 1986). But the effect seems limited to African-American males, at least in regard to academics.

Research by Hare (1977) and Osborne (1997) suggests that global self-esteem is maintained among African-American students by basing their self-esteem not on schooling but instead primarily on family and peer relations. White students in their research appeared to base their self-esteem primarily on school and, to a lesser extent, on family and peer interactions. These differences in self-definition have been observed even among students at highly elite universities. For example, Aronson, Fried, and Good (2002) asked African-American and White undergraduates at Stanford University how central academic achievement was to their self-definitions. Even after controlling for achievement and preparation, the Black–White difference was significant, with White students rating achievement as more important to making them "who I am as a person." In the same sample of students, Steele and Aronson (1995) found that African-Americans were more likely than Whites to rate peer relations as personally important, and this was particularly likely when they were confronted by a challenging and evaluative academic task. Thus, although theorists in this area have suggested that disidentification is likely to be an avenue of last resort, evidence that it occurs frequently is easy to come by. Psychological disidentification of this sort is thought to be maladaptive because reducing identification with academic achievement is likely to reduce effort and learning (Steele, 1997). Fortunately, interventions that mitigate disengagement and disidentification have been shown to boost academic achievement (Aronson, et al., 2002).

A subtler and thus more adaptive form of self-concept adjustment and coping occurs when an individual selectively disidentifies with either aspects of the domain or characteristics stereotypically associated with the minority group. For example, women majoring in math and science might alter their dress or behavior to avoid being pegged as overly feminine, and thus face less intense suspicions about their fitness for the major. As another example, Pronin, Steele, and Ross (2004) found that female college students who had taken a number of math courses rated certain female characteristics – like flirtatiousness or the desire to have children – as less self-defining than others, presumably because these characteristics were seen as incompatible with future math success. These women did not disavow female traits like empathy and nurturance, because these were not seen as incompatible with success in math. Moreover, Pronin et al. found essentially the same results in experimental studies. In their experiments women who strongly identified with math distanced themselves from characteristically feminine traits seen as irrelevant to math prowess (flirtatiousness, emotionality, wearing make-up, etc.) when threatened with information suggesting that women were less naturally gifted in math than men. Women who were less identified with math did not show this "identity bifurcation" response to stereotype threat. Thus, students who suspect that certain traits are stigmatized in a domain may feel considerable pressure, induced by social-identity threat, to modify their self-definitions. Such modifications presumably allow them to reduce the relevance of stereotypes; they can acknowledge the existence and validity of the stereotype yet simultaneously escape its more damning implications by creatively reconstruing their self-concepts.

Rejection Sensitivity, Self-Knowledge, and Self-Efficacy

As reviewed earlier, some targets of discrimination are significantly more prone than others to expect, perceive, and be psychologically bothered by stereotypes impugning their group's academic competence – an individual difference known as status-based rejection sensitivity (e.g., RS-race; cf. Pinel, 1999). It is presumed that RS-race is itself a self-concept coping response to prejudice, one that is partly an adaptation to either past or anticipated negative treatment. Chronic expectations of prejudice can have both negative and positive effects. For example, those individuals who are high in RS-race perform worse on tests framed as measures of ability (Aronson & Inzlicht, 2004) and have greater difficulty adjusting to college (Mendoza-Denton et al., 2002). At the same time, attributing negative outcomes to prejudice can buttress self-esteem. Crocker et al. (1991) have found, for example, that the self-esteem of stereotype targets is generally unaffected by negative performance feedback, particularly when there are objective grounds to suspect that prejudice is possible, such as when students know the evaluator to be aware of their race or gender.

More recent research (Aronson & Inzlicht, 2004) has revealed two further effects of RS-race among African-American college students. First, high RS-race students were far less sensitive to their actual strengths and weaknesses when evaluating their own academic performances than were low RS-race students. Specifically, all other things being equal, Black students with high RS-race scores were less able than their low RS-race counterparts to correctly estimate the number of items solved on a laboratory task a few minutes after completing it. Second, they were far less stable over time in their academic self-efficacy (Bandura, 1977) or their confidence in their abilities to achieve, learn, and accomplish important academic tasks. A diary study in which they reported their self-efficacy twice daily for 8 days revealed them to be to be riding a virtual rollercoaster of self-confidence, extremely high in confidence at one point in time, and extremely low in confidence a few hours later. In contrast, low RS-race students were far more stable in their self-efficacy, showing less sensitivity to the vagaries of academic life. Thus, suspicion about racial prejudice can significantly predict one's self-perceived academic ability. Both effects – miscalibration and temporal instability – suggest a lack of academic self-knowledge on the part of high RS-race students.

There is a clear parallel here with work on unstable self-esteem. Two studies (Kernis, Cornell, Sun, Berry, & Harlow, 1993; Campbell, 1990) find that unstable self-esteem is associated with an unclear self-concept. Importantly, Kernis et al.'s research shows that individuals with unstable self-esteem are highly influenced by external feedback; they respond more favorably to positive and more defensively to negative feedback than do individuals with stable, firmly grounded self-esteem. And they experience the rollercoaster-like effects of positive and negative feedback. Thus, given the parallel findings, it seems reasonable to make the same argument for the stability of academic self-efficacy: Clarity and stability go hand in hand. How exactly RS-race creates this lack of clarity remains to be established, but one possibility is that the link between prior discrimination and stability/

calibration is mediated by how much a person feels able to trust feedback about the self as veridical and valuable.

REMEDIATION OF THREAT: SOCIETAL ADJUSTMENTS

In this chapter, we've discussed how stigma can hurt, threaten, and impede. But what can we do to help people overcome these threats? How can we neutralize threats present in the environment? There is increasing evidence from both laboratory and field studies that the decrements in performance engendered by social-identity threat can be overcome with careful attention to how tasks are framed and to what students can be taught.

As the foregoing discussion should make clear, minority status is a reality: Some groups will always be underrepresented. Yet many studies show that minority status need not result in stereotype threat, which, as indicated in the preceding text, can impair academic achievement. For example, simply having the person administering the exam be of the same race or gender as the test-taker can reduce the test score differential between minority and the majority students (Marx & Roman, 2002; Marx & Goff, 2005). Famous interventions such as the "jigsaw classroom" (e.g., Aronson & Patnoe, 1997) and Treisman's Emerging Scholars Program (e.g., College Board, 2001) show that classroom cooperation and group work can improve minority student's performance by perhaps alleviating social-identity threat. In *The jigsaw classroom*, lessons are broken up into several pieces and one piece is distributed to each member of the group who must learn the material and teach it to the others. To perform well, therefore, students must cooperate, because the piece of the puzzle held by each student is vital to everyone's successful learning. Studies show that the technique typically raises the minority students' grades (by about one letter grade), raises their self-esteem, increases friendships between ethnic group members, and leads to greater enjoyment among students of all backgrounds. To the extent that the academic underperformance and self-concept effects seen in real classrooms are partially produced by social-identity threat, the jigsaw technique may be particularly helpful to minority students. In Treisman's program, there is also cooperative group study outside of class in special homework sessions, but the cooperation is not as rigidly structured as jigsaw. Moreover, the work is very challenging, going beyond what is covered in class. Treisman's program lifted the African-American students' achievement to surprising levels; they earned grades as high as the Asian students in the class. Recent research by Rosenthal and Crisp (2006) suggests that one can easily create the kind of communal mind-set that these interventions enjoy in surprisingly easy ways. They found that simply having women list a handful of ways that men and women are similar before taking a math test raised women's test performance and eliminated the classic stereotype threat effect.

Two recent studies suggest that people's awareness of their susceptibility to social-identity threat can reduce the negative effects, presumably by helping them make more situational (and thus anxiety-reducing) attributions for their difficulties. Simply informing students about the dynamics of stereotype threat before being tested improved the test scores of both African-American college students taking a verbal test (Aronson & Williams, 2004) and female college students taking a math test (Johns, Schmader, & Martens, 2005). Inspired by the research of Carol Dweck (e.g., Dweck, 1999), Aronson and colleagues have conducted several studies showing that framing tests as measuring improvable dimensions (as opposed to nonimprovable ones) appears to reduce the effects of stereotype threat. This has been demonstrated both in laboratory studies in which tests are presented as measuring malleable versus fixed skills, and in interventions in which students are taught to see all academic abilities as highly learnable. The results are consistent across studies: Students score better on evaluative tests and get better grades when they are led to see their abilities as malleable as opposed to fixed (Aronson, 1999; Aronson et al., 2002; Good, Aronson, & Inzlicht, 2003).

CONCLUSION

In the past 15 years, social psychological research on prejudice and discrimination has started focusing on the plight of the target. During this time, research has taught us that stigma has a far-ranging effect on its target. By focusing on a model of threatening environments, we have provided a framework in which to understand this research and to stimulate further research. The bottom line is that environmental cues, which on the surface appear benign, can communicate social devaluation and exclusion. When this message is received it can result in underperformance, mistrust, disidentification, and self-unclarity. Some people are particularly sensitive to stigma-relevant cues and experience the full brunt of social-identity threat as a result. The good news is that the effects of stigma can be mitigated and that there is much that educators and policy makers can do to help. Once this is done, we may be able to inoculate students against prejudice and create resilience among individuals belonging to socially devalued groups.

REFERENCES

Allison, K. W. (1998). Stress and oppressed social category membership. In J. K. Swim & C. Stangor (Eds.), *Prejudice: The target's perspective* (pp. 145–170). San Diego, CA: Academic Press.

Anderson, N. B. (1989). Racial differences in stress-induced cardiovascular reactivity and hypertension: Current status and substantive issues. *Psychological Bulletin, 105,* 89–105.

Aronson, E., & Patnoe, S. (1997). *The jigsaw classroom.* New York: Longman.

Aronson, J. (1999). *The effects of conceiving ability as fixed or improvable on responses to stereotype threat.* Unpublished manuscript, New York University.

Aronson, J. (2002). Stereotype threat: Contending and coping with unnerving expectations. In J. Aronson (Ed.), *Improving academic achievement: Impact of psychological factors on education* (pp. 279–301). San Diego, CA: Academic Press.

Aronson, J., & Inzlicht, M. (2004). The ups and downs of attributional ambiguity: Stereotype vulnerability and the academic self-knowledge of African-American students. *Psychological Science, 15,* 829–836.

Aronson, J., & Williams, J. (2004). *Stereotype threat: Forewarned is forearmed.* Manuscript in preparation: New York University.

Aronson, J., Fried, C., & Good, C. (2002). Reducing the effects of stereotype threat on African American college students by shaping theories of intelligence. *Journal of Experimental Social Psychology, 38,* 113–125.

Bandura, A. (1977). Self-efficacy: Toward a unifying theory of behavioral change. *Psychological Review, 84,* 191–215.

Baumeister, R. F., Heatherton, T. F., & Tice, D. M. (1994). *Losing control: How and why people fail at self-regulation.* San Diego, CA: Academic Press.

Ben-Zeev, T., Fein, S., & Inzlicht, M. (2005). Stereotype threat and arousal. *Journal of Experimental Social Psychology, 41,* 174–181.

Blascovich, J., Spencer, S. J., Quinn, D., & Steele, C. (2001). African Americans and high blood pressure: The role of stereotype threat. *Psychological Science, 12,* 225–229.

Bowlby, J. (1988). *A secure base: Parent-child attachment and healthy human development.* New York: Basic Books, Inc.

Brown, R. P., & Pinel, E. C. (2003). Stigma on my mind: Individual differences in the experience of stereotype threat. *Journal of Experimental Social Psychology, 39,* 626–633.

Cadinu, M., Maass, A., Rosabianca, A., & Kiesner, J. (2005). Why do women underperform under stereotype threat? Evidence for the role of negative thinking. *Psychological Science, 16,* 572–578.

Campbell, J. D. (1990). Self-esteem and clarity of the self-concept. *Journal of Personality and Social Psychology, 59,* 538–549.

Cohen, G. L., Garcia, J., Master, A., & Apfel, N. (2005). *Valuing the self before being evaluated: A brief intervention to reduce the racial achievement gap.* Paper presented at the Society of Experimental Social Psychology Conference, San Diego, CA.

College Board (2001). *Calculus and community: A history of the emerging scholars community.* Retrieved September 9, 2004, from http://www.collegeboard.com/repository/calcandcomm_3947.pdf

Crocker, J., & Knight, K. M. (2005). Contingencies of self-worth. *Current Directions in Psychological Science, 14,* 200–203.

Crocker, J., & Major, B. (1989). Social stigma and self-esteem: The self-protective properties of stigma. *Psychological Review, 96,* 608–630.

Crocker, J., Major, B., & Steele, C. (1998). Social stigma. In D. T. Gilbert, S. T. Fiske, & L. Gardner (Eds.), *The handbook of social psychology* (pp. 504–553). New York: McGraw Hill.

Crocker, J., Voelkl, K., Testa, M., & Major, B. (1991). Social stigma: The affective consequences of attributional ambiguity. *Journal of Personality and Social Psychology, 60,* 218–228.

Croizet, J. C., & Claire, T. (1998). Extending the concept of stereotype threat to social class: The intellectual underperformance of students from low socioeconomic backgrounds. *Personality and Social Psychology Bulletin, 24,* 588–594.

Davies, P. G., Spencer, S. J., & Steele, C. M. (2005). Clearing the air: Identity safety moderates the effects of stereotype threat on women's leadership aspirations. *Journal of Personality and Social Psychology, 88,* 276–287.

Demo, D. H., & Parker, K. D. (1987). Academic achievement and self-esteem among Black and White college students. *Journal of Social Psychology, 127,* 345–355.

Devine, P. G. (1989). Stereotypes and prejudice: Their automatic and controlled components. *Journal of Personality and Social Psychology, 46,* 5–18.

Downey, G., & Feldman, S. I. (1996). Implications of rejection sensitivity for intimate relationships. *Journal of Personality and Social Psychology, 70,* 1327–1343.

Dweck, C. (1999). *Self-theories: Their role in motivation, personality, and development.* Philadelphia, PA: Psychology Press.

Elliot, A., & McGregor, H. (2001). A 2 x 2 achievement goal framework. *Journal of Personality and Social Psychology, 80,* 501–519.

Engle, R. W. (2002). Working memory capacity as executive attention. *Current Directions in Psychological Science, 11,* 19–23.

Fordham, S., & Ogbu, J. U. (1986). Black students' school success: Coping with the "burden of acting White." *Urban Review, 18,* 176–206.

Good, C., Aronson, J., & Inzlicht, M. (2003). Improving adolescents' standardized test performance: An intervention to reduce the effects of stereotype threat. *Journal of Applied Developmental Psychology, 24,* 645–662.

Goffman, E. (1963). *Stigma: Notes on the management of spoiled identity.* Englewood Cliffs, NJ: Prentice-Hall.

Higgins, E. T. (1997). Beyond pleasure and pain. *American Psychologist, 52,* 1280–1300.

Hare, B. R. (1977). Black and White child self-esteem in social science: An overview. *Journal of Negro Education, 46,* 141–156.

Inzlicht, M., Aronson, J., Good, C., & McKay, L. (2006). A particular resiliency to threatening environments. *Journal of Experimental Social Psychology, 42,* 323–336.

Inzlicht, M., & Ben-Zeev, T. (2000). A threatening intellectual environment: Why females are susceptible to experiencing problem-solving deficits in the presence of males. *Psychological Science, 11,* 365–371.

Inzlicht, M., & Hickman, L. (2005). *Stereotype threat affects persistence in non-stereotyped domains.* Unpublished manuscript, University of Toronto.

Inzlicht, M., & Good, C. (2006). How environments threaten academic performance, self-knowledge, and sense of belonging. In S. Levin & C. Van Laar (Eds.), *Stigma and group inequality: Social psychological approaches* (pp. 129–150). Mahwah, NJ: Erlbaum.

Inzlicht, M., McKay, L., & Aronson, J. (2006). Stigma as ego-depletion: How being the target of prejudice affects self-control. *Psychological Science, 17,* 262–269.

Johns, M., Schmader, T., & Martens, A. (2005). Knowing is half the battle: Teaching stereotype threat as a means of improving women's math performance. *Psychological Science, 16,* 175–179.

Kaiser, C. R., Vick, S. B., & Major, B. (2006). Prejudice expectations moderate preconscious attention to cues that are threatening to social identity. *Psychological Science, 17,* 332–338.

Kernis, M. H., Cornell, D. P., Sun, C. R., Berry, A. J., & Harlow, T. (1993). There's more to self-esteem than whether it is high or low: The importance of stability of self-esteem. *Journal of Personality and Social Psychology, 65,* 1190–1204.

Keller, J., & Dauenheimer, D. (2003). Stereotype threat in the classroom: Dejection mediates the disrupting threat effect on women's math performance. *Personality and Social Psychology Bulletin, 29,* 371–381.

Lazarus, R. S., & Folkman, S. (1984). *Stress, appraisal, and coping.* New York: Springer.

London, B., Downey, G., Rattan, A., & Velilla, E. (2004). *Sensitivity to gender-based rejection: Theory, validation, and implications for psychosocial well-being.* Paper presented at the 5th Annual meeting of the Society of Personality and Social Psychology, Austin, TX.

Major, B., Quinton, W. J., & McCoy, S. K. (2002). Antecedents and consequences of attributions to discrimination: Theoretical and empirical advances. In M. Zanna (Ed.), *Advances in experimental social psychology* (Vol. 34). San Diego, CA: Academic Press.

Major, B. N., & O'Brien, L. T. (2005). The social psychology of stigma. *Annual Review of Psychology, 56,* 393–421.

Marx, D. M., & Goff, P. A. (2005). Clearing the air: The effects of experimenter race on target's test performance and subjective experience. *British Journal of Social Psychology, 44,* 645–757.

Marx, D. M., & Roman, J. S. (2002). Female role models: Protecting women's math test performance. *Personality and Social Psychology Bulletin, 28,* 1183–1193.

McConahay, J. B. (1986). Modern racism, ambivalence, and the modern racism scale. In J. F. Dovidio & S. L. Gaertner (Eds.), *Prejudice, discrimination, and racism* (pp. 91–125). San Diego, CA: Academic Press.

McGuire, W. J., McGuire C. V., Child, P., & Fujioka, T. (1978). Salience of ethnicity in the spontaneous self-concept as a function of one's ethnic distinctiveness in the social environment. *Journal of Personality and Social Psychology, 36,* 511–520.

Mendoza-Denton, R. (2003, January). *Sensitivity to status-based rejection: Implications for minority students' college experience.* Colloquium presentation, University of California, Santa Cruz.

Mendoza-Denton, R., Downey, G., Purdie, V., Davis, & Pietrzak, J. (2002). Sensitivity to status-based rejection: Implications for African American students' college experience. *Journal of Personality and Social Psychology, 83*, 896–918.

Mendoza-Denton, R., Page-Gould, E., & Pietrzak, J. (2005). Mechanisms for coping with race-based rejection expectations. In S. Levin & C. Van Laar (Eds.), *Stigma and group inequality: Social psychological approaches* (pp.151–169). Mahwah, NJ: Erlbaum.

Mendoza-Denton, R., Shaw-Taylor, L., Chen, S., & Chang, E. (2009). Ironic effects of explicit gender prejudice on women's test performance. *Journal of Experimental Social Psychology, 45*, 275–278.

Muraven, M., & Baumeister, R. F. (2000). Self-regulation and depletion of limited resources: Does self-control resemble a muscle? *Psychological Bulletin, 126*, 247–259.

Muraven, M., Tice, D. M., & Baumeister, R. F. (1998). Self-control as limited resource: Regulatory depletion patterns. *Journal of Personality and Social Psychology, 74*, 774–789.

O'Brien, L. T., & Crandall, C. S. (2003). Stereotype threat and arousal: Effects on women's math performance. *Personality and Social Psychology Bulletin, 29*, 782–789.

Osborne, J. W. (1995). Academics, self-esteem, and race: A look at the assumptions underlying the disidentification hypothesis. *Personality and Social Psychology Bulletin, 21*, 449–455.

    (1997). Race and academic disidentification. *Journal of Educational Psychology, 89*, 728–735.

Pinel, E. C. (1999). Stigma consciousness: The psychological legacy of social stereotypes. *Journal of Personality and Social Psychology, 76*, 114–128.

Pronin, E., Steele, C. M., & Ross, L. (2004). Identity bifurcation in response to stereotype threat: Women and mathematics. *Journal of Experimental Social Psychology, 40*, 152–168.

Purdie-Vaughns, V., Stelle, C. M., Davies, P. G., Dittlmann, R., & Crosby, J. R. (2008). Social identity contingencies: How diversity cues signal threat or safety for African Americans in mainstream institutions. *Journal of Personality and Social Psychology, 94*, 615–630.

Rosenthal, H. E. S., & Crisp, R. J. (2006). Reducing stereotype threat by blurring intergroup boundaries. *Personality and Social Psychology Bulletin, 32*, 501–511.

Ross, L., & Nisbett, R. E. (1991). *The person and the situation: Perspectives of social psychology*. New York: McGraw Hill Book Company.

Schmader, T., & Johns, M. (2003). Converging evidence that stereotype threat reduces working memory capacity. *Journal of Personality and Social Psychology, 85*, 440–452.

Seibt, B., & Förster, J. (2004). Stereotype threat and performance: How self-stereotypes influence processing by inducing regulatory foci. *Journal of Personality and Social Psychology, 87*, 38–56.

Sekaquaptewa, D., & Thompson, M. (2002). The differential effects of solo status on members of high and low-status groups. *Personality and Social Psychology Bulletin, 28*, 694–707.

Spencer, S. J., Steele, C. M., & Quinn, D. (1999). Stereotype threat and women's math performance. *Journal of Experimental Social Psychology, 35,* 4–28.

Steele, C. M. (1997). A threat in the air. How stereotypes shape intellectual identity and performance. *American Psychologist, 52,* 613–629.

Steele, C. M., & Aronson, J. (1995). Stereotype threat and the intellectual test performance of African Americans. *Journal of Personality and Social Psychology, 69,* 797–811.

Steele, C. M., Spencer, S., & Aronson, J. (2002) Contending with images of one's group: The psychology of stereotype and social identity threat. In M. Zanna (Ed.), *Advances in experimental social psychology* (Vol. 34). San Diego, CA: Academic Press.

Swim, J. K., & Stangor, C. *Prejudice: The Target's Perspective.* San Diego, CA: Academic Press.

Turner, M. L., & Engle, R. W. (1989). Is working memory capacity task dependent? *Journal of Memory and Language, 28,* 127–154.

Vorauer, J. D., Main, K. J., & O'Connell, G. B. (1998). How do individuals expect to be viewed by members of lower status groups? Content and implications of meta-stereotypes. *Journal of Personality and Social Psychology, 75,* 917–937.

Zanna, M. P., & Cooper, J. (1974). Dissonance and the pill: An attribution approach to studying the arousal properties of dissonance. *Journal of Personality and Social Psychology, 29,* 703–709.

2

"To Climb or Not to Climb?" When Minorities Stick to the Floor

MARGARITA SANCHEZ-MAZAS
AND ANNALISA CASINI

INTRODUCTION

Laura,* about 40-years-old, is a cultivated and resourceful woman. She has a university degree, fluently speaks four languages, and has spent a large part of her working life as a top manager within motor and financial corporations. Despite the fact that she reached a high status and a consequent economic condition, a few years ago she decided suddenly to give up her brilliant career to turn to a precarious and poorly paid job in social work. Since her working life changed, she has been faced with several employment contracts that were limited in time and quite meager in terms of salary. The case of Laura, who has moved from a secure working position to an uncertain one, could seem odd, given that no one forced her to leave her last corporate position and she hasn't been a victim of either moral or sexual harassment in the workplace. Moreover, people engaged in the struggle for women's economic emancipation might be shocked at the idea that a highly successful person abandoned her position. Hence, why did Laura make such a decision?

As far as this question is concerned, any potential answer should take into account two main arguments: First, professions are differentially evaluated in accordance with socially shared criteria, and those evaluations affect earnings and employment stability. Second, despite a generalized tendency for women to be emancipated from their traditional roles, women still tend to orient their working lives toward social concerns. The first issue raises the very general question of the social – and gendered – division of labor, while the second seems to address a "feminine" psychological propensity to engage in professions or activities characterized by what has been called the "ethic of care" (Gilligan, 1982).

* This is a fictitious name for a real person.

Our ambition in the research program described here was to understand better the informal impediments, currently called the "glass ceiling," that women often face while seeking positions of power or high responsibility. First, we will suggest that the differential valuation of professions is determined by normative principles that have been historically institutionalized. Second, we will interpret women's tendency to orient themselves toward "feminine" activities in the light of the also historically institutionalized division between private and public spheres and their correspondence with normative constraints and aspirations. Third, we will make explicit the main hypothesis that is currently guiding our empirical work, namely the idea of a normative discordance that most women face between a "feminine" principle underlying their socialization and large parts of contemporary social arrangements, and a "masculine" principle predominant in most of Western organizations and the political domain. Finally, we will present a research paradigm designed to capture this cleavage and some initial empirical findings that will be discussed in the light of our theoretical proposal.

THE SOCIAL DIVISION OF LABOR AND
MODERN FORMS OF RECOGNITION

Starting from the idea that the human being is a relational animal, the philosopher Axel Honneth posits that the individual owes his/her integrity and identity to being recognized by similar others (Honneth, 2003). But this human dependence on intersubjective recognition varies with the forms into which mutual recognition is shaped in different societies. In modern societies, intersubjective recognition grants individuals with a positive relation to themselves, that is to say, with the capacity to be sure of their personal integrity, their competencies, and their rights. In contrast with traditional societies where different forms of recognition were intertwined, the novelty of modern society has been to distinguish and institutionalize three different forms of recognition – love, rights, and esteem – that provide individuals with self-confidence, self-respect, and self-esteem, respectively. Each form of recognition is distributed according to a specific principle. While self-confidence is granted by attitudes of care that appeal to the principle of *need*, self-respect and self-esteem are granted by two forms of recognition that have emerged in modern societies and that are grounded in radically distinct, and even discordant, principles, namely *equality* and *achievement*. These distinctions parallel social psychological work on different justice rules governing specific social contexts, namely need, equality, and equity (Clémence & Doise, 1998; Roux, 2001). According to Honneth, legal equality is one form of recognition since it provides in principle each individual with equal rights. The second is achievement, a form of recognition that rests on the differential principle of equity. Whereas in traditional societies social prestige was highly dependent upon birth, individual achievement became, in modern times, the new and unique means to obtain social esteem. Along with the institutionalization of the principle of legal equality, "individual achievement emerged as a leading cultural idea [...] so that individual social standing became normatively independent of origin and possessions" (Honneth, 2003, p. 140). Indeed, the organized division of labor, as well as the very demarcation of professions along a graduated scale of prestige, can be seen as the results of the cultural valuation of specific capacities and abilities. In turn, this cultural valuation of professions determines the amount of resources that are allocated to the individual.

Moreover, this development established what was distinguished as "work" or "achievement" in the first place. The differential valuation of social activities – notably between paid and unpaid, domestic and professional work – traces back to a fundamental division between private and public spheres, which also characterizes modern society. For feminist historian Joan Scott (1996), this division implies that modernity has invented two universalisms instead of one, since besides the universal of human rights, the naturalization of the woman stands as a universal principle of a new fundamental divide based on biology (see also Guillaumin, 1992). Indeed, the gender divide has not only dictated the respective places and activity spheres for men and women, but also precisely defined the abilities and talents that are required in the private and public spheres. As Honneth points out in reference to the rise of the bourgeois-capitalist society, "the extent to which something counts as 'achievement,' as a cooperative contribution, is defined against a value standard whose normative reference point is the economic activity of the independent, middle-class, male bourgeois" (Honneth, 2003, p. 141). In this way, the naturalization of women transforms the activities of the housewife and mother into the mere realization of her "innate" nature. When entering the labor market, therefore, women's professional work is not believed to be as valuable and productive as that of men. The inheritance of this institutional framework, which provides the principles for the evaluation of professions and the criteria for distributing resources, can be found in the still-prevalent gendered vertical and horizontal division of labor (for a comprehensive report, see Eurostat, 2003). Even today, gender serves as a criterion for determining the value of a given profession independently of the actual content of the work. Moreover, this naturalist thinking is still recognizable in the present day in several explanations of the gender imbalance in the professional field, attributing the peculiarity of women's careers to biological differences in skills and aptitudes (Deady & Law Smith, 2006; Geary, 1998), as well as to psychological blockages such as a supposed "fear of success" (Horner, 1969a) or a weaker orientation toward social dominance (Sidanius, Pratto, & Rabinowitz, 1994). As we will argue subsequently, the principles guiding the modern forms of recognition, love, rights, and achievement are also to be regarded as principles governing distinctively the feminine and masculine universes that have been institutionalized as private and public spheres.

PUBLIC AND PRIVATE SPHERES AND THE GENDER NORM

The historical perspective adopted here incites to bridge the psychological – and professional – "relational" orientations, shown by most women, to the profound and lasting implications of women's relegation to the private sphere at the beginning of the *modernity*. Indeed, this relegation made them noneligible for equal rights and social esteem, the forms of recognition that are governed by the principles of equality and equity, respectively. This means that these two principles have not penetrated the domestic universe, which is, in turn, solely governed by the "ethic of care" (Gilligan, 1982) or the principle of need. We can find in Ulrich Beck's analysis a similar view that the distribution of social roles as a function of sexual belonging, as well as the very existence of the nuclear family, are at the basis of the industrial society and not a residue from the past or the result of some essentialist properties (Beck, 1992). The idea that conflicting logics are found in activities, attitudes, and values, and even as Honneth puts it, in "substantive modes of interaction," differ sharply between private and public spheres and embody distinct underlying principles at the heart of our conceptualization of the discrepancy between men's and women's professional destinies. Along this line, rather than abandoning the notion of women's psychological propensity to have a "feminine"-type career (Butterfield & Grinnell, 1999) or ascribing gender inequalities solely to the effects of discrimination or sexism (Bulard, 1999; Glick & Fiske, 1999; Swim, Aikin, Hall, & Hunter, 1995), we propose an interpretation in terms of the operation of discordant principles governing spheres that have been socially constructed as "feminine" versus "masculine" (Sanchez-Mazas & Casini, 2005). This approach may contribute to the incorporation into the interpretation of gender differences the analysis of the principles guiding organizations and institutions along with the analysis of individuals' gender orientations according to the classical instrumental/relational duality.

Hence, the qualities or aptitudes distinguished as "instrumental" versus "relational" should be regarded in the light of the normative framework of our Western modern societies, which has produced both the social construction of professional fields and the development of "masculine" and "feminine" social identities.

As far as social identity is concerned, the notion of gender (Oakley, 1972) reflects the socially learned components of masculinity and femininity rather than the aspects derived from biological sex. In this perspective, men and women are conceived as individuals who, in the process of socialization, have been "enculturated" to adopt gender organizing principles of *instrumentality* and *relatedness*, socially constructed, respectively, as *masculine and feminine* (Bem, 1993). Following this point of view, gender functions as an "actual culture" that offers "gender lenses" through the internalization of which biological males and females are progressively transformed into *masculine* and *feminine* adults who evaluate and enact behaviors and attitudes in different ways according to their perceived gender appropriateness (Bem, 1993).

Gender as a culture, that is, as a socially shared representation and a basis for self-definition, can thus be viewed as a set of powerful norms guiding social actions and interactions. However, as happens for other cultural norms, individuals can either "construct a conventionally gendered self, or resist acquiring those gender lenses and thereby become a gender subversive" (Bem, 1993, p.133). Even in the latter case, however, gender undeniably influences the construction of the self (Cross & Madson, 1997; Eagly & Steffen, 1984; Josephs, Markus, & Tafarodi, 1992; Wood, Christensen, Hebl, & Rothgerber, 1997). Considering the gendered dimension of professions and identities in terms of compatibilities or incompatibilities between norms in organizations and norms underlying the construction of the self, individuals may face more or less tension. Such tension may arise, in particular, in situations involving a discrepancy between organizational norms and the person's own gendered identity. According to this logic, a career option can appear as more or less suitable and attractive. Indeed, normative discrepancies are most likely to appear when a lack of fit exists between the qualities and aspirations derived from a "feminine" internalized gender norm and those required in professional sectors or positions organized according to a "masculine" norm (or vice versa). Following Morton Deutsch's analysis, the main hypothesis here is that there is a causal link between the different forms of social organization and individuals' psychological orientations, defined as a composite set of cognitive, motivational, and moral orientations that guide individuals' behaviors and reactions to given situations.

More precisely, Deutsch posits that "typically, the psychological orientation of the individual fits the situation and a lack of fit induces pressures from the situation and/or the self to reduce the misfit" (Deutsch, 1990, p. 157). This is probably what happened to Laura. Along with perhaps personal reasons, her shift from the commercial context to the social one – with the high costs that this implied in terms of financial outcome and social status – may have been due to the "clash" between a rather *masculine* work setting (relying on instrumentality) and her personal, more *feminine* social orientation (relying on relatedness).

Following this line of thought, we suggest that women's reluctance to strive to enter the top of the business, professional, or political hierarchy is at least partially due to a lack of perceived fit between the feminine *relational* norm and the meritocratic one. In contrast, most men, or at least the normatively "masculine" ones, benefit from an almost perfect fit between their psychological orientation and the masculine instrumental meritocratic norm.

GENDER DIFFERENCE AND GENDER HIERARCHY

The empirical study of the "glass ceiling" phenomenon as implying a fundamental discrepancy between norms in organizations and the individual's internalization of a gender norm required us to design a new paradigm. The first step was to assess the gendered dichotomy through the traits and attributes that have been found in the social science literature to differentiate men and women. These included, among others, *instrumentality* versus *expressiveness* (Parsons & Bales, 1955); *agentic* versus *communal* orientation (Eagly, 1987); a justice-based versus care-based moral sense (Gilligan & Attanucci, 1988); and *individualism* versus *collectivism* (Triandis, 1995). While our approach stresses the historical and social construction of these dualities (Marková, 2003; Sanchez-Mazas & Licata, 2005), we acknowledge that these polarized dimensions are actually reproduced, albeit with variability and evolution, by living men and women. However, these dichotomies are often approached in terms of the "difference" between men and women, whereas our concern, beyond gender differences, was gender hierarchy.

The conjunction of difference and hierarchy, which is typical of the gender divide, has been regarded as an anthropological universal that systematically attributes a higher value to what has been distinguished, in a given society, as symbolizing the masculine (Héritier, 1996, 2002). In our culture, professional prestige and power positions are mostly invested with traits that involve the masculine principles of instrumentality and orientation toward the task (Maier, 1999). Therefore, bringing together the gendered aspects of organizations and of social identities implies a consideration of the masculine and feminine polarities in a vertical top/down order according to which the masculine is at the top and the feminine at the bottom, instead of treating them as the opposed poles of an horizontal continuum. One way to explore the "glass ceiling" phenomenon is thus to assess the impact, upon social-mobility strategies, of an experimentally induced variation of the feminine and masculine dimensions at the top – that is, in the dimensions of organizations presented to a potential candidate for a leader position – and at the bottom, by measuring the psychological orientations of this potential candidate. Our contention was that psychological impediments to upward social mobility would be most likely in cases of incompatibility rather than compatibility between the two dimensions and specifically when a feminine individual is confronted with a masculine-typed professional position or organizational culture. It should be stressed that this hypothesis holds specifically for women. Not only is the "glass ceiling" a phenomenon that affects specifically women, but a male's career in female-dominated jobs has been described as a ride on a "glass escalator" (Acker, 1990; Budig, 2002; Williams, 1992, 1995): "Often, despite their intentions, they face invisible pressures to move up in their professions. Like being on a moving escalator, they have to work to stay in place" (Williams, 1995, p.87).

EXPERIMENTAL ILLUSTRATIONS

To test these assumptions, we set up a series of studies in which we tried to systematize the interaction between gender-related variables and work-setting variables to investigate individual willingness to climb the social ladder. We started from the idea that the willingness to undertake a particular position at work is influenced by the representation individuals hold about the working context itself (Schneider, 2001; van Vianen & Fischer, 2002). Indeed, through the observation of "key symbols," such as the firm's vocation (i.e., major goal), brand, or language (Hatch, 2000), individuals can become aware of the organizational culture and then decide whether to engage in it. Translating this into our analysis of the "glass ceiling," we hypothesized that males' and females' willingness to seek a particular career position partially depends upon the representation the person holds about a particular organizational culture and specifically whether this culture reflects mainly a *relational* or an *instrumental* norm (Casini & Sanchez-Mazas, 2005).

STUDY 1

In a first study (N = 153, N_{female} = 89; average age = 19), we evaluated men's and women's willingness to become a manager in a company as a function of the content – relational or instrumental – of the organizational norm operationalized as the "vocation of the organisation," that is, the main goal of a hypothetical company (Casini & Sanchez-Mazas, 2005, study 1). The method we followed was to present participants (first-year students from social sciences faculties at the Université Libre de Bruxelles) with a self-administered questionnaire ostensibly composed of two supposedly independent sections. The purpose of the first section was to assess participants' psychological orientations in terms of instrumentality versus relatedness. We used for this the "need for achievement/need for affiliation" scale, which is specifically designed to measure individuals' tendency to value either personal outcomes or relationships with others (Lindgren, Moritsch, Thulin, & Mich, 1986; Sid & Lindgren, 1982). Indeed, according to our hypothesis, this individual difference variable was expected to play an important role in willingness to engage in upward mobility and, more precisely, in the decision to become a manager in a particular work setting framed in either instrumental versus relational terms. Thus, the second part of the questionnaire was designed to induce the organizational norm through a description of the "vocation of the company" where the participants were asked to function as managers. To induce different representations of the organizational vocation, we used the Blau and Scott typology (1962) of distinctive forms of organizations according to the category of beneficiaries that is targeted, identified on the basis of the question "*cui bono?*" (i.e., "Who benefits?"). The *instrumental norm* was induced through the description of an organization whose priority was material benefit (e.g., financial organizations) – "instrumental company vocation" condition. The *relational norm* was made salient through the description of an organization aimed at alleviating the suffering of unfortunate human beings (e.g., humanitarian organizations) – "relational company vocation" condition. These contrasting "company vocations" were reflected in the names selected for the specific organization in which participants might take a managerial position: The instrumental vocation company was called "Leader Financial Consulting," and the relational vocation company was called "Handicap Aid International." The

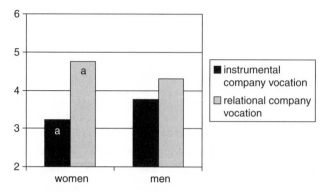

FIGURE 2.1. Men's and women's willingness to assume a managerial position as a function of the company vocation (Study 1).

Note: Scores marked by the index (a) are different at p <0.001.

main dependent variable in this study was the degree of participants' motivation to become manager in the described company.

Results showed first a significant interaction between the participants' gender and the organization's vocation: While the men's motivation to become a manager did not differ as a function of organizational vocation, the women's motivation was significantly higher for the relational organization (Handicap Aid International) than for the instrumental organization (Leader Financial Consulting) (Figure 2.1). This effect strongly suggests a female propensity to favor an altruistic over an instrumental type of organization when asked to engage in a leadership position. Furthermore, it reveals that, at least under some conditions, women are quite willing to assume a managerial role, a finding that questions the idea of a basic feminine reluctance toward power (Horner, 1969a, 1969b).

Interestingly, although the variable "sex" does not interact with the "need for achievement/need for affiliation" measure of participants' psychological orientation, this latter variable appears to moderate the participants' intention to become manager. More specifically, a higher "affiliation" motive – that is, the participants' orientation toward the relationship rather than the outcome – strengthens the willingness to accept the managerial role, albeit only within the relational context of Handicap Aid International. In the instrumental context of Leader Financial Consulting, the same "affiliation" motive weakens the motivation to become a manager. These findings confirm the importance of taking into account the general normative orientations of individuals, an issue that we address more explicitly in a second study involving the individual gender norm.

The second study addressed the general issue of intragender variability in upward social-mobility strategies. For if it is true that Laura gave up her career as an executive because she did not want to climb the social ladder and that many women resist climbing the social ladder, it is also true that a growing number of women can be found in leading positions in the professional, business, and political fields. One way to explain such intragender variability is to distinguish the fact of being a man or a woman from the ideological, symbolic, and representational dimensions that contribute to experiencing oneself as masculine or feminine (Héritier, 1996). Sandra Bem's conceptualization of gender psychological orientations as being the result of the internalization of gender norms (Bem, 1993) helps to account for this intragender variability in the professional domain. Of particular interest for our own perspective is the shift she proposes from a bipolar conceptualization of *masculinity* and *femininity*, which tends to deny the possibility for men and women to develop what she calls a "gender-subversive psychological orientation," to a more complex view of gender orientations, which recognizes individuals' potential to deviate from polarized masculine and feminine gender norms. Indeed, in her *psychological androgyny* approach (Bem, 1974), besides the "orthodox" orientations of *masculinity* and *femininity*, Bem includes two additional categories represented by individuals who either endorse both masculinity and femininity norms or who reject both norms; these are labeled *androgynous* and *undifferentiated*, respectively.

Drawing upon this differentiated gender-orientation typology, the purpose of Study 2 ($N = 154$, $N_{female} = 117$; average age = 20) was to test the hypothesis that highly gender-normative individuals – those who could be classified into the unambiguous masculine and feminine categories – would show particular reluctance to engage in upward social mobility within a normative context that would appear incongruent rather than congruent with their personal gendered identity (Casini & Sanchez-Mazas, 2005, study 2). Such incompatibility was assumed to be clear-cut in situations where a masculine individual has to make his/her way in a relational-type organizational culture or, conversely, where a feminine individual confronts an organizational culture framed in instrumental terms.

As far as the organizational culture is concerned, there are many variables that might evoke the gendered dimension. In this second study, we focused on the instrumental versus relational *style of management* to assess the impact upon the motivation to become a manager, of the induced representation of a task-oriented versus relation-oriented manager (see, e.g., Blake & Mouton, 1964).

Following the same method as in Study 1, we used the first part of a similar questionnaire to measure (along with other variables of interest) respondents' gender psychological orientations. Bem's Sex-Role Inventory (BSRI) (Bem, 1974) comprises a series of gendered and nongendered (filler) psychological traits aimed at assessing individual gender orientation and classifying respondents into one of four categories as a function of their responses. Thus, participants who scored high on the "masculine" traits (e.g., forceful, self-reliant, etc.) and low on the feminine (e.g., warm, gentle, etc.) were assigned to the masculine category ($n = 44$), whereas those who scored low on masculine but high on feminine traits where identified as feminine ($n = 34$). In addition, the androgynous category was composed of individuals scoring high on both kinds of traits ($n = 32$), whereas the undifferentiated category was composed of those scoring low in both kinds of traits ($n = 43$).

In the second section of the questionnaire, a sample of participants with the same characteristics to those questioned in Study 1 were presented with the same manager-recruitment scenario, except that the variable of organizational vocation was replaced by the variable of *style of management* to make salient the organization's *instrumental* versus *relational norm*. Hence, one half of participants were led to believe that they were expected to endorse a "directive" style of management (*instrumental* norm condition), described performing their role in an individualistic and task-oriented way, involving a top-down decision-making process. Conversely, the other half of participants was presented with a "collaborative" style of management (*relational* norm condition), described as involving a group-based, democratic decision-making process and a concern for the well-being of subordinates. Again, the main dependent variable was the extent to which respondents were willing to become a manager given the type of management they were expected to develop. Moreover, for the analysis of these data, only the masculine and feminine individuals were retained because of their strong adherence to a gender norm.

The results of this study show a significant interaction between the two independent variables (Figure 2.2), individual gender orientation and style of management, indicating that individuals classified as feminine and masculine exhibited different degrees of motivation to become a directive manager (*instrumental* norm condition). In contrast, no significant difference

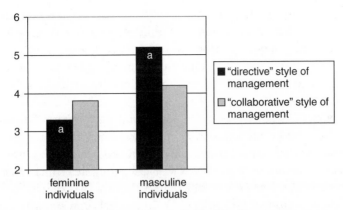

FIGURE 2.2. Feminine and masculine individuals' willingness to assume a managerial position as a function of the imposed style of management (Study 2).

Note: Scores marked by the index (a) are different at $p < 0.001$.

appeared in participants' motivation to become a collaborative manager (*relational* norms condition). That is, *feminine* individuals showed more reluctance to adopt the "directive" management role than did *masculine* individuals, but both groups were equally disposed to adopt the collaborative type of management. This finding suggests that the hypothesized incompatibility between organizational norms and gender norms obtains specifically in the confrontation between an instrumental organizational norm and a feminine-gendered identity. The implication of such an incongruent situation for women's propensity to endorse leadership positions may well be one of the keys to improve our understanding of the "glass ceiling" phenomenon.

DISCUSSION

Taken together, the results of these studies lend some support to the theoretical perspective adopted here and hence shed some new light on the factors underlying the imbalance between men and women with respect to power in business, professional, and political fields. In line with Tajfel's (1972) concern for the incorporation of relevant contextual variables into experimental settings, our findings in the study of the "glass ceiling" phenomenon should encourage the development of an approach connecting the values, norms, and particular arrangements that characterize the work setting to the symbolic dimensions underlying the elaboration of social identity. Such an approach suggests that, beyond the currently identified and well-documented impediments to women's careers stemming from the unequal distribution of housework and family tasks, the operation of norms and the implication of gender identity contribute to the reluctance that some women show in endorsing high positions in various fields.

Of course, this experiment is but one among many methods that should be used to explore the complexity of the relations between individuals and organizations, and discourse analysis methods are highly needed in this respect because of their efficacy in highlighting the actual contents of socially shared representations. The steps we have been taking in this direction provide additional evidence for the differential approach that men and women develop as far as their expectations for a successful life are concerned. Responding to the general open question of "what it means for you to lead a successful life?," men and women show quite diverse representations of the very notion of success. Specifically, while female participants in our study ($N = 49$; $N_{female} = 21$; average age = 28) show generally a strong concern for the creation and the realization of goals in general, personal well-being, and kinship, men value everyday life experiences and symbols of both material and status success (e.g., money).

Beyond its influence in general expectations for life, the "relational norm" may also contribute to the "glass ceiling" effect in other subtle ways. Hence, for example, the concern for relations with fellows and friends has been identified as a factor affecting girls', but not boys', lesser performance when they are evaluated publicly rather than privately (Huguet & Monteil, 1995), and girls' tendency to interrupt a game more often than do boys when tensions appear (Lever, 1976, cited in Gilligan, 1982). It may also be operating among spouses, such as when the woman decides not to accept a position or to undertake a competition that would place her above her companion in terms of earning and/or status, so as to avoid "spoiling the relationship" (Fortino, 2002). These few examples strongly evoke the notion of an "habitus," in Bourdieu's sense, which is acquired through the socialization process and determines in a rather unconscious way women's "feminine" destiny (Bourdieu & Passeron, 1964). However, it is important to stress that women are often very much aware of the high costs they may endure in terms of social relations when they enter domains or positions that have long been consensually defined as "masculine." On the basis of their awareness of sexist stereotypes and representations, many women *choose* not to risk being seen as a renegade from their identity group (Chryssochoou & Sanchez-Mazas, 2000) or as putting a social distance between themselves and other women (Ellemers, van den Heuvel, de Gilder, Maass, & Bonvini, 2004). This is particularly so if we consider not so much women's supposedly "collectivist" orientation (Triandis, 1995), but rather the growing evidence of women's distinctive "relational self" (Sedikides & Brewer, 2001). Very often, however, women search for compromises in an attempt to reach both social success and satisfactory social relations and personal lives (Heinich, 2003).

The vigor of what we have called here the "relational norm" therefore seems to deserve special attention, not only because it forms the normative context of forces that "retain" women at home and make them content with housework inequality (Roux, 2001), but also because it appears to be strongly implicated in the broader work expectations of women. Yet, "relational" concerns are often very much undervalued and badly implemented in many domains. Indeed, we should consider the weight that such a norm may have in diverse contexts, such as school life, professional orientation, atypical careers, and political involvement. In addition, we should stress the necessary changes that should be proposed not only for promoting women's upward mobility, but also for changing the norms and practical arrangements within the professional life. The still evident gendered division of labor cannot be illuminated solely in the light of women's own choices but must also consider women's hesitations in front of domains that have been organized on the basis of a socially constructed masculinity defining specific abilities, talents, interests, attitudes, and values. If an improvement of women's position is indeed a cherished aspiration, we cannot avoid questioning these masculine dimensions and rethinking the constraints of private and public spheres in the first place.

REFERENCES

Acker, J. (1990). Hierarchies, jobs, bodies: A theory of gendered organizations. *Gender & Society, 4*(2), 139.

Beck, U. (1992). *Risk society: Towards a new modernity.* London: Sage Publications.

Bem, S. L. (1974). The measurement of psychological androgyny. *Journal of Consulting and Clinical Psychology, 42*(2), 155, 162.

(1993). *The lenses of gender: Transforming the debate on sexual inequality.* New Haven: Yale University Press.

Blake, R. R., & Mouton, J. S. (1964). *The managerial grid; key orientations for achieving production through people.* Houston, TX: Gulf.

Blau, P. M., & Scott, W. F. (1962). *Formal organizations.* San Francisco, CA: Chandler Publishing Company.

Bourdieu, P., & Passeron, J.-C. (1964). *Les héritiers : les étudiants et la culture.* Paris: Editions de Minuit.

Budig, M. (2002). Male advantage and the gender composition of jobs: who rides the glass escalator? *Social Problems, 49*(2), 258–277.

Bulard, M. (1999, May). Désert féminin dans les lieux des pouvoir. Sexisme ordinaire au travail. *Le Monde Diplomatique*, 24–25.

Butterfield, D. A., & Grinnell, J. P. (1999). "Re-viewing" gender, leadership, and managerial behavior: Do three decades of research tell us anything? In G. N. Powell (Ed.), *Handbook of gender and work* (pp. 223–238). Thousand Oaks, CA, US: Sage Publications Inc.

Casini, A., & Sanchez-Mazas, M. (2005). " Ce poste n'est pas fait pour moi ! " l'impact de la culture d'entreprise et de l'adhésion aux rôles de genre sur la mobilité professionnelle ascendante. *Cahiers Internationaux de Psychologie Sociale, 67/68*, 101–112.

Chryssochoou, X., & Sanchez-Mazas, M. (2000). Modèle ou renégat? Une étude sur les perceptions de la "personne-alibi" dans un contexte méritocratique. *Cahiers Internationaux de Psychologie Sociale, 47/48*, 34–43.

Clémence, A., & Doise, W. (1998). Representation of human rights across different national contexts: The role of democratic and non-democratic populations and governments. *European Journal of Social Psychology, 28*(2), 207–226.

Cross, S. E., & Madson, L. (1997). Models of the self: Self-construals and gender. *Psychological Bulletin, 122*(1), 5–37.

Deady, D. K., & Law Smith, M. J. (2006). Height in women predicts maternal tendencies and career orientation. *Personality and individual differences, 40*(1), 17–25.

Deutsch, M. (1990). Forms of social organization: psychological consequences. In H. T. Himmelweit & G. Gaskell (Eds.), *Societal psychology* (pp. 157–176). Newbury Park, CA: Sage Publications Inc.

Eagly, A. H. (1987). *Sex differences in social behavior: a social-role interpretation*. Hillsdale, NJ: Lawrence Erlbaum Associates.

Eagly, A. H., & Steffen, V. J. (1984). Gender stereotypes stem from the distribution of women and men into social roles. *Journal of Personality and Social Psychology, 46*(4), 735–754.

Ellemers, N., Van den Heuvel, H., De Gilder, D., Maass, A., & Bonvini, A. (2004). The underrepresentation of women in science: Differential commitment or the queen bee syndrome? *British Journal of Social Psychology, 43*(3), 315–338.

Eurostat, E. C. (2003). *How women and men spend their time: Results from 13 European countries.* © European Communities, 2003. Retrieved 19/08/2003, from the World Wide Web: http://europa.eu.int/comm/eurostat/

Fortino, S. (2002). *La mixité au travail.* Paris: La Dispute/SNÉDIT.

Geary, D. C. (1998). *Male, female: The evolution of human sex differences* (1st ed.). Washington, DC: American Psychological Association,.

Gilligan, C. (1982). *In a different voice: Psychological theory and women's development.* Cambridge, MA: Harvard University Press.

Gilligan, C., & Attanucci, J. (1988). Two moral orientations: Gender differences and similarities. *Merrill Palmer Quarterly, 34*(3), 223–237.

Glick, P., & Fiske, S. T. (1999). Sexism and other "isms": Independence, status, and the ambivalent content of stereotypes. In W. B. J. Swann, J. H. Langlois & L. Albino Gilbert (Eds.), *Sexism and stereotypes in modern society: The gender science of*

Janet Taylor Spence (pp. 193–221). Washington, DC: American Psychological Association.

Guillaumin, C. (1992). *Sexe, race et pratique du pouvoir : l'idée de nature.* Paris: Côté-femmes.

Hatch, M. J. (2000). *Théorie des organisations : de l'intérêt de perspectives multiples.* Paris, Bruxelles: DeBoeck Université.

Heinich, N. (2003). *Les ambivalences de l'émancipation féminine.* Paris: Éditions Albin Michel.

Héritier, F. (1996). *Masculin/féminin : la pensée de la différence.* Paris: Odile Jacob.

(2002). *Masculin/féminin II: dissoudre la hiérarchie.* Paris: Odile Jacob.

Honneth, A. (2003). Redistribution or recognition: A response to Nancy Fraser. In A. Honneth (Ed.), *Redistribution or recognition? A political-philosophical exchange* (pp. 110–197). London: Verso.

Horner, M. S. (1969a). Fail: Bright women. *Psychology Today, 3*(6), 36, 38, 62.

(1969b). Sex differences in achievement motivation and performance in competitive and non-competitive situations. *Dissertation Abstracts International., 30*(1 B), 407.

Huguet, P., & Monteil, J. M. (1995). The influence of social comparison with less fortunate others on task performance: The role of gender motivations or appropriate norms. *Sex Roles, 33*(11–12), 753–765.

Josephs, R. A., Markus, H. R., & Tafarodi, R. W. (1992). Gender and self-esteem. *Journal of Personality and Social Psychology, 63*(3), 391–402.

Lever, J. (1976). Sex differences in the games children play. *Social Problems, 23*(4), 479–488.

Lindgren, H. C., Moritsch, B., Thulin, E. K., & Mich, G. (1986). Validity studies of three measures of achievement motivation. *Psychological Reports, 59*(1), 123–136.

Maier, M. (1999). On the gendered substructure of organization: Dimensions and dilemmas of corporate masculinity. In G. N. Powell (Ed.), *Handbook of gender and work* (pp. 69–94). Thousand Oaks, CA: Sage Publications Inc.

Marková, I. (2003). *Dialogicality and social representations. The dynamics of mind.* Cambridge, UK: Cambridge University Press.

Oakley, A. (1972). *Sex, gender and society.* London: Temple Smith.

Parsons, T., & Bales, R. F. (1955). *Family, socialization and interaction process.* Glencoe, IL: Free Press.

Roux, P. (2001). Perception of discrimination, feelings of injustice and women's resistance to gender equality. In F. Butera & G. Mugny (Eds.), *Social influence in social reality: Promoting individual and social change* (pp. 165–190). Ashland, OH: Hogrefe & Huber Publishers.

Sanchez-Mazas, M., & Casini, A. (2005). Egalité formelle et obstacles informels à l'ascension professionnelle : les femmes et l'effet "plafond de verre". *Social Science Information/sur les sciences sociales, 44*(1), 141–173.

Sanchez-Mazas, M., & Licata, L. (Eds.). (2005). *L'Autre: regards psychosociaux.* Grenoble: Presses Universitaires de Grenoble.

Schneider, B. (2001). Fits about fit. *Applied Psychology: An International Review, 50*(1), 141–152.

Scott, J. W. (1996). *Only paradoxes to offer. French feminists and the rights of man.* Cambridge, MA: Harvard University Press.

Sedikides, C., & Brewer, M. B. (Eds.). (2001). *Individual self, relational self, collective self.* Philadelphia, PA: Psychology Press.

Sid, A. K., & Lindgren, H. C. (1982). Achievement and affiliation motivation and their correlates. *Educational and Psychological Measurement, 42*(4), 1213–1218.

Sidanius, J., Pratto, F., & Rabinowitz, J. L. (1994). Gender, ethnic status, and ideological asymmetry: a social dominance interpretation. *Journal of Cross Cultural Psychology, 25*(2), 194–216.

Swim, J. K., Aikin, K. J., Hall, W. S., & Hunter, B. A. (1995). Sexism and racism: Old-fashioned and modern prejudices. *Journal of Personality and Social Psychology, 68*(2), 199–214.

Tajfel, H. (1972). Experiments in a vacuum. In J. Israel & H. Tajfel (Eds.), *The context of social psychology : A critical assessment* (pp. 69–119). London: Academic Press.

Triandis, H. C. (1995). *Individualism & collectivism.* Boulder, CO: Westview Press.

van Vianen, A. E. M., & Fischer, A. H. (2002). Illuminating the glass ceiling: the role of organizational culture preferences. *Journal of Occupational and Organizational Psychology, 75*(3), 315–337.

Williams, C. (1992). The glass escalator: hidden advantages for men in the "Female" professions. *Social Problems, 39*(3), 253–267.

(1995). *Still a man's world: men who do women's work.* Berkeley, CA: University of California Press.

Wood, W., Christensen, P. N., Hebl, M. R., & Rothgerber, H. (1997). Conformity to sex-typed norms, affect, and the self-concept. *Journal of Personality and Social Psychology, 73*(3), 523–535.

3

Managing the Message: Using Social Influence and Attitude Change Strategies to Confront Interpersonal Discrimination

JANET K. SWIM, SARAH J. GERVAIS, NICHOLAS PEARSON, AND CHARLES STANGOR

Members of stigmatized groups frequently find themselves as targets of interpersonal discrimination (e.g., Swim, Hyers, Cohen, & Ferguson, 2001; Swim, Hyers, Cohen, Fitzgerald, & Bylsma, 2003; Swim, Pearson, & Johnston, 2007). Interpersonal discrimination is defined as unfair or derogatory treatment based on social group membership (e.g., sex, race, age, sexual orientation, religion, or disability) that emerges within interpersonal contexts. It includes overtly hostile acts, covert acts designed to hide prejudices, and more subtle acts based upon, for example, habitual or normative behavior (Benokraitis & Feagin, 1986). For instance, the stigmatized may experience poor service in public establishments, be the target of racist jokes, experience sexually objectifying street comments, or assumptions of heterosexuality. Perhaps not surprisingly, targets of discrimination and bystanders often feel a desire to confront interpersonal discrimination, and one primary goal of such confrontation is to reduce prejudice, stereotyping, and discrimination (Feagin & Sikes, 1994; Hyers, 2007). However, the extent to which confronters are successful may depend upon factors that are related to attitude and behavior changes more generally.

The purpose of this chapter is to consider ways that individuals can strategically manage interpersonal confrontations of discrimination to reduce prejudice.[*] We define confrontation as any behavior or verbalization that indicates disagreement with another's behavior or comments. We focus on prejudice reduction, rather than other possible social goals (e.g., enhance personal control) because it acknowledges the agency that confronters can have in reducing prejudice (Swim, Hyers, & Cohen, 1998). Additionally, focusing on prejudice reduction allows us to draw upon theories of attitude

---

[*] For the purposes of simplicity, we refer to prejudice reduction, stereotype reduction, and discrimination reduction as *prejudice reduction.*

change and social influence, which provide a theoretical framework to understand how confronters can manage their messages to address this goal successfully. This literature points to strategic responses that may be particularly helpful for prejudice reduction. Taken together, research and theory about attitude change, social influence, and confronting indicate that individuals can increase the probability that their confrontations will reduce prejudice by crafting messages to maximize attitude change.

By strategically considering and selecting the types of responses they could give, confronters may maximize the likelihood of reducing prejudice while minimizing the costs of confronting. Potential costs include possible retaliation, revealing a stigmatized identity, negative evaluations, or further ostracism or discrimination (Kaiser & Miller, 2001; Swim, Johnston, & Pearson, under review; Swim & Thomas, 2006). Although people may choose to accept these costs to obtain the benefits of confronting, they may also be able to strategically manage the confronting message in such a way that they can obtain the benefits of confronting, such as prejudice reduction, while at the same time minimize the costs of confronting.

OVERVIEW

We structure our review within the classic message-learning framework developed by earlier attitude change researchers (e.g., Hovland, Janis, & Kelley, 1953; McGuire, 1985). This framework places confronters' messages within the social constraints of situations that influence the impact of the message on attitude and behavior changes. In this early research, attitudes were conceptualized as evaluative responses, beliefs, and behavioral tendencies. Similarly, when we consider prejudice reduction, we are considering changes in affect, cognitions, and behaviors, including different types of affect, stereotypes, and behaviors. The message-learning framework contrasts with other theories of attitude change that are more focused on the cognitive and motivational processes involved in attitude change that occur within recipients of messages. Although these latter theories are informative with regard to the consequences of confrontations, our review is limited to the literature that speaks to how confronters of discrimination can manage their messages within interpersonal contexts.

The message-learning approach indicates that in order for attitudes and beliefs to change, recipients of the message must *attend to* the message (which includes being exposed to and interested in the message), *comprehend* the message, and *accept* the message. And, for attitudes and beliefs to affect behaviors, individuals must *retain* the message and *act* on it later.

Therefore, in order for confronters to persuade others, they must first gain the audience's attention and then get the audience to understand what they are trying to say, such as what they see as problematic about the offending incident or the offensiveness of the underlying attitudes and beliefs. The confronters must then get the offenders to accept the message by agreeing, for instance, that the offenders' attitudes, beliefs, and/or behaviors are problematic, and that there are acceptable alternatives. Finally, for lasting change, the recipients of the message must remember the message at a later date and apply it to their behaviors.

According to the message-learning approach, the likelihood that individuals are able to take an audience through these processes is a function of the characteristics of the source, the message, the audience, the medium through which the message is given, and the effect of the message on the audience. These five factors are summarized in the following phrase, "*Who* (source), says *what* (message), to *whom* (audience), through what *channel* (medium), with what *effect* (message effect)." In the present domain, the source is the person doing the confronting and the message is the content of the confrontation. The medium is the way in which confronters convey their message (e.g., in writing, verbally, or behaviorally). The audience is the perpetrator and/or bystander to the source's confrontation, and the effect of the message is the psychological consequences that can either increase or decrease prejudice in the audience.

In the following three sections of the chapter, we use these characteristics to understand how confronters can manage their messages to decrease prejudice. In the first section, we examine possible effects on perpetrators and bystanders that confronters may seek. We then turn to the role of source and message characteristics by examining the ways that confronters can use messages to manage the impression they have on others. Finally, we examine features of audiences that might make confrontations most successful. Throughout these three sections, the confrontations we consider are through one medium, verbal interpersonal confrontation.

MESSAGE CHARACTERISTICS AND EFFECTS ON OTHERS

If confronters have the time, resources, and energy to develop their arguments, their messages could include arguments for their position and could refute counterarguments to effectively persuade their audience that underlying attitudes are prejudicial, beliefs are stereotypical, or behaviors are discriminatory. This may be particularly effective if their audience is deeply processing the information (Cialdini, Petty, & Cacioppo, 1981;

Greenwald, 1981; Petty, 1998). However, we are assuming that in interpersonal exchanges, individuals are not likely to be in the situation to construct such arguments. Rather, individuals likely need to make split-second judgments about whether to respond, what they want to target in their message, and how to respond. If individuals decide to respond, they may choose to target perpetrators' attitudes and beliefs, their behaviors, or both. Their responses may also involve attempts to influence how individuals think about situations or to influence their motivations by, for instance, targeting particular emotions or by changing social norms.

Changing Attitudes, Beliefs, and/or Behaviors

Successful direct attempts to reduce prejudice may depend upon whether confronters craft the message to address people's attitudes and beliefs or behaviors. Like links from attitudes and beliefs to behaviors more generally, prejudice and stereotypes are weakly linked to discrimination (Dovidio, Brigham, Johnson, & Gaertner, 1996). Thus, if confronters want to reduce offensive comments and behaviors, they may wish to focus the message on the comments and behaviors themselves. Confronters may need to explicitly state that they are addressing a behavior and not an attitude, because judging persons as prejudiced and judging their behaviors as discriminatory are highly correlated (Swim, Sechrist, Campbell, & Stangor, 2003). An audience may assume that confronters are addressing both when confronters only intend to address a behavior. A focus on behaviors has the potential to be even more effective if it directs a conversation toward improving future interactions rather than focusing on past wrongs (Smith & Ross, 2007). Moreover, as cognitive dissonance literature has shown, changing behaviors may have the added benefit of subsequently changing attitudes and beliefs (Festinger, 1957).

Confronters often target behaviors rather than attitudes and beliefs. For instance, when women respond to an alleged fellow participant or an interviewer who makes sexist remarks, women often focus on the perpetrator's behavior and not the perpetrator's attitudes and beliefs (Shelton & Richeson, 2005; Swim & Hyers, 1999). They may do this because they perceive that focusing the message on behaviors is more effective than focusing on attitudes and beliefs. Alternatively, however, confronters may choose to address behaviors because they feel more confident that the person's behavior is discriminatory and less confident that the person is prejudiced (Swim et al., 2003). As a result, they may believe that the safer or easier option is to focus on a particular concrete behavioral incident rather than on broader attitudes. This may lead to a confrontation that focuses on the problematic nature of the behavior (e.g., expressing the sentiment that the perpetrator's behavior was offensive or hurtful), rather than pointing a finger at the perpetrator of that behavior (e.g., expressing the sentiment that the perpetrator is prejudiced).

If targets choose to focus on attitudes and beliefs rather than behaviors, they may benefit from attending to the extent to which a behavior in question matches an attitude or belief (Ajzen & Fishbein, 1977; Fishbein & Ajzen, 1974). Research on attitude-behavior links indicate that general attitudes are more likely to be associated with an aggregation of similar behaviors rather than associated with a specific behavior (Fishbein & Ajzen, 1974). Thus, if a person is successful at changing a general attitude, the person may not necessarily see changes in a specific behavior at a specific time or place, but may be successful at changing general patterns of behaviors. As another example of matching attitudes and behaviors, research indicates that implicit prejudices tend to be associated with nonverbal behaviors, whereas explicit prejudices tend to be associated with verbal behaviors (Dovidio, Kawakami, & Gaertner, 2002). Thus, if confronters want to address a nonverbal behavior, they may be more successful if they consider ways to change implicit attitudes than ways to change explicit attitudes. Changing implicit attitudes could be difficult, given that this could involve repeated exposure to disconfirming associations (e.g., Kawakami, Dovidio, Moll, Hermsen, & Russin, 2000). When attempting to change implicit associations, it may be more effective to address motivations, so that the perpetrator makes efforts to break old associations and form new ones (Monteith, Ashburn-Nardo, Voils, & Czopp, 2002).

Of course a person could try to address attitudes, beliefs, *and* behaviors in an effort to cover all bases. We are not aware of research that examines the consequences of this tactic. This tactic could be ineffective if an audience reacts defensively to any accusation that they are prejudiced. When attitudes and beliefs are addressed along with behaviors, then the less-accusatory aspect of addressing a behavior may be lost. Also, practically, it may be difficult to respond to both within the course of an interpersonal interaction.

Changing Thoughts

It may be necessary or, at a minimum, helpful to inform individuals that particular behaviors are discriminatory or harmful to alter their beliefs or behaviors (Becker & Swim, 2008). One characteristic of many forms of modern discrimination is that discriminatory behaviors go unnoticed because they are habitual or ingrained in everyday life so that they seem normal or natural. Another characteristic of certain types of discrimination is that it appears positive, such as paternalistic behavior, even though it can still be harmful. Educating individuals about modern forms of discrimination can help reduce prejudice. For instance, Becker and Swim (2008) demonstrated that having individuals attend to everyday forms of sexism in their daily lives, providing information about the prevalence of sexism, and explaining the harm that can be caused by benevolent sexism, can help reduce endorsement of modern and benevolent sexist beliefs.

Confrontations can be a source of information about what types of behaviors are considered to be discriminatory or harmful, at least from the point of view of the person doing the confronting. Research by McClelland and Hunter (1992) reveals that the content of a confrontation can influence whether individuals define incidents as discriminatory. Specifically, they found that responses to discrimination influenced whether other individuals label such behavior as problematic. In one study, individuals read about several incidents of racial harassment that varied in severity but were still within the range of typical, everyday racism that college students might encounter. The target of the harassment gave different responses that varied in the extent to which the responder felt the behaviors were offensive. Specifically, the Black confronter either said nothing or said, "What?!," or "Stop! What the hell are you saying?" Participants were more likely to label the incident as serious with the third type of response, when the Black student directly asked the offender to stop.[†] It is possible that the more extreme response was needed to convey to observers that the behavior was insulting or harmful enough to be problematic. It is also possible that a more effective method may have been to more explicitly state how another person's behavior has caused distress in oneself (which has been referred to as an I-message), rather than making accusatory statements. More research, however, is needed to establish the consequences of different expressions of anger, as any negative emotion may elicit negative reactions from an audience and the effects of expressions of emotion may differ by different types of relationships (Bippus & Young, 2005).

[†] The effectiveness of confrontations for labeling incidents as prejudicial or discriminatory may depend upon the type of prejudice or discrimination involved. For instance, McClelland and Hunter (1992) found that the type of response women made to sexual harassment did not influence the perceived severity of the harassment. The two studies are not directly comparable, so it is difficult to know why one response was more effective than the other at influencing participants' perceptions of the events. However, supporting the difference in type of discrimination involved, Czopp and Monteith (2003) found that participants were more likely to take confrontations of racism more seriously than confrontations of sexism.

Changing Emotions

Emotions are powerful motivators for behavior. Thus, confronters may attempt to change perpetrator's emotions to alter behavior, which may subsequently change attitudes and beliefs. One powerful motivator can be feelings of personal guilt for having stereotyped another or engaged in discriminatory behavior (Monteith & Mark, 2005). This process was illustrated by Czopp, Monteith, and Mark (2006). Participants were given brief descriptions of individuals and were asked to describe the individual to another ostensible participant who was actually a confederate. Included in these stimuli was ambiguous information about three Black people that typically led to a stereotypical description of the person. For instance, participants were told that a Black person had spent time "behind bars" and the stereotypical response was to describe the person as a criminal. Across three similar types of information, nearly all participants gave at least one stereotypical description to a confederate. The confederate confronted them if they gave a stereotypical description. For instance, the confederate noted that the person behind bars could be a bartender, rather than a criminal. Czopp et al. found that being confronted led to negative self-evaluations, including feelings of guilt, annoyance, disappointment, and anger toward the self. These negative feelings were then related to less stereotypical responding on a similar subsequent task. This study also revealed that effects of confrontation generalized to decreased endorsement of negative beliefs about Blacks as measured by Brigham's (1993) Attitude toward Blacks scale. (They do not, however, report whether this latter decrease was mediated by either guilt or changes in behavior.)

Emotions can also operate on a group level (Mackie, Devos, & Smith, 2000). For example, some Whites report feeling group-based guilt when they reflect on their group's social, cultural, and economic advantages in comparison to the disadvantages that Blacks are more likely to have (Swim & Miller, 1999). This may occur for other groups as well, such as when women and men consider their gender-based advantages and disadvantages (Mallett & Swim, 2007). Additionally, group-based guilt is associated with endorsement of policies and engagement in collective action to reduce prejudice and discrimination (Mallett, Huntsinger, Sinclair, & Swim, 2008; Swim & Miller, 1999). If confronters are aware of these associations, then messages that elicit group-level guilt (independent of one's personal feelings of guilt) may also be an effective means for prejudice reduction via, for instance, making a target feel responsible for supporting policy changes that would reduce discrimination. This strategy may also be a way to motivate bystanders to support confronters' efforts to change perpetrators. Thus, confrontations that include messages that aim at group-based guilt could also contribute to prejudice reduction in perpetrators and bystanders.

Attempting to elicit group-based guilt, however, could backfire. First, confronters may inadvertently produce other group-based emotions such as group-based shame, which is associated with different behaviors than group-based guilt (Schmader & Lickel, 2006). Approach-related tendencies (e.g., efforts to repair the event) follow from group-based guilt, but avoidance-related tendencies (e.g., efforts to distance from the event or own group) follow from group-based shame. Because of the link between group-based guilt and approach-related tendencies, group-based guilt may motivate others to take action to reduce their own or other's prejudice. However, because of the link between group-based shame and avoidance-related tendencies, group-based shame may inhibit such actions. Second, like fear appeals, "guilt appeals" may lead to reactance (Witte & Allen, 2000). For instance, taking the perspective of Blacks after a hate crime incident increases feelings of White guilt but only if the Whites do not identify with Whites (Mallett et al., 2008). If they identify with Whites, White guilt decreases rather than increases. Finally, group-based guilt may backfire because of its association with group norms. Group-based guilt is presumably a result of perceiving that members of one's group have done something they should not have done. Yet information that indicates this may inadvertently make discriminatory group norms salient. If an individual's personal norms to not discriminate are weak, making group norms salient may lead to increases in discrimination, as discussed in the next section. However, just as fear appeals can be constructed to be more effective (Witte & Allen, 2000), it is possible that guilt appeals may also be constructed to be more effective.

Altering Social Norms

Another way to reduce prejudice is to alter social norms about what is inappropriate behavior. The goal would be to construct a message that reminds an audience of existing nondiscriminatory social norms or alters social norms to be nondiscriminatory. For instance, noting the inconsistent nature of someone's stereotypic comments or discriminatory behavior with egalitarian norms may alter behaviors (Grube, Mayton, & Ball-Rokeach, 1994; Rokeach & Cochrane, 1972). Confronters may wish to target both prescriptive and descriptive social norms (Cialdini & Trost, 1998). Prescriptive norms refer to what people *should* be doing in a given situation, whereas descriptive norms refer to what people *are* doing in the situation.

Prescriptive Norms

The power of a prescriptive norm lies in perceptions of what other people value. In the context of relations among many types of groups, many people recognize and internalize a social norm against prejudice (Crandall, Eshleman, & O'Brien, 2002). Additionally, many public and private establishments, such as classrooms and work places, are governed by such norms. For example, in a classroom setting, the professor may lay out egalitarian norms at the onset of the semester. This sends the message that students will be rewarded for making respectful and thoughtful comments, whereas they may be scolded or punished for disrespectful and thoughtless comments. Having explicit egalitarian norms can result in individuals being less tolerant of (Blanchard, Crandall, Brigham, & Vaughan, 1994) and less likely to express prejudice (Monteith, Deneen, & Tooman, 1996). Moreover, reminding individuals of prescriptive norms, or ways in which people are expected to behave, after observing interpersonal discrimination could prompt people to consider their own internal motivation to not be prejudiced or could heighten their external motivation to not be prejudiced (Plant & Devine, 1998). For example, in a seminal piece on confronting and prejudice reduction, Citron, Chein, and Harding (1950) found that confrontations that appealed to egalitarianism (e.g., fairness for everyone regardless of race and creed) and individualism (e.g., people from the same social group are not the same and should be judged as individuals) effectively reduced anti-Semitism in bystanders.

Descriptive Norms

Descriptive norms are beliefs about the types of behaviors people do. For interpersonal confrontations, norms could address the low quantity and frequency that people engage in discriminatory behaviors and indicate that a particular offensive behavior does not fit with descriptive norms. Confrontation may also alter perceptions of the group consensus about what is considered prejudicial, stereotypical, or discriminatory. The mere act of confronting may alter the extent to which perpetrators appear to represent others' opinions (Swim & Hyers, 1999). Hearing a dissenting view may influence the perceived prevalence of the perpetrator's view, and can influence others' willingness to follow a perpetrator's behavior, as long as the dissenter is respected by others (Swim, Ferguson, & Hyers, 1999). Likewise, silence after a prejudiced remark can indicate tacit agreement with the prejudice and result in others miming the perpetrator. In practice, it may be difficult to separate prescriptive from descriptive norms. For instance, informing individuals that they are not behaving like others could be experienced as being informed that one is not behaving as one should.

Summary

Although confronters may share the goal of reducing prejudice, the specific effects individuals seek to obtain may vary and this could influence the content of their confrontation. Their confrontation may vary depending on whether the individual attempts to change attitudes and beliefs versus behaviors. They may be most effective at changing behaviors, which may then change attitudes and beliefs. The content may also vary if confronters are attempting to alter people's thoughts or motivate change. In some cases it may be sufficient to alter people's thoughts. However, in other cases motivating individuals to behave differently may be necessary, which could occur through addressing personal, and possibly group-based, emotions, such as guilt, and addressing prescriptive or descriptive egalitarian norms.

SOURCE AND MESSAGE CHARACTERISTICS: MANAGING IMPRESSIONS OF THE SOURCE OF CONFRONTATION

Classic research on attitude change reveals that characteristics of the source can affect the extent to which messages are effective at changing an audience's attitudes. For instance, Czopp and Monteith (2003) provide evidence that confrontations are more effective if they come from members of a dominant group that is not adversely affected by the prejudice (e.g., Whites for racism and men for sexism) than if they come from members of the target group (e.g., Blacks for racism and women for sexism). Thus, some confronters may be more effective than others even if they deliver the same message.

Within any particular exchange, the source of the message could be considered fixed. However, confronters may alter how others see them by crafting the content of their message. For instance, one principle of inducing compliance is to have the message recipients see themselves as similar to the message deliverer (Cialdini & Trost, 1998). To do this, confronters could, for instance, agree with a perpetrator's inoffensive remarks before disagreeing with the perpetrator about the prejudice, stereotypes, or discrimination displayed. Another principle of compliance is to convince an audience that the message deliverer is an authority (Cialdini & Trost, 1998). To do this, confronters could attempt to present themselves as in charge and their message as authoritative and rational.

Thus, although source factors might normally be considered moderators of the effect of a message on persuasion, we consider source factors as something that confronters can attempt to manipulate by strategically presenting their message. Subsequently, we examine the ways that confronters manage their impressions by the way they choose to confront. Then we examine evidence of the effects of these impressions on reducing prejudice.

Impressions of Confronters

Targets of discrimination may be concerned about the impression they will have on other people should they choose to confront. There is evidence to support such concerns. Individuals who attribute negative outcomes to discrimination are typically liked less and seen as complainers, relative to those who do not make such claims (Kaiser & Miller, 2001). This is particularly true when confronting subtle rather than more blatant forms of discrimination (Dodd, Giuliani, Boutell, & Moran, 2001).

Yet, impressions may be influenced by the way that individuals choose to confront. If the tone of one's confrontation is friendly, then confronters may get a friendly response back. If the tone of their confrontation is hostile, then confronters may get a hostile response back. Research has documented that different styles of confronting can influence perpetrator's impressions of confronters. Czopp et. al. (2006) found that confronters whose message was less accusatory were liked more than those whose message was more accusatory. In this research, participants were confronted by another participant for making a stereotypic inference about Blacks in an experimental task. The less-accusatory confrontation included questions about the perpetrator's responses and suggestions for changes, and placed the stereotyped comments within a larger context of other forms of group-based mistreatment. The more accusatory confrontation indicated that perpetrators should behave differently and accused the perpetrators of being racist. Participants had more favorable evaluations of confronters who used less-accusatory styles of confronting.

Hyers (2000) similarly found that assertiveness influenced impressions of confronters. In this research, participants were members of a three-person discussion group where a confederate made a heterosexist comment in response to a discussion question about living with a gay roommate. A second confederate responded in one of three ways. In one condition, the confederate took offense to the comment and said "I don't see why it is such a *damn* problem. I am gay and I had a straight roommate in the past. Anyone who has a problem with it should get over it." In a second condition, the confederate indicated he was gay and he did not think it would be a problem based upon his past experiences. In a third condition, the confederate indicated he was gay and made a noncommittal response to the situation. The most direct confronter was rated as the most sensitive, least polite, and most likely to "speak his or her mind."

The Effect of Directness of Confronters on Impressions
The Czopp et al. (2006) and Hyers (2000) studies were conducted primarily to assess the effects of different types of confronting on prejudice reduction, rather than to assess different ways that confronting may influence impressions of the confronter. To assess this latter issue, we conducted research that was specifically designed to assess the effects of different ways of confronting. In one study we examined impressions of women who used confrontations that had frequently been used in our observational research on confronting sexism (Swim & Pearson, 2006). These observations indicated that three frequent ways of confronting were to make a joke, question the logic of the sexist remark, and point out the sexist content of each of the male character's statements (Swim & Hyers, 1999). These responses, as rated by other participants, fall along a continuum from least to most direct. Additionally, there was a condition where confronters started with less direct confrontations and then moved on to more direct confrontations. We reasoned that increasing directness in this manner could realistically represent the way that individuals are likely to approach situations (Goffman, 1963).

Three different types of impressions were examined: likeability, being seen as a complainer, and competence. We were interested in likeability of confronters and being perceived as a complainer because these have been proposed as costs of confronting that could inhibit confrontation (Kaiser & Miller, 2001). We anticipated that judging confronters as complainers would be linked to the directness of the confrontations, such that more direct confronter would be seen as complainers. We also predicted that being perceived as dislikable and as a complainer could be mitigated if the confronter started with a less direct response and moved to a more direct response.

We were interested in perceptions of competence because this might be related to an audience agreeing with the content of messages, even if the audience did not like the confronter. Impressions can often be categorized as falling within two dimensions, one representing how likable individuals appear and how competent they appear (Fiske, Cuddy, & Glick, 2007; Rosenberg, Nelson, & Vivekananthan, 1968). Our past research indicates that individuals who claim that the negative outcomes they experience are a result of discrimination are disliked more than those who do not make these claims, but they are also perceived to be more competent (Stangor, Swim, Sechrist, DeCoster, Van Allen, & Ottenbreit, 2003). We predicted that more direct responses may be associated with greater competence, even though they would simultaneously be associated with less likeability.

We created five vignettes that paralleled the group task that participants experienced in Swim and Hyers (1999, Study 1). In all of the vignettes, a male participant made sexist comments in the presence of two females. In one condition, neither of the females responded. In three conditions, one of the females confronted, using one of the three types of confronting styles for each comment noted earlier. In the final condition, the confronting female gave responses that increased in directness by first saying a joke in response to the first sexist comment, then questioning the second sexist comment, and finally by saying the comment was sexist.

One hundred and thirty-one female and 96 male undergraduate students were randomly assigned to one of five conditions and then answered questions about the characters in the scenario. Participants rated the characters in the scenario in terms of how *competent* (independent, responsible, intelligent, level headed, and successful), how *nice* (friendly, fun, good friend, likeable, and nice), and how *much of a complainer* (argumentative, complaining, whiney, hypersensitive, and irritating) they perceived the confronter to be. Principal components analysis revealed that all items loaded as predicted on these three dimensions. Finally, participants rated each of the statements made by the male in terms of how sexist they were. All ratings were on a five-point Likert scale (+2 = strongly agree; –2 = strongly disagree).

The results from this study are presented in Figure 3.1. Replicating past research, contrasts tests comparing those who made one of the four types of responses versus those who made no response revealed that those who confronted were more likely to be described as complainers [$F(1,186) = 5.68$, $p = .02$] and as unlikable [$F(1, 186) = 3.32, p = .07$], than those who did not confront. Confronters were, however, seen as equally competent as non-confronters. Thus, although confronters were seen as complainers and disliked, they were not perceived as incompetent.

We also tested differences in impressions within type of confrontation on these impressions. Consistent with predictions, those who told jokes were seen as less complaining than those who used the other forms of confrontations ($p = .06, p < .01, p = .01$ for comparisons with questioning, direct comments, and combination of all three, respectively). Similarly, if they told jokes, they were seen as less competent than if they asked a question ($p = .07$) or made a direct comment ($p = .05$). The means did not differ

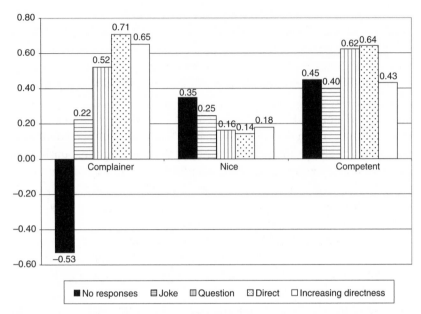

FIGURE 3.1. Effect of type of confronting responses on perceptions that confronter is a complainer, is nice, and is competent.

for how nice confronters were perceived to be, however, when we coded the conditions such that jokes are coded as 1, questioning as 2, and direct as 3; correlations indicated that more direct confrontations tended to be associated with being perceived as less nice ($r = -.14, p = .07$).

We did not find differences in impressions of confronters who used the two more-direct forms of confronting. Although the pattern of results indicated that those who directly accused the perpetrator of being sexist were seen as more complaining than those who questioned the perpetrator, differences in means were not statistically significant. Interestingly, we also did not find support for our prediction that starting with indirect confrontations and moving to more direct confrontations would mitigate negative impressions of those who made direct responses. Those who used this strategy were seen as equally complaining and nice as those who consistently used a direct response. Moreover, the pattern of means suggested that there could be a cost to this strategy because they were seen as less competent than those who questioned or directly accused the perpetrator.

In sum, this research indicates that individuals can alter the type of impression that audience members will have of confronters by the way in which they choose to confront. Yet the results still point to costs of confronting versus not confronting and cost-benefits associated with different confrontation styles. All confronters were seen as more complaining and less likeable than if individuals said nothing. Telling a joke decreased the likelihood of these negative impressions, but those who told jokes were seen as less competent than those who made more direct confrontations. Although, the joke could possibly have other effects that would help prejudice reduction, such as conveying that the perpetrator has strayed past a prescriptive norm, the light-hearted nature of a joke may make this violation seem trivial. In contrast, those who made more direct responses were seen as more competent than those who told jokes. Yet direct confronters were seen as more complaining and less likable than those who told a joke.

The Effect of Self-Presentation Strategies on Impressions

This study suggests that individuals could alter the impression that others have of them based upon how they confront. Extending this to types of confrontations that are designed to alter other people's opinions rather than simply stating an objection to someone's comments, Quinlivan, Gervais, and Swim (2008) applied Jones and Pittman's (1982) theory of strategic self-presentation to confronting. This theory indicates that there are a number of impressions, including being likeable, competent, threatening, moral, or helpless, that confronters may aim to obtain, and that these impressions are tied to particular self-presentation strategies. Not all of these impressions are favorable to the presenter, but they may still be used for prejudice reduction. For instance, being seen as threatening could potentially increase compliance with egalitarian social norms. We conducted three studies to examine whether strategic self-presentations would influence impressions of confronters and may reduce prejudice.

In this research, participants read about individuals who were observers or victims of racist or antifatist statements and who gave different responses to these incidents (Quinlivan et. al., 2008). The responses were pretested to represent one of five strategic, self-presentation strategies outlined by Jones and Pittman (1982). These strategies consisted of: *ingratiation* (eliciting the attribution of likeability), *self-promotion* (eliciting the attribution of competence), *intimidation* (eliciting the attribution of threatening), *exemplification* (eliciting the attribution of moral superiority), and *supplication* (eliciting the attribution of helplessness). Control participants read about people who made nonconfrontational responses.

The results from this research indicate that the strategy that confronters use affect whether they are viewed as likeable, competent, threatening, moral, and helpless. Specifically, in Study 1, we found that confronting racist remarks using each of the five self-presentation styles elicited the desired attribution. For instance, those who used an intimidating self-presentation style in their confrontation were perceived to be more threatening than those in the control condition. In some cases, such as when using ingratiation, confronters were liked as much as nonconfronters. In Study 2, we found a similar pattern of effects for confronters of antifatism. Additionally, we examined whether the effectiveness of the self-presentation strategy would vary as a function of whether the participant was high (vs. low) in antifatism. We found that these impressions were not affected by participants' levels of prejudice. Finally, in Study 3, we again examined confrontations of racist statements. In Study 3, however, we varied the degree to which the statement was prejudiced (definitely or possibly) and the race of the confronter (White or Black). Replicating Study 1 and Study 2, we found that confronting racist remarks using each of the five self-presentation styles elicited the expected attributions. Degree of prejudice and race of the confronter, however, did affect the attributions in some instances. For example, we found a three-way interaction among degree of prejudice, race of the confronter, and self-presentation style, indicating that Whites were perceived as more moral when confronting statements that were possibly racist compared to definitely racist. This interaction suggests that white confronters may be viewed as morally superior when they confront prejudice that could be racist. This is not, however, the case for Black confronters.

The aforementioned findings are consistent with the original theory of strategic self-presentation that aligns self-presentation with power and influence, suggesting that there are a number of ways in which people can strategically present themselves with varying degrees and types of influence. These connections show that individuals who are able to demonstrate these different types of influence in their confrontations may be able to effectively reduce prejudice and discrimination. Additionally, this research suggests that confronters need not sacrifice perceptions of likeability when they confront. This research also suggests that even low-power people, who are typically not considered particularly credible sources, may be able to effectively confront others by using self-presentation styles that do not involve displays of power (and are congruent with their low role). Specifically, people in low-power positions may be able to increase their social influence by portraying themselves as helpless or likable. Yet, there are potential costs to using strategies that elicit these attributions. Supplication and ingratiation could also induce paternalistic behavior. Thus, although these strategies could be effective at reducing discrimination in a given situation, they may further reinforce and maintain power structures (Glick & Fiske,

1996; Jackman, 1994; Jost & Banaji, 1994). Finally, the findings from Study 3, indicate that not all confronters may use each strategy equally effectively. The interactions from Study 3 indicated that some perceptions of confronters using the different strategies may vary as a function of the degree to which the behaviors are perceived as problematic and the identity of the confronter.

Effects of Type of Confrontation on Attitude and Behavioral Change

The Studies Reported earlier indicated that the way that people confront can influence the impression others draw about them. The question remains, however, whether different messages and impressions actually matter in terms of reducing prejudice. Data on the effect of different types of confrontation on impressions indicate that the answer to this question is mixed.

In some cases it may be helpful to be perceived as more hostile. For instance, in the McClelland and Hunter (1992) study described earlier, where participants learned that a confronter either responded to a racist remark by saying either nothing, "What?!," or "Stop! What the hell are you saying?," it would seem likely that observers would have thought the confronter who made the last remark was perceived to be the most hostile. But it was also this perpetrator who was most able to convey the offensiveness of the comment. This study did not assess the extent to which the comment reduced prejudice in others. Yet, it suggests that in some cases, it may be necessary to be extreme to convey the extent of harm a comment has on another person.

In contrast, results from Czopp et al. (2006) suggest that hostility may not be necessary to reduce prejudice. In this study, where participants were confronted in accusatory or nonaccusatory ways for having given stereotypical descriptions of targets, both confrontation styles were equally effective at reducing stereotype use. Both accusatory and nonaccusatory confrontations decreased the likelihood that participants made stereotypic responses on a similar subsequent task, even though those who confronted in an accusatory manner were perceived as less likable than those who were less accusatory. Thus, the unfavorable evaluations of confronters who were more accusatory did not interfere with their ability to effectively alter perpetrators behaviors. Or put another way, confronters can be as effective if they respond in a friendly way as when they respond in a more hostile way.

The results from Hyer's (2000) study point to the possibility that certain types of confronting can appear to be effective but may only be partially effective. In Hyers' study, a confederate made an antigay remark in front of the participant and another confederate. The second confederate then confronted the first confederate. However, this second confederate waited to allow the participant to say something before confronting. In about half the cases, the participant also said an antigay remark and in the other half did not say anything. Thus, when the confronting confederate made their remark, they were confronting both the confederate and the participant, particularly when the participant joined in with the first confederate. Of interest was the impact of confrontation on the participant. In this study, participants were most likely to engage in interpersonal repair (e.g., being friendly or apologizing) after being confronted by the person who gave the least hostile response (i.e., only revealed their sexual orientation rather than challenging the heterosexist comments). Yet these individuals were also most likely to privately express concerns about having a gay roommate after being confronted by a person who gave the least hostile response. Thus, the friendly confrontation appeared to be the most effective confrontation during the interaction, but backfired when it came to private thoughts.

The results from our study that examined impressions of confronters of sexism also indicate that confronting can backfire. When a confronter made a joke, questioned the perpetrator, or directly accused the perpetrator of being sexist, participants appeared to be more sympathetic toward the perpetrator if he had been confronted than if he had not been confronted, even though they perceived his behavior to be sexist. Specifically, confronting did not influence women's willingness to call the comments sexist or offensive, with most participants calling the comments sexist both when the perpetrator had been confronted and when he had not been confronted ($M = 1.36$ and 1.38, respectively, on a -2 *to* $+2$ scale where higher numbers indicate greater sexism and offensiveness). In contrast, confronting did influence ratings of whether the man was sexist [$F(1,186) = 3.592, p = .01$]. Participants were *less* likely to call the man sexist if they read about a man who was confronted ($M = 1.51$) than a man who was not confronted ($M = 1.16$). There was no difference in ratings of the man within the four different confrontation conditions. Yet, the studies suggest that it is important to consider the possibility that confronting can make observers sympathetic to perpetrators, and it is possible that in some cases more hostile forms of confronting might increase this likelihood.

In sum, different confrontation styles can alter the impression that confronters have on others. This is related to source variables in research on attitude change because it indicates that confronters may be able to manipulate source variables as a means of encouraging prejudice reduction. Yet, given the variability in effectiveness of confronting on reducing prejudice across studies, the conditions under which confronting and different forms of confronting effect prejudice reduction is yet to be understood.

AUDIENCE CHARACTERISTICS: SELECTING AUDIENCES FOR CONFRONTATIONS

Confrontations may be more or less effective dependent upon who is receiving the message, that is, who is in the audience. For instance, Kaiser (2006) found that individuals who endorse Protestant work ethic values are more likely than those who do not endorse such ideologies to derogate a man who claims he has been the victim of discrimination. Claims of discrimination presumably threaten dominant ideologies (e.g., social dominance orientation or Protestant work ethic) and create less receptivity to the messages by those who endorse the dominant ideologies.

However, audiences include more than just perpetrators. If more than one person is present during the exchange, confronters may choose to target the most appropriate audience member. Confronters may serve as a dissenter and encourage sympathetic bystanders to also confront (Blanchard, Crandall, Brigham, & Vaughn, 1994), particularly if the association with the dissenter is not seen as undesirable (Swim et al., 1999). Research on conformity indicates that if bystanders believe that even one other person does not agree, conformity reduces considerably. Extending this to interpersonal confrontations, if even one person indicates that a prejudiced statement is offensive, bystanders may feel more comfortable expressing subsequent disagreement with the perpetrator. As a result, bystanders' responses may build upon the original confrontation. For instance, if one person indicates that the comment is insulting, then another may join in and indicate that the comment was offensive. Even if the audience is not initially sympathetic to a confronter's message, confronting may reduce the likelihood of problematic behavior emerging from the others, regardless of its effect on the perpetrator.

Power and Choosing One's Audience

Gervais and Vescio (2005) examined how confronters in positions of power can influence the extent to which their responses are perceived to be influential by altering who they choose to be recipients of their message. In their study, confronting responses were made to the perpetrator either in the presence or absence of either high- or low-power others. Specifically, Gervais and Vescio had participants imagine the following scenario: During a staff meeting at a company, which prides itself on being fair and treating every-one equally, a male employee made a sexist statement directed at a female employee. The manager wished to tell people that the statement was inap-propriate and problematic, and had to decide to whom to convey this mes-sage. Participants were asked to rate how likely responding to (1) everyone, (2) the perpetrator and managers, (3) the perpetrator and other employees, (4) the perpetrator only, or (5) no one would stop future sexist events and convey that the manager was in charge. Responses to the perpetrator in the presence of both managers and employees were seen as most likely to stop future sexist events and to show that the manager was in charge, followed by confrontations of the perpetrator in the presence of other employees or managers, followed by the perpetrator only, followed by no one.

These results suggest that confronting in the presence of different people may produce varying degrees of change. For example, when high-power people convey the problematic and inappropriate nature of prejudice directly to the perpetrator, they will likely stop future expressions of prejudice from the perpetrator. Confronting the perpetrator in the presence of high- and/or low-power others, however, can also establish egalitarian norms, set a standard for rejecting prejudice, and ameliorate the damaging effects of prejudice (e.g., reassuring all female employees that they are in a supportive environment where sexism is promptly stopped). Thus, the latter approach may be more influential than confronting the perpetrator alone.

TOWARD A MORE COMPREHENSIVE THEORY OF CONFRONTING

By framing our discussion of interpersonal confrontation with the mes-sage-learning approach to persuasion, we hoped to elucidate the many fea-tures, including the message, source, and audience that confronters may use when attempting to reduce prejudice. We examined the types of messages confronters may use, the effects they may try to obtain from their messages, the ways they may strategically present themselves as the source, and the audiences they may select.

In this chapter, we integrated the existing interpersonal confrontation literature into the message-learning approach to persuasion. This integra-tion points to many novel directions that could be expanded in several ways. Most of the existing literature has focused on one particular point in the message-learning framework – the point in which the message recipient either accepts or rejects the message. In the aforementioned discussions, the implicit assumption was that the audience was aware that they have been confronted. However, as the message-learning approach indicates, persuasive messages begin with audiences attending to a message, and it is possible that confrontations may be ignored. For instance, if confronters are members of low-status groups, people may not even notice the message. Another possibility is that if confronters are timid or qualify their responses, their confrontations may be ignored. The message-learning approach also indicates that the audience must comprehend the message. Thus, if confronters do not clearly label the behaviors in question as discrimination but instead state, for instance, that a behavior is simply "offensive," the audience may not define their responses as confronting the prejudicial nature of their behavior. They may change their behavior but, if the goal was to change their attitudes or beliefs, this may not happen. In other cases, audiences may realize that they have been confronted but they may not sufficiently understand the message. For instance, confronters may have the goal of getting perpetrators to understand the problematic nature of their behavior. An audience, however, may miss this message and assume that the confronter is accusing the perpetrator of being prejudiced. Finally, at the end of the message-learning process, an audience must remember an attitude and act on it later. Research on confronting has not examined long-term consequences of confronting, such as whether an audience remembers the confrontation later and whether the effectiveness of confronting generalized to other situations.

Research on the effects of confronting would be further extended by considering features of actual interactions that may be missing from the current paradigms being used. First, much of the existing literature has focused on what people *could* do in interpersonal situations more so than what they *actually* do in these situations. Second, most existing theory and research has examined confronting strangers or observing confrontations of strangers. The message-learning framework suggests that the source and the audience are important features. Thus, the type of relationship between confronter and perpetrator may influence the effectiveness of confrontation. It is possible that friends and co-workers may respond differently, perhaps more sympathetically, to confrontations than strangers. Moreover, confrontations within established relationships may be effective over the long term, for instance, if confronters continue to confront perpetrators.

Third, it is important to consider the impact of the context on the way that individuals choose to confront. In our review, we have assumed that confronters are able to strategically manage their messages. Confronters may find it difficult to come up with effective confrontations *in the moment*. Individuals may find themselves surprised – even stunned! – by the comments of others, and these comments can be distracting and cognitively taxing. If potential confronters are in positions of low power, they may not feel they are able to interrupt the flow of a conversation to address problematic points of the discussion. However, we suspect that on many occasions, people walk away from offensive situations and ask themselves what they could have changed. It may be the case that individuals need to practice confronting to be able to best respond to confrontations (Plous, 2000).

Fourth, when considering interpersonal discrimination and confrontations as part of an ongoing conversation, it would be useful to consider perpetrator's reactions to the confrontation. Perpetrators' responses may be supportive, such as when they engage in interpersonal repair, and these behaviors may help encourage social norms of egalitarianism. On the other hand, perpetrators may defend themselves and counterargue the confrontation. For instance, McClelland and Hunter (1992) found that when perpetrators made excuses for their interpersonal forms of discrimination, others were less likely to label racial harassment as serious. Similarly, expressions of lack of intent to discriminate can decrease the likelihood that observers perceive the perpetrators as prejudiced and the perpetrator's behavior as discriminatory (Swim, Scott, Sechrist, Campbell, & Stangor, 2003). Thus, perpetrator's responses could lead others to redefine incidents as not being based in prejudice and, by implication, their behaviors may also not be defined as discriminatory and thus there would be no subsequent reduction in prejudice, stereotypes, stereotyping, and discrimination.

It is also important to situate the goal of reducing prejudice and discrimination within the context of confronters' other possible goals. We have purposely constrained our review of the research to situations where confronters have the goal of reducing prejudice. However, a comprehensive theory would examine this goal within the context of other goals. For instance, a more comprehensive theory would consider how this particular goal may have been activated and how individuals weigh this goal versus other goals that they may see as important (see Swim & Thomas, 2006).

In addition to considering ways to theoretically broaden the study of confrontation, it is important to make attempts to address methodological hurdles when studying selection and effects of different forms of confrontations. If one wants to study the effects of confrontation on perpetrators of discriminatory behavior, the perpetrators must freely engage in discriminatory behavior that can be confronted. It may be difficult to get perpetrators to make prejudicial comments, particularly in lab contexts where they know they are being observed. Additionally, it is virtually impossible to manipulate intent to discriminate. The research by Czopp et al. (2006), where participants were confronted for saying stereotypical remarks, and by Hyers (2000) where participants were confronted for saying antigay remarks, provided creative solutions to this problem. But even these studies have limitations. In Czopp et al.'s study, where participants made stereotypical comments about Blacks, they may not have realized that they were making such comments so they may have interpreted their behavior as unintentional. In Hyers' (2000) study, participants self-selected into conditions where they either joined in or did not join in with a confederate's heterosexist comments about having a gay roommate.

CONCLUSION

The aforementioned research indicates that confronting discrimination can be a fruitful way to understand methods that individuals can use to reduce prejudice, change stereotypes, and reduce stereotyping and discrimination in interpersonal interactions. Research on prejudice reduction often does not indicate what initiates prejudice reduction in perpetrators. Confrontations can be a powerful impetuous for these processes by either directly addressing others' prejudices and behaviors, indirectly addressing them through mechanisms that theoretically lead to changes in prejudices and behaviors, or by influencing descriptive and prescriptive social norms. Moreover, research on the role of intergroup contact on prejudice reduction, one of the most productive lines of research on prejudice reduction (Tropp & Pettigrew, 2005), does not typically examine specific behaviors and responses to behaviors that can emerge within these contact situations. Research on confrontations provides an analysis of the ways that confronters can effectively respond when interpersonal discrimination emerges in these contexts. This research can, for instance, examine the ways that confronters may strategically manage impressions and whether different types of responses influence impressions and ultimately changes in attitudes, beliefs, and behaviors.

The ways that individuals respond to discrimination can have an important impact on future discrimination. The success of these attempts at social influence is likely to be a function of many factors including characteristics of confronters and target audiences, as well as characteristics of the actual behavior being confronted. Yet, the way that confronters manage their messages can potentially adjust to these factors and even take advantage of them in ways that can maximize social influence processes dictating behaviors and attitude change.

REFERENCES

Ajzen, I., & Fishbein, M. (1977). Attitude-behavior relations: A theoretical analysis and review of empirical research. *Psychological bulletin, 84*(5), 888–918.

Benokraitis, N. V. & Feagin, J. R. (1986). *Modern sexism: Blatant, subtle, and covert discrimination.* Englewood Cliffs, NJ: Prentice-Hall.

Becker, J. C. & Swim, J. K. (2008). *Legi, intellexi, condemnavi (I have read, comprehended, and condemned): Differential effects of attending to sexism and its harm on reducing modern, neo- and benevolent sexist beliefs.* Manuscript under review.

Bippus, A. M., & Young, S. L. (2005). Owning your emotions: Reactions to expressions of self- versus other-attributed positive and negative emotions. *Journal of Applied Communication Research, 33*(1), 26–45.

Blanchard, F. A., Crandall, C. S., Brigham, J. C., & Vaughn, L. A. (1994). Condemning and condoning racism: A social context approach to interracial settings. *Journal of Applied Psychology, 79*(6), 993–997.

Brigham, J. C. (1993). College students' racial attitudes. *Journal of Applied Social Psychology, 23*(23), 1933–1967.

Cialdini, R. B, Petty, R. E., Cacioppo, J. T. (1981). Attitude and attitude change. *Annual Review of Psychology, 32*, 357–404

Cialdini, R. B., & Trost, M. R. (1998). *Social influence: Social norms, conformity and compliance.* New York: McGraw-Hill.

Citron, A. F., Chein, I., & Harding, J. (1950). Anti-minority remarks: A problem for action research. *Journal of Abnormal & Social Psychology, 45*, 99–126.

Crandall, C. S, Eshleman, A., & O'Brien, L. (2002). Social norms and the expression and suppression of prejudice: The struggle for internalization. *Journal of Personality and Social Psychology, 82*, 359–378.

Czopp, A. M., & Monteith, M. J. (2003). Confronting prejudice (literally): Reactions to confrontations of racial and gender bias. *Personality and Social Psychology Bulletin, 29*(4), 532–544.

Czopp, A. M., Monteith, M. J., & Mark, A. Y. (2006). Standing up for a change: Reducing bias through interpersonal confrontation. *Journal of Personality and Social Psychology, 90*(5), 784–803.

Dodd, E. H., Giuliano, T. A., Boutell, J. M., & Moran, B. E. (2001). Respected or rejected: Perceptions of women who confront sexist remarks. *Sex Roles, 45*, 567–577.

Dovidio, J. F., Brigham, J. C., Johnson, B. T., & Gaertner, S. L. (1996). Stereotyping, prejudice, and discrimination: Another look. In C. N. Macrae, C. Stangor, & M. Hewstond (Eds.), *Stereotypes and stereotyping* (pp. 276–319). New York: Guildord.

Dovidio, J. F., Kawakami, K., & Gaertner, S. L. (2002). Implicit and explicit prejudice and interracial interaction. *Journal of Personality and Social Psychology, 82*(1), 62–68.

Feagin, J. R., & Sikes, M. P. (1994). *Living with racism: The black middle-class experience.* Boston, MA: Beacon Press, Inc.

Festinger, L. (1957). *A theory of cognitive dissonance.* Oxford, UK: Row, Peterson.

Fishbein, M., & Ajzen, I. (1974). Attitudes towards objects as predictors of single and multiple behavioral criteria. *Psychological Review, 81*(1), 59–74.

Fiske, S. T., Cuddy, A. J. C., & Glick, P. (2007). Universal dimensions of social cognition: Warmth and competence. *Trends in Cognitive Sciences*, 11(2), 77–83.

Gervais, S. J., & Vescio, T. K. (2005) Confronting as leadership. Manuscript in preparation.

Glick, P., & Fiske, S. T. (1996). The ambivalent sexism inventory: Differentiating hostile and benevolent sexism. *Journal of Personality and Social Psychology*, 70(3), 491–512.

Goffman, E. (1963). *Stigma: Notes on the management of spoiled identity*. New York: Simon & Schuster.

Greenwald, A. G. (1981). Cognitive response analysis: An appraisal. In R. E. Petty, T. M. Ostrom, & T. C. Brock (Eds.). *Cognitive responses in persuasion* (pp. 127–133). Hillsdale, NJ: Lawrence Erlbaum Associates.

Grube, J. W., Mayton, D. M., & Ball-Rokeach, S. J. (1994). Inducing change in values, attitudes, and behaviors: Belief system theory and the method of value self-confrontation. *Journal of Social Issues*, 50(4), 153–173.

Hovland, C. I., Janis, I. L., & Kelley, J. (1953). *Communication and persuasion*. New Haven, CT: Yale University Press.

Hunter, C., & McClelland, K. (1991). Honoring accounts for sexual harassment: A factorial survey analysis. *Sex Roles*, 24, 725–752.

Hyers, L. L. (2000). *Interpersonal confrontation as a means to prejudice reduction: When oppressed group members challenge the prejudices of dominant group members*. (Doctoral dissertation, ProQuest Information & Learning). Dissertation Abstracts International: Section B: The Sciences and Engineering, 61 (2-B).

Hyers, L. L. (2007). Resisting prejudice every day: Exploring women's assertive responses to anti-black racism, anti-semitism, heterosexism, and sexism. *Sex Roles*, 56(1–2), 1–12.

Jost, J. T., & Banaji, M. R. (1994). The role of stereotyping in system-justification and the production of false consciousness. *British Journal of Social Psychology. Special Issue: Stereotypes: Structure, Function and Process*, 33(1), 1–27.

Kaiser, C. R. (2006). Dominant Ideology Threat and the Interpersonal Consequences of Attributions to Discrimination. S. Lavin & C. Van Laar (Ed.). *The Claremont Symposium on Applied Social Psychology*.

Kaiser, C. R., & Miller, C. T. (2001). Stop complaining! the social costs of making attributions to discrimination. *Personality and Social Psychology Bulletin*, 27(2), 254–263.

Kawakami, K., Dovidio, J. F., Moll, J., Hermsen, S., & Russin, A. (2000). Just say no (to stereotyping): Effects of training in the negation of stereotypic associations on stereotype activation. *Journal of Personality and Social Psychology*, 78(5), 871–888.

Jackman, M. R. (1994). *The velvet glove: Paternalism and conflict in gender, class, and race relations*. Berkeley, CA: University of California Press.

Jones, E. E., & Pittman, T. S. (1982). Toward a general theory of strategic self-presentation. In J. Suls (Ed.), *Psychological perspectives on the self* (Vol. 1, pp. 231–262). Hillsdale, NJ: Lawrence Erlbaum Associates.

Mackie, D. M., Devos, T., & Smith, E. R. (2000). Intergroup emotions: Explaining offensive action tendencies in an intergroup context. *Journal of Personality and Social Psychology*, 79(4), 602–616.

Mallett, R. K., Huntsinger, J. R., Sinclair, S., & Swim, J. K. (2008). Seeing through their eyes: When group-based guilt motivates collective action on behalf of an outgroup. *Group Process and Intergroup Relations, 11*(4), 451–470.

Mallett, R. K., & Swim, J. K. (2007). The influence of inequality, responsibility and justifiability on reports of group-based guilt for ingroup privilege. *Group Processes and Intergroup Relations, 10*(1), 57–69.

McClelland, K., & Hunter, C. (1992). The perceived seriousness of racial harassment. *Social Problems, 39*(1), 92–107.

McGuire, W. J. (1985). Attitudes and attitude change. In G. Lindzey & E. Aronson (Eds.) *Handbook of social psychology* (3rd ed., Vol. 2, pp. 233–346). New York: Random House.

Monteith, M. J., Ashburn-Nardo, L., Voils, C. I., & Czopp, A. M. (2002). Putting the brakes on prejudice: On the development and operation of cues for control. *Journal of Personality and Social Psychology, 83*(5), 1029–1050.

Monteith, M. J., Deneen, N. E., Tooman, G. D., (1996). The effect of social norm activation on the expression of opinions concerning gay men and Blacks. *Basic and Applied Social Psychology, 18*, 267–288.

Monteith, M. J., & Mark, A. Y. (2005). Changing one's prejudice ways: Awareness, affect, and self-regulation. *European Review of Social Psychology, 16*, 113–154.

Petty, R. T. (1998). *Attitude change: Multiple roles for persuasion variables.* New York: McGraw-Hill.

Plant, E. A., & Devine, P. G. (1998). Internal and external motivation to respond without prejudice. *Journal of Personality and Social Psychology, 75*(3), 811–832.

Plous, S. (2000). Responding to overt displays of prejudice: A role-playing exercise. *Teaching of Psychology, 27*, 198–200.

Rokeach, M., & Cochrane, R. (1972). Self-confrontation and confrontation with another as determinants of long-term value change. *Journal of Applied Social Psychology, 2*(4), 283–292.

Rosenberg, S., Nelson, C., & Vivekananthan, P. S. (1968). A multidimensional approach to the structure of personality impressions. *Journal of Personality and Social Psychology, 9*(4), 283–294.

Quinlivan, E., Gervais, S. J., & Swim, J. K. (2008). It's not what you say, it's how you say it: Self-presentational strategies and confronting prejudice. Manuscript in preparation.

Schmader, T., & Lickel, B. (2006). The approach and avoidance function of guilt and shame emotions: Comparing reactions to self-caused and other-caused wrongdoing. *Motivation and Emotion, 30*(1), 43–56.

Shelton, J. N., & Richeson, J. A. (2005). Intergroup contact and pluralistic ignorance. *Journal of Personality and Social Psychology, 88*(1), 91–107.

Smith, J., & Ross, H. (2007). Training parents to mediate sibling disputes affects children's negotiation and conflict understanding. *Child Development, 78*(3), 790–805.

Stangor, C., Swim, J. K., Sechrist, G. B., DeCoster, J., Van Allen, K. L., & Ottenbreit, A. (2003). Ask, answer and announce: Three stages in perceiving and responding to discrimination. *European Review of Social Psychology, 14*, 277–311.

Swim, J. K., Ferguson, M. J., & Hyers, L. L. (1999). Avoiding stigma by association: Subtle prejudice against lesbians in the form of social distancing. *Basic and Applied Social Psychology, 21*(1), 61–68.

Swim, J. K., & Hyers, L. L. (1999). Excuse me – what did you just say?!: Women's public and private responses to sexist remarks. *Journal of Experimental Social Psychology, 35*(1), 68–88.

Swim, J. K., Cohen, L. L., & Hyers, L. L. (1998). *Experiencing everyday prejudice and discrimination.* San Diego, CA: Academic Press.

Swim, J. K., Hyers, L. L., Cohen, L. L., & Ferguson, M. J. (2001). Everyday sexism: Evidence for its incidence, nature, and psychological impact from three daily diary studies. *Journal of Social Issues, 57*(1), 31–53.

Swim, J. K., Hyers, L. L., Cohen, L. L., Fitzgerald, D. C., & Bylsma, W. H. (2003). African American college students' experiences with everyday racism: Characteristics of and responses to these incidents. *Journal of Black Psychology, 29*(1), 38–67.

Swim, J. K., Johnston, K. E., & Pearson, N. B. (under review). Day to day experiences with heterosexism: coping with heterosexist hassles. Unpublished manuscript.

Swim, J. K., Pearson, N. B., Johnston, K. E. (2007). Daily encounters with heterosexism: A week in the life of lesbian, gay, and bisexual individuals. *Journal of Homosexuality, 53*, 18–31

Swim, J. K., & Miller, D. L. (1999). White guilt: Its antecedents and consequences for attitudes toward affirmative action. *Personality and Social Psychology Bulletin, 25*(4), 500–514.

Swim, J. K., & Pearson, N. B. (2006). Effect of types of confrontation on impressions of confronters. Unpublished data.

Swim, J. K., Scott, E. D., Sechrist, G. B., Campbell, B., & Stangor, C. (2003). The role of intent and harm in judgments of prejudice and discrimination. *Journal of Personality and Social Psychology, 84*(5), 944–959.

Swim, J. K., & Thomas, M. A. (2006). Responding to everyday discrimination: A synthesis of research on goal-directed, self-regulatory coping behaviors. In S. Levin & C. van Laar (Eds.), *Claremont symposium on applied social psychology, 2004, Claremont, CA, US* (pp. 105–126). Mahwah, NJ, US: Lawrence Erlbaum Associates Publishers.

Tropp, L. R., & Pettigrew, T. F. (2005). Differential relationships between intergroup contact and affective and cognitive dimensions of prejudice. *Personality and Social Psychology Bulletin, 31*(8), 1145–1158.

Witte, K., & Allen, M. (2000). A meta-analysis of fear appeals: Implications for effective public health campaigns. *Health Education & Behavior, 27*(5), 591–615.

4

A New Representation of Minorities as Victims

SERGE MOSCOVICI AND JUAN A. PÉREZ

A DIALOGUE BETWEEN CHOMSKY AND FOUCAULT

To convey the general meaning of this study, we must first clarify the question
it seeks to answer and then delineate the observations that served as its initial impetus. What, then, is the question with which we are concerned? For
a short answer, let us go back to the famous 1971 debate between Chomsky
and Foucault on the subject of "human nature." From the very outset, there
is a sharp difference of opinion. Foucault asserts that human nature has a
social basis and is founded on the drive for dominance and power, while
Chomsky stresses its innate character, which is the true basis, the absolute foundation of justice. Here are just a few excerpts from this exchange.
Foucault is certain that justice is an instrument of power, "an idea invented
and applied in different types of society as an instrument of a certain political and economic power, or as a weapon against this power" (Chomsky &
Foucault, 2002, p. 69).

After voicing his disagreement, Chomsky not only reformulates his
arguments by including justice as one of man's most deep-seated needs,
but also asserts that justice can be ensured by legal means. "In my view,"
he states, "it is a bit hasty to characterize our current judicial systems as
simple instruments of class oppression; I don't believe that to be the case.
While they may incarnate other forms of oppressions, they also incarnate
a genuine quest for true concepts of justice, honor, love, goodness, and
understanding" (ibid, p. 70). Hence, we would have a democracy in which
individuals, in Rawls' description, might lead a life "beyond all reproach"
(1971, p. 70).

This research was supported by the Spanish Ministerio de Cienciay Tecnologia SEJ2007–
61414 / PSCE and the Balzan Foundation.

These quotations suffice to convey the bitterness of the conflict about justice as opposed to power, and to stress the irreconcilable character of Foucault's and Chomsky's views. Foucault sees a power relationship between rulers and ruled, whereas to Chomsky, this relationship is an ethical question, a matter, one might say, of moral values. The German poet Novalis best describes this antinomy. We borrow his words to express our provisional conclusion – "the most dangerous rivals to moral ideals are the ideals of a superior force, of a supremely abundant life, which have also been called the ideal of aesthetic grandeur." Our study broaches the question of influence exerted by minorities on majorities in the framework of a "moral ideal." We must now detail how and why we approach the question from this angle.

REPRESENTATION OF THE SOCIAL DOMAIN IN FULL FLUX

This study rests on three assumptions, none of them self-evident. The *first assumption* is that relationships among groups or individuals – to the extent that one believes in their existence – are declared to exist and that people share the representation of the social domain that defines these relationships. This is tantamount to saying that individuals or groups are not *res* or things, they are *res cogitans*, thinking things in a "thinking society" (Moscovici, 2000, p. 29). On the whole, we act by sharing feelings, interests, and conversations about what is hurtful to us or what is similar to something else or what constitutes a norm within a given social framework. But this process rests on continuous evaluations and reflections, practices that are at times a judgment, and at others an explanation of how our society operates and how to conduct oneself in it. These cogitations presuppose and entail a representation of the social domain. We are neither saying nor implying that there are no external sources or external influences affecting this process. But, contrary to what is often assumed, there is no such thing as mindless and detached acceptance. It would be just as erroneous to say that we can predict how such a process unfolds as it would be to trivialize it by regarding it simply as a matter of "common sense," as though groups or individuals made their decisions solely on the basis of palpable evidence. Our most serious mistake with respect to political and social thinking may lie in the way we move from an ephemeral and discontinuous world to a permanent and quite clearly represented social world.

The *second assumption* relates to the changed backdrop for our representation of the social domain. Even before the social sciences came into being, the central theme of modern representation was that people inevitably set aside religious or moral principles in the pursuit of their self interests or their exertion of power when these principles are incompatible with their goals, or that religion and morality are not inherently superior criteria for determining what constitutes a just life for mankind (Berlin, 1991, p. 8). Herein lies the origin of and the explanation for the distinction between facts and values that underpins the representation of the social domain in our social sciences and in our culture. From this perspective, society, like its individual members, came to be envisaged as complex pieces of machinery rationally assembled by an engineer. As Gellner wrote on this point, "Rationality does not merely identify a supposed path to the discovery of truth or legitimization of principles. It is also a life-style. The two aspects are intimately connected" (Gellner, 1992, p. 136).

What really characterizes their relationships in plain and simple words? Mainly the habit of distinguishing between the means and the ends of common actions. Let us look at this distinction by considering the possibility that means can be calculable and ascertainable according to certain rules. Rationality in the social realm is indeed an instrumental rationality of means and ends, relating to the exercise of power over humans or nature. The lack of flexibility in the choice of means explains why historical figures in the 20th century were so enamored with the maxim "the ends justify the means," thus unleashing the terrible consequences that we all know only too well. The English sociologist Baumann, at the end of a lucid analysis in which he referred to Milgram's experiments, pointed out that the noble belief in reason graciously absolved both the victims and the participants of the accusation of immorality and freed them of a guilty conscience. Having reduced human life to a calculus of self-preservation, rationality strips human life of its humanity (Bauman, 2001).

He could not have said it better. This is barbarity carried to its ultimate. And the continent-wide obliteration of millions of individuals and of their culture stimulated new thinking about the social realm in its wake. Undoubtedly human holocausts had taken place at previous times, but not at the height of modern Europe, and never so rationally and scientifically, so secretly, and with such total disregard for ethical norms. These events gave rise to a completely new concept, that of a crime directed not only against the life of a nation, hence the crime of genocide, but of a crime against mankind as a whole. A crime against humanity is both an ethical and legal crime, so that it is impossible to reduce the *questio facti* to a *questio juris*. Since that time, collective responsibility – which the philosopher Jaspers (1946) assumed in his famous book – and ethical responsibility have taken on many meanings. Legal and ethical categories become blurred in the sanction of crimes against humanity by its transformation into an absolute imperative. In the process, we move from the "is" to the "ought," since the crime in question – Kant (1781) calls it the quintessential evil – is an ethical notion on which the fate of democracy depends.

The second source of our thinking and of the reevaluation of the representation of the social domain is the big explosion of social movements in the 1970s, notably the "civil rights" movement. Given a world undergoing rapid change, civil rights proponents advocated the extension of democracy – hitherto limited to certain nations, to certain institutions – to all groups, all aspects of public and private life, particularly the most traditional institutions such as the family and schools. We do not claim that they have all been successful, but for most of these movements, emancipation and liberation were steps in bringing about change that affected "the moral nature of human existence," as the civil rights movement proclaimed.

Furthermore, the universal declaration of the rights of men, of which so little was expected, turned into a political factor from the 1970s onward and became ingrained in the anonymous throng of our beliefs and social representations (Doise, 2002). It is important to understand why we paid no attention to the paradoxical character of the rights of men, which henceforth apply to groups just as much as to individuals. What is this imperative that has been imposed on each one of us? It has to do with our ordinary feeling of a link between "ourselves" and "others," which may be associated with certain social regulations or constraints. The practice of appealing to human rights is subject to abuses, just like any other practice. Still, whenever these rights are invoked, it is reasonable to assume that they express an idea of justice that is common to the human species and to human society. The encompassing character of these rights, which makes them the object of universal respect and, simultaneously, of universal transgression, emphasizes the ethical component of our social interactions.

We make no claim to have offered a complete history of our time. All we have done is to recall its themes – genocide, the movement for the rights of men – that have opened up a whole series of collective ideas related to ethics and changed our representation of the social domain.

The *third assumption* is the idea that groups, societies that are propelled toward their ends by a power that is often completely instrumental, more or less unwittingly pay obeisance to "higher," that is to say, to ethical and historical, ends. In the face of conflicts, suffering, conquests, these ends impart a sense of injustice and sacrifice in the service of something that is meant as a great and progressive human fulfillment of its historic movement toward a higher standard. No matter how we feel about it, this ethical

perspective has penetrated all spheres of existence. This process, to which
we have become habituated, has affected our ordinary speech as well as
the representations that groups have of themselves. It has even affected the
priorities of social movements. We do not have to look far afield to see
its effect on our approach to social problems: Sociology itself highlights it
for us through the concept of deviance or marginality. Durkheim (1893)
devotes admirable pages to anomic groups that inevitably spring from the
social division of labor and addresses himself to the preservation of solidarity. Parsons (1951) and Merton (1968) speak of individuals who do not conform to prevailing norms, failing in their roles as fathers and citizens, and
sliding toward the margins of society, of strangers, members of minorities
subject to discrimination, the ailing, and other "misfits."

We have reached a turning point in the last 20 years that has changed the
features of the social problem by our replacing the old figure of the deviant and the excluded with that of a new figure, the figure of the victim. We
actually find groups trying to define themselves anew by discarding their
old shame about handicaps of a physical, social, ethnic, political, and so on,
nature, feelings that used to be their defining characteristic. They now present themselves in the guise of victims who are under the protection of the
rights of men, who spell out the values of justice and compassion that are
their due. No wonder that, by contrast, the previously dominant or "normal"
groups are now identified by their degree of social guilt in the genesis of
these sufferings and these shames. According to an American historian, "this
new sense of guilt is different. It is something congenital, intrinsic, collective,
something that is probably ineradicable" (Williams, 1993, p. 222).

But is this not a new way of expressing the old belief that the strong are
intrinsically unjust and the weak intrinsically just? Williams certainly has
this new status of victim in mind when he call self-evident the proposition that "it must be a virtue inherent in culpability that by taking a stance
against shame, it focuses our attention on the victim of our wrongdoings;
thus the victims and their feelings of shame should remain an element in
the construction of culpability" (Williams, 1993, p. 222).

It is difficult to believe that Benjamin was right to assert that the concept
of fault, rather than of cause and effect, is "the supreme category of universal
history that guarantees the univocity of the course of events. Every moment
in universal history commits a fault and results from a fault" (Benjamin,
2001, p. 101).

By recognizing the victim, we recognize and designate the guilty: Women
point to men, Indians to the Spanish, Blacks to the Whites, the colonized to
the colonizers, all of whom, in a Dostoevskian universe, are responsible "for

everybody and before all men ....." To free oneself of guilt, one must repent, that is, express remorse as a way of forgiving oneself. The only one who can pardon the offender is the offended victim by concluding that the offender is sincere in his or her repentance or determination to make amends. For, we must remember, the victim is also a person or a group that defines itself by the wrong that it has suffered and that insists on compensation.

A clue to the transformation of deviants into victims is the related change in representation of the social domain, which reveals itself by the presence of compassion, the upswing of charitableness. And above all, the admission of a social culpability, as witnessed by the request for pardon and expiation. In this respect, the action taken by the Catholic Church is all the more striking because of its lack of precedents. After the first *mea culpa* for the persecutions inflicted by the Inquisition, John Paul II begged forgiveness for the excesses committed by missionaries during colonization, for injury done to the Indians, the native African populations, and for the Holocaust.

In a recent article, the anthropologist Terray (2005), an African specialist, cites innumerable victims: descendants of slaves, populations decimated if not exterminated by genocide, natives of the Republic who have suffered from colonialism. All of them at the very least demand the symbolic recognition of their sufferings, the equivalent of repentance. In this context, France has designated May 10th for its annual commemoration of its colonial past. And France is not alone in making this gesture: Queen Elizabeth II recently apologized to the Maoris of New Zealand for the mistreatment inflicted on them by the British Empire, as one example.

The widespread practice (Barkan, 2000) of admitting past injustices by urging repentance may seem absurd, like any other practice. Although accepting blame for the political aspects of shame and culpability may be a mere show, asking the victims for forgiveness also holds a promise for future action. The verbal action is held out as an ethical commitment to refrain from inappropriate, inconsiderate deeds toward the group of victims. It may give rise to the impression that the past cannot be undone and that there is no way to transcend resentment or the desire to avenge old offenses, since it is impossible to modify the past (Colonomos, 2005; Margalit, 2002).

Even so, it is possible to change our representation of the past. In the light of the expression of repentance, culpability is seen in a new context, a context that allows reconciliation with the past and the transcendence of the sense of humiliation. It is not surprising that some countries have gone a step further. In 2004, France recognized the status of victims by creating a special ministry for victims and a new victims' right, which supersedes the normal judicial procedure (Lévy, 2005). Things have reached a point where the newspaper *Le Monde* (2004, October 10) calls French society a "society obsessed by victims." And a sociologist notes that minorities "are engaged in a fierce competition for the title of most disadvantaged group" (Todorov, 2005, p. 155).

We realize that these assumptions merely scratch the surface, but even so they should suffice to indicate where our research is heading. Obviously one needs to study, case by case, as is being done, the different components of shame and culpability, the characteristics of the victims – all these are matters of the most basic observations. Our approach takes a different notion as its starting point; namely, that changes in the representation of the social domain, like changes in the concepts of motion, space, or time, give new meaning to old phenomena and lead to the discovery of new phenomena. And the modifications we have outlined throw a new light on the interdependence of group members, the processes of categorization, and group interactions. They also affect the cultural atmosphere within which, according to Lewin, answers are given to questions raised by individuals in trying to solve the problems of our times. Our research takes as its point of departure such changes in the interdependence between majorities and minorities.

ACTIVE MINORITIES AND VICTIMIZED MINORITIES

It is no accident that research on the psychology of minorities first concentrated on active minorities. These minorities were matched to historical descriptions, but they also applied to the groups that at that time were leaving their mark by provoking conflicts, rejecting the norms and beliefs of the majority, and even transgressing prohibitions. And they thereby accepted the ultimate risk of a break with the group or their exclusion from it. That was the cost the active minority had to pay to convert the majority to an unfamiliar, original point of view or to an alternative lifestyle, of which the most recent examples are the social movements and dissident minorities of the late 20th century (Moscovici, 1976).

From the very outset, minority theory envisaged social culpability, that is, an ethical factor, as one of the two reasons for the innovative influence exerted by a minority over the majority. But on the one hand, there was no model or specific example of minorities arousing social culpability. And on the other hand, it would have been difficult to confirm this finding empirically, in view of the representation of the social domain in everyday existence. It is perfectly obvious that the concept of social culpability could only be tested with a concrete prototype of a victimized minority in place. At the same time, a different representation of the social domain had to become anchored in daily life.

We must now examine the reasons why victimized minorities arouse social culpability. This is tied to the fact that collectivities or groups were considered inferior, deprived not only of political or economic rights, but even denied their basic human identity. They were shunted aside from society by a biased application of laws, of economic regulations or work rules, of family or neighborhood treatment. In each case, beliefs, human rights, or the values on which society is founded were violated openly or surreptitiously, just as colonization violated the principles of emancipation or the Dreyfus affair (Reinach, 1901) the right to a fair trial. Whenever a discrepancy arises between the principles of a society or the maxims of a religion on the one hand and reality on the other, internal conflicts are aroused that end up creating a sense of guilt, with the consequences that we have noted.

To understand why in our time victimized minorities exert an influence or an effect on the majority, and why this effect or influence differs from that of an active minority, we offer as a first hypothesis that the minority that claims the status of victim is recognized and even legitimized, so that the majority can and is even obliged to accept its demands or share its opinions. In terms of influence, these victimized minorities will receive an overt social recognition (Moscovici & Paicheler, 1978). Such an influence can occur when the message of the victimized minority is rooted in an ethical relationship with the majority. The message of the victimized minority is more likely to trigger a conflict within the majority than with the majority. Hence, the conflict takes the form of culpability: between its beliefs, ideas, and principles on the one hand, and its actions or prejudices and its behaviors toward the minority on the other. This may be due to the fact that these actions and prejudices are publicly forbidden or condemned, or because they are thought to be so. By its requests for actions that make amends, the victimized minority offers the majority the opportunity to resolve this internal conflict, to make a new start after all the harm it has done. An active minority, on the other hand, is more likely to create an external conflict that would lead to a change in the way the minority is judged or preconceived.

STUDIES ON THE POLITICAL AND ETHICAL RELATIONS BETWEEN MAJORITY AND MINORITY

We have done a series of studies on these two types of minorities and the corresponding influence processes (Moscovici & Pérez, 2007) by using Gypsies as a victimized or active minority. At the outset, the participants read a one-page summary on the true history of Gypsy persecution in Europe. After recalling the dates on which the Gypsies reached the different European countries, the summary divided the fate of the Gypsies into three phases: a favorable reception (objects of curiosity, treatment as pilgrims); a phase in which they were evicted from each country; and a final phase of intensified Gypsy persecution – enforced slavery in Rumania before 1860, defenceless slaughter while roaming in Germany, Austria, Switzerland; Charles VI's edict to hunt down all men and cut off an ear on all women and children; enforced name change, enforced residence in specific places; enforced attire differing from that of other people; prohibition against speaking their own language; and, finally, a reference to the 250,000 Gypsies exterminated by the Nazis. This historical report was identical for the three experiments that we summarize subsequently.

Our first experiment (Moscovici & Pérez, 2007), with 94 students at the University of Valencia as subjects, followed a 2 x 2 factorial design. The first independent variable consisted of manipulating the presentation of the Gypsy minority either as an active or as a victimized minority. For the *victimized minority* condition, participants were told that they were reading an "abstract of a report about the Gypsy population by a Gypsy representative," while in the *active minority* condition they were informed that it was an "abstract of a report about the Gypsy population by the Gypsy Political Party." In addition, the conclusion of this summary was formulated so as to stress the contrast between the two types of minorities. The victimized minority emphasizes the history of its persecution and its suffering to seek a compensation: "*We ask ourselves: should we Gypsies not seek compensation from the State, given that this society has inflicted such grave sufferings on us in the past and continues to make us suffer?*" Conversely, the active minority uses this history of persecution to seek a change in society so that it will never again be a victim of such a persecution: "*We ask ourselves: should we Gypsies not mobilize and fight actively until we achieve a radical change in this society, which has persecuted us so grievously and continues to persecute us?*" The victimized minority, we might say, asks for nothing but a pacifying ad hoc gesture on the part of the majority society at the present time; the active minority, on the other hand, expresses its desire to engage firmly in an action which one day will lead to a change in the representation of the minority in society.

We assumed, it may be recalled, that the victimized minority would evoke a sense of guilt in the participants with respect to the Gypsies, while the active minority would arouse a feeling of conflict with the Gypsies.

To try to reinforce or to counteract these two feelings, of culpability or of conflict, that are assumed to be operating, we made use of the emotional semiotics of colors. It is no great revelation that every society associates certain emotional or affective states with certain colors (Bousoño, 1952). We believed that in Europe and especially in the southern part of the continent, black is usually a sign of grief, evil, sadness, or mourning. Red, on the other hand, is most often a symbol of revolution or conflict, or of a certain amount of violence. A second independent variable was therefore created by varying *the affective and symbolic context* within which the main idea about the minority (compensation request for past suffering vs. the slogan for a radical social change) was introduced: on a *black* background for half the participants and on a *red* one for the other half. These two colors could be envisaged as a latent emotional context accompanying the overt messages addressed to the majority. The victimized minority was expected to have a greater overt influence when its message was presented on a black background, reinforcing guilt feelings, while the active minority was expected to strengthen its influence when its message was presented on a red background, accentuating the conflict with the majority.

That was the schema for the experiment, conceived to test the idea that there are in fact two distinct types of minorities: active minorities, which maintain a political relationship with the majority, and the – new – victimized minorities that tend to maintain an ethical relationship. The first question was to determine whether the Gypsies could be represented in these two guises in these two reports to the majority. It should be kept in mind that we told largely the same story about the Gypsies and only at the very end varied the potential strategy taken by the political or victimized minority. We speculated that if the Gypsies participated in these new relationships that were taking shape between the majority and the minority, contrasting thoughts and feelings based only on the conclusion that the minority draws from the history of its persecution should be elicited in the subjects.

The first dependent variable was measured by asking the participants to write down all the feelings and ideas that came spontaneously to mind when they read the plea of the Gypsy minority. Analyses of these associations showed that the victimized minority induced more ideas related to compensation than the active minority ($p < .03$; for further statistical details, see Moscovici & Pérez, 2007); it also elicited more associated ideas referring to "injustice" and "suffering," which invoked the pain, inequality, repression experienced by the Gypsy minority in the course of its history than did the active minority ($p < .007$). The active minority, for its part, more frequently elicited significantly more ideas explicitly referring to "mobilization and change" than the victimized minority ($p < .0001$). Moreover, compared to the victimized minority, the active minority more frequently ($p < .0001$) elicited a category related to struggle, conflict, and courage, reflecting the adversarial relationship between an active minority and the repressive majority described in the historical account. It is thus apparent that the associations of ideas or values chosen by the subjects after reading the historical account of Gypsy oppression in Europe formed a relatively consistent semantic field, which was a rather faithful reflection of our Zeitgeist.

The victimized minority drew the subjects' attention to the repression and suffering unjustly inflicted by the majority on the minority, on the amends to be made to minority, and on the compensation requested for earlier injuries. All of this is part of a new representation of the social domain. But where the active minority expressed an urge or a desire to change the relationships between the minority and the Spanish majority, it triggered a more traditional but still potent layer of associations relating to putting up a struggle and the courage needed to reach a goal. Two relationships with the majority thus emerge. In the case of the victimized minority, an ethical relation was elicited; for the active minority, an antagonistic, that is, a conflicted relationship, was evoked. Our initial hypothesis with respect to influence is that this conflicted relationship is required to produce a latent change and conversion in the majority; by contrast, the ethical relationship is adequate for obtaining compensation, without necessarily persuading the majority to accept the point of view of the minority.

OVERT CULPABILITY AND LATENT REPRESENTATION

What influence does each of these two minorities actually exert on the majority? An attitude scale intended to measure the overt attitude toward the Gypsies and another scale to measure the latent attitude was devised to observe this influence. For the manifest attitude scale, the participants were asked to state whether they approved or disapproved of a series of institutional measures explicitly favoring or compensating the Gypsies (*One must grant special rights to the Gypsies to erase the memory of this horrible past; The Gypsies must be given 2% of the leadership positions in public institutions; There should be a ministry devoted solely to the Gypsy question*). The subject could tell immediately if he or she was expressing a favorable or unfavorable attitude toward compensating the Gypsies to make amends for past wrongs. The latent attitude scale followed a different logic. On this scale were items such as: *Gypsies are less concerned about their children's education than the Gadje (i.e., Spaniards, "payos" in Spanish); Gypsies care less about technological progress in our society than the Gadje.* Here a set of values known to prevail among the Gadje (the value of education, development of political life, technological progress) was emphasized. It may well be true that the Gypsies are actually less interested in these matters, which are more likely to be highly valued by the Gadje. The logic of this scale was that the more the Gypsies are perceived as lacking interest in whatever is highly valued by the Gadje, the more they will be perceived as "valueless" from the Gadje point of view. The latent aspect of this scale was that the subjects are not necessarily aware of the fact that their agreement or disagreement with these factual statements is being correlated with their overt attitudes toward the Gypsies.

Analysis of these scales yields a first result concerning the interaction between the type of minority and overt versus latent attitude ($p < .008$): The victimized minority had a more favorable impact on overt attitudes toward the Gypsies than on latent attitudes, while the active minority had a more favorable influence on attitudes at the latent than at the overt level. This finding confirms our hypothesis as to the field of influence of each type of minority.

But we also started out from the hypothesis that each of these two minorities would exert its influence by a different mediating process. We postulated, as mentioned earlier, that the mediating factor would be culpability in the case of victimized minorities and conflict in the case of active minorities. The results partially confirm this hypothesis (for further details, see Moscovici & Pérez, 2007). It is true that in the context of symbolic guilt expressed by the black background, the victimized minority elicited, as expected, a much more favorable response to Gypsy claims for compensation than it did in the context of symbolic conflict expressed by a red background ($p < .007$). The response was also much more favorable in the symbolic guilt context than it was for an active minority in the same guilt context ($p < .04$, one-tailed). These results certainly agree with the hypothesis that guilt acts as mediator for the influence of victimized minorities. They also confirm that the active minority induces more favorable latent attitudes toward the Gypsies than the victimized minority ($p < .002$), but, contrary to our expectations, this difference was independent of the symbolic context of guilt or conflict within which the message is presented to the participants.

CULPABILITY AS A MEDIATOR OF OVERT ATTITUDES

At the end of this first experiment, we were not entirely convinced that our manipulations of culpability (black background color) and conflict (red background color) were effective, and we thus were unable to tell whether, in fact, culpability was the mediator for the overt influence of victimized minorities and conflict the mediator for the latent influence of active minorities. To clarify this point, we undertook a second experiment ($N=51$ students at the University of Valencia). Nearly the same procedure was followed as in the preceding experiment, except for adding the following two variations. We eliminated the manipulation involving the background color on which the central argument of each type of minority was presented, and thus only kept the variable about the type of minority, victimized versus active minority. We then added a measure for social guilt feelings, which we borrowed from recent research by Powell, Branscombe, and Schmitt (2005).

With respect to our two focal points, the representation of the victimized minority and that of the active minority, and the type of influence induced by each of these two minorities, we reproduced the same major results as in the previous experiment. On the one hand, the subjects were fully aware of the difference between the victimized Gypsy minority and the active Gypsy minority, almost in the same way as in the previous experiments. On the other hand, the victimized minority elicited more favorable overt attitudes toward the Gypsies than the active minority ($p < .03$). Conversely, the active minority aroused more favorable latent attitudes toward the Gypsies than the victimized minority ($p < .041$). On the new social guilt scale, the victimized minority appeared to induce greater social guilt than the active minority ($p < .014$).

We then made a series of analyses seeking to test whether social guilt was the mediator of overt influence and conflict the mediator of latent influence. Following regression analysis procedures proposed by Baron and Kenny (1986), we found that social guilt significantly predicted overt attitudes ($p < .001$), because when these feelings were introduced in the equation, the type of minority (victimized vs. active) ceased to be significant ($p > .42$). This shows that social guilt feelings mediate the more favorable overt attitudes obtained by the victimized minority. Using a similar procedure, however, we determined that social guilt feelings did not mediate the influence of the type of minority on latent attitudes.

We then tested whether thoughts related to "struggle, conflict" could play a role in latent influence, depending on the type of minority. Results showed that while the effect of the type of minority was significant before control for "struggle, conflict" ($p < .041$), it was no longer a significant predictor of latent attitudes ($p > .28$). At the same time, while "struggle, conflict" had a significant direct effect on latent attitudes before control for the effect of the type of minority ($p < .047$), it no longer was a significant predictor of latent attitudes after controlling for the effect of the type of minority ($t < 1$). These results confirm that the participants' responsiveness to the militant and confrontational social style characteristic of active minorities was related to its positive influence on latent attitudes. But at the same time, it cannot be asserted that the effect of the active minority on latent attitudes can only be explained by a perception of its confrontational style.

THE MAJORITY'S *MEA CULPA*: RECONCILIATION WITH THE MINORITY? OR ACT OF PURIFICATION OF ITS OWN MEMORY?

The purpose of our new study was to delve into the difference between minorities as activists, so to speak, and minorities as victims. When the majority is confronted with a minority that takes an active stand, that is, an active minority, its attention is focused on that minority. The minority gives rise to a conflict with the majority and instigates a validation context. The majority is challenged to demonstrate an active resistance until it finds new ways of grasping or experiencing the values of the minority. Conversely, when the majority is confronted with a minority in the role of victim, the majority centers on its own ego. Here the focal point is not the behavior or the value of the minority, but the majority's past behavior toward the minority. In this context of what one might call soul-searching, the majority may feel an internal conflict between its principles and its behaviors and may seek to lighten its social guilt. Whatever change occurs in the majority, if any, reflects its repentance and its judgment about its own past behavior, and not a new increased esteem for the minority as such.

To summarize, the hypothesis examined in this third study deals with the following question: To what degree does minority influence on the act of penitence depend on the quasi-ritual character of doing penance or asking for forgiveness? These practices are not exactly acts of *mea culpa*, since strictly speaking culpability is attributed to generations preceding the one that recognizes a moral and material responsibility. What, then, impels this majority to do second-hand penance for wrongs perpetrated by its ancestors? It is the same motivation that impels the victims to ask for redress, not only for themselves but also for and in the name of their ancestors. One might thus say that the majority performs what one calls a duty to memory, which produces beneficial effects. It could also be said that today's majority, by recognizing the wrongs inflicted on the minority in the past, in some way purifies its own memory, and, at the same time demonstrates that it disapproves of the wrongs attributed to its ancestors, thereby giving the victimized minority a chance to free itself of a resentment passed on from generation to generation.

"To repent is to modify the past," said Oscar Wilde. In this third study we tried to answer the question whether the majority offers a gesture of recognition to the victimized minority or whether it acts to clear its memory, thus inducing a change in its own past and, at the same time, presumably presenting a less racist image of itself. To elucidate these points, some of the subjects participating in the experiment were told that their responses to a questionnaire would be passed on to a minority group (a Gypsy association), while the remaining subjects were led to believe that their responses would be used by a European institution in a study devoted to anti-Gypsy racism on our continent.

Fifty-two students at the University of Valencia, who were evenly divided into the four conditions described later, participated in this study. The same procedure as in the previous studies was followed. As in the previous studies, the participants read a one-page summary on the true history of the persecution of the Gypsies in Europe. This report reflected the style of a victimized minority in one-half of the conditions and that of an active minority in the other half. The participants then jotted down the association of ideas or values that came to their minds when they read this report. Immediately thereafter, a new independent variable was introduced. It consisted of manipulating the public to which the subjects' opinions about the Gypsies were to be submitted. Half the participants were told that the study had been sponsored by the *Gypsy Association*, while the other half of the participants were told that it was sponsored by a *Commission of the European Union*, established in Brussels. The subjects were told that their opinions about the Gypsies would be shown directly either to the Gypsies or to a commission of experts of the European Union. Moreover, it was specified in all four conditions that a comparative analysis between the different European countries would be launched to see in which country racism against the Gypsies was strongest.

Let us begin with culpability expressed by the subjects in each of these conditions. The same social guilt scale used in the previous study was applied. In an ANOVA 2 (victimized minority vs. active minority) x 2 (public addressed: Gypsy minority vs. European Union), the only significant effect is that the subjects express greater guilt when their opinions are to be analyzed by a commission of the European Union than when they are to be submitted to the Gypsies themselves ($p < .04$). This result agrees with the hypothesis that the sense of social guilt is more likely to manifest itself in the face of an international authority than in the face of the minority, though it is the target of the subjects' opinions. We thereby confirm that the minority on its own has no control over whether the majority feels or fails to feel guilty, as though it were unable to be both judge and litigant. Only under the eyes of a third party does the history of minority persecution evoke a sense of culpability in the majority.

Given the centuries-long persecution of the Gypsies, what are the conditions under which the subjects are the most favorably inclined toward compensation? In this study, the compensation scale is similar to the overt attitude scale of the previous studies. The only modification is that now all the items solely refer to the various compensation measures in favor of the Gypsies. The scale consists of nine items (Cronbach Alpha = .75). ANOVA 2 (victimized minority vs. active minority) x 2 (public addressed: Gypsy minority vs. European Union) shows that there is an interaction ($p < .04$) between the two manipulated variables (see Figure 4.1). When the subjects' opinions are to be directly judged by the Gypsies, the subjects are more inclined to compensate the victimized minority ($m = .29$) than the active minority ($m = -56$; $p < .05$). When the subjects' opinions are to be examined by the E.U. Commission, the fact that the minority is presented as active ($m = .30$) or as victimized ($m = .02$) has no significant effect ($t < 1$) on the inclination to compensate it. The new result with respect to our previous studies is thus that the customary overt rejection of an active minority no longer manifests itself when the relationship between majority and minority is evaluated by another supranational majority (the averages –.56 and .30 do differ significantly; $p < .02$).

What becomes of the representation of the minority? In this study, the so-called latent scale of the previous studies was expanded by an equal number of new items. It should be remembered that the measure for the latent attitude toward the Gypsies is the extent to which the Gypsies are held not to share the Gadje's values (concern for educational opportunities, technological progress, etc.). We added other items that referred more explicitly to Gadje values and to values generally recognized as more characteristic of the Gypsies (*"Gypsies are more concerned about taking care of old people than the Gadje"; Gypsies teach us a different way to treat old persons in the family"; "Gypsies represent anti-progress in our country"; "Gypsies suffer discrimination because non-Gypsies know little about their culture"*). The new scale consists of ten items in all (Cronbach's Alpha = .74). The average was calculated, and the pertinent items were calculated as their inverse so as to make a high score correspond to a greater recognition of Gypsy values.

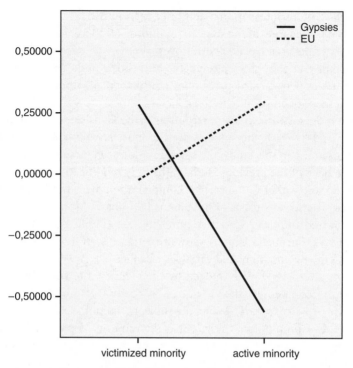

FIGURE 4.1. Attitude toward compensations for the Gypsies. (A positive score means that one favors compensation.)
Note: EU, European union.

ANOVA 2 (victimized minority vs. active minority) × 2 (public addressed: Gypsy minority vs. European Union) on this scale shows an interaction between the two variables ($p < .03$; see Figure 4.2). In the condition where interaction with the minority is direct, the active minority induces a greater recognition of the Gypsies' having positive values ($m = .27$) than the victimized minority ($m = -.13$). By contrast, when the participants think that they are addressing themselves to the E.U. Commission, the subjects assign greater value to the Gypsies when they are presented as a victimized minority ($m = .35$) than as an active minority ($m = -.49$).

This third study confirms once again that the minority's strategy of presenting itself as a victim does predispose the majority to grant it compensations in recognition of the discrimination it experienced, whereas the majority changes its representation of the minority in the face of an active minority that deploys a strategy of contention and struggle, and recognizes the minority's existence as having an intrinsic cultural value. It may be

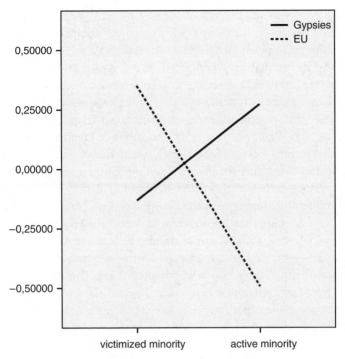

FIGURE 4.2. Recognition of Gypsy values. (A positive score means that one recognizes Gypsy values.)

Note: EU: European union.

interesting to observe that there is no correlation ($r = +.04$) in the attitude scale between compensation for the minority and representation of the minority as a bearer of values.

Delving a little further in our analysis, we recognized that such a response pattern toward victimized and active minorities basically presupposes that the opinions and attitudes of the participants are geared to two different audiences. It would seem that social guilt toward a victimized minority, which predisposes the majority toward compensation of the minority, would never arise in the first place in the absence of a third authority that acts as a protector toward the minority and incites the majority to do this soul-searching. By contrast, the active minority itself challenges the majority directly.

We can now understand why the subjects expressed greater culpability when their responses were going to be judged by an international authority (the E.U. Commission) than by the minority itself. Compensation and culpability are positively correlated ($r = +.47$, $p < .001$); hence, the greater the guilt one experiences, the more readily one gives compensation. But such a correlation, significant as it is, allows considerable margin as to whether culpability is automatically converted into compensation. Undoubtedly people sometimes resist agreeing to compensation because they do not wish to admit more guilt than necessary. This phenomenon has been carefully studied in a series of recent experiments on social guilt (Branscombe & Doosje, 2004). When the degree of the subject's identification with the group is taken into account, for instance, not all the members of the majority group feel culpability for the wrongdoings of their group according to these experiments. In fact, those for whom group identity is very important and who identify strongly with the group may have trouble admitting the group's wrongdoings; they are reluctant to accept the group's responsibility and deny its having violated moral standards. Here, denial of guilt serves to retain a positive self-image, insofar as one thereby avoids recognizing the responsibility of the group to which one belongs. The complexity of the process becomes apparent, when, *mutatis mutandis*, the individuals with the lowest group identification prove to be equally unwilling to express collective guilt for acts of which the group was the perpetrator: They do not feel sufficiently tied to their group to compromise themselves by assuming any responsibility for wrongdoings committed by other members of this group.

All this raises the difficult question of collective responsibility in a society in which the law recognizes only individual responsibility. We must realize that the subjects who believe that their responses will be judged by the E.U. Commission will be less inclined to offer compensation to the victimized minority, even when they express a high degree of culpability. According to Terray, "to present oneself as a victim, to display one's traumatism and suffering openly is the best way to attract the public's esteem, the media's sympathy, and favorable treatment by the authorities...but as the reservoir of attention and kind feelings at their disposal is not inexhaustible, competition is inevitable" (Terray, 2006, p. 56).

It is likely that what we are seeing is a competition among the penitents to avoid the compensations from piling up, a situation that would be detrimental to the image of their national or professional group. This is exactly what occurred when Swiss banks were asked to pay compensations for the accounts belonging to wartime victims of Nazi persecutions: It was a serious blow to their image. But, to keep within the limits of our theory for the moment, it is obviously easier to admit that compensation is justified in a relationship between two partners, the majority and the minority, than in a three-fold relationship, with the intervention of an outside adjudicator. To be sure, the presence of a third partner in a relationship among groups introduces a reality principle, namely, that in our societies, criminal culpability can be imputed only to individuals who are present or to their legal representatives. And finally, it is much easier to agree to compensation when one knows the continuous history of minority persecutions (though this history is told to the subjects in the active minority condition as well as in the victimized minority condition), but the active minority is not seen as victimized, so that the majority does not play the part of executioner.

CONCLUSION

It has been the purpose of this research to elucidate and to confirm a fundamental concept in the theory of innovation by minorities and, in the process, to broaden its field of application by taking into account the evolution of the representation of the social domain, or even of our *ethos* (Moscovici, 2004). Until now, no one has realized its importance with respect to relationships in other fields, notably in our own area of knowledge. An experiment like Milgram's, for example, could not have been carried out today. To the extent that considerations of this kind are an accurate reflection of our experiments, our hypothesis about the emerging phenomenon of minorities recognized as victims will seem natural.

This may be a result of circumstances – their living in a setting where repressions and discriminations abound – but a more important factor is a happy change in the ethics of democracy, in the diffusion of the human rights. Given these circumstances, discrimination and repressions are envisaged with a view to granting equality and liberation to the groups that suffer from them. This entails the admission of a social guilt that at times has historical roots. More specifically, it requires the recognition of the majority's social guilt, which reveals, in a historical context, the contradiction or the conflict between the majority's principles or values and its real behavior, the distance separating it from the minorities, its lack of knowledge about the conditions under which these minorities are living, or the violent acts that they must endure. As recognized victims, minorities can arouse the social guilt of majorities, whose internal conflicts they intensify, one might say, legitimately. We were able to confirm this hypothesis in the three studies. The victimized minority received a favorable response from the study subjects to its request for redress of past wrongs, and this redress seems to be mediated by culpability. The active minority, by contrast, did not receive a similar concession from the majority.

The question arises whether minorities are seeking the status of victim at the very time when collective action is stymied by difficulties, and mobilization of the "masses" to transform the state of affairs, the relation between minorities and majorities, society, is no longer a viable option. In other words, to the extent that the old political strategy of attaining transformations in the system as a whole has come to a dead end, a new, we might say, ethical-legal path is now being pursued to change people's mentality and social representation, to improve human interactions and to readjust the system accordingly. In other words, being unable to modify the police, we are now attempting to modify policemen.

Finally, though victimized minorities do obtain redress in the form of compensation, they do not succeed in modifying the opinions of the majority, in this case, in changing its conception of Gypsies, in gaining insight into the essence of their being. We therefore wonder whether the victimized minority's lack of latent influence, its failure to change the representations it elicits, in short, its failure to convert the majority, might not represent a danger, a future threat. To take a familiar analogy, it would be as though women were to find that they had been granted equal wages and social standing with men, without a concomitant change in men's image of women and in their prejudices against them. Or, to take another example, it would be as if the Jews had been emancipated, granted the same political and civil rights as all other citizens, without the simultaneous disappearance of the old anti-Semitic attitudes toward them. We certainly know that we are dealing here with psychic and social forces that tend to endure and to resurface when circumstances are propitious. For most minorities that have suffered from discrimination and oppression, the unleashing of these forces is a threat that hangs over them in perpetuity. This second question may transcend the field of social psychology and reach beyond our field of research. Or perhaps it lies within our reach, for, with a reliable theory at our disposal, we may be able to discover an approach for studying these difficult, uncertain phenomena by applying to them the necessary mental acuity, curiosity, and empathy. They are surely of crucial importance for understanding what is happening under our very eyes and for seeing more lucidly in this age of minorities.

REFERENCES

Barkan, E. (2000). *The guilt of nations: Restitution and negotiating historical injustices*. New York: Norton.

Baron, R. M., & Kenny, D. A. (1986). The moderator-mediator variable distinction in social psychological research: Conceptual, strategic and statistical considerations. *Journal of Personality and Social Psychology, 51*, 1173–1182.

Bauman, Z. (2001). *The individualized society.* Cambridge, UK: Polity Press.

Benjamin, W. (2001). *Fragments.* Paris: P.U.F.

Berlin, J. (1991). *The crooked timber of humanity.* London: John Murray.

Bousoño, C. (1952). *Teoría de la expresión poética [Theory of the poetic expression].* Madrid: Gredos.

Branscombe, N. R., & Doosje, B. (2004). *Collective guilt. International perspectives.* Cambridge, UK: Cambridge University Press.

Chomsky, N., & Foucault, M. (2002). *Sur la nature humaine.* Bruxelles: Aden.

Colonomos, A. (2005). *La morale dans les relations internationales.* Paris: Odile Jacob.

Doise, W. (2002). *Human rights as social representations.* London: Routledge.

Durkheim, E. (1893). *De la division du travail social.* Paris: Presses Universitaires de France.

Gellner, E. (1992). *Reason and culture.* Oxford, UK: Blackwell.

Jaspers. K. (1946). *Die Schuldfrage.* Heidelberg: Schneider.

Kant, I. (1781/1993). *Kritik der reinen Vernunft.* Frankfurt & Main: Suhrkamp Verlag.

Levy, T. (2005). *Eloge de la barbarie judiciaire.* Paris: Odile Jacob.

Margalit, A. (2002). *The ethics of memory.* Cambridge, MA: Harvard University Press.

Merton, R. (1968). *Social theory and social structure* (2nd revisited ed.). New York: Free Press.

Moscovici, S. (1976). *Social influence and social change.* New York: Academic Press.
(2000). *Social representations.* Cambridge, UK: Polity Press.
(2004). The shame and guilt ethos. Mimeographed.

Moscovici, S., & Paicheler, C. (1978). Social comparison and social recognition: Two complementary processes of identification. In H. Tajfel (Ed.), *Differentiation between social groups* (pp. 251–266). London: Academic Press.

Moscovici, S., & Pérez, J. A. (2007). A study of minorities as victims. *European Journal of Social Psychology, 37,* 725–746.

Parsons, T. (1951). *The social system.* New York: Free Press.

Powell, A. A., Branscombe, N. R., & Schmitt, M. T (2005). Inequality as ingroup privilege or outgroup disadvantage: The impact of group focus on collective guilt and interracial attitudes. *Personality and Social Psychology Bulletin, 31,* 508–521.

Rawls, J. (1971). *A theory of justice.* Cambridge, MA: Harvard University Press.

Reinach, J. (1901). *Histoire de l'affaire Dreyfus.* Paris: Laffont.

Terray, E. (2005). La pitié et la raison. *Le Monde,* 20 Marz.
(2006). *Face aux abus de mémoire.* Paris: Actes Sud.

Todorov, T. (2005). *Mémoire du mal, tentation du bien.* Paris: Robert Laffont.

Williams, B. (1993). *Shame and necessity.* Berkeley, CA: University of California Press.

5

Marginalization Through Social Ostracism: Effects of Being Ignored and Excluded

KIPLING D. WILLIAMS AND
ADRIENNE R. CARTER-SOWELL

Humans rely on social interactions with others to fulfill fundamental social, psychological, and survival needs. These interactions provide basic survival needs for mating, food, and protection, but also provide the higher-order socioeconomic advantages of cooperation and reciprocity. Perhaps most importantly, however, social interactions provide individuals with a sense of belonging and recognition from their mates. Not all social interactions are pleasant, yet they still provide a sense of recognition, and in some cases belonging. For instance, aversive forms of interpersonal interaction such as bullying and overt forms of rejection still provide the individual with a sense of recognition and importance. Others must go out of their ways to bully, to overtly reject, and this expended effort alone is substantiation that one deserves recognition. However, another aversive interpersonal behavior deprives the individual of the sense of recognition and meaning: ostracism. We define ostracism as being ignored and excluded (Williams, 1997, 2001, 2007, 2009). Ostracism can occur through the physical banishment or exile of an individual or group to venues that are separate from the others. In this sense, extreme forms of segregation could be viewed as physical ostracism. Ostracism can also occur without physical separation. When society's actions communicate to individuals or groups that they are psychologically invisible and inaudible to the larger society, they become socially ostracized. By being marginalized in this way, they have no measurable impact on their society. They are not recognized, nor do they have voice. These effects translate into losing four fundamental needs: belonging, self-esteem, control, and meaningful existence. These basic needs nurture human survival, maintain motivation, and promote health and success.

In this chapter we describe our research program that illustrates the powerful impact that ostracism has on individuals. Admittedly, our research largely focuses on how individuals react to being ostracized by a few others, but we believe these studies lay an important foundation for understanding how minorities feel when marginalized by the dominant society. After reviewing our research program, we will speculate about specific effects of ostracism on minorities, at the individual and group levels.

OSTRACISM RESEARCH: AN OVERVIEW

We begin with brief descriptions of the paradigms used to manipulate and examine ostracism. Then, we present a model of ostracism that guided our research and summarized our findings (see Figure 5.1). Finally, we consider how ostracism is used to marginalize individuals and groups, and what consequences this might have on these individuals and groups and on society in general.

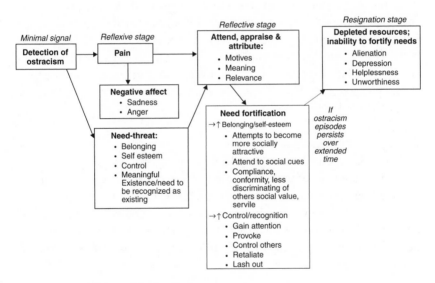

FIGURE 5.1. New model of ostracism.

Paradigms

The paradigms we use to examine ostracism are meant to create a sense of being ignored and excluded, while at the same time trying not to indicate failure, disagreement, and certainly not outright rejection, abuse, or bullying. Thus, our paradigms have purposefully attempted relatively minimal forms of ignoring and exclusion. We summarize them briefly here.

Ball Tossing
Actual participants arrive with two other ostensible participants, and while waiting for the experiment to begin, one of the confederates picks up a ball and starts tossing it around. Half the participants are included in a third of the tosses (inclusion), while the other half receive the ball a few times, but never again for the remaining 5 minutes or so (Warburton, Williams, & Cairns, 2006; Williams & Sommer, 1997).

Cyberball
A virtual analogue of the ball toss paradigm, Cyberball (Eisenberger, Lieberman, & Williams, 2003; Williams, Cheung, & Choi, 2000; Williams & Jarvis, 2006; Zadro, Boland, & Richardson, 2006; Zadro, Williams, & Richardson, 2004) is played on a computer over the Internet and appears to be an interactive tossing game. When the ball is tossed to the participant, the participant chooses to whom to throw the ball by clicking one of the other players. In the ostracism condition, the participant receives the ball twice and then is completely excluded from the game (i.e., they do not receive the ball again). In the inclusion condition, the participant randomly receives the ball approximately 33% of the time. In both conditions, there are no players other than the participant, since the tosses are programmed to control level of inclusion.

Cell-Phone Text Messaging
Unlike ball tossing and Cyberball, text messaging on cell phones cannot depict the level of inclusion among the other members of the group. Thus, being ignored and excluded through text messaging requires that the participant believes the others continue to interact. In this paradigm, after initial inclusion in a conversation, participants either continue to be included or receive no further messages from the others (Smith & Williams, 2004).

Chat Rooms
The chat room paradigm involves a three- or four-way conversation in a chat room on a computer. For several minutes, the two confederates engage the participant in conversation. In the inclusion condition, the confederates continue to engage the participant in the conversation. In the ostracism condition, the confederates ignore the participant. This is achieved by following a predetermined script – essentially a dialogue between the two confederates – with any comments made by the ostracized participants ignored (Williams, Govan, Croker, Cruickshank, Tynan, & Lam, 2002).

Role Playing
In these paradigms, participants are induced to either ostracize (or argue) with other participants. These methods allow examination of the sources of ostracism in addition to the targets of ostracism. In the "O Train" role play (Zadro, Williams, & Richardson, 2005; Zadro & Williams, 2006), participants role play an interaction with two or three others as though they are on a train ride. In the Scarlet Letter study, participants are fully aware of the entire process but each is selected to be ostracized by the others for a full day. Sources and targets keep a diary of their thoughts and reactions (Williams, Bernieri, Faulkner, Grahe, & Gada-Jain, 2000).

Recollection
In this paradigm, participants are asked to recall, in great detail, an episode of ostracism (or some other socially or physically painful event). They are then asked to indicate the levels of pain that they are currently experiencing after the recollection (Williams & Fitness, 2004).

A Model of Ostracism

Our research is guided by a model of ostracism that continues to evolve with our research (see Williams, 1997, 2001, 2009). The modified model is informed by the results of about 12 years of research. Although some versions of the model address factors that pertain to the sources of ostracism (Williams & Zadro, 2005), here we will focus on the model as it pertains to targets of ostracism.

Reactions to ostracism begin with detection of being ignored and excluded. While it is possible to separate these two experiences (i.e., one can feel excluded but not ignored, as would be the case if one was being bullied, and ignored but not excluded, as might be the case for an individual low on the totem pole within an organization), we intentionally link the two as necessary conditions for ostracism. Detection of ostracism may also be independent of the intentions of the others. Individuals may perceive ostracism when it is not intended, but we would predict the same sequence as when it was intended. If ostracism is not detected, we would predict that the individual would not proceed through the sequence of reactions.

REFLEXIVE REACTIONS TO OSTRACISM: UNIFORMLY PAINFUL

The results of numerous studies now provide strong support for the premise that the initial reflexive reactions to ostracism are uniformly distressing and painful, unlikely to be moderated by individual differences, situational forces, or causal attributions. Recent evidence suggests that recalled and re-lived ostracism experiences result in self-reported pain levels as high as those experienced with back pain or even child birth (Williams & Fitness, 2004). We regard reactions to ostracism much like reactions to being shocked by a cattle prod. Regardless of which traits an individual possesses, who holds the cattle prod, or why it is being used, the shock of the cattle prod will still be painful. So it seems to be with ostracism. Taking the cattle prod analogy further, French developmental psychologist Jacqueline Nadel (Nadel, Prepin, & Okanda, 2005) has shown that being totally unresponsive to an autistic child (using the "stillface" paradigm that has much in common with short-term ostracism) results in a temporary surge in social attention sought by that child, and a pleasant response once that responsiveness is provided. The result is chillingly similar to autistic children's reaction to receiving a shock in Ivar Lovaas's (Lovaas, Schaeffer, & Simmons, 1965) lab years ago, in which the shocked child would cease self-injurious or other injurious behaviors and would smile at and even hug the very person who shocked them. In some ways, then, we regard ostracism as a social shock that appears to serve the same function.

More direct evidence comes from an affective and cognitive neuroscience investigation of how the brain responds during a short episode of ostracism. Eisenberger, Lieberman, and Williams (2003) examined individuals in an fMRI chamber who were playing Cyberball on a computer screen with two other ostensible players who were thought to be in their own fMRI chambers in the adjoining rooms. Participants were told that the other two were already playing, and that the connection had not yet been made to allow them to participate, but that in a few minutes, they could join in. After a few minutes, the ball was thrown to participants so that they were included as much as the other two players. But, a little later, the other two players started throwing the ball only to each other. Following this game, participants filled out a post-experimental questionnaire. The results indicated a significant activation to the dorsal anterior cingulate cortex (dACC), the same region of the brain that is activated when individuals detect physical pain. Further, the level of activation was highly positively correlated ($r = .88$) with post-experimental self-reports of distress. Finally, even during the initial phase in which participants had a good explanation for their exclusion (their computer had not yet been connected to the other two players' computers), they still showed significant activation of the dACC. The results of this study suggest that even a very short episode of ostracism is detected as painful, and the painful reaction is not eliminated even when a plausible excuse is provided.

No Moderation by Individual Differences

Additional studies provide further support for the premise that reflexive reactions to ostracism are unmitigated by individual differences or situational factors. Nadasi (1992) found that introversion/extraversion did not moderate reactions to ostracism in a face-to-face ball-tossing game, and using the same paradigm, Warburton, Williams, and Cairns (2006) found no moderation by narcissism. Williams, Cheung, and Choi (2000) found that self-esteem differences did not moderate ostracism (in Cyberball); Smith and Williams (2004) found that differences in individualism–collectivism did not moderate negative reactions to cell phone text-messaging ostracism. Carter-Sowell, Chen, and Williams (2006) found that loneliness did not moderate reactions, nor did self-monitoring or need for belonging. Finally, Zadro, Boland, and Richardson (2006) found that even individuals who scored extremely high in social anxiety showed comparable levels of distress to individuals who scored at normal levels of social anxiety when they were ostracized during Cyberball.

No Moderation for Situational Factors

There are many possible reasons why being ostracized could be either more or less distressing. Yet, numerous studies have demonstrated that, like individual differences, situational factors appear not to moderate reflexive reactions to ostracism. For instance, it would seem logical to assume that being ostracized by ingroup members, people who share one's own social identity, would be more distressing than being ostracized by outgroup members. We should be able to easily dismiss outgroup ostracism, whereas ingroup ostracism should trouble us as to our place within our group. Nevertheless, several studies have manipulated the group membership of those who are ostracizing, and this has yet to make a difference. Williams et al. (2000) manipulated ingroup and outgroup by means of which computer platform the participants preferred (Mac or PC). Although there was ample evidence of negative outgroup stereotypes when participants were asked to describe people who used Macs or PCs, participants were no more likely to be distressed by being ostracized during Cyberball by ingroup members than by outgroup (or mixed-group) members. Ingroup/outgroup manipulations (e.g., being educated in public vs. private school) failed to emerge for chat room ostracism (Williams, Govan, Croker, Tynan, Cruickshank, & Lam, 2003) or for cell phone text-messaging ostracism (using smokers vs. non-smokers) (Smith & Williams, 2004). Even more striking, Gonsalkorale and Williams (2007) found that reflexive reactions to ostracism (via Cyberball) were strongly distressing, yet no more so for those ostracized by individuals with like-minded political leanings than by those with rival political leanings, or more surprisingly, by individuals purportedly from a despised out-group – the Ku Klux Klan!

Other studies underscore the unimportance of situational factors in moderating reflexive reactions to ostracism. Zadro, Williams, and Richardson (2004) found that ostracized individuals reacted with as much distress when convinced they were playing Cyberball with the computer as when they were convinced they were playing with two other humans. They also found it made no difference whether individuals were told the other players' were or were not operating under their own volition. Jones, Carter-Sowell, Kelly, and Williams (2009) have examined partial ostracism or being "out of the loop," where people perceive being uninformed of information mutually known by others. Findings indicate that compared to in-the-loop participants, out-of-the-loop participants, even without significant costs for being uninformed, experienced a variety of deleterious social and psychological effects (e.g. depleted fundamental needs), Finally, van Beest and Williams (2006a) loaded the dice so that being ostracized should be preferable to being included. Yet, ostracized participants were just as distressed when being the recipient of a tossed ball resulted in 50-cent deductions as they were for rewards of 50 cents. That is, even when ostracized participants went home with 5 euros while the other two players went home with nothing, they still felt bad. Van Beest and Williams (2006b) also found that when participants played Cyberbomb (in which a bomb was being tossed around in a three-person virtual game), ostracized individuals felt just as bad as those who were ostracized from Cyberball. The implications of this study are that people would even feel hurt not being invited by their friends to play Russian Roulette.

Thus, research to date suggests that it is quite difficult, if not impossible, to moderate the painful reflexive reactions to even short and relatively meaningless episodes of ostracism. We continue to search for moderation, but are left with the conclusion that, if we consider a flame rather than a shock as the analogy to ostracism, then we might predict that, just as wetting one's finger buffers the pain of the flame, so, too, might immersing the individual in a protective coating of need satiation – especially those needs most threatened by ostracism – temporarily protect against the pain of ostracism. For marginalized individuals, perhaps strong support from others who are also marginalized could offer such protection. We now discuss the four needs proposed to be most threatened by ostracism, and the supporting research.

OSTRACISM THREATENS FOUR FUNDAMENTAL NEEDS

Williams (1997, 2001, 2009) proposed that ostracism can threaten four basic needs: belonging, self-esteem, control, and meaningful existence. There is an abundance of research and theory that supports the importance of each of these needs for human motivation, efficacy, and survival. Humans need and seek to increase their sense of belonging (Baumeister & Leary, 1995), self-esteem (Steele, 1988; Tesser, 1988), control (Burger, 1992; Peterson & Seligman, 1984; Seligman, 1975), and meaningful existence (Greenberg, Pyszczynski, & Solomon, 1986; Greenberg et al., 1990, 1992). Ostracism may be particularly unique in that it simultaneously threatens all four of these basic human needs.

None of these needs or social motives is a new invention of the model; all enjoy considerable empirical support for their roles in sustaining and motivating human behavior. The novel aspect of the model is that usually the literature and interest in these four needs are separate and mutually exclusive. In some cases, there are attempts to engulf or subsume one or more needs under another, but in this model all four needs are unique and important, despite overlap and all being mutually influential.

Belonging

Most researchers and theorists in the area of ostracism, social exclusion, and rejection acknowledge that these related aversive interpersonal behaviors threaten a fundamental need to belong (see, for example, Gardner, Pickett, & Brewer, 2000; Gardner, Pickett, Jefferis, & Knowles, 2005). The need to belong (Baumeister & Leary, 1995) has been shown to be of such importance that without it, people suffer mental and physical illness, and are rendered virtually incapacitated. It was originally hypothesized that people need to feel a sense of belonging to no more than a few important others, but Williams posits that a threat to belonging, even to strangers, evokes a strong immediate warning. One might argue that any sort of aversive interaction threatens belonging, but we suggest that ostracism, in particular, threatens belonging more directly than other unpleasant social responses. Consider a comparison between being given the silent treatment (relational ostracism) and being the target of a heated argument. Both are clearly aversive, but within the argument, there is an interaction – one is still connected to the other(s). The connection is strained, but it exists. The same cannot be said for being the target of the silent treatment. There is an implicit, and perhaps explicit, divorce between the source(s) and the target. There is no back-and-forth, no playing field on which to relate to or feel a connection with the others. Thus, it is not surprising that the four needs are more highly thwarted when ostracized than when enduring a heated argument (Zadro, Williams, & Richardson, 2005).

Self-Esteem

Another need focused on by researchers is the threat to self-esteem, especially social self-esteem – how individuals think others perceive their goodness and worth (see Leary's sociometer theory; e.g., Leary, Tambor, Terdal, & Downs, 1995). Leary's perspective is that self-esteem is nothing more than a gauge for belonging and acceptance, thus self-esteem is a proxy for belonging. While this model of ostracism supports this idea to a degree, it is likely that there is more to the threat of ostracism to self-esteem than simply as a means for estimating inclusionary status. Once again, let's compare argument to the silent treatment. In an argument, it is usually relatively clear what the target has done or said that is disapproved. The offense in question is usually the subject matter of the argument: The husband came home late without calling; the co-worker did not contribute sufficiently to the group task. Thus, although damaging to one's self-esteem, there is a sense of containment that makes coping with the problem relatively manageable. Even if one feels bad about a misdeed, other positive self-concepts can be brought forth to affirm the self (Steele, 1988). Ostracism, however, often (but not always) occurs without much in the way of an explanation. Targets are left to surmise (a) whether they are being ostracized, and if so (b) for what reason(s). Without being given the specific reason, targets must generate plausible reasons for its occurrence. This list might consist of one or two obvious infractions, or might extend to three, four, or more possibilities. Actively generating a list of wrong doings that would warrant ostracism surely threatens self-esteem more than being able to focus on one offense. In this sense, self-esteem is threatened more by ostracism than by other forms of rejection.

Control

A third need or social motive that has received considerable attention in social and clinical psychology is the need to perceive *control* over one's (social) environment (Seligman, 1975, 1998). Compared to belonging and self-esteem, however, relatively few social exclusion researchers have acknowledged the threat to control that comes with being ostracized. To illustrate how control is affected by ostracism, let us again compare being the target of an argument with being the target of a silent treatment. In an argument, the target can influence its intensity and course. One can choose calming or inflammatory words, which can either douse the flames with water or gasoline. Likewise, the content can be redirected by bringing up different topics, different perspectives, and different points. Thus, in an argument, the target still has control over the course of the interaction. Such is not the case when being subjected to the silent treatment; nothing one does or says evokes a reaction from the source. This is reminiscent of the Uncle Remus fable, the tar baby (Harris, 1948), in which Brer Fox tries to capture Brer Rabbit by positioning a person made out of tar on a log. Brer Fox reasoned (correctly) that the gregarious Brer Rabbit would think the tar baby was a person and would try to engage it in friendly conversation. Brer Rabbit became incensed and aggressive when the tar baby was unresponsive to his friendly overtures, and after punching and kicking the tar baby, he became stuck, allowing Bref Fox to capture him.

Meaningful Existence

Finally, ostracism has the unique capacity to threaten one's sense of meaningful existence, and may even serve as a mortality salience cue. Relying on the extensive research and theory by the terror-management perspective (Greenberg, Pyzczynski, & Solomon, 1986), a prime motive for humans is to buffer the terror they feel in contemplating their mortality and insignificance. Even fleeting and subliminal exposures to various cues that remind people of their mortality have been shown to activate responses that shore up their world views, from which they derive worth and meaning. Why should ostracism be considered a mortality salience cue? To be ostracized is to not be recognized as existing. In many tribes around the world, social ostracism is the most extreme form of punishment (Case & Williams, 2004; Gruter & Masters, 1986). The translation for this punishment often refers to death or "social death." William James (1897) referred to the terror of being ignored and excluded as being "cut dead." Indeed, being ostracized is a glimpse into what life would be like if the target were nonexistent. To complete the comparison to argument, ostracism provides a very palpable metaphor for death, while argument does not.

Sadness and Anger

Our research on ostracism indicates that two affective states, sadness and anger, also increase with increasing levels of ostracism. It should be noted that mood changes are not always detected in research on social exclusion (see, for instance, research by Twenge, Catanese, & Baumeister, 2003). Apparently, certain types of social exclusion manipulations can be so strong as to cause a temporary state of cognitive deconstruction, a state resembling numbness following a concussion (Baumeister, Twenge, & Nuss, 2002). Thus, depending perhaps on the magnitude of the ostracism manipulation, negative affect might give way to emotional numbness.

REFLECTIVE REACTIONS TO OSTRACISM: FORTIFICATION OF THWARTED NEEDS

In addition to positing the initial pain and distress of ostracism, and the four fundamental needs thwarted by ostracism, the model also posits that once ostracized individuals have had time to reflect on the ostracism episode, they will attempt to fortify their threatened needs through cognitive, affective, and/or behavioral responses. In this regard, the ostracized individual copes with ostracism by elevating his or her sense of belonging, self-esteem, control, or meaningful existence.

Consistent with these predictions, ostracized individuals have been found to attend more carefully to social information (Gardner, Pickett, & Brewer, 2000; Pickett et al., 2004), to conform to unanimously incorrect others (Williams et al., 2000), to mimic others either consciously (Ouwerkerk, Kerr, Gallucci, & van Lange, 2005) or unconsciously (Lakin & Chartrand, 2005), to work harder on collective tasks (Williams & Sommer, 1997), to express more interest and liking for group leaders of even the most dubious groups (Wheaton, 2002), and to become more susceptible to compliance tactics (Carter-Sowell, Chen, & Williams, 2008). All of these responses could increase a sense of belonging or assist in making the individual more acceptable and likeable to others. Another form of ostracism, a time out, is used by teachers and parents worldwide as a means to correct the undesired behavior of children. The assumption behind this method is that removing social attention from children is aversive, and that children will avoid behaving in undesirable ways to reclaim the attention they desire (Heron, 1987).

ProSocial or AntiSocial Responses?

The aforementioned list of outcomes can all be characterized as relatively pro-social. That is, they appear to have as their eventual goal an outcome that will increase both belonging and self-esteem. This is not to say that these are all necessarily functional and healthy reactions. Indeed, it is most likely dysfunctional to be overly concerned with fitting in and being liked. Indeed, social susceptibility might not just lead to liking of bizarre group leaders or being easily duped by compliance tactics, but may result in being easy prey to cults and extremist groups. Nevertheless, all of these behaviors can serve to please others. But this is not always the route that ostracized individuals take to fortify needs, especially, we contend, needs for control and meaningful existence.

Ostracism may drive individuals to fortify basic control and existential needs by foreswearing attempts to be liked and included, and override them with attempts to exert control over their situations and to be recognized as existing (Case & Williams, 2004). Consistent with this reasoning, there have been observations of anti-social and aggressive behaviors (Leary, Kowalski, Smith, & Phillips, 2003; Twenge, Baumeister, Tice, & Stucke, 2001), and retrospective reports of suicide attempts (Williams & Zadro, 2001). Recently, Warburton, Williams, and Cairns (2006) conducted a study in which, following ostracism, some participants were allowed to fortify control by controlling the onset of a series of unpleasant noises, whereas other participants had to hear the same unpleasant noises without controlling their onset. Participants then had an opportunity to dole out as much hot sauce as they wished to a naïve participant (one not involved in the ostracism) who they knew had to eat the full amount they doled out, and who had indicated a strong dislike for hot sauce. The results showed that when control was fortified, participants were no more likely to be aggressive than those who were included. But ostracized participants who did not have an opportunity to exercise control gave five times as much hot sauce to the naïve, hot sauce-hating participant. These results suggest that control plays an important role in the ostracism-aggression effect.

By examining the other paradigms in which aggression has emerged following different methods of inducing social exclusion, we suggest that those methods are more likely to threaten a sense of control than our paradigms. For instance, being told by a psychologist that your personality-test results indicate that you will lead a life alone (Twenge et al., 2001) suggests that the individual has no control over altering this outcome. At this point, we suggest, becoming attractive to others takes a back seat to exerting control over others, even if the control is achieved by being aggressive.

DEPLETION OF COPING RESOURCES: REACTIONS TO LONG-TERM AND CHRONIC OSTRACISM

The model also predicts reactions to chronic exposure to ostracism over one's life. In real life, individuals are not so lucky as to endure only a 5-minute episode of ostracism in the form of not being tossed a real or imaginary ball. Many individuals, especially those who have been marginalized within their families, workgroups, or society, must endure a life-time of ostracism. What then? Obviously, our approach to finding answers to this question involves research conducted outside the laboratory. We have interviewed scores of individuals who answered advertisements looking for people who have experienced the silent treatment for long periods (either giving it or getting it) (see Williams, 2001; Zadro & Williams, 2000). Although open to alternative interpretations based on self-selection, our preliminary results indicate that, as expected, people who endure such long-term exposure to relational ostracism appear to no longer be able to effectively cope with it, either by improving their inclusionary status or by re-exerting control through retaliation. Instead, they tend to give up and accept that they are unworthy of attention. These individuals report health problems, suicidal ideation (and attempts), eating disorders, promiscuity, and other dysfunctional outcomes.

OSTRACISM AND MARGINALIZATION

Targets of ostracism are more likely to be members of stigmatized groups. Being social creatures, humans form social groups, some of which are stigmatized, hold minority status, and are marginalized by the society-at-large. For example, in the United States, consensual negative stereotypes exist toward African-Americans (Brigham, 1974; Hartsough & Fontana, 1970; Karlins, Coffman, & Walters, 1969; Samuels, 1973) and women (Broverman, Vogel, Broverman, Clarkson, & Rosenkrantz, 1972; Deaux & LaFrance, 1998; Heilbrun, 1976; Rosenkrantz, Vogel, Bee, Broverman, & Broverman, 1968), and discrimination is one consequence of these stereotypes. One form of discrimination is to give members of these groups less attention, to ignore and exclude them from important social tasks of everyday life. We suggest that our research pertains especially to individuals who themselves have been marginalized, or who are members of groups that have been marginalized. However, we are only in the beginning phases of research that can address these questions.

We are currently conducting research that examines two aspects of this marginalization process. One aspect is that marginalized group members might attribute their ostracism to their group membership rather than to personal characteristics. The results of research on discrimination based on gender or race membership suggests that attributing the discrimination to one's group membership can either exacerbate or ameliorate the negative impact of that discrimination. Crocker and Major (1989) found initial support for the idea that, because prejudice against one's group is an external attribution for negative consequences, this attribution should protect the self-esteem of stigmatized individuals. Schmitt and Branscombe (2002), however, argue that attributing discrimination to group membership is not necessarily an external attribution. If one identifies strongly with one's group, then a group-based attribution for discrimination will be essentially a personal internal attribution. They found support for this argument when examining individuals who identify highly with their groups. We are examining these ideas further in our studies of ostracism. If individuals can attribute their ostracism to group membership, will it be more or less distressing? And should it matter if they identify highly with their group?

The other aspect of examining marginalized groups' reactions to ostracism involves ostracism of more than one individual. Until now, the focus of ostracism/social exclusion research has been on the individual who finds him- or herself ostracized by two or three other individuals. But how should people react if their dyad is being ostracized by other dyads? On the one hand, having a co-target might buffer the negative impact of ostracism [see for example: Allen's (1975) work on social support in conformity situations]. Additionally, one could quickly fortify threatened needs by becoming more cohesive with one's co-target, resulting in ostracism's diminished impact. Still, other research suggests that groups relate to other groups with distrust, competitiveness, and perhaps even aggression [see for example: work by Insko and colleagues (1998) on the discontinuity effect]. Thus, we may see that groups who are ostracized by other groups might be simultaneously less distressed, yet more retaliative and aggressive.

CONCLUSION

When individuals feel marginalized within society they are likely to perceive (accurately or not) that they do not belong to the same social structure as the others, that they do not matter, that they are unable to contribute or effect change within society, and that, for all intents and purposes, they are invisible. Our empirical research to date has focused primarily on nonmarginalized individuals who are temporarily ostracized by strangers (but who are usually drawn from the same pool as the individuals, so they could be described as stranger-peers).

Based on our research, we conclude that the immediate impact of perceiving ostracism by *anyone* (i.e., friend, stranger, enemy) is painful and distressing, regardless of whether that ostracized individual is marginalized, stigmatized, or dehumanized. Furthermore, ostracism threatens four fundamental needs – belonging, self-esteem, control, and meaningful existence – and increases anger and sadness. Upon thoughtful reflection, however, in which targets of ostracism are able to generate attributions for the reasons behind the ostracism, to consider the relation of the ostracizers to themselves, and are influenced by such factors as whether they possess a stigma, hold a marginalized status, or possess particular personality traits, we expect differing routes to fortifying these threatened needs and managing the resulting emotions and moods.

The Functionality of Fortifying Needs

To the extent that belonging and self-esteem (especially self-esteem based on perceptions of acceptance and approval by others) are primarily threatened, then we expect individuals to think and behave in ways that will improve their inclusionary status. Although generally positive in valence, behaviors aimed to make one socially acceptable or likeable can be dysfunctional for the individual: He or she may become overly compliant, dependent, or susceptible to social influence. Similarly, to the extent that control and meaningful existence are primarily threatened, he or she is more likely to utilize behaviors to fortify these needs that may override desires to be liked. Thus, retaliative, aggressive, and violent behavior may appear to be effective means to achieve control and recognition by others. Although generally negative in valence, behaviors aimed at asserting control and recognition may also be functional. We are reminded of Ralph Ellison's (1980) *Invisible Man*, in which the protagonist (a nameless Black man) feels invisible within society, and exploits that invisibility to achieve goals to improve his situation.

We hope that we have alerted readers interested in marginalization that one factor that the marginalized must contend with is ostracism, and it may have far-reaching intra- and inter-personal consequences. We hope that others will consider this phenomenon as it pertains to their interests so that we can fully appreciate the consequences of living in a society in which one, or one's group, is excluded and ignored.

REFERENCES

Baumeister, R. F., & Leary, M. R. (1995). The need to belong: Desire for interpersonal attachments as a fundamental human motivation. *Psychological Bulletin, 117*, 497–529.

Baumeister, R. F., Twenge, J. M., & Nuss, C. K. (2002). Effects of social exclusion on cognitive processes: Anticipated aloneness reduces intelligent thought. *Journal of Personality and Social Psychology, 83*, 817–827.

Brigham, J. C. (1974). Views of Black and White children concerning the distribution of personality characteristics. *Journal of Personality, 42*, 144–158.

Broverman, I. K., Vogel, S. R., Broverman, D. M., Clarkson, F. E., & Rosenkrantz, P. S. (1972). Sex stereotypes: A current appraisal. *Journal of Social Issues, 28*, 59–79.

Burger, J. M. (1992). *Desire for control: Personality, social and clinical perspectives.* New York: Plenum Press.

Carter-Sowell, A. R., Chen, Z., & Williams, K. D. (2008). Ostracism increases social susceptibility. *Social Influence, 3*, 143–153.

(2006, May). *Loneliness and social monitoring in social interaction.* Presentation at the annual meeting of the Midwestern Psychological Association, Chicago, IL.

Case, T. I., & Williams, K. D. (2004). Ostracism: A metaphor for death. In J. Greenberg, S. L. Koole, & T. Pyszczynski (Eds.), *Handbook of experimental existential psychology* (pp. 336–351). New York: Guilford Press.

Crocker, J., & Major, B. (1989). Social stigma and self esteem: The self-protective properties of stigma. *Psychological Review, 96*, 608–630.

Deaux, K., & LaFrance, M. (1998). Gender. In D. T. Gilbert, S. T. Fiske, & G. Lindzey (Eds.). *The handbook of social psychology* (pp. 788–827). New York: McGraw-Hill.

Eisenberger, N. I., Lieberman, M. D., & Williams, K., D. (2003). Does rejection hurt? An fMRI study of social exclusion. *Science, 302*, 290–292.

Ellison, R. (1980). *Invisible man.* New York: Random House.

Gardner, W. L., Pickett, C. L., & Brewer, M. B. (2000). Social exclusion and selective memory: How the need to belong influences memory for social events. *Personality and Social Psychology Bulletin, 26*, 486–496.

Gardner, W. L., Pickett, C. L., Jefferis, V., & Knowles, M. (2005). On the outside looking in: Loneliness and social monitoring. *Personality and Social Psychology Bulletin, 31*, 1549–1560.

Gonsalkorale, K., & Williams, K. D. (2007). The KKK won't let me play: Ostracism even by a despised outgroup hurts. *European Journal of Social Psychology, 37*, 1176–1185.

Greenberg, J., Pyszczynski, T., & Solomon, S. (1986). The causes and consequences of the need for self-esteem: A terror management theory. In R. F. Baumeister (Ed.), *Public self and private self* (pp. 189–212). New York: Springer-Verlag.

Greenberg, J., Pyszczynski, T., Solomon, S., Rosenblatt, A., Veeder, M., Kirkland, S., & Lyon, D. (1990). Evidence for terror management theory, 2: The effects of mortality salience on reactions to those who threaten or bolster the cultural worldview. *Journal of Personality and Social Psychology, 58,* 308–318.

Greenberg, J., Solomon, S., Pyszczynski, T., Rosenblatt, A., Burling, J., Lyon, D., Simon, L., & Pinel, E. (1992). Why do people need self-esteem?: Converging evidence that self-esteem serves an anxiety-buffering function. *Journal of Personality and Social Psychology, 63,* 913–922.

Gruter, M., & Masters, R. D. (1986). Ostracism as a social and biological phenomenon: An introduction. *Ethology and Sociobiology, 7,* 149–158.

Harris, J. C. (1948). *The favorite Uncle Remus.* Boston: Houghton-Mifflin.

Hartsough, W. R., & Fontana, A. F. (1970). Persistence of ethnic stereotypes and the relative importance of positive and negative stereotyping for association preferences. *Psychological Reports, 27,* 723–731.

Heilbrun, A. B., Jr. (1976). Measurement of masculine and feminine sex role identities as independent dimensions. *Journal of Consulting and Clinical Psychology, 44,* 183–190.

Heron. T. E. (1987). Timeout from positive reinforcement. In I. O. Cooper, T. E. Heron, & H. Merrill (Eds.), *Applied behavior analysis* (pp. 439–453). Columbus, OH: Merrill.

Insko, C. A, Schopler, J., Pemberton, M. B, Wieselquist, J., McIlraith, S. A, Currey, D. P., & Gaertner, L. (1998). Long-term outcome maximization and the reduction of interindividual-intergroup discontinuity. *Journal of Personality and Social Psychology. 75,* 695–711.

James, W. (1897). *Principles of psychology (Vol. I).* New York: Dover Publications.

Jones, E. E., Carter-Sowell, A. R., Kelly, J. R., & Williams, K. D. (2009). 'I'm out of the loop': Ostracism through information exclusion. *Group Processes & Intergroup Relations. 12,* 157–174.

Karlins, M., Coffman, T. L., & Walters, G. (1969). On the fading of social stereotypes: Studies in three generations of college students. *Journal of Personality and Social Psychology, 13,* 1–16.

Lakin, J. L., & Chartrand, T. L. (2005). Exclusion and nonconscious behavioral mimicry. In K. D. Williams, J. P. Forgas, & W. von Hippel (Eds.), *The social outcast: Ostracism, social exclusion, rejection, and bullying* (pp. 279–296). New York: Psychology Press.

Leary, M. R., Kowalski, R. M., Smith, L., & Phillips, S. (2003). Teasing, rejection, and violence: Case studies of the school shootings. *Aggressive Behavior, 29,* 202–214.

Leary, M. R., Tambor, E. S., Terdal, S. K., & Downs, D. L. (1995). Self-esteem as an interpersonal monitor: The sociometer hypothesis. *Journal of Personality and Social Psychology, 2,* 518–530.

Lovaas, O. I., Schaeffer, B., & Simmons, J. Q. (1965). Building social behavior in autistic children by use of electric shock. *Journal of Experimental Research in Personality, 1,* 99–105.

Nadasi, C. (1992). The effects of social ostracism on verbal and non-verbal behavior in introverts and extraverts. Unpublished honors thesis, University of Toledo, Toledo, OH.

Nadel, J., Prepin, K., & Okanda, M. (2005). Experiencing contingency and agency: First step toward self-understanding in making a mind? *Interaction Studies: Special Issue on Making Minds, 6,* 447–462.

Ouwerkerk, J. W., Kerr, N. L., Gallucci, M., & van Lange, P. A. M. (2005). Avoiding the social death penalty: Ostracism and cooperation in social dilemmas. In K. D. Williams, J. P. Forgas, & W. von Hippel (Eds.), *The social outcast: Ostracism, social exclusion, rejection, and bullying* (pp. 321–332). New York: Psychology Press.

Peterson, C., & Seligman, M. E. P. (1984). Content analysis of verbatim explanations: The CAVE technique for assessing explanatory style. Unpublished manuscript, University of Pennsylvania, Philadelphia, PA.

Pickett, C. L., Gardner, W. L., & Knowles, M. (2004). Getting a cue: The need to belong and enhanced sensitivity to social cues. *Personality and Social Psychology Bulletin, 30,* 1095–1107.

Rosenkrantz, P., Vogel, S., Bee, H., Broverman, I., & Broverman, D. M. (1968). Sex role stereotypes and self-concepts in college students. *Journal of Consulting and Clinical Psychology, 32,* 287–295.

Samuels, F. (1973). *Group images.* New Haven, CT: College & University Press.

Schmitt, M. T., & Branscombe, N. R. (2002). The internal and external causal loci of attribution to prejudice. *Personality and Social Psychology Bulletin, 28,* 620–628.

Seligman, M. E. P. (1975). *Helplessness: On depression, development, and death.* San Francisco: Freeman & Company.

(1998). *Learned optimism* (2nd ed.). New York: Pocket Books Simon and Schuster.

Smith, A., & Williams, K. D. (2004). R U There? Ostracism by cell phone text messaging. *Group Dynamics: Theory, Research, and Practice, 8,* 291–301.

Steele, C. M. (1988). The psychology of self-affirmation: Sustaining the integrity of the self. In L. Berkowitz (Ed.), *Advances in experimental social psychology, Vol. 21: Social psychological studies of the self: Perspectives and programs.* (pp. 261–302). New York: Academic Press.

Tesser, A. (1988). Toward a self-evaluation maintenance model of social behavior. In L. Berkowitz (Ed.), *Advances in experimental social psychology, Vol. 21.* (pp. 181–227). San Diego, CA: Academic Press.

Twenge, J. M., Baumeister, R. F., Tice, D. M., & Stucke, T. S. (2001). If you can't join them, beat them: Effects of social exclusion on aggressive behavior. *Journal of Personality and Social Psychology, 81,* 1058–1069.

Twenge, J. M., Catanese, K. R., & Baumeister, R. F. (2003). Social exclusion and the deconstructed state: Time perception, meaninglessness, lethargy, lack of emotion, and self-awareness. *Journal of Personality and Social Psychology, 85,* 409–423.

van Beest, I., & Williams, K. D. (2006a). Cyberball: When inclusion costs and ostracism pays, ostracism still hurts. Unpublished manuscript. Leiden University, The Netherlands.

(2006b). Cyberbomb: Do we feel bad being excluded in a game of Russian Roulette? Unpublished manuscript. Leiden University, The Netherlands.

Warburton, W. A., Williams, K. D., & Cairns, D. R. (2006). When ostracism leads to aggression: The moderating effects of control deprivation. *Journal of Experimental Social Psychology, 42,* 213–220.

Wheaton, A. (2002). *Reactions of ostracized individuals to group leaders.* Unpublished Honours Thesis, Macquarie University, Sydney, Australia.

Williams, K. D. (1997). Social ostracism. In R. M. Kowalski (Ed.) *Aversive interpersonal behaviors* (pp. 133–170). New York: Plenum Press.

(2001). *Ostracism: The power of silence.* New York: Guilford Press.

(2009). Ostracism: A temporal need-threat model. In M. Zanna (Ed.), *Advances in Experimental Social Psychology, 41* (pp. 279–314). New York: Academic Press.

Williams, K. D., Bernieri, F., Faulkner, S., Grahe, J., & Gada-Jain, N. (2000). The Scarlet Letter Study: Five days of social ostracism. *Journal of Personal and Interpersonal Loss, 5,* 19–63.

Williams, K. D., Cheung, C., & Choi, W. (2000). Cyberostracism: Effects of being ignored over the Internet. *Journal of Personality and Social Psychology, 79,* 748–762.

Williams, K. D., & Fitness, J. (2004). *Social and physical pain: Similarities and differences.* Presented at the Society for Experimental Social Psychology, Ft. Worth, TX.

Williams, K. D., Govan, C. L., Croker, V., Tynan, D., Cruickshank, M., & Lam, A. (2002). Investigations into differences between social and cyberostracism. *Group Dynamics: Theory, Research, and Practice, 6,* 65–77.

Williams, K. D., & Jarvis, B. (2006). Cyberball: A program for use in research on ostracism and interpersonal acceptance. *Behavior Research Methods, Instruments, and Computers, 38,* 174–180.

Williams, K. D., & Sommer, K. L. (1997). Social ostracism by one's coworkers: Does rejection lead to loafing or compensation? *Personality and Social Psychology Bulletin, 23,* 693–706.

Williams, K. D, & Zadro, L. (2001). Ostracism: On being ignored, excluded, and rejected. In M. R. Leary (Ed.), *Interpersonal rejection* (pp. 21–53). New York: Oxford University Press.

(2005). Ostracism: The indiscriminate early detection system. In Williams, J. P. Forgas, & W. von Hippel (Eds.) *The social outcast: Ostracism, social exclusion, rejection, and bullying* (pp. 19–34). New York: Psychology Press.

Zadro, L., Boland, C., & Richardson, R. (2006). How long does it last? The persistence of the effects of ostracism in the socially anxious. *Journal of Experimental Social Psychology, 42,* 692–697.

Zadro, L., & Williams, K. D. (2000, June). *Ostracism in close relationships.* Presented at the joint ICCRP-IRPR conference on close relationships, Brisbane, Australia.

(2006). How do you teach the power of ostracism? Evaluating the train ride demonstration. *Social Influence, 1,* 1–24.

Zadro, L., Williams, K. D., & Richardson, R. (2004). How low can you go? Ostracism by a computer lowers belonging, control, self-esteem, and meaningful existence. *Journal of Experimental Social Psychology, 40,* 560–567.

(2005). Riding the 'O' train: Comparing the effects of ostracism and verbal dispute on targets and sources. *Group Processes and Interpersonal Relations, 8,* 125–143.

PART 2

COPING WITH EXCLUSION: BEING EXCLUDED FOR WHAT YOU THINK AND DO

6

Delinquents as a Minority Group: Accidental Tourists in Forbidden Territory or Voluntary Emigrées?

NICHOLAS EMLER

INTRODUCTION

The minority group in society represented by delinquents provides an interesting case for at least two reasons. One concerns the nature of moral norms for behavior and how they are defined. The other relates to the behavioral control mechanisms that ensure compliance with these norms and make societies viable. However, to appreciate what lessons may be derived from a consideration of this particular minority, it is important to understand why and how it recruits and retains members, and members' reactions to apparent pressure to renounce their minority status. These issues form the focus of this chapter.

DELINQUENCY AND THE SOCIAL ORDER

There is a view, rooted deeply in the psyche of the social sciences, that viable societies are constructed around norms of conduct to which the majority willingly adhere. Without this consensus there can be no orderly social life. The questions toward which the social scientist may then turn address the means by which this consensus is created and maintained. An important thread to the ensuing analysis has been provided by the observation that norms, and particularly norms of conduct, vary. That is, they show a tendency to differ across time and cultures. One response to this has been to conclude that all social norms are inevitably arbitrary and relative, and that their power and authority to secure compliance are based purely on the capacity they have at a particular time and in a particular place to attract a consensus.

Some of the most iconic studies in social psychology have earned this reputation on the basis of their apparent capacity to illustrate this as a fundamental phenomenon in social life. Thus Sherif's (1935) studies of the formation of norms established the effects of mutual dependence in the face of uncertainty, and the strong inclination to converge upon a common position – a norm. Asch (1956) revealed that the power unanimous majorities can exercise over individuals may be unrelated to the objective truth of the position these majorities support. Finally, Schachter (1951) illustrated responses of the majority to deviance. The story these studies collectively support is that it is the spontaneous human inclination to search for a consensus, to avoid dissensus, and to attempt its suppression should it appear. Subsequent research has confirmed the inclination of majorities to focus their communicative attention, and by implication their persuasive efforts, upon deviants, and to form an unfavorable view of individuals who do maintain deviant positions (Levine, 1989).

There has always been, however, another strand to this story. Human societies are distinctive for their reliance upon socialization to maintain their coherence. New members of any society are inducted into its particular ways of thinking and behaving, a socialization process that normally occurs across the course of childhood. Accounts of the socialization process are varied and numerous, but they are unified by a common assumption: Socialization generates internalized commitment to shared norms (Aronfreed, 1968; Hoffman, 1983). Society, in this view therefore, is sustained by the tandem forces of socialization and social influence.

Deviance poses a challenge for this view, encapsulated sometime ago by Wrong (1961) in the title of his essay, "The Oversocialized Conception of Man." Wrong's own target happened to be a functionalist sociology in which consensus was so over-determined as to render nonconformity of any kind theoretically impossible. But the argument applies equally to a "functionalist" social psychology (cf. Moscovici, 1976); compliance with norms looks to be so thoroughly ensured by the joint effects of socialization and social influence that it is difficult to see how deviance, whether creative or destructive, could occur.

NEGATIVE GROUP INFLUENCE

How then to explain the inexplicable? With respect to those forms of deviance that are delinquent, one kind of answer has always been available from within social psychology, and ironically has drawn on some of the same iconic studies to make its case. It can be summed up as the "groups are bad for you" response. There was always ambivalence behind social psychology's analysis of social influence. Hidden, and often only barely hidden, beneath the story of cohesive social groups, bound together by their shared norms and unity of purpose, has been a quite different sentiment, the idea that humans are properly independent. According to this sentiment, civilized society requires individual moral and intellectual autonomy; social influence constitutes the failure of such autonomy. Delinquency, understood as antisocial behavior, as conduct violating the deeper moral requirements of a civilized community, is an instance of just such failure.

This argument, that groups are in some way criminogenic, can be traced back to Le Bon's (1895/1947) vision of the crowd as exercising a malign influence upon the individuals within it, weakening their moral self-control and inducing irrational, destructive aggression. The theme is picked up again later in Zimbardo's (1969) concept of de-individuation within the group, Latane and Darley's (1970) idea that groups encourage diffusion of moral responsibility, and even Wallach, Bem, and Kogan's (1962) conclusion that the group pushes those within it to foolhardy risk taking. And Asch's studies of conformity can be, and often are, taken to demonstrate the power of the group to undermine independent objective judgment as to what is true. Milgram (1964) showed subsequently that the group can have the same destabilizing effect on choices as to what is right and decent.

This sentiment that group influence is an influence for ill, not good, is interestingly echoed in some of the more contemporary campaigns to rescue young people from other problematic forms of deviance, such as smoking, drug abuse, and excessive alcohol consumption. The "just say no" appeal is based on the premise that peer group pressure is the problem and a more robust independence is the remedy. There are various good reasons for concluding that this kind of analysis, as an explanation for delinquency, will not do. I shall return to the more important of these when I consider the phenomenon of adolescent delinquency in more detail later on.

INADEQUATE SOCIALIZATION

A different kind of explanation for criminal deviance locates the fault within development: The process of socialization does not always work perfectly enough to ensure internalized commitment to majority norms. One version of this answer emphasizes the link between delinquency and poor parenting, an answer that can also recruit adverse social conditions as the underlying culprits: Parenting can be poor because it is delivered by people unable or unwilling to do it well by virtue of their poverty, the poor housing they occupy, their immaturity (teenage mothers), their lack of social support (single mothers), or their lack of emotional investment (institutional employees substituting for absent parents). In sociological terms, this is the old social disorganization argument (cf. Shaw & McKay, 1931) with roots in concerns about the damage to family processes of mass urbanization. Within psychology, the inclination was to emphasize deficits internal to the individual as the proximal causes of deviance and delinquency, assuming (rather more often than demonstrating) that the causal chain could be traced back from these deficits to parenting failure. Over the years all kinds of deficits have been invoked, including personality deficits (Eysenck, 1970), motivational deficits such as low self esteem (Kaplan, 1980), deficits in a violence inhibition mechanism (Blair, 1995), social skill deficits (Gibbs, Potter, Barriga, & Liau, 1996; Spence, 1981), intellectual deficits (Hirschi & Hindelang, 1977; Moffitt, 1993), socio-cognitive deficits (Dodge, 1986), and moral deficits (Jennings, Kilkenny, & Kohlberg, 1983; Smetana, 1990). Note that although such deficits might be attributed to parenting failures, at least some can plausibly be linked to inherited dispositions. Parenting undoubtedly plays some part, and I shall later suggest what that part may be. For the moment, I note only that it has proved difficult to pin down the operation of many of the alleged proximal causes in the production of deviance (Emler & Reicher, 1995). But there are two other features of this answer to which I would like to draw attention. First, its general drift is to deny the delinquent a choice in the matter of his or (less commonly) her status. Second, the deficit model is a pathology model, and pathologies almost by definition afflict, in numerical terms, very small minorities.

The next answer I consider takes a very different view on this last point, though it shares with psychological deficit interpretations the assumption that delinquency is not a self-chosen status. However, it does directly address the response of the recipient to imposition of this minority status, a central theme of this volume. For this reason it merits more extended consideration. This is the answer provided by labeling theory.

LABELING THEORY

Labeling theory, unlike either the "criminogenic group" argument or any of the psychological deficit models, embodies an explicit view of delinquents as a minority defined by low power and prestige, together with an account of how this status is constructed and of its consequences. Labeling theory – more accurately an umbrella term for a number of analyses, none of them strictly qualifying as theory (ironically "theory" is an epithet more often applied by the critics of these analyses than by their advocates; Becker, 1991) – is defined by two propositions. First, the individuals and groups that hold power in a society determine what is to count as normative and what as deviant. In other words, deviance is a socially constructed category, the content of which is determined by societal power relations (Archer, 1985; Oplinger, 1990). In this respect it bears some resemblance to functionalist social psychology. The second basic proposition, and the more provocative, is that the label of "deviant," when successfully applied to actors, has the effect of a self-fulfilling prophecy; it causes their behavior to become more closely and consistently aligned with the terms of the label.

There is, of course, a difference between labeling the act and labeling the actor; the former does not require the latter. Thus, some analyses have taken the interesting question to be the power relations that lead certain categories of activity but not others to be defined and treated as deviant. History provides numerous examples that fit this notion of deviance as a socially constructed category and not an intrinsic quality of particular acts – homosexuality, witchcraft, the treatment of some kinds of drug use but not others as criminal, and so on. What the historical examples can show, depending on how well they are chosen, is something of the dynamics underlying the construction of deviant categories of action. Thus, whereas social psychology (cf. Sherif, 1935) has been less interested in *why* a particular norm should be adopted than in the idea that its adoption is independent of its intrinsic merits, the content of norms has been of interest to sociologists and social historians because content is relevant to the particular political-economic interests served by the norm promoted. One striking example is the manner in which powerful financial interests, those of the pharmaceutical industry, led to the exclusion of amphetamines from legislation defining proscribed drugs (Chambliss, 1974).

There is an interesting question here about the nature of the norms at stake. When sociologists talk of deviance, the term potentially embraces any activity currently proscribed by law. And so an argument for the social construction of deviance, which makes sense when it constructs certain forms of drug use but not others as deviant, is then extended to other legally sanctionable activities, such as robbery and property damage. But are delinquents, therefore, sensibly regarded simply as the losers in a struggle to decide where moral boundaries lie, individuals who have tastes and preferences in this respect no different from those of marijuana users (cf. Becker, 1991) or consenting participants in sadomasochistic practices (cf. Thompson, 1994)? I believe the answer is "no" but to understand why, we need to consider the nature of moral norms.

MORAL NORMS: RELATIVE OR ABSOLUTE?

Cultural and ethical relativism, probably the dominant position within the social sciences across the 20th century, sits well with the social constructivist view of deviance. However, the contrary position, namely that some moral standards are not arbitrary and certainly not culturally relative, has had several prominent champions over the last 100 years (Redfield, 1953), and has acquired added momentum from recent cross-cultural research. Cultural relativism was partly motivated by the honorable aspiration to avoid judging all other cultures by the standards of the one in which those otherwise tempted to make the judgments resided. And it proved relatively easy to identify substantial cross-cultural variation in norms (see Shweder, Mahapatra, & Miller, 1987). But the more recent research has employed a more sophisticated and differentiated notion of social norms.

Within moral psychology, the movement in this direction can be traced to Kohlberg's (1963, 1971) ambitious program to identify universal moral standards and then to show that these do indeed define the natural endpoints of moral development in *all* cultures. Among the inevitable critiques, an innovative response was assembled by one of Kohlberg's own students, Turiel (1983). Effectively, his response acknowledges truth in both universalist and relativist positions, but attributes the original argument to a confusion of two kinds of norm. Turiel argued the need to distinguish "moral" norms, recognized to be universals that admit of no exceptions, from "conventions" or social practices that can and do vary across times and places. Such conventional norms include dress codes and dietary rules. This is not to say that deviation from such practices generally fails to attract strong condemnation – indeed, quite the contrary can be the case. Nor should one conclude that the relativity of conventional practices is routinely recognized by those involved. Rather, it is a reminder that, just because some norms are relative to cultures, not all are. In a recent and striking demonstration of this point, Shweder and colleagues showed that in highly contrasting cultures, the United States and India, some of the same "moral" offenses consistently attract condemnation (Shweder et al., 1997). On this basis they go on to propose candidates for morally universal virtues (promise keeping, respect for others' property, fair allocations, protecting the vulnerable) and vices (arbitrary assault).

The point of this preamble is to make an observation about the particularity of delinquents as a minority. People whose minority status derives from their pursuit of minority *conventions* – styles of dress, forms of religious observance – are in a different position to those whose minority status derives from their pursuit of the illegal activities that are most characteristic of juvenile delinquency. Thus, within this latter group, those whose illegal activities include theft, vandalism, and assault with intent to injure are less ambiguously on the wrong side of a moral boundary than those whose illegalities are confined to drug use. The former pursue activities with evident victims (and which map on to Schweder and colleagues' list of universal vices), while the latter engage in activities lacking evident and immediate victims.

Two further points might be made here about delinquents and delinquency. First, official definitions of delinquency may make no distinction between forms of illegality in the way they have been made here. Activities that are illegal purely by virtue of the offender's age, such as buying cigarettes, sexual relations, truanting from school, gambling, or drinking alcohol, may be treated no differently than theft or malicious damage to private property. But these activities, sometimes called status offenses, have something of the arbitrariness of so-called "blue laws," for example, local legislation covering when shops can and cannot be open for business. More important, however, a distinction can also be made on empirical grounds. Status offenses are among the least typical of delinquency as a whole. The most typical are also the least morally ambiguous, namely those offenses with obvious and immediate victims, offenses involving theft, property damage, and violence toward others (Emler & Reicher, 1995).

The second point is that these most typically delinquent activities are nonetheless themselves not entirely without moral ambiguity. If one thinks of acts intended to cause others extreme pain and distress – acts, therefore, of violence – one may find no difficulty in classifying these as acts that should be outlawed. But some acts objectively in this category have, for example, been represented as "alternative interrogation techniques."*

Nonetheless, it would be a mistake then to conclude that any moral judgment about acts of violence against others is necessarily arbitrary. Rather one group, in this case politicians, has far more power and resources to manipulate language and blur moral clarity as to where the boundary lies. The interesting issues here concern the consequences of being on the wrong side of the moral boundary without these resources.

These issues have not passed unnoticed in the delinquency literature. On the contrary, most possibilities have had an airing. One possibility is that the culprits are simply unaware of where the boundaries lie or that these boundaries have been crossed; in the popular jargon, "they do not know the difference between right and wrong" (cf. debates about the age of criminal responsibility). A quite different possibility is contained in Matza's

---

* The term has been used by George W. Bush and members of his administration referring to practices objectively indistinguishable from torture as forbidden by the Geneva conventions (Andrew Sullivan, *The Sunday Times*, 24 September, 2006).

(1964) notion of "drift"; transgressions are occasional and temporary moral absences, recognized as such by perpetrators after the event and, in the recognition, requiring the employment of what Matza called techniques of neutralization (see also Sykes & Matza, 1957). These are accounts offered both to the self and to others that neutralize the moral import of the particular transgression. Such accounts might involve denying that anyone was actually injured by the action in question, or claiming that the victim deserved it. A related notion but with a more psychological gloss is that of cognitive distortion (Samenow, 1984), except that this latter has tended to be built into personality-based explanations: Cognitive distortions, such as denying real injury or blaming the victim, are treated as cognitive styles that allow delinquency rather than the techniques anyone would use when finding themselves unexpectedly on the wrong side of the moral boundary. Each of these possibilities deserves serious attention, but first there is more to be said about labeling theory. And on this particular point, labeling theory offers a quite distinctive view.

SUPPRESSING DEVIANCE: THE COMMON-SENSE VIEW

The more counter-intuitive claims of labeling theory, claims that are counter to much conventional wisdom about the effects of sanctions upon behavior, concern the consequences for individuals of being labeled deviant. Consider again for a moment two of those iconic studies in social psychology. Schachter (1951) described a two-stage response on the part of majorities when confronted with deviance in their midst. In the first phase, the deviant is put under pressure to conform. The pressure may be explicit, in the form either of blunt urging or reasoned arguments or both, but may also include the implicit threat of social rejection and ostracism. A second phase will be triggered by a recalcitrant deviant and takes the form of exclusion from the group. The value of Schachter's work is in illustrating something of the potential mechanisms of informal social control; it cannot tell us whether these mechanisms are potent because, in the experiments, the response of the deviant is scripted in advance by the experimenter. However, Asch's (1956) work does point in this direction, suggesting that dissent from the majority can be very difficult to sustain in the face of informal social pressure to comply.

This is consistent with a common-sense view of the effects of sanctions upon those to whom they are applied, or at least the common-sense bequeathed by the Enlightenment (cf. Bentham, 1789/1970): Negative sanctions are aversive. Actors will change their actions to avoid negative sanction, and even the anticipation of sanctions can be sufficient to discourage deviance. This is also the basic model of human motivation to be found in economics, in rational choice theories of crime, in the deterrence theory of crime, and in the law of effect or the theory of contingent reinforcement as applied to deviance (Akers, 1990): People respond to incentives. And this is the premise on which penal systems often appear to be based: Experience of punitive sanctions causes offenders to reform; furthermore, they are deterred from future deviance by the experience of this punishment and by the threat of its repetition.

Both labeling, as a theory of crime, and the brute evidence of recidivism rates among convicted offenders argue that simple faith in the power of punishment either to deter or to reform is misplaced. So did functionalist social psychology really get it so wrong? There are two issues here and they need to be distinguished. The first is whether deterrence is ineffective, the second whether the reasons for its lack of effect, and indeed its contrary effect as set out by labeling theorists, is correct. The question of sanctioning effectiveness, whether as instrument of reform or of deterrence, is the more difficult and I shall return to this later. Let us look first at the labeling argument in a bit more detail, this time with the focus upon the labeling of the actor.

LABELING ACTORS

Labeling theory can be traced back to Mead's (1934) symbolic interactionism, and probably even further to Cooley's (1902) "looking-glass self." Cooley proposed that people define themselves in terms of how they imagine others see them, a process that begins in childhood. However, where Cooley located the relevant "action" inside the heads of individuals imagining or anticipating others' impressions of them, Mead took the view that real interactions are involved. In these interactions, others communicate their impressions; individuals do not need to guess at them. And among the matters they communicate are the fit of individuals with particular "roles." The concept of role as a prescription for behavior is central to symbolic interactionism. Individuals as social actors learn that society contains a set of roles that can be occupied, much as a play contains specified parts and a football team a set of positions. Outside of these defined positions there is no coherent action – one is either a social actor in one of these roles or one is not a social being at all. But individuals are not free to inhabit any role; they must negotiate its occupancy with the society they inhabit. Labeling theory takes this to be a negotiation between unequal parties. Power in the negotiation typically rests with those who have power and status in society at large, and effectively they can assign or ascribe roles (labels) to those without power or status. "Deviant" is one such role and the individual labeled a deviant then acts out the assigned role; other roles, and therefore other options for action, are not thereafter available.

Who gets chosen for such a role and how does it happen? An important distinction here is that between primary and secondary deviance (Lemert, 1951, 1967). Primary deviance is any violation of a rule or norm that an individual commits before being labeled as a deviant. Secondary deviance refers to those violations that follow, and in one way or another amount to a response to, such labeling. The counter-intuitive proposition is that social control, and in particular the formal procedures of this control such as arrest, trial, conviction, sentencing, and incarceration, increase delinquency rather than reduce it. They are the building blocks of a labeling process that assigns some individuals but not others to the role of deviant and to membership of this minority category. And in performing this role, the individual so labeled is involved in deviance that follows from the role's requirements.

A presumption underpinning labeling theory is that many and perhaps most delinquent actions fail to result in the deviant label being attached to the perpetrator. But what was initially a presumption was soon to be strongly confirmed. It is probably no coincidence that the wider impact of the labeling perspective followed quite directly upon the diffusion into the social science community of self-report evidence concerning offending. Self-report was developed as a methodology in criminological research in response to the suspicion that the evidence for crime on which it had previously relied, namely official records of convictions, was tainted. The suspicion was that the official records exaggerated the involvement of some social categories in crime – in particular working class, ethnic minority, male juveniles – and downplayed the involvement of others. Self-report evidence began to provide some support for this suspicion, but of more significance it suggested that official records vastly underestimated the sheer volume of crime as a whole (e.g., Radzinowitz, 1964). In this it provided empirical foundation for a distinction between a high frequency and prevalence of undetected, unreported, unrecorded, and unpunished crime (the sphere of primary deviance) and a much smaller body of punished crime (a source of secondary deviance).

Additionally, however, primary deviance was regarded from the perspective of labeling theory as uninteresting because it was thought to flow from a large number of causes, because it predicted no consequences for the actor, and because, in the words of one labeling theorist, "everybody does it" (Schur, 1973). The important questions were instead about what causes a small minority of individuals to be plucked out from among a majority from whom they are behaviorally indistinguishable and labeled as deviants, how this labeling happens, and what its consequences are.

Even the first question has not invariably been treated as interesting, sometimes having been regarded as a matter of chance. Nonetheless, the self-report evidence gave comfort to the view that selection of candidates for the deviant label is systematically biased, and biased in the direction of people whose social characteristics – age, social class, ethnicity, gender, area of residence – together with visible markers of these, such as speech style, dress, and demeanor, make them a good fit with the stereotype of an offender.

However, self-report and other evidence points to the conclusion that primary deviants are a more differentiated category (West & Farrington, 1977) and, moreover, that differences within the category do affect the labeling process. To put it another way, some young people are rather more delinquent than others in advance of any public or formal labeling while the likelihood of being labeled is in part a consequence of conduct. That is to say, official labels are neither assigned at random nor assigned purely on the basis of extra-legal criteria. Instead, a young person's conduct also influences the probability that he or she will attract official attention. The self-report evidence does indicate that those young people whose offences are most serious and frequent are more likely to attract such attention and more likely to be convicted of some offense (Farrington, 1973; Jolliffe et al., 2003).

This, in turn, raises a question about how labeling happens. The original proposal was that there are watershed events – typically arrests, court proceedings, convictions, and sentences – that produce a sharp discontinuity in the public visibility of the offender (Tannenbaum, 1938). More recently a wider range of publicly disseminated decisions, such as exclusion or expulsion from school and even academic assessments and curriculum track placements, have been included as potentially contributing to the process. There is a case for going much further than this, however. A useful approach, I submit, is provided by the concept of reputation.

REPUTATIONS AND MORAL LABELING

Reputations can refer to a variety of personal characteristics, but the discussion here focuses upon reputations for moral virtue. If one regards these reputations as the moral labels that are attached to individuals by communities, then one may also appreciate that these labels are developed gradually over time. The features of a moral reputation that may change over time include its substance – whether the target is believed to be honest, law abiding, trustworthy, truthful, and so on; its clarity or how consistent and precise is the shared belief about an individual's moral character; and its reach or how many people share in this belief.

The long tradition of research on sociometry (cf. Moreno, 1934) has relied on the fact that children within a school classroom are known to their classmates. Or rather, classmates have formed impressions of one another that are sufficiently clear for them to nominate peers on various dimensions. A few years ago, discussion would have taken a different course from this point. The presumption was that impressions reflect peculiarities of the observer (Cronbach, 1955; Dornbusch et al. 1965); the impressions of different observers show no consensus or convergence. Reputation as a *shared* judgment, whether of the moral character or of any other quality of the observed, seemed to be ruled out (Bromley, 1993).

More recently, the picture has changed radically for two reasons. First, there is a more mature appreciation of the conditions under which converging impressions are likely to be formed (Cheek, 1982; Funder, 1999; Moskowitz & Schwartz, 1982). Second, more sophisticated research designs now provide better tests of the degree to which consensus exists (Kenny, 1994). Put simply, observers are more likely to share impressions of an individual the more extensively they are acquainted both with the individual and with each other (Malloy et al., 1997). And put another way, the clarity of reputations depends on the extent of association between those to whom they refer and those who share in them. Hence, one would anticipate that the longer a child retains membership of a community, the clearer that child's moral reputation will be within that community. Other things being equal, clarity of reputation will therefore be related to age. Other things, of course, are not equal in some quite important ways and in particular, there are significant breaks in the continuity of association over the life course, breaks that can have consequences for reputation (Emler, 2005), a point to which I shall return.

The fact of some measure of consensus in impressions does not by itself settle the matter of its origins. One possibility that must be taken seriously is that impressions converge through a process of mutual influence (Kenny, 1994), and do so much as norms emerge (cf. Sherif, 1935) and for similar reasons, namely because there is no objective evidence of character on which observers can draw. If this is entirely responsible for reputations, then reputations are potentially as arbitrary as the formal labeling process was originally conceived to be. And if reputations do reflect the reality of an individual's moral virtue they could do so only to the extent that they operate as self-fulfilling prophecies, effectively the position of labeling theory.

Funder (1999), among others, has outlined an alternative scenario. He describes his own version as a "realistic" model of person perception. Funder proposes that there are real differences in personality, reflected in conduct, and that these differences are perceived by others with varying degrees of accuracy. It is conduct that provides the raw behavioral data from which impressions are formed, and the larger the sample of these data available to the observer, the more closely will the observer's impression correspond with the reality. The size of the available sample of relevant data is coherently related to such matters as the amount of direct contact the observer has with the target, and the range of other valid observations on which the observer can draw, reflecting, for example, the number of mutual acquaintances and extent of informative contact with them.

It should be noted at this point that if Funder's argument is credible, we are now at a considerable distance from the classical labeling view. We are accepting the proposition that the labels applied to individuals can reflect something real about these individuals and the differences between them. This is not to say that no mutual influence lies behind agreements on labels or reputations but, as with social norms, the part played by such influence may be a function of observers' uncertainty. Accepting Funder's argument, we might also recognize that reputations (or impressions) will vary in their clarity because the individuals to whom they refer vary in the clarity and distinctiveness of the evidence they provide.

The evidence that can be provided can differ systematically in its diagnosticity for character, however. Skowronski and Carlston (1992) have shown that there is an asymmetry to judgments of moral character, such that people come to clearer conclusions when the evidence is negative. In other words, it is easier to provide evidence to others that will convince them of one's bad character than it is to provide evidence that will convince them of one's good character. This may be relevant to the ease with which a delinquent reputation is acquired and the difficulty with which it is shed.

If the "reach" of a reputation refers to the number of people sharing an impression of a target individual, then as this number increases, so will the proportion of people within this group whose knowledge of the target is partly if not completely mediated. That is, some will know this individual purely "by reputation." For example, the same elementary school class may contain some children known only to a few other members of the class but also children whose reputation has disseminated throughout the school, to pupils and teaching staff alike. Reach in this sense is likely to go with substance and clarity. Exceptionally, children may acquire a far-reaching reputation by virtue of extraordinary talents; more often, such reputations will be for problematic conduct.

A critical point in the argument has been reached here. I am proposing that reputations reflect (if imperfectly) reality. This is the implication both of Funder's realist model and of evidence concerning the validity of observer ratings, or reputational measures, of character (cf. Cheek, 1982; Moskowitz & Schwartz, 1982). Where does this leave the original labeling theory claim, that deviants as a category of people, as well as deviance as a category of action, are socially constructed? I would submit that criminal justice rituals do not pluck individuals from undifferentiated anonymity to place them in this category. These rituals are much more likely to reinforce already-established reputations, and serve mainly to increase their reach.

Emler and Reicher (1995), having come to the conclusion that reputations are not pure social constructions, considered the position of the individuals to whom reputations refer, and particularly the position of those with conventionally "bad" reputations. The options they considered included the possibility that bad reputations are unforeseen by those who acquire them, and if not wholly unforeseen then unwanted or at best, for them, incidental consequences of their actions. None of these possibilities was consistent with the evidence they reviewed. Most importantly, young people more extensively involved in delinquency were as aware of the reputations that attach to delinquent habits, and as aware of their own reputations, just as were those members of the peer group least involved in such behavior (see Emler & Reicher, 1995, for review). Emler and Reicher also found that being identifiable as the author of misdeeds, far from being a problem for delinquent teenagers, is actively sought. In a more recent study we have been able to confirm that delinquent teenagers are, if anything, even more attuned to their own reputations than their more law-abiding peers (Tarry & Emler, unpublished; see also Emler, Tarry, & St. James, 2007). The only reasonable conclusion would appear to be the one to which Emler and Reicher came, namely that reputations, including delinquent reputations, are in fact among the goals of action. So delinquency is not an ascribed status; it refers to an elective minority. But this conclusion just seems to raise new questions in its wake: Most obviously, why would anyone elect to join such a minority? The attractions of a reputation for virtue can seem so obvious as to need no further explanation. But the disadvantages of a delinquent reputation would appear to be even more obvious. The following draws upon and extends the arguments developed by Emler and Reicher (1995; 2005).

JOINING THE DELINQUENT MINORITY

There are two kinds of pull exerted upon young people by delinquency. First, delinquent and antisocial activities have intrinsic attractions. They can offer fun, excitement, challenge, and even material gratification. If no one was tempted to do these things, no point would be served in prohibiting them. But the fact of prohibition can provide additional appeal (cf. Matza, 1964). At this point, however, the reward shifts from something intrinsic to the activity toward the reputation acquired through engagement in the activity. The second and more complex pull of delinquency is more closely associated with the perceived advantages of this reputation. To understand this pull, we need to appreciate what problems confront young people and what solutions they perceive to be available to them. I have in mind here in particular the problems posed by relations with others.

While it is a truism that we are social animals, utterly reliant on our relations with others and therefore unavoidably interdependent, these other members of our shared environment are also potential threats, whether to our dignity, our well-being, or our prosperity. They may insult us, cheat us, exploit us, persecute us, injure us, or rob us. It is the normal expectation that, from birth, infants are protected from these hazards by their parents, though sadly this normal expectation is not invariably met. However, this form of protection, even when successfully provided, is not one children can rely upon entirely in the longer run. Increasingly, they come into contact with other children when they are beyond the direct supervision of parents or other adults, and these other children are usually the most significant source of threat. To manage this threat they must identify and come to trust other solutions.

One such solution is based on growing appreciation of the merits of reciprocity in social life (cf. Gouldner, 1960), a norm that enjoins actors not to harm those who have previously helped them, and encourages them not to harm others by reason of the future help and support they would otherwise forego. However, when others fail to respect this norm, the next line of defense should be provided by those in positions of authority; in schools it is the teaching staff, and beyond them the apparatus of the criminal justice system. As children grow older and their intellectual capacity to penetrate the functions of social institutions improves, they do begin to appreciate that the institutional apparatus of authority, rules, and procedures is, at least in principle, not primarily a source of prohibitions but of protection for individuals and their rights, and a source of redress for their legitimate grievances (Adelson, 1971).

Herein lies a difficulty, however. Formal authority, whether embodied in school staff or in the agents of criminal justice, does not provide perfect protection. Children continue to be assaulted, robbed, bullied, and otherwise victimized by their peers. Unsurprisingly some children conclude from this that they must look for other remedies. We found, for example, a very clearly social class difference here; working class children, compared to middle class, were much more likely to recommend direct action – retaliation – by the victim as an appropriate response to victimization, and correspondingly less likely to recommend appeal to authority (Emler & Ohana, 1992).

At some point in childhood a divide begins to open up in beliefs about formal authority, over and above the general age trend toward less positive views of law and of police benevolence (Hess & Torney, 1967). By age 12, children are beginning to differ from one another in their views of authority. On the one side are those who express confidence in the legal system to operate impartially, to treat them fairly, and to protect their interests. On the other are young people who feel ambivalent about this system, doubting its impartiality, lacking confidence that it provides them with meaningful protection, and even beginning to see it as a source of persecution (Gouviea-Pereira et al., 2002; Palmonari & Rubini, 1999; Reicher & Emler, 1985). This divide is in turn strongly associated with involvement in delinquency (Brown, 1974; Emler & Reicher, 1987, 1995; Heaven, 1993, Levy, 2001; West & Farrington, 1977).

It is not clear what causes this divide to start opening up. However, to address an issue raised earlier in the chapter, it seems plausible that poor parenting has an impact on later conduct, not because it generates psychological deficits but because it undermines or even fails to establish any sense of protection children have from victimization. Poor parenting may merely take the form of lack of manifest sympathy with the child's anxieties and fears. When it also involves harsh, inconsistent, and unfair punishment, parents move toward being the victimizers rather than the protectors. And at this point poor parenting shades into child abuse, the connection of which to delinquency is well established (e.g., Stouthamer-Loeber et al., 2001). The state is typically an even poorer parent; children growing up in care – and having no continuity of care (and not infrequently being neglected if not abused by the carers they do have) – are more likely to be offenders in adolescence (Anderson, 2005).

It is unlikely, however, that parenting quality is the only factor. Experience of harsh, inconsistent, or unjust treatment at the hands of anyone in authority will undermine confidence in authorities as sources of protection and redress. Remember more generally that certain categories of people, and significantly those categories that are overrepresented in the delinquent minority – children, males, those of working class background – are both more likely to be victims and to enjoy less-effective legal protection or redress (Black, 1983).

How then does a delinquent reputation take on the appearance of a solution? Delinquent reputations contain predictable elements relating to dishonesty, unreliability, and irresponsibility (Emler & Reicher, 1995). But they also contain the implication that one is strong, tough, brave, unemotional, and thus potentially a person willing to take direct and violent revenge, and therefore dangerous to offend against. Interestingly, delinquency is also associated with a perception that one is a person who stands up for one's rights (Emler & Reicher, 1995). Delinquent reputations, therefore, can seem, particularly to those who pursue them, to offer some protection against the risk of becoming another's victim. Once embarked upon this course as a deliberate policy, it has consequences that reinforce even deeper commitment to a delinquent reputation. In other words, a positive feedback loop is set up, though positive only in the technical sense of amplifying the original inclination. The feedback loop operates through several interlinked effects – on patterns of association, on group dynamics, on elaboration of norms, on intergroup dynamics, and on societal reactions.

First, patterns of affiliation increasingly reflect behavioral inclinations. One of the most reliable correlates of deviance, a finding to have emerged in study after study, is having friends who are similarly deviant (Baron, 2003; Dishion et al., 1991; Elliot & Voss, 1974; Haynie, 2002; Heinze et al. 2004; Hindelang, 1973; Hindelang et al, 1981; Hirschi, 1969; Jensen, 1972; Johnson, 1979; Menard & Morse, 1984; Tremblay et al., 1995; Voss, 1969). Young people whose inclinations are delinquent are disposed to affiliate with and spend time with peers who share this inclination, with the consequence that this minority forms *groups* in a meaningful sense. Whether this is purely a matter of attraction based on common interests is unclear.

Some work indicates it may be a choice enforced by the consequences of the delinquent behavioral style itself, a style that causes children who are more delinquent to be unattractive as associates to more law-abiding peers (Vuchnich et al., 1992). It is relatively easy to see how this might happen. Children who expect to rely upon direct action as a response to victimization by others are more likely to invest in negative reciprocity – or retaliation – as a policy in their conduct of interpersonal relations. Rose and Asher (1999) found that children who regarded retaliation as an important goal with respect to friends, had fewer friends and poorer quality relations with their friends, who presumably also did not last very long as friends. In the conventional terms of social psychology, their rejection of majority norms leads to their informal exclusion from the majority. This points to a degree of negative selection; law-abiding teenagers avoid choosing delinquents as close friends. For the latter, this kind of rejection reduces the field of available companions to kids who are more like themselves. In other words, the positive selections are made primarily by those young people who are not themselves delinquent.

Unpopularity, however, is not the same as social isolation. Cairns and colleagues (1988) discovered that, although aggressive 13 year olds were more frequently disliked by their peer group as a whole, they were as likely as their less-aggressive peers to be well integrated into friendship groups. The findings reported by Claes and Simard (1992) from their study of teenagers indicate that the more delinquent among them actually had more friendships than the less delinquent, though they did describe fewer of their friendships as close and reported more conflict with friends. On the other hand, Giordano, Cernovich, and Pugh (1986) observed that, in some respects, the strength and significance of personal ties to peer group members can be even greater for delinquent adolescents than for their nondelinquent peers (see also Houtzager & Baerveldt, 1999). We found that more-delinquent adolescents had as much contact with peers described as friends or close friends as did those who were less delinquent (Emler & Reicher, 1995). They also reported as much contact with parents and other family members, and as much intimacy and enjoyment in their interactions. In contrast to these indications, however, Poulin, Dishion, and Haas (1999) report that friendship/relationship quality is negatively associated with delinquency of groups.

Whatever the mechanisms producing differentiated patterns of association – and work remains to be done sorting these out – consequences do flow from group formation and from the composition of the groups so formed. Group homogeneity is often further reinforced by institutional practices, notably those of large high schools that sort children into streams according to ability but effectively also sort according to attitudes and behavior (Hargreaves, 1967; Willis, 1977). This is also one powerful reason why the simple "groups are bad for you" thesis will not do. All young people associate in groups to some extent. Antisocial conduct is not associated with the extent to which they do this; such conduct is, however, associated with the composition of the group. It is important also to underline, even if it might seem self-evident, that adolescent peer groups are friendship groups; they are not aggregations of mutually unacquainted individuals, a fact that is at odds with the de-individuation argument for negative effects of group context on conduct.

Group dynamics do nonetheless play a part in the generation of delinquent behavior. Groups develop, and attract commitment to, shared norms.

The more homogenous the group in terms of its members' initial behavioral inclinations, the more likely is the group to embody distinctive norms. And delinquency, it is important to note, is overwhelmingly a group, not a solitary activity (Emler, Reicher, & Ross, 1987; Erikson & Jensen, 1977; Shapland, 1978), underlining the role that group membership has in translating inclinations into more consistent habits of action. Effectively, groups have polarizing effects on behavioral tendencies.

If groups have a polarizing effect, this may in part flow from the discussions that occur among young people. Given that involvement in delinquency is associated with distinctive views of, for example, authority, one might expect that these shared views are further elaborated within the peer group. This is what some recent research has shown (e.g., Granic & Dishion, 2003; see also Dishion et al., 1997). And Shortt et al.(2003) report that antisocial talk is predictive of continued association with antisocial peers.

The group focus of adolescent activities has further consequences when these include delinquent activities. In particular, encounters with authority become intergroup encounters, with the associated consequences for intergroup perceptions. For young people in a delinquent peer group, individual representatives of authority, whether teaching staff in schools, police officers, or others, come to be categorized as members of an out-group to whom shared negative images of authority are generalized. We have found that these images include the perception that they, young people, are being picked upon by people in authority (Emler & Reicher, 1995). Undoubtedly this will be in part because they are indeed being singled out for attention and this happens because their conduct is seen to merit this attention. But the intergroup context of encounters with authority also shapes the response of those on the authority side. They are more likely to see collections of young people as homogeneous groups to which a negative image and negative expectations are appropriately attached. The risk is that individuals will be judged guilty by association, triggering in turn a strengthened perception of authority as biased and a source of persecution. Police perceptions of young people do seem to be sensitive to context in this way. A group is seen as more of a problem than a single individual and more likely to attract a police response (Hindelang, 1976). The intergroup dynamics then favor a more aggressive and defiant response from the targets of their action, driven in part by self-presentational concerns before an audience of peers (cf. Felson, 1982).

At some point, the positive feedback processes push conduct to the point at which some more formal response is triggered, the "societal reaction" that has traditionally formed the focus of labeling theory. My point is that such societal reactions are not at the origin of deviant careers; rather they occur only after delinquent career trajectories are well established. However, in one very important respect, labeling theorists were right. The consequences of formal labeling are not to correct or reverse these trajectories but to reinforce them. Labeling young people as delinquent or antisocial is associated with a subsequent *increase* in offending (Fisher & Erikson, 1973; Johnson et al., 2004). The open question concerns precisely what it is about labeling or its consequences that has this effect.

Becker (1963) argued that the deviant label has the effect of embedding the individual into deviant groups, the company of like-minded peers who, on the one hand, regard deviant activities as acceptable and, on the other, provide social shelter from the negative reactions of those who disapprove. However, where Becker sees that the "final step in the career of a deviant is movement into an organized deviant group" (p. 37), differential association, as I have argued, is likely to predate the kind of public labeling involved in arrest, court proceedings, sentence, or punishment.

How then does labeling of these kinds relate to the labeling process already in train, namely the more general labeling process entailed in the formation of a reputation? Informal labeling by teachers, parents, and peers as "bad boy," "troublemaker," "disruptive," or "rule-breaker" supports self-perception as a delinquent and encourages association with more delinquent peers and further involvement in delinquent activities (Adams & Evans, 1996; Heimer & Matsueda, 1994; Zhang, 1997). The more formal and public labeling of the criminal justice system would be expected to enhance the clarity and reach of delinquent reputations. It appears also to enhance differential association. There has always been a suspicion that when consequences of this labeling include incarceration, they greatly increase exposure to a more consistently delinquent peer group (those who are similarly incarcerated). Some recent publications providing analyses of longitudinal data sets confirm that contact with the criminal justice system leads to increased association with delinquent peers (Bernburg, Krohn, & Rivera, 2006; Johnson, Simons, & Conger, 2004). Of more significance, however, Bernburg et al. (2006) were able to show that the amplifying effects of system contact on subsequent delinquency were mediated by impact upon involvement in delinquent peer groups (see also Adams, 1996).

ESCAPING FROM THE VICIOUS CYCLE

The foregoing indicates that joining the delinquent minority can be a self-reinforcing process. The barriers to membership are not great; the boundaries are relatively permeable and easily breached. Movement from periphery to core appears to acquire an inexorable momentum. These observations pose three problems, one for policy, one for the individual member of this minority, and one for theory. The problem for theory is that membership of this minority is typically short-lived. Membership reaches its peak in mid-adolescence and declines thereafter. And according to Blumstein and Cohen (1987), the vast majority of offenders have stopped offending by their late twenties. But to the extent that movement into the category is readily explained through the co-action of attractive and exclusionary forces, movement out is correspondingly difficulty to explain. And yet it happens. The policy problem is that it does not happen often enough, early enough, or rapidly enough. But there are hints of answers to both of these problems in the solutions individuals find to their particular problems.

As a solution to the risk of victimization, a delinquent reputation is not conspicuously successful. The pattern of behavior required to support this kind of reputation, a pattern of reasonably consistent involvement in antisocial behavior, is closely associated with being victimized. Young people who engage in delinquency are themselves the category most at risk of being the victims of others' delinquencies. It is not entirely clear whether this association is noticed by young people and, if noticed, whether it reduces the attractions of a delinquent reputation.

What is noticed, albeit only toward the end of compulsory schooling, is the disadvantage of this reputation for future employment prospects A consistent theme in our interviews with 15 year olds was the need for a decent reference from the school to take to potential employers (Emler & Reicher, 1995). Thus, many of those with the more-extensive records of involvement in delinquency wished by this stage to present themselves as reformed sinners. These anxieties are well founded. Carrying a delinquent reputation forward from the end of schooling does serious damage to employment prospects (Davies & Tanner, 2003; Tanner et al., 1999).

If the intention is to reinvent a reputation that is currently delinquent as something else, this intention is not easily implemented. For example, the very cognitive bias that makes it relatively easy to provide evidence of "bad" character creates correspondingly substantial obstacles to the demonstration of virtue (Skowronski & Carlston, 1989), as Lofland (1969) anticipated. Given that reputations are the opinions of an audience, a better option than offering this audience new evidence is to cultivate the opinion of a different audience. Existing social relations can support this strategy. Most adolescents belong to networks containing both delinquent and nondelinquent friends (Haynie, 2002), offering some scope for shifting the focus of social attention. However, Haynie's analysis also showed that there will still be limits in these options; those more seriously and extensively involved in delinquency tend to have more densely interlinked networks and thus fewer options for building relations with nondelinquent audiences (Haynie, 2001).

A much better opportunity for audience change is provided by the end of formal education. Friendship networks are substantially derived from the institutions in which people routinely participate (Emler, 2000), and for adolescents, the single most significant institution in this regard is the school they attend. Leaving school has two advantages for the delinquent intent on reform. First, it can mean a loss of routine contact with those others who provided their companions in crime, making it somewhat easier to live a reformed life. Second, the discontinuity in relationships allows the young person to find a new audience with which a different reputation can be constructed (Emler, 2005).

Self-reinvention via this route will be less easily accomplished, however, if a delinquent reputation has extended its reach through formal processes of labeling; in this case, the audience with which the current reputation exists may be just too extended to change. At this point, individual aspirations need to be supported by policy initiatives. Thus, various commentators are beginning to recognize that effects of the rituals of arrest, trial, and conviction may only be undone by equally potent public rituals of "delabeling" (Braithwaite, 1989; Maruna et al., 2004), in effect rituals that formalize readmission of the repentant sinner to the majority.

Finally, some will never escape their delinquent reputations, whatever their wishes, and these are most likely to be the individuals who embarked upon the route into this minority earliest (Moffitt, 1993) and reached closest to its core. Just a few may find a route back through the happy luck of encountering a propitious "turning point" in life (Laub & Sampson, 2003), such as a close relationship with someone willing to discount the past and give them a new start.

At this point we should briefly revisit the issue of sanctions, whether formal or informal. Social psychology's potent experimental demonstrations of the power of informal sanctions (cf. Asch, 1956) actually show that they are only *relatively* potent. A significant experimental effect will normally reflect sensitivity to experimental manipulations of a majority of participants, but not all participants. What constitutes a sanction is relative to personal history, circumstances, and perceptions. An institutional regime that looks punitive to the majority can be, on the contrary, an invigorating challenge to a minority. Those who choose to pursue a delinquent reputation are not acting irrationally, but are exercising a choice that makes sense in light of the particular circumstances they face and their interpretation of the information available to them; it is a coherent response to the incentives they perceive. But equally, it is important to recognize that individuals do not have perfect control over their own fates; virtuous reputations are not equally accessible to all.

CONCLUSIONS

The chapter opened with the proposition that delinquents represent an interesting minority for two reasons, relating respectively to the nature of moral norms and to the control mechanisms through which compliance with these norms is secured. So what lessons can be learned from this case? I wish to draw attention to three.

The first is that norms of conduct need to be understood as means to secure desired ends. In this context, the desired ends are not arbitrary or group specific; they include protection of the self from harm or victimization, redress for grievances, and fair treatment. Correspondingly the difference between minority and majority is not in commitment to these desired ends. Instead, and this brings us to the second lesson, the difference would appear to be in views as to the effective means to achieve these ends.

Regarding norms of conduct as means to secure desired ends recalls Piaget's (1932) classic observations on the relationships children develop to the rules of their games. Children come to appreciate that behind these rules is a more general or abstract "spirit of the game" and particular rules attract their respect to the extent they believe that doing so promotes this more general principle. Much more recently, Tyler (2006) has shown that people obey the law in significant part because they believe doing so promotes fair procedures for deciding guilt and innocence. In other words, compliance with the norms derives from confidence in the means-ends relationship. Pursuit of delinquent activities is associated with a lack of confidence in this relationship. Thus, delinquency would appear to be a self-chosen and not an externally imposed status.

However, and this is the third lesson, the case of delinquency indicates that the relationship between minority and majority can be very complex. Recruitment to the delinquent minority has multiple determinants, among them the reactions of the majority. And although majority reactions appear to entail strong pressure to renounce minority membership, their effect more often is to strengthen commitment to that membership, reinforcing the sense these young people have that they are excluded from the conventional mechanisms of protection and justice. Nonetheless, one of the most striking features of this minority is that membership is typically transient, pointing to a need to appreciate not just how it recruits, but also how it loses members. There are indications that this happens in part because delinquency proves in the longer run to be an unreliable means to secure desired ends, but on this point further research would be of value.

REFERENCES

Adams, M. S. (1996). Labelling and differential association: Towards a general social learning theory of crime and deviance. *American Journal of Criminal Justice*, 20, 149–164.

Adams, M. S., & Evans, T. D. (1996). Teacher disapproval, delinquent peers and self reported delinquency: A longitudinal test of labelling theory. *Urban Review*, 28, 199–211.

Adelson, J. (1971). The political imagination of the young adolescent. *Daedalus*, 100, 1031–1050.

Akers, R. (1990). Rational choice, deterrence, and social learning theory in criminology: The path not taken. *Journal of Criminal Law and Criminology*, 81, 653–676.

Anderson, G. (2005). Family relations, adjustment and well-being in a longitudinal study of children in care. *Child and Family Social Work*, 10, 43–56.

Archer, D. (1985). Social deviance. In G. Lindzey & E. Aronson (Eds.), *Handbook of social psychology* (3rd ed., Vol. 2, pp. 743–804). New York: Random House.

Aronfreed, J. (1968). *Conduct and conscience: The socialization of internalized control over behavior*. New York: Academic Press.

Asch, S. (1956). Studies of independence and conformity: A minority of one against a unanimous majority. *Psychological Monographs*, 7(9), (Whole No. 416).

Baron, S. W. (2003). Self-control, social consequences and criminal behavior: Street youth and the general theory of crime. *Journal of Research in Crime and Delinquency*, 40, 403–425.

Becker, H. (1963). *Outsiders: Studies in the sociology of deviance*. New York: Free Press.

 (1991). *Outsiders: Studies in the sociology of deviance*. New York: Free Press. Revised edition. New York: Free Press.

Bentham, J. (1970). *An introduction to the principles of morals and legislation*. London: Athlone Press. (Original work published 1789).

Bernburg, J. G., Krohn, M. D., & Rivera, C. J. (2006). Official delinquency, criminal embeddedness and subsequent delinquency: A longitudinal test of labelling theory. *Journal of Research in Crime and Delinquency*, 43, 67–88.

Black, D. (1983). Crime as social control. *American Sociological Review*, 48, 34–45.

Blair, J. (1995). A cognitive developmental approach to morality: Investigating the psychopath. *Cognition*, 57, 1–29.

Blumstein, A., & Cohen, J. (1987). Characterizing criminal careers. *Science*, 237, 985–991.

Braithwaite, J. (1989). *Crime, shame and reintegration*. New York: Cambridge University Press.

Bromley, D. B. (1993). *Reputation, image and impression management.* Chichester: John Wiley.

Brown, D. (1974). Adolescent attitudes and lawful behaviour. *Public Opinion Quarterly, 38,* 96–106.

Cairns, R. B., Cairns, B. D., Neckerman, H. J., Gest S. D., & Gariepy, J.-L. (1988). Social networks and aggressive behaviour: Peer support or peer rejection? *Developmental Psychology, 24,* 815–823.

Chambliss, W. J. (1974). The state, the law, and the definition of behaviour as criminal or delinquent. In D. Glaser (Ed.), *Handbook of criminology* (pp. 7–43). Chicago: Rand McNally.

Cheek, J. (1982). Aggregation, moderator variables, and the validity of personality tests: A peer-rating study. *Journal of Personality and Social Psychology, 43,* 1254–1269.

Claes, M., & Simard, R. (1992). Friendship characteristics of delinquent adolescents. *International Journal of Adolescence and Youth, 3,* 287–301.

Cooley, C. H. (1902). *Human nature and social order.* New York: Charles Scribner's.

Cronbach, L. J. (1955). Processes affecting scores on "understanding others" and "assumed similarity." *Psychological Bulletin, 52,* 177–193.

Davies, S., & Tanner, L. (2003). The long arm of the law. *Sociological Quarterly, 44,* 385–404.

Dishion, T. J., Eddy, M., Haas, E., & Li, F. (1997). Friendships and violent behaviour during adolescence. *Social Development, 6,* 207–223.

Dishion, T. J., Patterson, G. L., Stoolmiller, M., & Skinner, M. L. (1991). Family, school and behavioral antecedants to early adolescent involvement with anti-social peers. *Developmental Psychology, 27,* 172–180.

Dornbusch, S. M., Hastorf, A. H., Richardson, S. A., Muzzy, R. E., & Vreeland, R. S. (1965). The perceiver and the perceived: Their relative influence on the categories of interpersonal perception. *Journal of Personality and Social Psychology, 1,* 434–440.

Dodge, K. A. (1986). A social information processing model of social competence in children. In M. Perlmutter (Ed.), *Minnesota Symposium on Child Psychology* (Vol. 18). Hillsdale, NJ: Lawrence Erlbaum.

Elliot, D. S., & Voss, H. (1974). *Delinquency and dropout.* Lexington, MA: Heath.

Emler, N. (2000). Social structures and individual lives: Effects of participation in the social institutions of family, education and work. In J. Bynner & R. K. Silbereisen (Eds.), *Adversity and challenge in the life course in England and the new Germany* (pp. 62–84). London: Macmillan.

(2005). Life course transitions and social identity change. In P. Levy, P. Ghisetta, J.-M. Le Goff, D. Spini, & E. Widmer (Eds.), *Towards an interdisciplinary perspective on the life course* (pp. 203–221). New York: Elsevier.

Emler, N., & Ohana, J. (1992). Responses au prejudice: Representations sociales enfantines. *Bulletin de Psychologie, 45,* 223–231.

Emler, N., & Reicher, S. (1987). Orientations to institutional authority in adolescence. *Journal of Moral Education, 16,* 108–116.

(1995). *Adolescence and delinquency: The collective management of reputation.* Oxford: Blackwell.

(2005). Delinquency: Cause or consequence of social exclusion? In D. Abrams, J. Marques, & M. Hogg (Eds.), *The social psychology of inclusion and exclusion* (pp. 211–241). Philadelphia, PA: Psychology Press.

Emler, N., Reicher, S., & Ross, A. (1987). The social context of delinquent conduct. *Journal of Child Psychology and Psychiatry, 28*, 99–109.

Emler, N., Tarry, H., & St. James, A. (2007). Postconventional moral reasoning and reputation. *Journal of Research in Personality, 41*, 76–89.

Erikson, M. L., & Jensen, G. F. (1977). Delinquency is still group behaviour. *Journal of Criminal Law and Criminology, 68*, 262–273.

Eysenck, H. J. (1970). *Crime and personality* (2nd ed.). London: Granada Press.

Farrington, D. (1973). Self reports of deviant behaviour: Predictive and stable? *Journal of Criminal Law and Criminology, 64*, 99–110.

Felson, R. (1982). Impression management and the escalation of aggression and violence. *Social Psychology Quarterly, 45*, 245–254.

Fisher, G., & Erikson, M. L. (1973). On assessing the effects of official reactions to juvenile delinquency. *Journal of Research in Crime and Delinquency, 10*, 177–194.

Funder, D. (1999). *Personality judgment: A realistic approach to person perception.* San Diego, CA: Academic Books.

Gibbs, J. C., Potter, G. B., Barriga, A. Q., & Liau, A. K. (1996). Developing the helping skills and prosocial motivation of aggressive adolescents in peer group programs. *Aggression and Violent Behavior, 1*, 285–305.

Giordano, P. C., Cernovich, S. A., & Pugh, M. D. (1986). Friendship and delinquency. *American Journal of Sociology, 91*, 1170–1201.

Gouldner, A. (1960). The norm of reciprocity: A preliminary statement. *American Sociological Review, 25*, 161–178.

Gouviea-Pereira, M., Vala, J., Palmonari, A., & Rubini, M. (2002). School experience, relational justice and legitimation of institutional authorities. *European Journal of Psychology of Education, 28*, 309–325.

Granic, I., & Dishion, T. J. (2003). Deviant talk in adolescent friendships: A step towards addressing a pathogenic attractor process. *Social Development, 12*, 314–334.

Hargreaves, D. H. (1967). *Social relations in a secondary school.* London: Routledge & Kegan Paul; Willis, 1977.

Haynie, D. L. (2001). Delinquent peers revisited: Does network structure matter? *American Journal of Sociology, 106*, 1013–1057.

(2002). Friendship networks and delinquency: The relative nature of delinquency. *Journal of Quantitative Criminology, 18*, 99–134.

Heaven, P. (1993). Personality predictors of self-reported delinquency. *Personality and Individual Differences, 14*, 67–76.

Heinze, H. J., Toro, P. A., & Urberg, K. A. (2004). Antisocial behaviour and affiliation with delinquent peers. *Journal of Clinical Child and Adolescent Psychology, 33*, 336–346.

Heimer, K., & Matsueda, R. L. (1994). Role-taking, role commitment and delinquency: A theory of differential social control. *American Sociological Review, 59*, 365–390.

Hess, R. D., & Torney, J. V. (1967). *The development of political attitudes in children.* New York: Aldine.

Hindelang, M. J. (1973). Causes of delinquency: A partial replication and extension. *Social Problems, 17,* 502–517.

(1976). With a little help from their friends: Group participation in reported delinquent behaviour. *British Journal of Criminology, 16,* 105–125.

Hindelang, M. J., Hirschi, T., & Weiss, J. G. (1981). *Measuring delinquency.* Beverly Hills: Sage.

Hirschi, T. (1969). *Causes of delinquency.* Berkeley, CA: University of California Press.

Hirschi, T., & Hindelang, M. J. (1977). Intelligence and delinquency: A revisionist review. *American Sociological Review, 42,* 571–587.

Hoffman, M. (1983). Affective and cognitive processes in moral internalization. In E. T. Higgins, D. N. Ruble, & W. W. Hartup (Eds.), *Social cognition and social development: A socio-cultural perspective* (pp. 236–274). Cambridge: Cambridge University Press.

Houtzager, B., & Baerveldt, C. (1999). Just like normal: A social network study of the relation between petty crime and the intimacy of adolescent friendships. *Social Behavior and Personality, 27,* 177–192.

Jennings, W. S., Kilkenny, R., & Kohlberg, L. (1983). Moral development theory and practice for youthful and adult offenders. In W. S. Laufer & J. M. Day (Eds.), *Personality theory, moral development and criminal behavior.* Lexington, MA: Lexington Books/ Heath.

Jensen, G. F. (1972). Parents, peers and delinquent action: A test of the differential association hypothesis. *American Journal of Sociology, 78,* 562–576.

Jolliffe, D., Farrington, D. P., Hawkins, J. D., Catalano, R. F., Hill, K. G., & Kosterman, R. (2003). Predictive, concurrent, prospective and retrospective validity of self-reported delinquency. *Criminal Behaviour and Mental Health, 13,* 179–197.

Johnson, R. E. (1979). *Juvenile delinquency and its origins.* Cambridge: Cambridge University Press.

Johnson, L. M., Simons, R. L., & Conger, R. D. (2004). Criminal justice system involvement and continuity of youth crime: A longitudinal analysis. *Youth and Society, 36,* 3–29.

Kaplan, H. B. (1980). *Deviant behavior in defence of the self.* New York: Academic Press.

Kenny, D. A. (1994). *Interpersonal perception: A social relations analysis.* New York: Guilford.

Kohlberg, L. (1963). The development of children's orientation toward a moral order, I: Sequence in the development of human thought. *Vita Humana, 6,* 1–33.

Kohberg, L. (1971). From is to ought: How to commit the naturalistic fallacy and get away with it in the study of moral development. In T. Mischel (Ed.), *Cognitive development and epistemology* (pp. 151–236). New York: Academic Press.

Latane, B., & Darley, J. (1970). *The unresponsive bystander: Why doesn't he help?* New York: Appleton-Century-Crofts.

Laub, J. H., & Sampson, R. J. (2003). *Shared beginnings, divergent lives: Delinquent boys to age 70.* Cambridge, MA: Harvard University Press.

Le Bon, G. (1947). *The crowd: A study of the popular mind.* London: Ernest Benn. (Originally published 1895).

Lemert, E. M. (1951). *Social pathology: A systematic approach to the theory of socio-pathic behaviour.* New York: McGraw Hill.

(1967). *Human deviance, social problems and social control.* Englewood Cliffs, NJ: Prentice-Hall.

Levine, J. (1989). Reaction to opinion deviance in small groups. In P. B. Paulus (Ed.), *Psychology of group influence* (2nd ed., pp. 187–231). Hillsdale, NJ: Lawrence Erlbaum.

Levy, K. S. (2001). The relationship between adolescent attitudes toward authority, self-concept, and delinquency. *Adolescence, 36,* 333–346.

Lofland, J. H. (1969). *Deviance and identity.* New Jersey: Prentice-Hall.

Malloy, T. E., Albright, L., Kenny, D., Agatstein, F., & Winquist, L. (1997). Interpersonal perception and metaperception in nonoverlapping social groups. *Journal of Personality and Social Psychology, 72,* 390–398.

Maruna, S., LeBel, T. P., Mitchell, N., & Naples, M. (2004). Pygmalion in the reinte-gration process: Desistance from crime through the looking glass. *Psychology, Crime and Law, 10,* 271–281.

Matza, D. (1964). *Delinquency and drift.* New York: John Wiley.

Mead, G. H. (1934). *Mind, self and society.* Chicago: University of Chicago Press.

Menard, S., & Morse, B. J. (1984). A structuralist critique of the IQ-delinquency hypothesis: Theory and evidence. *American Journal of Sociology, 89,* 1347–1378.

Milgram, S. (1964). Group pressure and action against a person. *Journal of Abnormal and Social Psychology, 69,* 137–143.

Moffitt, T. E. (1993). Adolescent-limited and life-course persistent antisocial behav-iour: A developmental taxonomy. *Psychological Review, 100,* 675–701.

Moreno, J. L. (1934). *Who shall survive?* Washington: Nervous and Mental Disease Pub. Co.

Moscovici, S. (1976). *Social influence and social change.* London: Academic Press.

Moskowitz, D. S., & Schwartz, J. C. (1982). Validity comparison of behaviour counts and ratings by knowledgeable informants. *Journal of Personality and Social Psychology, 42,* 518–528.

Oplinger, J. (1990). *The politics of demonology: The European witch crazes and the mass production of deviance.* Selinsgrove, PA: Susquehanna University Press.

Piaget, J. (1932). *The moral judgment of the child.* London: Routledge.

Poulin, F., Dishion, T. J., & Haas, E. (1999). The peer influence paradox: Friendship quality and deviancy training within male adolescent friendships. *Merrill Palmer Quarterly, 45,* 42–61.

Radzinowitz, L. (1964). The criminal in society. *Journal of the Royal Society of Arts, 112,* 916–929.

Redfield, R. (1953). *The primitive world and its transformations.* Ithaca, NY: Cornell University Press.

Reicher, S., & Emler, N. (1985). Delinquent behaviour and attitudes to formal authority. *British Journal of Social Psychology, 3,* 161–168.

Rose, A. J., & Asher, S. R. (1999). Children's goals and strategies in response to con-flicts within a friendship. *Developmental Psychology, 35,* 69–79

Samenow, S. E. (1984). *Inside the criminal mind.* New York: Random House.

Schachter, S. (1951). Deviation, rejection and communication. *Journal of Abnormal and Social Psychology, 46,* 190–207.

Schur, E. (1973). *Radical non-intervention: Rethinking the delinquency problem.* Englewood Cliffs, NJ: Prentice Hall.

Shapland, J. (1978). Self reported delinquency in boys aged 11 to 14. *British Journal of Criminology, 18,* 256–266.

Shaw, C. R., & McKay, H. D. (1931). *Social factors in juvenile delinquency.* Washington, DC: U.S. Government Printing Office.

Sherif, M. (1935). A study of some social factors in perception. *Archives of Psychology, 2,* 187.

Shortt, J. W., Capaldi, D. M., Dishion, T. J., Bank, L., & Owen, L. D. (2003). The role of adolescent friends, romantic partners, and siblings in the emergence of adult antisocial lifestyle. *Journal of Family Psychology, 17,* 521–533.

Shweder, R., Mahapatra, M., & Miller, J. C. (1987). Culture and moral development. In J. Kagan & S. Lamb (Eds.), *The emergence of morality in young children* (pp. 1–83). Chicago: University of Chicago Press.

Skowronski, J., & Carlston, D. (1989). Negativity and extremity biases in impression formation. *Psychological Bulletin, 105,* 131–142.

(1992). Caught in the act: When impressions based on highly diagnostic behaviours are resistant to contradiction. *European Journal of Social Psychology, 22,* 435–442.

Smetana, J. (1990). Morality and conduct disorders. In M. Lewis & S. M. Miller (Eds.), *Handbook of developmental psychopathology.* New York: Plenum.

Spence, S. H. (1981). Differences in social skill performance between institutionalised juvenile male offenders and a comparable group of boys without offence records. *British Journal of Social and Clinical Psychology, 20,* 163–171.

Stouthamer-Loeber, M., Loeber, R., Hornish, D. L., & Wei, E. (2001). Maltreatment of boys and the development of disruptive and delinquent behaviour. *Development and Psychopathology, 13,* 941–955.

Sykes, G., & Matza, D. (1957). Techniques of neutralisation. *American Sociological Review, 22,* 664–670.

Tannenbaum, F. (1938). *Crime and community.* Boston: Ginn.

Tanner, J., Davies, S. & O'Grady, B. (1999). Whatever happened to yesterday's rebels? Longitudinal effects of teenage delinquency on education and occupational outcomes. *Social Problems, 46,* 250–274.

Tarry, H., & Emler, N. (unpub.) *Delinquency, moral reasoning and reputation management.* Unpublished manuscript, University of Surrey.

Thompson, B. (1994) *Sadomasochism.* London: Cassell.

Tremblay, R. E., Masse, L. C., Vitaro, F., & Dobkin, P. L. (1995). The impact of friends' deviant behaviour on early onset of delinquency: Longitudinal data from 6 to 13 years of age. *Development and Psychopathology, 7,* 649–667.

Turiel, E. (1983). *The development of social knowledge: Morality and convention.* Cambridge: Cambridge University Press.

Tyler, T. (2006). *Why people obey the law* (2nd ed.). Princeton, NJ: Princeton University Press.

Voss, M. L. (1969). Differential association and containment theory: A theoretical convergence. *Social Forces, 47,* 381–391.

Vuchnich, S., Bank, L., & Patterson, G. R. (1992). Parenting, peers and the stability of antisocial behaviour in preadolescent boys. *Developmental Psychology, 28,* 510–521.

Wallach, M. A., Kogan, N., & Bem, D. J. (1962). Group influence on risk taking. *Journal of Abnormal and Social Psychology, 65,* 76–86.

West, D. J., & Farrington, D. P. (1977). *The delinquent way of life.* London: Heinemann.

Willis, P. (1977). *Learning to labour: How working class kids get working class jobs.* Farnborough: Saxon House.

Wrong, D. H. (1961). The oversocialized conception of man in modern sociology. *American Sociological Review, 26,* 183–193.

Zhang, L. (1997). Informal reactions and delinquency. *Criminal Justice and Behavior, 24,* 129–150.

Zimbardo, P. (1969). The human choice: Individuation, reason and order versus deindividuation, impulse and chaos. In W. J. Arnold & D. Levine (Eds.), *Nebraska Symposium on Motivation* (Vol. 17). Lincoln, NE: University of Nebraska Press.

7

Minority-Group Identification: Responses to Discrimination When Group Membership Is Controllable

JOLANDA JETTEN AND NYLA R. BRANSCOMBE

In any given era, there may be a widespread consensus concerning what groups are seen as deserving of negative treatment. Indeed, such social-group memberships can represent a negative identity for those who are categorized as "one of them" (e.g., murderers, child abusers, smokers; see Crandall, Eshleman, & O'Brien, 2002). Likewise, groups that are consensually agreed upon as being positive (e.g., volunteer groups) have the potential to confer a positive social identity on their members. Social psychologists have assumed that a basic human desire to achieve and maintain a positive identity motivates people to seek membership in groups that are seen as positive and to avoid membership in groups that are seen as negative (Cialdini et al., 1976; Tajfel & Turner, 1979). Because people derive their identity in part from the groups to which they belong, it might seem, at first glance, to be rather contradictory to this central tenet in the field to find that some people remain loyal to groups that are seen as negative by other social groups or by society as a whole. Yet, clearly, many people choose to belong to a group even though they know they may face discrimination as a result.

What is more, we can point to many examples of people joining groups fully aware that this may make them vulnerable to discrimination (e.g., joining a feminist group or gay rights movement). In some extreme cases, people might even join such groups *precisely because of their devaluation by the powers that be.* Consider, for instance, people who seek out body piercings and identity markers such as tattoos; teenagers involved in youth cultures (e.g., Goths); or people who join various outlaw and rebel groups or political activist groups (including terrorist organizations) that may be perceived as radical, criminal, or dangerous by the general public. Such groups often emerge as a counterforce to those in power, and their raison d'être is to challenge mainstream culture. In such instances, differentiation from the mainstream can be a goal in itself (e.g., punks). At other times, such delineations may be best understood as part of a larger struggle for social change. While the amount of derision a person can expect can differ dramatically depending on what group he or she joins, it is almost inevitable that choosing to belong to a devalued group will be psychologically costly because it exposes the self to discrimination and exclusion from the dominant groups. Because the benefits of membership in a devalued group may not be apparent, outsiders may struggle to understand the motivation of people who choose to identify with such groups.

Why people maintain loyalty to groups that are devalued by others when they have a choice to leave the group is the central issue we address in this chapter. We propose that membership in a devalued group can serve different functions, which are contingent upon and determined by processes that are not different from general self-categorization processes – the perception of intragroup similarity and intergroup difference (Turner, Hogg, Oakes, Reicher, & Wetherell, 1987). However, the meaning that can be derived from emphasizing intragroup similarity and intergroup difference may differ for devalued groups compared with groups that are consensually defined as positive. For example, when members of valued groups stress intergroup differentiation, they underscore positive distinctiveness. For devalued groups, however, an emphasis on intergroup differentiation should be understood in the light of the exclusion that these groups experience. For devalued group members, emphasizing "us" versus "them" can serve to raise awareness of their group's devaluation. Such heightened salience of the ingroup's identity and the treatment it receives from other groups, facilitates the development among group members of a sense of common fate. This may be an important first step toward the development of a "politicized identity" in which groups respond to their devalued status collectively rather than individually (Simon & Klandermans, 2001).

Our starting assumption – that the reasons people choose to identify with devalued groups differ from the motivations for identifying with positively valued groups – raises some novel and interesting social-psychological issues. What processes underlie self-categorization as a member of a devalued group? Does the reason and function of self-categorization with a devalued group affect the nature of group identification? And, if it does, can we identify processes that are uniquely associated with choosing to identify with a devalued group? We draw on social identity theory (Tajfel, 1978a; Tajfel & Turner, 1979) and self-categorization theory (Turner et al., 1987) as we explore these questions. We start with an overview of research on the effects of choice of group membership on group identification, and then we examine whether identifying with a devalued group is compatible with core social identity theory principles.

SELF-SELECTED GROUP MEMBERSHIPS

Before examining why people may choose to identify with devalued groups, it is prudent for us to consider the effects of choosing one's group membership on group identification. To our knowledge, only a few studies have examined the effects of control over group membership on identification, and even fewer have examined choice of joining groups. For instance, Lindeman and Koskela (1994) examined the effect of group status and control over group membership on ingroup bias. Group status was manipulated by varying the size of the group with the numerical minority low in status and the numerical majority high in status. Lindeman and Koskela manipulated controllability of group membership by providing participants with false feedback that membership in a minimal group was under voluntary control or not (i.e., a permeability of group-boundaries manipulation). Because uncontrollable settings are, presumably, more threatening to high-status groups than to low-status groups, the researchers found that majority-group members displayed more ingroup bias in uncontrollable group-membership settings than in controllable group-membership settings. This effect was reversed for minority-group members, who showed more bias when group membership was controllable than when it was not controllable. Lindeman and Koskela (1994) explained their findings by assuming that minority-group identity becomes especially salient when group membership is controllable (compared to when it is not controllable). Enhanced ingroup bias in controllable settings may reflect perceptions of enhanced cognitive alternatives, which can result in a positive reevaluation of a perceived minority status. This finding is in line with other research showing that when individual mobility to a more desirable group is possible (permeable group boundaries), identification with the minority group is lower than when this option is not available (Ellemers, Van Knippenberg, & Wilke, 1990; Ellemers, Wilke, & Van Knippenberg, 1993; Tajfel & Turner, 1979).

Lindeman and Koskela examined controllability of group membership as perceptions of permeability of group boundaries *after* participants were categorized as group members. Ellemers, Kortekaas, and Ouwerkerk (1999) and Perreault and Bourhis (1999) examined more specifically whether or not choice of group membership *before* being categorized affected identification and ingroup bias. In both lines of research, participants were, following the typical minimal-group procedure, either assigned to a group or were given the chance to self-select a group. Perreault and Bourhis (1999) found that participants who chose their minimal group identified more with their group and also showed stronger ingroup bias than participants who did not have a choice. In a similar vein, Ellemers et al. (1999) showed that participants identified more strongly with self-selected groups than with groups whose membership was assigned by the experimenter. Ellemers and colleagues (1999) argued that the element of choice may help to explain why people typically identify more strongly with natural groups than with experimental or minimal groups.

However, other research has found that among natural groups the effects of self-selection on identification may not be that straightforward (Jetten, Schmitt, Branscombe, & McKimmie, 2004). We asked participants ($N = 199$) to think of a specific group to which they belonged that met the following criteria: First, participants were asked to think of a group that they joined either voluntarily or involuntarily. Half of the participants were also asked to select a group that was perceived "negatively by most other people," while the other half were asked to identify one that was "positively valued by those who do not belong to this group." This procedure allowed us to independently and interactively consider the effects of choice of group membership and valence of the group across a wide variety of natural-group memberships.

Two coders classified the participants' groups into four categories: (1) social groups (e.g., sports teams, group of friends; 35.2%); (2) work or study groups (23.1%); (3) social categories (e.g., sexual orientation, gender, class, ethnic group; 23.6%); and (4) belief-based groups (e.g., church groups, political groups; 18.1%). In addition, the two coders rated the size of the groups (small or large). A third, independent coder resolved the few disagreements that occurred between the other two coders.

We first examined the effects of choice on group identification. Controlling for the size of the groups, we did not replicate the Ellemers et al. (1999) finding where identification was higher in self-selected groups compared to those where membership was imposed. Identification did not differ in the self-selected groups and in the involuntary-membership groups. One reason for the different findings of our study and the Ellemers et al. (1999) results may concern the different procedures used in these different investigations. The choice manipulation in the study by Ellemers et al. (1999) may have heightened participant involvement: because participants experienced a sense of control this could well have led them to take a more active interest in the group and consequently to value it more. Rather than clarifying the effects of choice, the higher identification for self-selected groups found in the Ellemers et al. (1999) study may inform us about what happens when the experimenter hands over some control to the participant. Our findings suggest that choice per se may not be a strong predictor of group identification.

The second finding from our study that is relevant here is that valence of the group had no effect on the extent to which group members identified with it. Furthermore, the interaction between valence and choice of group membership on group identification was not significant. This suggests that devalued self-selected group memberships are not less meaningful or important to participants than other groups they belong to that are not devalued or not self-selected. However, even though the manipulation checks of the choice and value manipulation confirmed the success of these manipulations, it is important to be cautious in drawing strong conclusions from this study because there may be other methodological reasons why we found no effect of these manipulations on identification.

WHEN MEMBERSHIP IN A DEVALUED GROUP IS CONTROLLABLE

One of the core tenets of social identity theory is that group members are motivated to achieve positive intergroup distinctiveness because doing so reflects positively on the self (Tajfel & Turner, 1979). According to this reasoning, it should be more difficult for devalued groups to compare favorably with other groups than it is for positively valued groups to do so. Thus, group identification should be negatively affected by membership in a devalued group to the extent that such groups cannot provide a positive intergroup comparison. As a result, members of devalued groups should aim to improve their status or to rid themselves of their devalued status, either individually or as a group. However, this implied relationship between public regard and importance attached to the devalued identity has not been supported in a variety of correlational studies (see Ashmore, Deaux, McLaughlin-Volpe, 2004). What is more, when significant correlations have been found, they are not positive, as one might expect. Instead, the correlations are negative: the lower the public regard for the group, the more identity is perceived as important for self-definition. This relationship between public regard and self-definition has been repeatedly found in a host of groups for which membership is not controllable, including gender and ethnic groups (see Branscombe, Schmitt, & Harvey, 1999; Schmitt, Branscombe, Kobrynowicz, & Owen, 2002).

At first glance, the observation that people maintain identification with devalued groups may appear inconsistent with the emphasis in social identity theory on positive distinctiveness. Specifically, why would people identify with a group when they can avoid the devalued-group membership, and when they can engage in individual mobility? There are at least two reasons why it would be erroneous to suggest that social identity theory predicts a straightforward positive relationship between the positive distinctiveness opportunities an identity provides and group identification. First, such a reading of social identity theory implies a rather simplistic account of the core motivations underlying devalued-group members' behavior. Even though an analysis focusing on the search for positive distinctiveness has proven to be useful for understanding certain group processes, it also runs the danger of providing a fairly mechanistic analysis of devalued groups' motivations. Second, even if the motivation to seek out positive differentiation is prevalent among those maintaining identification with devalued groups, the way this motivation affects behavior is likely to be determined by the broader sociostructural context in which the groups are situated. That is, perceptions of permeability of group boundaries, perceptions of legitimacy of the devalued status and discrimination against individual group members, and the likelihood that intergroup relations may change in the future all affect the meaning and content of a devalued-group identity (Branscombe & Ellemers, 1998; Tajfel & Turner, 1979)

Interestingly, Tajfel (1978b) warned against assuming a straightforward relation between-group status and identification. He argued that social-change beliefs may be perfectly compatible with having ample opportunities for individual mobility (i.e., being able to avoid membership in a devalued group). Indeed, Tajfel pointed out that group members may emphasize and intensify collective attempts to address status inequality, even though individual mobility is clearly an option available to them (1978b, p. 55). Precisely because there is a choice, cognitive alternatives to the low-status position become salient, which reinforces the need for a collective rather than individual approach. As Tajfel put it, "the problems of social identity of the inferior group would not necessarily express themselves in social behavior until and unless there is some awareness that the existing social reality is not the only possible one and that alternatives to it are conceivable and perhaps attainable" (1978b, p. 94). He then outlines a number of strategies that devalued groups can engage in to construct such alternative representations. One such strategy involves the creation of a new identity via engaging in social action that allows for differentiation from the dominant group.

Accordingly, the proposed tension between membership in a devalued group and the search for a positive identity is more apparent than real. Paradoxically, as Tajfel discussed, opportunities for social mobility can reinforce the motivation to engage in social change. On this basis, we will explore a social identity theory and self-categorization theory account of controllable devalued-group memberships. In particular, we are interested in addressing the question of whether people identify with groups precisely *because* they are devalued.

Before addressing this question, it is important to highlight two points. First, maintaining identification with a devalued group does not necessarily involve a conscious, well-reasoned choice at one moment in time. It often involves a slow process of becoming increasingly immersed in a minority group over time as a result of an interactive dynamic where initial exclusion by the mainstream leads to distancing from it, and this in turn invites further discrimination and exclusion by the mainstream. For instance, people may sympathize with the feminist cause and become increasingly involved in it over time to the point that it becomes an important aspect of self-definition. It is only at these later stages that the perception of the mainstream as an outgroup is strengthened and the us-versus-them categorization becomes more salient (Emler & Reicher, 2005; Tajfel, 1978b).

Second, membership in a devalued group cannot always be clearly defined; there is often a grey area consisting of people who sympathize with the devalued group but will not openly self-define as members. For instance, Griffin (1989) discusses the difference between women who openly identify as feminist and those who sympathize with feminist ideals but do not self-identify as feminist ("I'm not a women's libber, but ..."). Thus, whereas the former group has signed up for a collectivist struggle, the latter group embraces the ideology in a more covert and individualist way, and disavows the group identity. This distinction can be traced to the negative image of feminism; some women will not take on the feminist label in order to avoid the negative consequences of being associated with this group, whereas other women will self-define as feminists despite, or even because of, the negative label. That is, a negative response from society may come to epitomize for feminists the need for a collective response and strengthen the perceived collective nature of the cause.

WHY PEOPLE IDENTIFY WITH GROUPS THAT ARE DEVALUED

We propose that in order to understand identification with a devalued group, one has to examine the more basic process of how self-categorization is affected by external threats (i.e., discrimination). Self-categorization theory posits that forces within the group (intragroup cohesion or the extent to which "we are in this together") and forces between groups (us-versus-them dynamics) concurrently affect self-categorization (Turner et al., 1987).

Self-categorization as a group member is strengthened when perceived within-group similarities and between-group differences are maximized (comparative fit and the metacontrast principle).*

Previous research has provided empirical evidence that threats to the group's identity enhances perceptions of intragroup similarity and intergroup differentiation. For instance, when the value of the ingroup is threatened, high identifiers, in particular, emphasize the homogeneity of the ingroup (Doosje, Ellemers, & Spears, 1995; Ellemers, Spears, & Doosje, 1997) and self-stereotype as a group member to a greater extent (Spears, Doosje, & Ellemers, 1997). More generally, research testing the rejection-identification model has shown how perceptions of discrimination are associated with increased group identification and belonging. Increased identification, in turn, has been found to protect well-being (Branscombe et al., 1999; Jetten, Branscombe, Schmitt, & Spears, 2001). There is also evidence that self-categorization is strengthened by emphasizing intergroup differentiation (e.g., setting one's own group apart, signaling to all that it is different). For instance, Mlicki and Ellemers (1996) showed that Polish participants expressed their national identification by underlining their distinctiveness from participants from other European countries (even though this meant engaging in a negative intergroup comparison). Likewise, African-Americans who live primarily in contexts with other Blacks differentiate their experiences from Whites more and self-categorize in racial terms compared with African-Americans who spend their lives among White Americans (Postmes & Branscombe, 2002).

The view that intragroup and intergroup processes (in particular, those relating to perceived intergroup distinctiveness) mutually affect identification has received considerable attention in recent research. For instance, research by Jetten et al. (2001) showed that identification with other people with body piercings following an expectation of discrimination was determined jointly by perceptions of intragroup similarity and intergroup differentiation (being different from the mainstream). In a similar vein, Postmes and Branscombe (2002) demonstrated that identification as African-American was determined, not only by perceptions of acceptance by the ingroup (intragroup), but also by perceived rejection by the outgroup (intergroup). Finally, Branscombe, Spears, Ellemers, and Doosje (2002) found the highest group identification when members felt respected by their ingroup and when their ingroup was devalued by another group.

---

* Interestingly, in previous research, group identification has been primarily assessed by items referring to similarity to other ingroup members and commitment to the group. Questions assessing how identification is affected by comparisons with other groups are frequently lacking (see Jackson & Smith, 1999).

Experimental evidence further shows that intragroup and intergroup processes jointly determine group identification following threats to the value of a group (Jetten, Schmitt, Branscombe, & McKimmie, 2005). We provided participants with false feedback that other groups viewed their state (Queensland, Australia) positively or negatively. We then assessed identification with Queensland, intragroup processes relating to the extent to which people felt respected by other ingroup members, and intergroup differentiation (i.e., perceived differences between Queensland and other Australian states).

We found that threats to the value of the group did not significantly affect group identification. However, the relationship between the presence of threat to the group value and group identification changed when we took into account the mediating role of self-categorization processes. Specifically, as predicted, the two components of self-categorization (intergroup and intragroup processes) were emphasized when the group value was threatened. That is, value threat led participants to emphasize that their state was different from other Australian states and that they received respect from their fellow Queenslanders. Both intergroup differentiation and intragroup respect, in turn, affected group identification positively. Mediational analyses revealed a suppressor effect: when controlling for the indirect positive effect from a value threat to group identification (through intergroup differentiation and intragroup respect), a direct negative effect between value threat and group identification emerged. It thus appears that intergroup differentiation and intragroup respect counteracted any direct negative effect of threats to the group value on group identification.

In other words, emphasizing intragroup respect and intergroup differentiation appear to be distinct means by which group members maintain or enhance social identity. For those who belong to a group whose value is under threat, self-categorization as a group member can buffer against such threat, and protect identification against their negative effects. This process involves emphasizing both the rewards derived from group belongingness and the gulf between "us" and "them." Such enhanced perceptions of intragroup rewards and intergroup differentiation increase group identification, which in turn counteracts the negative relation between threats to group value and group identification. Because self-categorization processes hide harmful effects of threats to the group value on group identification, the direct relation is only revealed when controlling for the influence of intragroup reward and intergroup differentiation.

It is likely that perceived intragroup similarity and intergroup differentiation are central to self-categorization and identification with most social groups (Tajfel & Turner, 1979), although the relative strength of these

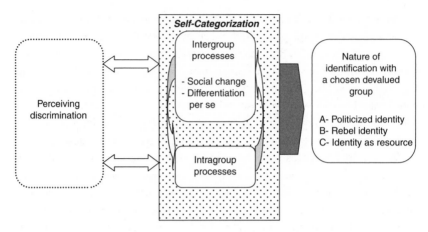

FIGURE 7.1. The relationship between perceiving discrimination and nature of group identification: The role of intragroup processes and intergroup differentiation in self-categorization.

processes may differ. We propose that the relative strength of these processes is an important determinant of the type of collective identity that emerges following perceptions of discrimination. That is, the nature of identification is likely to differ depending on whether categorization stems from an emphasis on intergroup differentiation or from emphasis on intragroup similarity. These processes are represented in Figure 7.1. Importantly, perceptions of intergroup differentiation and intragroup similarity are intertwined and mutually affect each other. That is, when groups emphasize their distinctiveness from other groups, this is likely to affect intragroup processes and perceptions, and vice versa.

Below, we outline the influence of perceiving discrimination on self-categorization that is driven predominantly by an emphasis on intergroup differentiation versus a focus on intragroup processes. We then turn to the nature of identification and how it may be affected by the different motivations underlying the choice of devalued group membership.

INTERGROUP DIFFERENTIATION UNDERLYING
IDENTIFICATION WITH A DEVALUED GROUP

Those who perceive themselves as discriminated against may identify with a devalued group in order to emphasize the ingroup's difference from the people who are doing the discriminating. Regardless of whether or not group membership in the devalued group is controllable, polarization away from the dominant group via emphasizing intergroup differences may be an important first step to prepare for collective action (Simon & Klandermans, 2001). This is nicely illustrated in the following interchange between a court judge and the Black activist Steve Biko during South Africa's apartheid period:

> JUDGE BOSHOFF: But now why do you refer to you people as blacks? Why not brown people? I mean you people are more brown than black.
> BIKO: In the same way as I think white people are more pink and yellow and pale than white.
> [General laughter in the court]
> JUDGE BOSHOFF: Quite ... but now why do you not use the word brown then?
> BIKO: No, I think really, historically, we have been defined as black people, and when we reject the term non-white and take upon ourselves the right to call ourselves what we think we are, we have got available in front of us a whole number of alternatives,... and we choose this one precisely because we feel it is most accommodating. (Biko, 1978, p. 121)

Thus, when provided with the opportunity to downplay intergroup differences, Steve Biko instead chooses to emphasize the distinctiveness of categories. In this way, Biko strengthens the us-versus-them distinction and paves the way for a collective response to discrimination. The identity becomes politicized because the group's aim is to challenge those in power. Intergroup-distinctiveness perceptions strengthen collective identification that is ultimately aimed at improving the status of the devalued group (see also Haslam, Postmes, & Jetten, 2004; Simon & Klandermans, 2001).

The processes at play for people who choose membership in a devalued group are not any different. Like members of classic minorities whose identity is politicized (e.g., Blacks), people who have chosen their devalued group membership are not interested in finding ways of avoiding stigma or downplaying their stigmatized identity. Rather, they are motivated to emphasize their group membership and differences from the mainstream (see Jetten et al., 2005). What the case of controllable devalued-group membership makes clear is that, under some conditions, intergroup differentiation per se may be sought out. That is, emphasizing intergroup differentiation may not only result from a long history of persecution and discrimination that demands a collective response (as Steve Biko's case exemplies); differentiation itself may be the goal.

In those cases where differentiation is the goal, the basis of identification and self-definition is not so much related to emphasizing similarity to other ingroup members; rather, the focus is on the outgroup and how the self and similar others differ from it. By contrasting the ingroup from relevant outgroups, the ingroup is more clearly defined. Thus, knowing *who one is not* may be just as important to establishing a meaningful identity as is knowing whom the self is similar to or *who one is*. Spears, Jetten and Scheepers (2002) label this type of intergroup differentiation "creative distinctiveness." Groups that perceive themselves as insufficiently distinct from other groups may seek out ways to differentiate themselves. This process may be driven by a motivation to gain a more meaningful identity, but it may also be a response to discriminatory treatment (see Jetten et al., 2001).

INTRAGROUP PROCESSES UNDERLYING IDENTIFICATION WITH A DEVALUED GROUP

Social identity theory was developed in an attempt to counteract individual-level explanations of social phenomena. It has accordingly focused on the relations between groups, particularly how broad socio-structural variables (e.g., group status) affect group identification. As a result, social identity theorizing has mainly focused on the role of intergroup processes, and theorizing with respect to intragroup processes has only recently captured the attention of social identity theorists (e.g., research on the role of intragroup respect in maintaining group identification, see Branscombe et al., 2002; Hogg, 1996; Postmes & Jetten, 2006; Simon & Stürmer, 2003).

Research examining the consequences of perceptions of discrimination has focused on how group identification can counteract and act as a buffer against the negative consequences of perceiving discrimination (see Branscombe et al., 1999; Postmes & Branscombe, 2002). For instance, Jetten et al. (2005) show how group members emphasize the respect they receive from fellow ingroup members following threats to the value of the group. Perceptions of ingroup respect in turn relate positively to group identification. More generally, identities can be resources that members draw upon when confronted with negative treatment, and they can be a source of stress buffering and resistance in times of intergroup turmoil (see Haslam, 2004).

Membership in some devalued groups may occur because individuals are victimized and then join others for support and solidarity. Thus, rather than accepting the negative treatment they face, they respond by seeking out others who face a similar fate. At other times, however, people may not face discrimination as individuals, but only experience discriminatory treatment when they voluntarily join a devalued group (e.g., taking on body piercings). However, even for these individuals, identification may still be an important resource. By making themselves vulnerable to becoming targets of discrimination, identification with similar others will be strengthened over time. This dynamic is likely to overshadow and become more important than the fact that membership in the devalued group was avoidable.

THE NATURE OF IDENTIFICATION WITH DEVALUED GROUPS WHEN MEMBERSHIP IS CONTROLLABLE

We propose that the relative emphasis on intragroup versus intergroup processes affects, not only the strength, but also the nature of identification with a devalued group. That is, if identification with a devalued group is mainly driven by intergroup processes, the consequences and the way the identity is experienced are likely to differ from when an identity is mainly embraced because it represents a resource. Specifically, we propose that because the nature of identification is affected by the strength of intragroup versus intergroup factors, this will have consequences for the content and meaning of the identity (e.g., ideology) and for the willingness of group members to engage in collective action.

In the remainder of this chapter, we consider how the interplay between intragroup and intergroup self-categorization can affect the nature of identification, and we identify three different bases of identification. Although there may be considerable overlap among these three bases of identification, and processes associated with them may occur simultaneously, it is worthwhile to theoretically tease apart these processes in order to examine their unique effects. We propose that when self-categorization is predominantly determined by intergroup differentiation, identification can either reflect a social-change ideology (politicized identity) or be driven by intergroup differentiation per se, harnessing a "being different" identity (e.g., rebel identity). When intragroup processes are the main drivers of self-categorization, identification with a group mainly reflects and captures a resource function.

The differences between these three different bases of identity are quite subtle, but we argue that the function of identification is slightly different for each one of these three types of devalued groups, affecting the way they respond to negative treatment. Specifically, we will argue that devalued groups with a politicized identity aim to draw attention to differences in order to increase broad acceptance of "being different." In contrast, being different is a goal in itself for the second cluster of devalued identities – rebel groups. Emphasizing intergroup differences serves the function of providing meaning and differences are nourished because they provide the main reason for existence for these minority groups. The third cluster brings together devalued groups where identification is a response to being discriminated against. The three different bases of identification are discussed in more detail below.

POLITICIZED IDENTITIES: DRAWING ATTENTION TO DIFFERENCES TO INCREASE ACCEPTANCE

The motivation of group members whose identity is politicized as a means of facilitating social change has been at the heart of social identity theorizing, and the processes involved are reasonably well understood. For instance, Simon and Klandermans (2001) describe how groups develop a more politicized identity only when they become aware of (a) shared grievances that lead to (b) the identification of a group that is to blame for the suffering that ingroup members face, and (c) society at large or a third party is involved in the power struggle. This analysis is quite compatible with our proposal that perceptions of discrimination lead to increased salience of the intergroup context in which the ingroup is perceived as separate and distinct from the outgroup.

Even though there may be costs associated with maintaining membership in groups that face devaluation (e.g., feminist groups, the gay rights movement), people may be willing to pay a price in order to facilitate collective action and social change. Because membership is associated with a collective struggle, group membership is not aimed at downplaying differences, but on drawing attention to differences to increase broad acceptance of "being different."

We propose that people will remain members of a politicized group if the social-change agenda remains strong and if the ideology is reinforced over time. In these cases, the potential costs of being discriminated against are compensated for by the psychological benefits of membership in a group with a cause that is worth fighting for. Indeed, perceptions of collective efficacy are often not the best predictor of identification with these groups. Drury and Reicher (2005) found in an ethnographic study of two collective-action movements that the emotions associated with the action were not reducible to success of the actions. Rather, taking part in collective action and expressing social identity reinforced feelings of empowerment and identity, independent of success at bringing about the desired change.

It may even be the case that the motivation to remain a member of that particular devalued group may wane when social change has successfully been achieved (e.g., greater equality or mainstream acceptance of "being different"). That is, precisely when discrimination against the group comes to be seen as something of the past (e.g., is no longer pervasive), there may be less need for individuals to engage in a collective struggle. As a result, the nature of identification with such groups may change over time. Group actions may no longer be directed at emphasizing intergroup differentiation or at challenging outgroups.

REBEL IDENTITIES: WHEN BEING DIFFERENT IS A GROUP'S RAISON D'ETRE

When being different lies at the heart of the group identity, the choice to join the group is often associated with rebellion against the mainstream (Jetten, Branscombe, & Spears, 2006). Rather than trying to convince the majority of the ingroup's value, members may take pride in and emphasize their "differentness." Indeed, devalued status itself can provide distinctiveness and meaning, with relevant differences being nourished and further cultivated. When members of such groups encounter discrimination, the motivation to be different is strengthened and emphasized. For groups whose main purpose is to differentiate from the mainstream, it is likely that not being noticed by the majority (and therefore not being seen as different) will be disempowering and undermine the identity. Whereas collective action stemming from perceptions of pervasive discrimination among some devalued groups may be directed at reducing discriminatory treatment, for rebel groups, discrimination is very much needed to reinforce the rebel identity. This has been demonstrated quantitatively (see Jetten et al., 2001), but it is also evident from qualitative reports of people who perceive hostility from others because of their body piercings. Wojcik (1995) reports, from interviews with people with body piercings: "When I asked if experiences like that (being discriminated) ever made him question the types of body adornments he had chosen, he firmly responded, 'No, it made me want to do it more…It made me want to be more extreme'" (p. 32).

When being different is the basis of social identification with a devalued group, any attempts to undermine intergroup distinctiveness are likely to be perceived as identity threats. For instance, the ultimate threat for subcultures and groups that embrace a rebel identity may be being copied, particularly by the mainstream. Irwin (2003), for example, notes that many core members of the tattoo world are waiting for the "time when tattoos will go out of fashion" (p. 38). Thus, the main motivation of these groups may be to keep the boundaries clear and to keep out others who may popularize and undermine the rebel status of the group. The focus is very much on keeping the us-versus-them distinction alive; joining the majority group is not a desirable option.

Paradoxically, however, the way that distinctiveness is sought out by rebel groups may be informed by and rely heavily on mainstream culture. For example, Irwin (2003) describes how tattoo collectors (an elite subgroup in the tattoo community) strive to express many of the fine-art forms (typically associated with high class) in their tattoos. Thus, these tattoo collectors seek differentiation from the mainstream while simultaneously conforming to its standards of artistic merit. It is unlikely, however, that tattoo collectors perceive this as conforming to the mainstream. Rather, intergroup distinctiveness is emphasized by making use of the mainstream's standards of art and transforming them into ingroup beauty. The fact that the tattoo art is often recognized as high-quality by the mainstream can add to the status of the tattoo collector within the rebel group.

IDENTITIES AS RESOURCE: MINORITY IDENTIFICATION AS A BUFFER AGAINST DISCRIMINATION

At times, people's motivation to join a devalued group mainly reflects the psychological rewards associated with membership. Whereas some people may turn to a devalued group for support in dealing with negative treatment (Tajfel & Turner, 1979), for others, the function of identification may relate to facilitating meaning construction, identity formation, and the development of a politicized or rebel identity. That is, group identification may not only serve the function of counteracting the negative effects on well-being, it may also be associated with developing, cultivating, and nourishing a new identity as a way of being different from other groups. In particular for groups that have a strong politicized identity (e.g., feminist groups), membership and identification is a resource because it allows for the collective development of an identity that can act as a counterforce against the dominant group.

The broader sociostructural context plays an important role in determining the nature of the resource function of group identification. In particular, perceptions of the legitimacy or illegitimacy of the discrimination plays an important role in determining whether devalued-group identification is aimed at facilitating collective action or whether it is merely a support resource (see Schmitt & Branscombe, 2002). Of course, many forms of discrimination are perceived to be illegitimate, particularly those that are often studied (e.g., Branscombe et al., 1999; Crandall et al., 2002). However, there are also examples of discrimination that is perceived by both the victim and the perpetrator as legitimate. Consider, for example, the exclusion of people who are HIV positive from blood donation or excluding smokers from doing so in public buildings. Researchers have rarely addressed the extent to which perceptions of legitimacy might moderate the identity consequences of discrimination. We conducted a series of studies examining the moderating role of the perceived legitimacy of discrimination. We argued that perceptions of discrimination might have very different consequences depending on whether it is perceived as legitimate or as illegitimate.

We predicted that when group members perceive discrimination to be illegitimate, they are more likely to respond collectively to discriminatory treatment and to directly challenge the majority group. Increasing awareness of shared discriminatory experiences with other ingroup members should lead to increased group-identity commitment. Conversely, any collective response to discrimination should be weaker when the ingroup perceives the discrimination they experience as justified. Because legitimate discrimination is likely to erode the collective basis of responding to exclusion, group identification may wane because the devalued group has lost its utility as a resource.

We recently obtained evidence in a series of studies in groups whose membership is not controllable (Mexican-Americans) and groups where membership is, at least to some extent, controllable (people with body piercings and smokers) that legitimacy of discrimination perceptions moderate the extent to which group identification can be seen as a resource to counteract discriminatory treatment (Jetten, Schmitt, Branscombe, Garza, & Mewse, 2009). We found that discriminatory treatment only led to greater ingroup commitment in contexts in which ingroup members face pervasive and illegitimate exclusion. In contrast, in contexts in which group-based discriminatory treatment was perceived as legitimate, pervasive discrimination undermined group commitment.

It is important to note that our predictions concerning the effects of pervasiveness and legitimacy were confirmed in all samples, regardless of whether or not group membership was controllable. This supports our argument that, even when an exit strategy is available to members of devalued groups, as is the case when group membership is controllable, people may not select this option. Paradoxically, our results suggest that, even when members have an individual exit option, the conditions under which discrimination is most likely to affect the individual negatively (pervasive and illegitimate discrimination), may lead members to further increase their identification with the devalued group and to respond collectively to the threat they face (Tajfel, 1978).

These results highlight the important role of perceptions of legitimacy of discrimination when responding to discrimination. Increased awareness of shared discriminatory experiences with other ingroup members affected the nature of group commitment. It reflected a more politicized identity and was aimed at facilitating collective action when discrimination was perceived as illegitimate and pervasive. When discrimination is perceived as illegitimate, devalued groups can redefine the intergroup context by taking on an identity that allows them to turn a shameful label into pride (see Schmitt, Spears, & Branscombe, 2003). Such meaning-seeking may not be limited to devalued groups where membership is controllable, but may also be found among minority groups for whom group membership is uncontrollable. Such groups may seek out new identities that emphasize rather than downplay aspects of the devalued status. For instance, Ben-Eliezer (2004) discusses how responding to discrimination can also involve choosing to emphasize the devalued identity. New identities can emerge because old identities appear not capable of meeting intergroup distinctiveness needs. He found that Ethiopian Jews in Israel who do not feel that they are accepted as Jews cope with that exclusion by emphasizing their Black identity (resurrecting their ethnic language and music and by taking on African names). As Ben-Eliezer puts it: "It was in Israel that Ethiopian Jews became black" (2004, p. 259). Interestingly, Ethiopian Jews emphasize the dimension of comparison that sets them apart from White Jews and that is the very basis of the discrimination they face. This example suggests that other ingroup members are not sought out to provide social support per se; rather, the emphasis is on identity development and intergroup differentiation. This may be a social creativity strategy (e.g., seeking out new dimensions of comparison; Tajfel & Turner, 1979), but it is also clear that this could be the first step towards mobilizing the group to engage in social change (Simon & Klandermans, 2001, see also Tajfel, 1978).

CONCLUDING COMMENTS

We started this chapter with the observation that, while research has often focused on the conditions under which devalued group members take the opportunity to leave a group (individual mobility), there is not much research that explores what keeps people in groups when devalued group membership is under their own control. Perhaps this question has largely been left unexplored because researchers and lay people alike start from the assumption that people avoid membership in groups that may attract negative treatment from others. Thus, joining a devalued group is not seen as something that people do, or would do, if they had a choice. However, it is not hard to find devalued groups where membership is voluntary and controllable. What is more, research shows that people may cherish their devalued identities (chosen or not) just as much as they cherish their valued identities. We started this chapter with the assumption that, to fully understand issues surrounding voluntary membership in devalued groups, we should not just be asking when members stay or leave devalued groups. It is important to also consider why they identify with such groups.

We proposed that the same self-categorization processes that drive identification with valued groups can lead people to seek out membership in a consensually defined devalued group. Identification with such groups is affected jointly by intragroup and intergroup processes and follows meta-contrast principles (see Turner et al., 1987). We considered how the strength of intragroup versus intergroup processes affects the nature of identification with a devalued group. At times, intergroup differences are emphasized in order to pave the way for a collective response to negative treatment by other groups. Other devalued groups, however, attract members because they provide differentiation per se from the mainstream. Finally, devalued groups may attract members because identifying with these groups provides a resource to counteract negative treatment.

Even though these processes may not be unique to the study of why people join devalued groups – and they are likely to play a role in any type of context where people identify with groups that are under threat – it is nonetheless evident that these processes may become especially visible when controllable or voluntary devalued group memberships are examined. This is because it becomes immediately clear when we examine these groups that simply assuming that identification merely reflects positive differentiation opportunities is not sufficient. Moving beyond such processes, previously unexplored motivations of those who are confronted with discrimination become more obvious. For instance, differences are not downplayed but emphasized following discrimination, and identification with these devalued groups can be seen as an indirect way of coping with perceived discrimination and protecting group-based esteem (Branscombe et al., 1999). The different responses to group-based discrimination outlined in this chapter are important in their own right if we are to understand the psychology of devalued groups.

REFERENCES

Ashmore, R. D., Deaux, K., & McLaughlin-Volpe, T. (2004). An organizing framework for collective identity: Articulation and significance of multidimensionality. *Psychological Bulletin, 130,* 80–114.

Ben-Eliezer, U. (2004). Becoming a black Jew: Cultural racism and anti-racism in contemporary Israel. *Social Identities, 10,* 245–266.

Biko, B. S. (1978). *I write what I like.* London, UK: Penguin.

Branscombe, N. R., & Ellemers, N. (1998). Coping with group-based discrimination: Individualistic versus group-level strategies. In J. K. Swim & C. Stangor (Eds.), *Prejudice: The target's perspective* (pp. 243–266). New York: Academic Press.

Branscombe, N. R., Schmitt, M. T., & Harvey, R. D. (1999). Perceiving pervasive discrimination among African-Americans: Implications for group identification and well-being. *Journal of Personality and Social Psychology, 77,* 135–149.

Branscombe, N. R., Spears, R., Ellemers, N., & Doosje, B. (2002). Intragroup and intergroup evaluation effects on group behavior. *Personality and Social Psychology Bulletin, 28,* 744–753.

Cialdini, R. B., Borden, R., Thorne, A., Walker, M., Freeman, S., & Sloan, L. (1976). Basking in reflected glory: Three (football) field studies. *Journal of Personality and Social Psychology, 34,* 366–375.

Crandall, C. S., Eshleman, A., & O'Brien, L. (2002). Social norms and the expression and suppression of prejudice: The struggle for internalization. *Journal of Personality and Social Psychology, 3,* 359–378.

Doosje, B., Ellemers, N., & Spears, R. (1995). Perceived intragroup variability as a function of group status and identification. *Journal of Experimental and Social Psychology, 31,* 410–436.

Drury, J., & Reicher, S. (2005). Explaining enduring empowerment: A comparative study of collective action and psychological outcomes. *European Journal of Social Psychology, 35,* 1–22.

Ellemers, N., Kortekaas, P., & Ouwerkerk, J. W. (1999). Self-categorization, commitment to the group and group self-esteem as related but distinct aspects of social identity. *European Journal of Social Psychology, 29,* 371–389.

Ellemers, N., Spears, R., & Doosje, B. (1997). Sticking together or falling apart: Group identification as a psychological determinant of group commitment versus individual mobility. *Journal of Personality and Social Psychology, 72,* 617–626.

Ellemers, N., Van Knippenberg, A., & Wilke, H. (1990). The influence of permeability of group boundaries and stability of group status on strategies of individual mobility and social change. *British Journal of Social Psychology, 29,* 233–246.

Ellemers, N., Wilke, H., & van Knippenberg, (1993). Effects of the legitimacy of low group or individual status on individual and collective status-enhancement strategies. *Journal of Personality and Social Psychology, 64,* 766–778.

Emler, N., & Reicher, S. (2005). Delinquency: Cause or consequence of social exclusion. In D. Abrams, M. A. Hogg, & J. M. Marques (Eds.), *The social psychology of inclusion and exclusion* (pp. 211–242). New York: Psychology Press.

Griffin, C. (1989). "I'm not a women's libber, but …" Feminist consciousness and gender identity. In S. Skevington & D. Baker (Eds.), *The Social Identity of Women* (pp. 173–193). London: Sage.

Haslam, S. A. (2004). *Psychology in organizations: The social identity approach* (2nd ed.). London, UK: Sage.

Haslam, S. A., Postmes, T., & Jetten, J. (2004). Beyond balance: To understand 'bias', social psychology needs to address issues of politics, power and social perspective. *Behavioral and Brain Sciences, 27*, 341–342.

Hogg, M. A. (1996). Intragroup processes, group structure and social identity. In W. P. Robinson (Ed.), *Social groups and identities: Developing the legacy of Henri Tajfel* (pp. 65–93). Oxford: Butterworth Heinemann.

Irwin, K. (2003). Saints and sinners: Elite tattoo collectors and tattooists as positive and negative deviants. *Sociological Spectrum, 23*, 27–57.

Jetten, J., Branscombe, N. R., Schmitt, M. T., & Spears, R. (2001). Rebels with a cause: Group identification as a response to perceived discrimination from the mainstream. *Personality and Social Psychology Bulletin, 27*, 1204–1213.

Jetten, J., Branscombe, N. R., & Spears, R. (2006). Living on the edge: Dynamics of intragroup and intergroup rejection experiences. In R. Brown & D. Capozza (Eds.), *Social identities: Motivational, emotional and cultural influences* (pp. 91–108). London, UK: Sage.

Jetten, J., Schmitt, M. T., Branscombe, N. R., & McKimmie, B. M. (2004). *Social creativity strategies as a way to maintain group identification.* Paper presented at a small group meeting: Hoping and Coping. Grenoble, France.

Jetten, J., Schmitt, M. T., Branscombe, N. R., & McKimmie, B. M. (2005). Suppressing the negative effect of devaluation on group identification: The role of intergroup differentiation and intragroup respect. *Journal of Experimental Social Psychology, 41*, 208–215.

Jetten, J., Schmitt, M. T., Branscombe, N. R., Garza, A. A., & Mewse, A. J. (2009). *Group commitment in the face of discrimination: The role of legitimacy appraisals.* Manuscript submitted for publication.

Lindeman, M., & Koskela, P. (1994). Group size, controllability of group membership, and competitive dimension as determinants of intergroup discrimination. *European Journal of Social Psychology, 24*, 267–278.

Mlicki, P., & Ellemers, N. (1996). Being different of being better? National stereotypes and identification of Polish and Dutch students. *European Journal of Social Psychology, 26*, 97–114.

Perreault, S., & Bourhis, R. Y. (1999). Ethnocentrism, social identification and discrimination. *Personality and Social Psychology Bulletin, 25*, 92–103.

Postmes, T., & Branscombe, N. R. (2002). Influence of long-term racial environmental composition on subjective well-being in African Americans. *Journal of Personality and Social Psychology, 83*, 735–751.

Postmes, T., & Jetten, J. (2006). *Individuality and the group: Advances in social identity.* London, UK: Sage.

Schmitt, M. T., & Branscombe, N. R. (2002). The meaning and consequences of perceived discrimination in disadvantaged and privileged social groups. *European Review of Social Psychology, 12*, 167–199.

Schmitt, M. T., Branscombe, N. R., Kobrynowicz, D., & Owen, S. (2002). Perceiving discrimination against one's gender group has different implications for well-being in women and men. *Personality and Social Psychology Bulletin, 28,* 197–210.

Schmitt, M. T., Spears, R., & Branscombe, N. R. (2003). Constructing a minority group identity out of shared rejection: The case of international students. *European Journal of Social Psychology, 33,* 1–12.

Simon, B., & Stürmer, S. (2003). Respect for group members: Intragroup determinants of collective identification and group-serving behavior. *Personality and Social Psychology Bulletin, 29,* 183–193.

Simon, B., & Klandermans, B. (2001). Politicized collective identity: A social psychological analysis. *American Psychologist, 56,* 319–331.

Spears, R., Doosje, B., & Ellemers, N. (1997). Self-stereotyping in the face of threats to group status and distinctiveness: The role of group identification. *Personality and Social Psychology Bulletin, 23,* 538–553.

Spears, R., Jetten, J., & Scheepers, D. (2002). Distinctiveness and the definition of collective self: A tripartite model. In A. Tesser, D. A. Stapel, & J. Wood (Eds.), *Self and motivation: Emerging psychological perspectives* (pp. 147–171). Washington, DC: American Psychological Association.

Tajfel, H. (1978a). *The social psychology of minorities.* London: Minority Rights Group.

Tajfel, H. (1978b). *Differentiation between social groups: Studies in the social psychology of intergroup relations.* London: Academic Press.

Tajfel, H., & Turner, J. C. (1979). An integrative theory of intergroup conflict. In W. G. Austin & S. Worchel (Eds.), *The social psychology of intergroup relations* (pp. 33–47). Monterey, CA: Brooks/Cole.

Turner, J. C., Hogg, M. A., Oakes, P. J., Reicher, S. D., & Wetherell, M. S. (1987). *Rediscovering the social group: A self-categorization theory.* Oxford, UK: Blackwell.

Wojcik, D. (1995). *Punk and neo-tribal body art.* Jackson, MS: University Press of Mississippi.

8

Coping with Stigmatization: Smokers' Reactions to Antismoking Campaigns

JUAN MANUEL FALOMIR-PICHASTOR, ARMAND
CHATARD, GABRIEL MUGNY, AND ALAIN QUIAMZADE

Smoking is bad! Few ideas have achieved such a consensus: Today, every-body agrees that smoking is deleterious to health and damaging to the self and others. Antismoking campaigns promulgated by health author-ities and health-related organizations are frequently considered effective and valuable. Their influence is thus of considerable interest for social influence researchers, who have long been interested in the way peo-ple's attitudes and behaviors are shaped by social influence from expert sources. Furthermore, antismoking campaigns have indubitably contrib-uted to the emergence of a negative reputation of smoking and smokers. Indeed, these campaigns provide cogent rationalizations for the ostra-cism, stigmatization, and discrimination smokers receive. However, very little research has sought to examine the influence of antismoking cam-paigns on smokers' reactions to their social stigmatization (Falomir & Mugny, 2004). In part to redress this neglect, we report in this chapter on a research program investigating the influence of antismoking campaigns by expert sources on smokers' reactions and, particularly, on their inten-tion to quit smoking.

SMOKERS AS A STIGMATIZED GROUP

For a long period, smoking was associated with such positive social val-ues as adulthood, masculinity, and intellectualism, and smokers benefited from a positive image (Escohotado, 1989). However, a large body of publi-cations since the 1950s – documenting that tobacco consumption is related to health hazards and damages – has changed the perception of smokers

This research program was supported by the National Foundation for Scientific Research, Switzerland.

and smoking (e.g., World Health Organization, 1996). A lot of countries have become increasingly interested in promoting actions, including information campaigns and governmental policies, against smoking (Roemer, 1993). For example, smoking is currently constrained by policies that render tobacco purchase difficult, increase cigarette taxes, reduce the number of smoking areas in public places, and, sometimes, seek discriminatory treatment of smokers in the form of social and health-insurance taxes. As a consequence, most people nowadays are aware of the negative consequences of cigarette smoking (e.g., Cecil, Evans, & Stanley, 1996; Goldman & Glantz, 1998). Smoking is largely seen as an unjustified, unsuitable, and illegitimate behavior, and smokers have become a minority, stigmatized social group. As a matter of fact, smokers now endure a negative stereotype (Echebarria, Fernández, & Gonzalez, 1994; Keller, Krebs, & Hornung, 2003), and hostile attitudes toward them are often observed in various domains (e.g., Gibson, 1998; Hines, 1996; Malouff & Schutte, 1990).

Ironically, smokers do not often respond to their low status by denying the existence of prevention information or by actively defending their social identity. Smokers as well as nonsmokers are sensitive to the negative consequences of cigarette smoking (Brownson, Jackson-Thompson, Wilkerson, Davis, Owens, & Fisher, 1992). Smokers provide arguments against tobacco consumption, and they attribute greater importance to factors that are at odds with tobacco consumption (i.e., health and dependence), than to factors that are in line with it (i.e., pleasure and relaxation) (Falomir, Mugny, & Pérez, 2000). Furthermore, most smokers share with nonsmokers a negative representation of their ingroup. For instance, smokers perceive themselves, and are perceived by others, as being psychologically unstable, disturbed people (Echebarría et al., 1994). Smokers are also concerned about their behavior's lack of legitimacy (Falomir et al., 2000). In sum, smokers are confronted with an existential dilemma: they continue to smoke, even if they agree that tobacco consumption is "bad" and that there are no "good" reasons to smoke (see the concept of "dissonant smoker"; e.g., Joossens, 1992).

Considering the fact that smokers recognize both their own stigmatization and that smoking-prevention campaigns are generally produced by legitimate, expert sources (e.g., health authorities, scientific institutions), one might expect that their resistance to prevention campaigns would be low. On the one hand, it has been shown that expert sources are generally influential (e.g., Wilson & Sherrell, 1993). On the other hand, research has also documented that people who are led to question their own position react more positively toward a counterattitudinal argument (Eagly &

Chaiken, 1998; Edwards & Smith, 1996; Pratkanis, 1989; Sherif & Hovland, 1961). Therefore, conditions favoring change would be met when stigmatized smokers are confronted with a persuasive antismoking message.

However, most smokers continue to smoke for a long period. Some progress has been achieved in reducing the number of smokers, but several studies point out that this change is not proportional to the change in knowledge and consciousness of the negative consequences of smoking (e.g., Chassin, Presson, & Sherman, 1990; Leventhal & Cleary, 1980). Thus, one crucial goal for current research is to identify factors that produce smokers' resistance to antismoking campaigns. Why does smokers' stigmatization not constitute a stimulus to change? Why do experts not strengthen this process?

An obvious major determinant of resistance is physiological and psychological dependence, which makes it very difficult for smokers to quit (USDHHS, 1988). In this chapter we argue that, beyond this powerful factor, smokers' resistance is, at least to some extent, the outcome of their low social status and the social-influence contexts fostered by antismoking campaigns. Insofar as they constitute a minority and stigmatized social group in society, smokers have to manage their negative social image, which is strengthened by most antismoking campaigns. Indeed, antismoking programs repeatedly expose smokers to their own deviance. Generally speaking, antismoking programs present smokers in negative terms: They are depicted, either implicitly or explicitly, as being unaware of the consequences of their behavior, dependent, selfish, influenced by others, and easily manipulated by tobacco firms. In other words, being a smoker may be threatening to one's identity and integrity, and this threat may be strengthened when smokers are exposed to persuasive antismoking information (see also Sherman, Nelson, & Steele, 2000). Although these campaigns may be seen as legitimate, we argue that there are strong reasons to believe that they generate resistance more often than they generate change.

This chapter provides evidence concerning this assumption by taking into account two factors: (a) the status of the influence sources used in antismoking campaigns and (b) the fact that most smokers acknowledge their social stigmatization (e.g., they are dissatisfied with their own image as smokers). We will first review the research documenting that even a high-status expert source does not generate the amount of influence that might be expected when it introduces a threat to targets' identity and freedom. Next, we will present a line of research documenting that antismoking campaigns induce a defensive motivation among smokers, especially those who are the most dissatisfied with their own smokers' identity, which prevents the influence message from having a strong impact.

EXPERTS' INFLUENCE AND PERSUASIVE CONSTRAINT

Our previous work has demonstrated that expert sources are often perceived by targets as introducing an *external constraint* when they try to change their attitudes and behaviors (Falomir, Butera & Mugny, 2002). An external constraint refers to any factor perceived as emphasizing the legitimacy of an alternative point of view (i.e., that of the source) and as compelling the target to endorse it. For instance, an external constraint can be provided by the perceived high quality of the persuasive arguments or by heuristics offering support for its validity (e.g., source expertise, Chaiken, 1987). External constraint is opposed to the need to be autonomous and self-determined in any process of personal change (Brehm & Brehm, 1981). When the external constraint is low, people perceive themselves as free, autonomous, and respected by others. They are intrinsically motivated (see Williams et al., 2002, 2006) to change in the direction others expect, and thus change is less conflictual and more likely to occur. In contrast, when the external constraint is high, and people are externally pressed to change, they feel a lack of freedom and respect for themselves. This identity threat is expected to be the core motivation that induces targets to resist to expert influence (Brehm & Brehm, 1981).

According to this theoretical position, we develop two main arguments in this chapter: The first is that antismoking campaigns, which are frequently associated with expert sources, may be perceived by smokers as introducing a heightened external constraint to change. This, in turn, may increase smokers' resistance rather than motivation to change. Indeed, some past research confirmed the idea that experts are perceived as introducing a high external constraint to change. For instance, it has been observed that expert sources render their communication not only more valid and legitimate (Falomir et al., 2000) but also more salient and explicit (Falomir, Mugny, & Pérez, 1996). As a consequence, smokers attribute to expert sources more persuasive intentions (Falomir et al., 2002). These findings are also consistent with another line of research showing that high-status actors (e.g., experts) are frequently perceived as assertive and directive (Holtgraves, 2002).

Furthermore, perceived external constraint to change may result in defensive motivation and resistance to expert influence, especially when core aspects of the targets' identity are at stake (Invernizzi, Falomir, Muñoz,

& Mugny, 2003). Indeed, Invernizzi et al. observed that experts obtain less influence than nonexperts among highly identified smokers, who perceive themselves as "real" smokers. Furthermore, such resistance to influence was paradoxically correlated with the perception of experts as competent, as providing strong arguments against smoking, and as particularly motivated to influence smokers. This finding confirms our main argument that source credibility and argument strength do not always increase influence and suggests that the defensive motivation frequently observed in threatening contexts (e.g., Lieberman & Ckaiken, 1992; Sherman et al., 2002) may in some circumstances be a specific reaction to the high external constraint introduced by expert sources. More specifically, the findings of the aforementioned studies suggest that expert sources introduce a high external constraint, which elicits a defensive motivation among smokers that may lead them to resist to the influence.

Finally, a great deal of experimental evidence has documented that expert sources exert more influence when the external constraint they introduce is reduced in some way. For example, several studies have found that expert sources are perceived as less constraining when their argumentation is framed in a flexible style, rather than in a rigid style, and that they obtain greater influence in the former condition than in the latter one (Falomir & Mugny, 1999; Falomir, Invernizzi, Mugny, Muñoz, & Quiamzade, 2002). In the same way, several experiments indicate that expert sources are perceived as less constraining and as obtaining greater influence when their persuasive intent is less salient (i.e., when they are not perceived at the origin of the recipient's change; Falomir, Mugny, Invernizzi, & Muñoz, 2001; Falomir, Mugny, Quiamzade, & Butera, 2000).

The second main argument we develop in this chapter is that smokers' resistance to change appears specifically when they acknowledge their stigmatized condition (e.g., when they are dissatisfied with their own image as smokers) and thus are particularly sensitive to influence attempts aimed at changing their behaviors. As already mentioned, dissatisfied smokers should be more internally motivated to change than satisfied smokers. However, dissatisfied smokers would be more susceptible to change only if they perceive themselves as responsible for their decision and effort to stop smoking. In this case, they should perceive the influence attempt as more congenial and less harsh. When external constraint to change is made salient or strengthened, however, dissatisfied smokers will interpret their internal motivation as being the product of such an external constraint. Thus, if expert sources introduce a high external constraint, smokers may misattribute their internal motivation to change and will perceive a rather low internal motivation to change. This should not be the case for nonexpert sources because they are expected to induce less external constraint.

This reasoning has been examined in several experiments. For instance, a first study examined these concerns by considering smokers' internal motivation as a dispositional factor (Falomir, Mugny, & Invernizzi, 2006, study 1). Participants were first asked to indicate their satisfaction with their self-image as smokers. Satisfaction was low, generally. According to a median split of the distribution, participants were divided in two groups: "strongly dissatisfied smokers" and "moderately satisfied smokers". Then, they were asked to read an antismoking essay focusing on social and psychological motives for smoking that was attributed either to professors in social psychology (expert source) or to professors in art history (nonexpert source). Because moderately satisfied smokers are presumably less motivated to change than dissatisfied smokers, the only constraint to change imposed upon them was the one deriving from the influence attempt. Accordingly, we expected that both sources should be perceived as motivated to convince by moderately satisfied smokers. Indeed, results showed that dissatisfied smokers overall perceived the source's attempt to influence them as less constraining than moderately satisfied smokers. Furthermore, this study also showed that while the experts were perceived by all participants as trying to persuade them, only moderately satisfied smokers perceived the nonexperts as trying to do so. This result indicates that dissatisfied smokers (i.e., those who initially questioned their own behavior) perceived the expert source as trying more to convince (and less to inform) them than did the nonexpert source.

Another study replicated these findings, taking into account smokers' perception of the influence relationship (Falomir et al., 2006, study 2). Dissatisfied smokers, compared to moderately satisfied smokers, evaluated the authors of the message as being more respectful of their freedom. However, this effect was qualified by the degree of source expertise. Dissatisfied smokers perceived the nonexpert source as more respectful of smokers than did moderately satisfied smokers. This difference was not significant for the expert source. Finally, dissatisfied smokers perceived nonexperts as more respectful than experts.

Finally, another study examined these concerns by experimentally manipulating the internal motivation to change (Falomir, Butera, & Mugny, 2002). Smokers were asked to list important personal reasons for smoking before reading an influence message. Half of them, in a condition of low internal motivation to quit smoking, were told that, "several studies conducted in various countries have concluded that if a smoker can give at least two reasons for smoking, s/he has a very clear idea of the reasons why s/he smokes" (all participants gave two or more reasons). The other half, in a condition of high internal motivation to quit smoking, were told that a smoker should give at least eight reasons (all participants gave fewer than eight arguments). Smokers in the high internal-motivation condition, as compared to those in the low internal-motivation condition, acknowledged having fewer reasons, and fewer good reasons, to smoke. Next, the participants were exposed to an antismoking message that described smokers as manipulated by tobacco industry, attributed to either an expert (professors of political economy) or a nonexpert (ordinary citizens) source, and they were asked to indicate the perceived intention of the source on a continuum ranging from "to inform you" to "to convince you". Results showed that, overall, participants perceived the expert source as more motivated to persuade them than the nonexpert source. Furthermore, whereas smokers in the high internal-motivation condition perceived both sources as trying to persuade them, smokers in the low internal-motivation condition interpreted the source's intention as a function of its expertise. They were more inclined to attribute a persuasive intention to the source when it was an expert than a nonexpert. Further results showed that participants were more inclined to acknowledge that smokers should yield (rather than resist) the antismoking message when the source was nonexpert, whereas the opposite was observed when the source was expert.

In sum, we argue that, because they acknowledge the challenge to their behavior and identity (i.e., they express a clear dissatisfaction with their image as smokers), a lot of smokers have internalized the stigmatized status of their group. The findings reported here suggest that these smokers have a high motivation to change but that they may change the origin of this motivation by attributing it to the influence relationship, especially when the source is perceived as exerting a strong external constraint. Accordingly, this misattribution is more likely to appear in the case of expert sources than in the case of nonexpert sources. Since experts are expected to influence others, smokers may attribute their own motivation to change to the experts' intention to persuade them, and this misattribution may decrease their own motivation to change.

IDENTITY THREAT AND RESISTANCE TO THE INFLUENCE OF EXPERT SOURCES

In the previous section, we documented that the influence of expert sources is mainly characterized by an external persuasive constraint. The next step in our reasoning is to show that expert sources generate less influence when the overall external constraint associated to the influence context is high (versus low). Since external persuasive constraint has been conceptualized as a function of the salience of the influence relationship, experts should lose their influence specifically when the influence relationship is made salient. However, they should obtain some influence when the salience of the influence relationship is reduced. According to the previously reviewed literature, several studies were carried out to examine this possibility, especially among the most dissatisfied smokers.

In a first study (Falomir et al., 2001), two variables were used to manipulate both internal and external constraint associated to the influence context: (a) the smokers' threat (low versus high) to their social identity and (b) the salience (low versus high) of the influence relationship. Whereas smokers' threat corresponds to what we have called the internal motivation to change, the salience of the influence relationship corresponds to external constraint. To activate the threat, smokers were asked to list the three out of eight available negative characteristics (e.g., malodorous, nervous, dependent, disrespectful) that corresponded the most with their personal dissatisfaction as smokers. In the condition in which threat was not induced, participants were asked to list the three positive characteristics out of eight (e.g., sociable, convivial, independent, likeable) that corresponded the most with their personal satisfaction as smokers. Next, participants were exposed to an antismoking message focusing on social, political, and economical reasons why people smoke, attributed to an expert source (i.e., a group of professors in political economy). They were then asked to describe themselves as they were presently (i.e., smoker) and as they wished to be in the future (i.e., nonsmoker), using a list of dimensions (positive or negative) included in the influence message. To induce a low versus high salience of the influence relationship with the source, participants were asked to describe themselves using either their own viewpoint or the expert source's viewpoint, respectively. The main dependent variable was change in the intention to quit smoking, assessed before and after the influence phase.

According to our previous theoretical considerations, we expected that, compared with smokers who focused on characteristics leading them to feel *satisfied* with the smoker's image, smokers who focused on characteristics leading them to feel *dissatisfied* with this image would be more motivated to change in the direction of quitting smoking, but only when the salience of the influence relationship was low. In contrast, the opposite pattern was expected in the condition of high salience of the influence relationship,

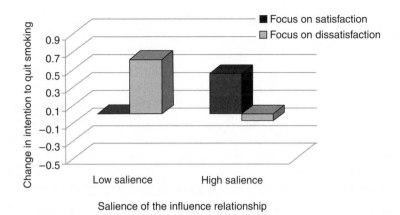

FIGURE 8.1. Change in the intention to quit smoking (positive scores mean greater intention).

Source: Adapted from Falomir et al., 2001.

since the internal motivation to change should be misattributed (i.e., attributed to the external constraint introduced by the expert source). Results were supportive of these general expectations (see Figure 8.1). In addition, further analyses indicated that the salience of the influence relationship led smokers who were dissatisfied with their image to perceive tobacco consumption as less problematic. This study also showed that the salience of the influence relationship with expert sources may constitute a limitation to their influence, in particular when targets have to deal with a threat to their identity (i.e., focus on dissatisfaction), but not when the perceived threat is reduced because of the focus on their satisfaction with their image as smokers.

According to our theoretical considerations, the defensive reactions observed when smokers have to deal with a threat to their smoker's identity should not appear when the influence message is promulgated by a nonexpert source. Because in this case the source is not expected to induce a high external constraint, no differences should be observed in relation to the intensity of the identity threat.

Another study may help to illustrate this point (Falomir, Mugny, Maggi, & Sanchez-Mazas, 2000). In this study, smokers anticipated a discussion with a group of either experts (i.e., university professors) or nonexperts (i.e., undergraduate students) that explicitly argued against smoking. All participants were informed that the group had chosen three out of six arguments that criticized tobacco consumption. According to the second experimental induction, these arguments introduced either a low threat (e.g., "smoking prohibition may contribute to a better way of life") or a high threat (e.g., "smokers are the puppets of tobacco firms since they relinquish their freedom to tobacco advertisements") to smoker's identity. The researchers used two dependent variables: (a) intention to criticize the antismoking arguments and (b) disagreement with these arguments. Intention to criticize was used to measure smokers' defensive motivation, and disagreement was used to assess resistance toward the influence attempt.

Results revealed that participants were more likely to criticize the experts' arguments in the high-threat condition than in the low-threat condition. More interestingly, such a difference did not appear with the nonexperts. Specifically, participants criticized the nonexperts' arguments more than they criticized those of the experts in the low-threat condition, but they were more likely to criticize the experts' arguments than the nonexperts' arguments in the high-threat condition (see Figure 8.2). Similar results were observed when considering the disagreement measure. In the low-threat condition, participants disagreed less with antismoking arguments presented by experts rather than nonexperts. In contrast, the expert's arguments produced more disagreement than the nonexpert's arguments in the high-threat condition. This finding corroborates the proposal that

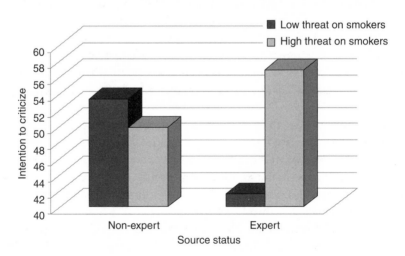

FIGURE 8.2. Intention to criticize the antismoking arguments (higher scores mean greater intention).

Source: Adapted from Falomir, Mugny, Maggi, & Sanchez-Mazas, 2000.

identity threat is at the origin of smokers' defensive motivation and resistance to influence when confronted with experts but not when confronted with nonexperts.

Further results from an aforementioned study provided converging evidence that experts motivate smokers to resist the influence attempt in particular when smokers' identity is at stake (Falomir et al., 2006, study 2). Let us remember first that dissatisfied smokers are expected to be more ready to quit smoking after exposure to an antismoking persuasive message than are satisfied smokers. However, our theoretical argument suggests that, although such a facilitated influence should appear if the source does not make salient the influence relationship (i.e., a nonexpert source), such a facilitated influence should not appear when the source does make salient the influence relationship (i.e., an expert source). Accordingly, an expert source can obtain less influence than a nonexpert source among smokers with a negative self-image.

During a pretest, smokers were asked to indicate the extent to which they were satisfied with their image as smokers. Based on a median split, they were divided in two groups: moderately satisfied and strongly dissatisfied. As in the previous studies, all participants were next exposed to an antismoking message focusing on social and psychological motives for smoking, attributed either to an expert (professors in social psychology) or a nonexpert source (professors in history of art). The main dependent variable was change in the intention to quit smoking, assessed before and after the influence phase.

The results were consistent with our predictions (see Figure 8.3). The expert source produced greater influence among moderately satisfied smokers than among strongly dissatisfied smokers, whereas the nonexpert source was more influential among strongly dissatisfied smokers than among moderately satisfied smokers. In addition, the expert source produced greater influence than the nonexpert source among moderately satisfied participants, while the nonexpert source produced marginally greater influence than the expert source among strongly dissatisfied participants. Therefore, we can conclude that expert sources generate a defensive reaction among smokers acknowledging a threat to their identity (i.e., dissatisfied smokers), which does not appear when the source is nonexpert.

In sum, these findings suggest that antismoking campaigns associated with expert sources may not be as powerful as one might intuitively expect them to be. On the one hand, antismoking campaigns associated with expert sources may obtain greater influence but only among moderately satisfied smokers. On the other hand, dissatisfied smokers,

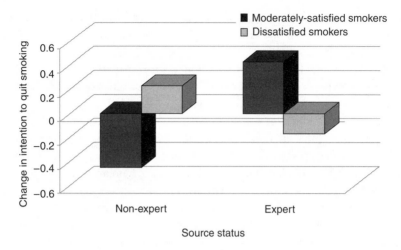

FIGURE 8.3. Change in the intention to quit smoking (positive scores mean greater intention).

Source: Adapted from Falomir et al., 2006.

who should more easily engage in a smoking-cessation process, appear to do so only when confronted with a nonexpert source. Our explanation is that dissatisfied smokers need to perceive that their motivation is autonomous and self-directed rather than elicited by an external persuasive attempt. They thus react positively to an antismoking message when it is attributed to a source that is not perceived as compelling them to change (i.e., a nonexpert source), but they react negatively when such a message is attributed to a source introducing a high external constraint to change (i.e., an expert source). This source changes how they perceive their internal motivation to change. Why does the expert source elicit at the opposite an influence on moderately satisfied smokers? We consider that these smokers are less motivated to change and react less defensively to the antismoking essay. In the sections that follow, we examine these considerations in more detail.

SMOKERS' REACTIONS TO THREATENING SOCIAL COMPARISONS

Smokers' social stigmatization is also related to the fact that they are involved in various forms of social comparison that can be more or less threatening to their identity. The most obvious and threatening comparison occurs when smokers engage themselves, or are engaged, even unintentionally, in intergroup comparisons with nonsmokers. This kind of social comparison contributes to the smokers' stigmatization and should be threatening to their identity and integrity. However, other comparisons may be less threatening. For instance, smokers may perceive themselves in more positive terms after social comparison with other ingroup members (i.e., other smokers).

It can also be argued that smokers' intrapersonal comparison with themselves, as they would be if they quit smoking, may be less personally threatening than intergroup comparisons with other smokers. As previously noted, most smokers wish to quit smoking in the future, and thus their ideal self (nonsmoker) may be more positively evaluated and satisfying than their actual self (smoker) (Higgins, Tykocinski, & Vookles, 1990). The intrapersonal comparison may allow them a partial escape (i.e., at the individual level) from the threat to their social identity as smoker. As a consequence, we predict that smokers should react more defensively after social comparison with nonsmokers (intergroup comparison) than after social comparison with themselves as nonsmokers (intrapersonal comparison). Two studies examined these hypotheses.

In a first study (Falomir & Mugny, 2009a), smokers were asked to indicate their degree of satisfaction as smokers. They were then divided in two groups according to a median split: strongly dissatisfied or moderately satisfied smokers. Next, they were asked to read an antismoking essay focusing on social and psychological motives for smoking that was written by an allegedly expert source (professors in social psychology), and they completed a self-report questionnaire assessing their perception of themselves as smokers on positive and negative dimensions. Some of these dimensions were part of the antismoking essay (independent, manipulated), whereas other dimensions were typical of smokers (social, nervous) or nonsmokers ("up-tight", healthy). On each of these dimensions, each participant was asked to compare himself or herself with a nonsmoker (intergroup comparison: *Please describe yourself in comparison with a nonsmoker*) or with himself or herself as nonsmoker (intrapersonal comparison: *Please describe yourself in comparison with how you could be as a nonsmoker*). The main dependent variables were the defensive motivation during the comparison task (i.e., the motivation to favor their smoker image); their intention to engage in collective actions to preserve smokers' rights (e.g., participation in public debates, signing a petition for smokers' rights); and their attitude toward the antismoking essay (e.g., personal agreement and evaluation of the arguments).

Participants' defensive motivation and intention to engage in collective actions were rather low. However, as might be expected, they were lower among strongly dissatisfied smokers than among moderately dissatisfied smokers. In addition, whereas moderately satisfied smokers were unaffected by the social comparison, strongly dissatisfied participants were less likely to manifest a defensive motivation and to engage in collective actions in the intrapersonal-comparison condition than in the intergroup-comparison condition. Finally, when the social comparison was intrapersonal, strongly dissatisfied participants were less motivated defensively and manifested a lower intention to engage in collective actions than did moderately satisfied participants.

Regarding the measure of influence (i.e., the attitude toward the antismoking essay; see Figure 8.4). However, strongly dissatisfied participants reported a more positive attitude toward the antismoking essay in the intrapersonal-comparison condition than in the intergroup-comparison condition. The results also indicated that agreement with the antismoking essay was higher among strongly dissatisfied participants than it was among moderately satisfied participants, but only under the intrapersonal-comparison condition. These findings provide a first illustration that strongly dissatisfied participants may be influenced by the expert source, but only when the social comparison allows them to avoid an identity threat.

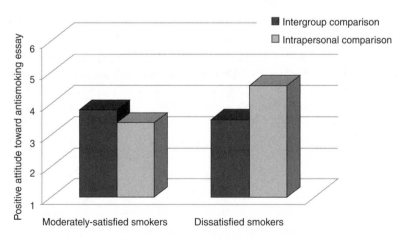

FIGURE 8.4. Attitude toward the antismoking essay (higher scores mean a more positive attitude).

Source: Adapted from Falomir & Mugny, 2009a.

In sum, these findings confirm that expert sources generate a self-protective strategy among strongly dissatisfied participants, specifically when they are stigmatized through a social comparison with nonsmokers. In other words, experts obtain less influence when smokers have to cope with an identity threat. This threat may result from unfavorable comparisons with a nonsmoker. At the opposite pole, this resistance appears to be attenuated when the social comparison allows them to restore a positive identity through the projection of an ideal self. This is the case with intrapersonal comparisons through which participants attributed positive characteristics to themselves as nonsmokers, while criticizing themselves as smokers.

In the previous study, the antismoking essay was attributed to an expert source. In the case of a nonexpert source, however, we can expect that the same dynamics would not be observed. To test this hypothesis, we conducted a second study introducing four main differences. First, smokers were exposed to the same antismoking essay focusing on social and psychological motives for smoking, attributed either to an expert (professors in political economy) or to a nonexpert (ordinary citizens) source. Second, the degree of satisfaction was considered as a continuous variable rather than a dichotomous variable. Third, this time the main dependent measure concerned the personal attitude toward smoking cessation (i.e., the change in the intention to quit smoking). Finally, a thought-listing task was also introduced to examine cognitive responses elicited during the reading of the persuasive essay. The manipulation of the social comparison (intrapersonal versus intergroup) was the same as in the previous study.

The analysis revealed a significant interaction between the three factors. Consistent with the previous study, there was a reliable interaction between the degree of satisfaction and the social-comparison condition as regards with the expert conditions (see Figure 8.5). The more the participants were dissatisfied, the more they attempted to quit smoking when the comparison was intrapersonal, but not when the comparison was intergroup. Regarding the nonexpert source, the results showed the opposite effect, but the interaction between the degree of satisfaction and the social-comparison condition was only marginal: The more participants were dissatisfied, the more they wanted to quit smoking when the comparison was intergroup but not when it was intrapersonal.

Examining the reported thoughts, we also observed a different picture for the expert and nonexpert sources. The relation between the degree of satisfaction and the reported thoughts was moderated by the social-comparison condition only when the source was expert. The more participants

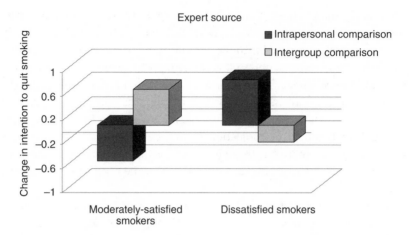

FIGURE 8.5. Change in the intention to quit smoking (estimated means for 1SD over and above smokers' satisfaction; positive scores mean greater intention).

Source: Adapted from Falomir & Mugny, 2009a.

were dissatisfied, the more they generated thoughts consistent with the antismoking essay when the social comparison was intrapersonal, but they generated more ideas that were at odds with the antismoking essay when the social comparison was intergroup. Finally, in the intrapersonal condition, the less the dissatisfied smokers generated thoughts that were at odds with the essay, the more they increased their intention to quit smoking. Again, this pattern of findings was not observed when the source was nonexpert.

In sum, the results of this study extended those of the previous study to the intention to quit smoking and the cognitive responses elicited during the persuasive attempt. They confirm that expert sources induce some resistance among dissatisfied smokers and that influence appears only when these smokers can preserve a positive identity (i.e., when they attributed positive characteristics to themselves as nonsmokers through an intrapersonal comparison). These findings provide additional support for the hypothesis that expert influence decreases when a threat is salient in the persuasive context. Thus, one can predict that expert influence may appear when smokers have the opportunity to restore a positive image of themselves (in this case, as nonsmokers), rather than taking into account the identity threat resulting from their social stigmatization as smoker.

In addition, because the underlying dynamics were not observed and even tended to be reversed in the case of a nonexpert source, this study points out the specificity of the expert source. Consistent with the results of the Falomir et al. (2006) study, the results of the present study revealed that a nonexpert source may obtain greater influence among smokers dissatisfied with their image as smokers. However, this finding appeared here specifically when dissatisfied smokers strengthened the threat to their smoker image through the negative comparison with a nonsmoker. Indeed, nonexperts may, paradoxically, obtain more influence than experts when the identity threat is high, that is, when both chronic (personal dissatisfaction with their image as smokers) and situational (intergroup comparison) factors converge.

SELF-ESTEEM RESOURCES AND IMAGE OF THE SMOKER

In the precedent studies, smokers appeared particularly motivated to defend their social identity and to resist influence when the threat stemming from the persuasive message was coupled with an unfavorable intergroup comparison. In contrast, some influence was observed when targets were able to maintain a positive personal self-esteem because of either the low expertise of the source or the intrapersonal comparison with themselves as nonsmokers.

If this interpretation is correct, we should observe similar dynamics when we more directly manipulate the threat to the targets' personal self-esteem. For instance, it could be expected that the defensive motivation and the resistance to the expert influence should be enhanced when smokers are focused on their negative personal characteristics but reduced when smokers are asked to focus on positive personal characteristics. Two studies (Falomir & Mugny, 2009b) examined this hypothesis regarding smokers' defensive motivation (i.e., evaluation of the image of the smoker) and regarding attitude towards tobacco consumption.

In a first study, two independent variables were considered: (a) the opportunity for participants to describe themselves personally using positive versus negative traits and (b) the expert versus nonexpert social status of the source. Smokers were asked to participate in two ostensibly unrelated studies. The first one was the usual research about tobacco consumption and was divided into two parts, a pretest and a posttest, but participants were told that this study required a break between the two parts. The second one was introduced during this break and was presented as a very short study carried out by another researcher. Participants were told that this short study focused on general positive and negative characteristics of people. Half of the participants were asked to indicate two of their most important positive characteristics (positive-characteristics condition), while the other half were asked to indicate two of their most important negative characteristics (negative-characteristics condition). In both cases, participants were also asked to justify their answers. Afterwards, they were redirected to the main study about tobacco consumption. The booklet included the antismoking essay used in previous studies attributed to either an expert (professors in social psychology) or a nonexpert source (professors in art history). The main dependent variable of this study was the evaluation of smokers, on the one hand, and of nonsmokers, on the other hand. A composite score was computed by subtracting evaluation of smokers from evaluation of non-smokers: High scores reflected a negative evaluation of smokers compared to nonsmokers and hence a tendency to endorse a negative image of the participants' ingroup.

As expected, the results showed that the expert source induced a stronger depreciation of the ingroup in the positive-characteristics condition than in the negative-characteristics condition. In contrast, this difference was not significant when the source was nonexpert. Figure 8.6 presents the observed means. What we learn from these findings is that, after exposure to an expert source, participants were more likely to question their own social identity as smokers when they could attribute positive characteristics to themselves (i.e., when they could maintain a positive personal self-esteem). This finding provides additional evidence for the hypothesis that antismoking efforts by experts may cause smokers to question their identity (and, therefore, potentially, their behavior) only when smokers can maintain positive personal self-esteem. When personal self-esteem is not positive, experts' efforts can contribute to smokers' resistance to antismoking campaigns.

The last study that we shall discuss was aimed at testing whether it is smokers' maintenance of their personal self-esteem or their social identity that leads to a decrease of defensive motivation. To this end, this study introduced a new operationalization of social-identity questioning and of the influence measure. The social-identity questioning measure was assessed by smokers' answers to a question about their self-respect ("Overall, what is your self-esteem as smoker?"). They then read the same antismoking message attributed to an expert source (professors in social psychology). As with the induction of personal versus social positive self-esteem, participants indicated the three most important features they possessed, either personally or as smokers. To do so, they selected them from nine positive characteristics (i.e., sociable, bon vivant, independent, nice, relaxed, warm, dynamic, interesting, and self-assured).

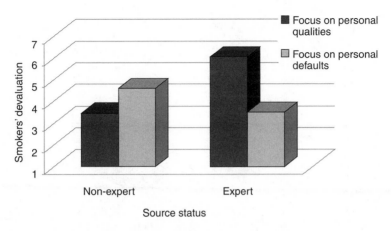

FIGURE 8.6. Smokers' evaluation of smokers and nonsmokers image (higher scores mean a higher devaluation of smokers as compared to nonsmokers).
Source: Adapted from Falomir & Mugny, 2009b.

The main dependent variable was attitude towards smoking cessation (i.e., evaluation of smoking cessation, intention to quit, and intention to decrease smoking) measured before and after exposure to the antismoking persuasive message (using 15-point scales). Analyses showed a significant interaction between the two independent variables (Figure 8.7). Focusing on personal qualities increased expert influence among smokers with negative self-esteem as smokers. This result confirms previous findings, and suggests that smokers' defensive motivation and resistance to the influence of expert sources are reduced when they benefit from positive resources for their personal self. The reverse pattern of results appeared when these smokers focused on their qualities as smokers. Thus, these findings confirm that it is the salience of a positive personal self-esteem and not of a positive social identity as smoker per se that causes expert influence among initially dissatisfied smokers.

Overall, these findings suggest that smokers with negative self-esteem are internally motivated to change. However, expert influence may occur only when smokers benefit from positive self-related resources. Indeed, these resources allow them to feel more comfortable despite the source expertise. Conversely, the focus on positive smoker-related resources may block this process since these resources may motivate them to increase their smoker self-esteem, rather than to question their smokers' identity and behavior.

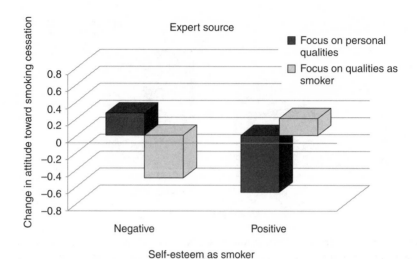

FIGURE 8.7. Change in positive attitude toward smoking cessation (estimated means for 1SD over and above self-esteem mean; positive scores mean positive attitude).

Source: Adapted from Falomir & Mugny, 2009a.

CONCLUSION

Nowadays, smokers constitute a stigmatized social minority. Several studies have shown that smokers' stigmatization is observed in smokers' negative stereotype and in discriminatory treatment of smokers (e.g., Echebarria et al., 1994; Gibson, 1998; Hines, 1996; Keller et al., 2003; see also Roemer, 1993). Contrary to other stigmatized groups (e.g., foreigners), smokers' stigmatization rests on behavior, and this is frequently perceived as amenable to change. As a consequence, smoking is not perceived as simply an alternative behavior in a pluralistic society, but rather as an unjustified behavior that society should legitimately fight and banish. Not to smoke or stop smoking, rest on the perception of nonsmokers (and exsmokers) as the dominant societal model, which means that measures and campaigns are required to change the behavior of current smokers.

The aim of this chapter was to provide experimental illustrations of how smokers react as a stigmatized social group to societal efforts against smoking. Of course, one possible reaction for smokers in this situation is to make efforts to move away from the stigmatized group and to stop smoking as a form of individual mobility (Tajfel & Turner, 1986). However, exposure to health messages is frequently associated with defensiveness and resistance to change (e.g., Liberman & Chaiken, 1992; Weinstein & Klein, 1995), and both dependence and identity threat (e.g., Kunda, 1990; Liberman & Chaiken, 1992; Sherman et al., 2002) may prevent smokers from making the advocated change. Indeed, several theoretical models consider that people can react in two ways when confronted with negative information about themselves (Trope, Ferguson, & Raghunathan, 2001; Trope & Neter, 1994) or about their group membership (Hornsey, 2005). They may be defensively oriented or not.

Within this framework, the key challenge is to identify moderators that determine when an individual will or will not react to challenging information defensively. We have examined the effect of the threat to smokers' identity introduced by antismoking efforts by considering three factors: (a) smokers' initial questioning of their identity as smokers (i.e., smokers' acknowledgment of their social stigmatization); (b) the threat introduced by the antismoking persuasive essay; and (c) the threat to smokers' personal self-esteem introduced in the persuasive context (i.e., associated with the external constraint introduced by the source expertise).

Overall, the results of the studies described here support the main argument that, whereas stigmatized smokers should be more ready to question their identity and behavior after being exposed to an antismoking essay, they become more defensively motivated when this essay is attributed to an expert source. Indeed, the threat associated with smokers' initial acknowledgement of their social stigmatization, together with exposure to the antismoking essay, might be considered a factor increasing the influence. However, this pattern was not found when the influence attempt was associated with an expert source. The reason we provided for that dynamic involved threat to personal identity introduced by the external constraint associated with the expert source. In agreement with this reasoning, the persuasive attempt is successful only when smokers are allowed to maintain a positive view of themselves. This was the case, for instance, when the influence source was nonexpert (i.e., which introduces a lower external persuasive constraint) or when the influence context allowed either intrapersonal comparisons (i.e., which allows the maintenance of a positive comparison for the self, while challenging the value of the smoker identity) or smokers' focus on personal qualities. In such situations, smokers' defensive motivation is reduced at the same time as the questioning of the smoker social identity and behavior is maintained.

We have here the indication that scientific or expert discourse, which is mostly used in prevention campaigns to increase their credibility and influence, turns out to be problematic from a psychological viewpoint because it forces the smoker to elaborate the threat to his or her social status as a smoker in relation to a threat to personal identity. Without any possibility of maintaining a worth view of themselves, smokers respond defensively to maintain their identity and behavior. These findings are important from a theoretical viewpoint because they question the idea supported in the literature that expert sources produce more influence than nonexpert sources. They are also important from an applied point of view because in some cases they question a means frequently considered to be effective in the fight against unhealthy behaviors, which is, however, not necessarily appropriate when trying to change unhealthy behaviors associated with stigmatized groups.

REFERENCES

Brehm, S. S., & Brehm, J. W. (1981). *Psychological reactance: A theory of freedom and control.* San Diego, CA: Academic Press.

Brownson, R. C., Jackson-Thompson, J., Wilkerson, J. C., Davis, J. R., Owens, N. W., & Fisher, E. B. (1992). Demographic and socioeconomic differences in beliefs about the Health effects of smoking. *American Journal of Public Health, 82,* 99–102.

Cecil, H., Evans, R. I., & Stanley, M. A. (1996). Perceived believability among adolescents of health warning labels on cigarette packs. *Journal of Applied Social Psychology, 26,* 502–519.

Chaiken, S. (1987). The heuristic model of persuasion. In M. P. Zanna, J. M. Olson, & C. P. Herman (Eds.), *Social influence: The Ontario symposium* (Vol. 3, pp. 3–39). Hillsdale, NJ: Lawrence Erlbaum.

Chassin, L., Presson, C. C., & Sherman, S. J. (1990). Social psychological contributions to the understanding and prevention of adolescent cigarette smoking. *Personality and Social Psychology Bulletin, 16,* 133–151.

Eagly, A. H., & Chaiken, S. (1998). Attitude structure and function. In D. Gilbert, S. Fiske, & G. Lindzey (Eds.), *The handbook of social psychology* (4th ed., pp. 266–322). New York: McGraw-Hill.

Echebarría Echabe, A., Fernandez Guede, E., & Gonzalez, J. L. (1994). Social representations and intergroup conflicts: Who's smoking here? *European Journal of Social Psychology, 24,* 339–355.

Edwards, K., & Smith, E. E. (1996). A disconfirmation bias in the evaluation of arguments. *Journal of Personality and Social Psychology, 71,* 5–24.

Escohotado, A. (1989). *Historia de las drogas [History of drugs].* Madrid: Alianza Editorial.

Falomir, J. M., Butera, F., & Mugny, G. (2002). Persuasive constraint and expert vs. non-expert influence in intention to quit smoking. *European Journal of Social Psychology, 32,* 209–222.

Falomir, J. M., Invernizzi, F., Mugny, G., Muñoz-Rojas, D., & Quiamzade, A. (2002). Social influence on intention to quit smoking: The effect of the rhetoric of an identity relevant message. *International Review of Social Psychology, 15,* 81–96.

Falomir, J.M. & Mugny, G. (1999). Influence sociale et resistance au changement chez les fumeurs. *Alcoologie*, 21, 25–29.

Falomir, J.M. & Mugny, G. (2004). *Société contre fumeur: Analyse psychosociale de l'influence des experts.* Grenoble: Presses Universitaires de Grenoble

(2009a). *Expert vs. non-expert influence and threatening social comparison.* Unpublished manuscript.

(2009b). *Smokers' self-esteem and expert versus nonexpert influence.* Unpublished manuscript.

Falomir, J.M., Mugny, G., & Invernizzi, F. (2006). Smokers' (dis)satisfaction, persuasive constraint, and influence of expert and nonexpert sources. *Swiss Journal of Psychology*, 65, 7–14.

Falomir, J.M., Mugny, G., Invernizzi, F., & Muñoz-Rojas, D. (2001). Influencia social y disociación: Elaboración interna versus externa de la amenaza de la identidad. *Revista de Psicología Social*, 16, 331–348.

Falomir, J.M., Mugny, G., Maggi, J., & Sanchez-Mazas, M. (2000). El efecto del estatus de la fuente de influencia en función de la amenaza de la identidad y de la interdependencia de las posiciones. *Anuario de Psicología*, 31, 59–76.

Falomir, J.M., Mugny, G., Quiamzade, A., & Butera, F. (2000). Social influence and control beliefs in identity threatening contexts. In W.J. Perrig & A. Grob (Eds.), *Control of Human Behavior, Mental Processes and Consciousness* (pp. 443–455). Mahwah, NJ: Lawrence Erlbaum.

Falomir, J.M., Mugny, G., & Pérez, J.A. (1996). Social Influence and threat to identity: Does the fight against tobacco use require a ban on smoking? *International Review of Social Psychology*, 8, 95–108.

(2000). Social influence and identity conflict. In D. Terry & M. Hogg (Eds.), *Attitudes, behavior, and social context: The role of norms and group membership* (pp. 245–264). London: Lawrence Erlbaum.

Gibson, B. (1998). Nonsmokers' attributions for the outcomes of smokers: Some potential consequences of the stigmatization of smokers. *Journal of Applied Social Psychology*, 28, 581–594.

Goldman, L.K., & Glantz, S.A. (1998). Evaluation of antismoking advertising campaigns. *Journal of the American Medical Association*, 279, 772–777.

Higgins, E., Tykocinski, O., & Vookles, J. (1990). Patterns of self-beliefs: The psychological significance of relations among the actual, ideal, ought, can, and future selves. In J.M. Olson & M.P. Zanna (Eds.). *Self-inference processes: The Ontario symposium* (Vol. 6, pp. 153–190). Hillsdale, NJ, England: Lawrence Erlbaum.

Hines, D. (1996). Nonsmoking college students' attitudes toward smokers and smoking. *Psychological Reports*, 78, 860–862.

Holtgraves, T.M. (2002). *Language as social action.* Mahwah, NJ: Lawrence Erlbaum.

Hornsey, M. (2005). Why being right is not enough: Predicting defensiveness in the face of group criticism. *European Review of Social Psychology*, 16, 301–334.

Invernizzi, F., Falomir, J.M., Muñoz, D., & Mugny, G. (2003). Social influence in personally relevant contexts: The respect attributed to the source as a factor increasing smokers' intention to quit smoking. *Journal of Applied Social Psychology*, 33, 1818–1836.

Joossens, L. (1992). Fumeurs consonants et fumeurs dissonants: les perspectives d'action [Consonant smokers and dissonant smokers: Perspectives for action]. In K. Slama, S. Karsenty & A. Hirsch (Eds.), *La lutte contre le tabagisme est-elle efficace?* Paris: INSERM (Institut National de la Santé et de la Recherche Médicale) et CFES (Comité Français d'Education pour la Santé).

Keller, R., Krebs, H., & Hornung, R. (2003a). *Tabakmonitoring. Bericht über den Tabakkonsum der Schweizer Wohnbevölkerung in den Jahren 2001 und 2002. Im Auftrag des Bundesamtes für Gesundheit* [Enquête sur la consommation de tabac en Suisse 2001–2002 (Monitoring tabac). Sur mandat de l'Office Fédéral de la Santé Publique]. Zurich : Psychologisches Institut der Universität Zürich, Sozialpsychologie II.

Kunda, Z. (1990). The case for motivated reasoning. *Psychological Bulletin, 108,* 480–498.

Leventhal, H., & Cleary, P.D. (1980). The smoking problem: A review of the research and theory in behavioral risk modification. *Psychological Bulletin, 88,* 2, 370–405.

Liberman, A., & Chaiken, S. (1992). Defensive processing of personality relevant health messages. *Personality and Social Psychology Bulletin, 18,* 669–679.

Malouff, J., & Schutte, N.S. (1990). The employment disadvantage of being a smoker. *Journal of Drug Education, 20,* 329–336.

Pratkanis, A.R. (1989). The cognitive representation of attitudes. In A.R. Pratkanis, S. J . Breckler, & A.G. Greenwald (Eds.), *Attitude structure and function.* Hillsdale, NJ: Lawrence Erlbaum.

Trope, Y., Ferguson, M., & Raghunathan, R. (2001). Mood as a resource in processing self-relevant information. In J.P. Forgas (Ed.), *Handbook of affect and social cognition* (pp. 256–274). New York: Erlbaum Press.

Roemer, R. (1993). *Legislative action to combat the world tobacco epidemic* (2nd ed.). Geneva: World Health Organisation.

Sherif, M., & Hovland, C.I. (1961). *Social judgment.* New Haven, CT: Yale University Press.

Sherman, D.A.K., Nelson, L.D., & Steele, C.M. (2000). Do messages about health risks threaten the self? Increasing the acceptance of threatening health messages via self-affirmation. *Personality and Social Psychological Bulletin, 26,* 1045–1058.

Tajfel, H., & Turner, J.C. (1986). The social identity theory of intergroup behaviour. In S. Worchel & W.G. Austin (Eds.), *Psychology of intergroup relations* (pp. 7–24). Chicago: Nelson-Hall.

Trope, Y., & Neter, E. (1994). Reconciling competing motives in self-evaluation: The role of self-control in feedback seeking. *Journal of Personality and Social Psychology, 66,* 646–657.

U. S. Department of Health and Human Services (USDHHS) (1988). *The health consequences of smoking: Nicotine addiction. A report of the Surgeon General.* Rockville, MD: Offices on Smoking and Health, DHHS Publication No. (CDC) 88–8406.

Williams, G.C., Gagné, M., Ryan, R.M., & Deci, E.L. (2002). Facilitating autonomous motivation for smoking cessation. *Health Psychology, 21,* 40–50.

Williams, G. C., McGregor, H. A., Sharp, D., Levesque, C., Kouides, R. W., Ryan, R. M., & Deci, E. L. (2006). Testing a self-determination theory intervention for motivating tobacco cessation: Supporting autonomy and competence in a clinical trial. *Health Psychology, 25*, 91–101.

Wilson, E. J., & Sherrell, D. L. (1993). Source effects in communication and persuasion research: A meta-analysis of effect size. *Journal of the Academy of Marketing Science, 21*, 101–112.

World Health Organization. (1996). *The tobacco epidemic: A global public health emergency first global report on tobacco*. Geneva: WHO.

9

Terrorism as a Tactic of Minority Influence

XIAOYAN CHEN AND ARIE W. KRUGLANSKI

Since the late 1970s, the topic of minority influence has constituted an important research issue for social psychologists. Introduced by Serge Moscovici's seminal papers (Moscovici, 1980, 1985), minority influence research exemplified minority influence in that it innovated and deviated from the tendency to view social influence phenomena predominantly from the majority's perspective.

As Moscovici aptly noted, majority influence serves to preserve existing knowledge (by which we mean widely received views or shared realities) whereas new knowledge, germinating as it typically does in the mind of one person or in the discussions of a small group of people, presupposes the influence of a minority on a dominant majority. The typical metaphor for much minority influence research was nonviolent influence by the minority through socially sanctioned means, such as debates, publications, media appearances, lawful protests, and licensed public demonstrations. The prototypical cases of minority influence phenomena were innovations in science and technology, minority-prompted change in political attitudes, and shifts in the world of fashion, and so on.

But in the past several decades, a very different type of influence tactic has captivated the world's attention and mobilized the resources of nations; it goes by the name of "terrorism" and is considered by many the scourge of our times. Many different definitions of terrorism have been proposed over the years (Schmid & Jongman, 1988). For the present purpose, we will define terrorism as the deliberate targeting of civilians by nonstate actors with the aim of advancing political objectives through the induction of fear (Ganor, 2005). Though a small group of social scientists (primarily political scientists, sociologists, and psychiatrists) has been studying terrorism since the early 1970s (Crenshaw, 1978; Fields, 1979;

Hutchinson et al., 1972), the events of 9/11 catapulted the topic to the very top of the social sciences research agenda.

The number of symposia, solid-authored books and edited-volumes on terrorism has mushroomed (almost overnight) and multiple disciplinary perspectives in both the natural and the social sciences are intensely being brought to bear on the terrorism issue, in the hope of offering a better understanding and, hopefully, identifying effective ways of dealing with this unsettling problem.*

The social psychological research on terrorism is relatively sparse and in its infancy. But, clearly, terrorism as a phenomenon is both social and psychological. One would expect, therefore, that social psychology should offer important insights into the antecedents of terrorism, its internal dynamics, and its consequences. The present volume because it is devoted to the ways in which minorities cope with their social environments, affords an opportunity to examine terrorism as a *social psychological phenomenon*, and more precisely as a *form of minority influence*. Such a framing of the problem begs the question of whether it makes sense to lump terrorism together with other forms of minority influence. To address it, it may be well to clarify first what features terrorism shares with other forms of minority influence and what its unique features are. If we deem it justifiable, after all, to consider terrorism as a form of minority influence, it may be of interest to consider how effective it is as a form of minority influence and the limits of its efficacy. In the pages that follow, we address these issues.

TERRORISM'S DISTINCTIONS FROM OTHER FORMS OF MINORITY INFLUENCE

Actions versus Beliefs

In contrast to alternative forms of minority influence that have used verbal arguments to alter majority attitudes and beliefs, terrorism has used the argument of action that "speaks louder than words," which, it was hoped, would elicit some desired reaction from the targeted majority, such as release of prisoners, withdrawal of forces, territorial concessions, etc. Nineteenth-century anarchists, for instance, coined the term "propaganda of the deed" (Johann Most, 1885), which was used to refer to an act

---

* A recent count revealed that as of 9/11/01 over 5,000 books have been published on the topic of terrorism, an immense amount indeed (Kruglanski & Fishman, 2006)

of *insurrection* as a "powerful means of arousing popular conscience" and the materialization of an idea through actions" (Crenshaw, 1998, p. 252). In the modern era, in particular, bloodcurdling deeds perpetrated by terrorists have been amplified considerably by the attention they naturally attract from the mass media and, most recently, the Internet. From a psychological perspective, the power of actions (over words) rests on the logic that actions signify personal investment and commitment (whereas "words are cheap"). In addition, actions, particularly unusual or extreme actions, are salient and noticeable. In that regard, not only violent actions, but also other committing or unusual actions, such as hunger strikes or other forms of nonviolent resistance, may be credited with the power to convince one's audience of one's dedication and seriousness of purpose.

Various terrorist groups have exploited these opportunities for gaining the world's attention to their causes. For instance, each act of suicide terrorism in Chechnya, Russia has been accompanied by a last testament and video, prepared in advance by the "martyr," and capable of inciting considerable interest when subsequently shown on television or the Internet (Speckhard, 2005). In one case, Chechen terror organizations riveted world attention while staging, in the Dubrovka Theater House takeover, a spectacular dram, in which 19 women dressed in black were shown in a premade video that, horrifyingly, displayed the bombs that were prominently strapped to their bodies. Not only did the spectacle create a sense of horror in the wider witnessing audience, but it may well have prompted many people to question what could drive Chechen women to such desperate measures and to lend an ear to their side of the story (Speckhard & Akhmedova, 2005).

Admittedly, the distinction between actions, the operating mode of the terrorists, and the beliefs that are targeted in more traditional forms of minority influence, isn't very sharp: Actions are intelligible forms of human conduct. As such, they are based on, or implied by, relevant beliefs. For instance, joining a terrorist organization or volunteering for a terrorist mission may be based on the beliefs that the injustice that has been done to one's group is unbearable and that it warrants the most extreme of measures, including suicide killings of innocent civilians.

Furthermore, the reactions that terrorists hope to elicit from a majority aren't divorced from the expected impact of terrorist activities on the majority's attitudes and beliefs. For instance, terrorist-perpetrated violence and the victims it may claim may support the belief that adherence to a given governmental policy isn't worth the damage that results. In turn, such belief may motivate individuals and/or governments to accede to the terrorists' demands by releasing prisoners or withdrawing forces from a given territory.

The Contents of Attitude/Belief Change

In a prototypical case of minority influence, the minority attempts to convince the majority to adopt the minority's opinions, attitudes, and so on. Such is the case with scientific innovations, such as when proponents of a novel theory or a methodological approach (e.g., a social-cognitive neuroscience) attempt to convince a skeptical majority to accept it as valid. Such is also the case with religious proselytizers (e.g., Jehovah's Witnesses) who attempt to convince others to accept a given religious credo; it is also typically the case with political debates.

In the case of terrorism, by contrast, there is less of an attempt to convince the majority to accept the minority's opinion (partly because the opinion discrepancy is simply too large). For instance, even though an ultimate goal of radical Islamists might be to spread the Muslim belief system across the world or of radical Marxists, to spread Marxism, such goals may appear too unattainable in the foreseeable future to be seriously adopted. Rather than persuading the majority to join the minority in its unique brand of "shared reality," the terrorist minority typically attempts to alter the majority beliefs about the desirability of making concessions to minority demands. For instance, the terrorism perpetrated by the Palestinian organizations is intended to bring about the withdrawal of Israeli forces from the West Bank and the Gaza Strip; activities of Al-Qaeda are intended to affect the withdrawal of the U.S. forces from the Middle East, and so on.

Terrorism as a Form of Minority Influence

Despite these obvious differences between terrorism and more "conventional" forms of minority influence, there are good reasons to consider terrorism as a tactic of minority influence. One such reason is the considerable power it places in the minority hands in its struggle against some majority.

Terrorism's Equalizing Potential

The term "minority" is usually taken to connote a weaker faction as compared to the majority. Indeed, terrorism has often been considered the weapon of the weak, though not exclusively so. In fact, the term "terrorism" was originally invented to refer to state terrorism, namely, Le Regime de la Terreur (The Reign of Terror) of 1793–1794, conceived of by Maximilien Robespierre and his colleagues in the French Revolution as "an instrument of governance wielded by the recently established revolutionary *state*" (Hoffman, 1998, p. 15). Similarly, terrorism has been pervasively used by totalitarian states and their despotic leaders against their own citizens (Rummel, 1996). Hitler's Nazi Germany, Stalin's Soviet Union, right-wing military dictatorships that rose to power in Argentina, Chile, and Greece, as well as elected governments in El Salvador, Guatemala, Colombia, and Peru have all used terror against domestic populations to keep them in check.

Some authors reserve the term terrorism to violence committed by nonstate entities, using instead the term "terror" for state-committed violence. Be that as it may, it is of interest that, in the 20th century, nearly 169 million people were the victims of state terrorism, including 130 million people who were killed by their own governments. The remaining 39 million is the estimated number of civilians killed by enemy forces during various wars, whereas merely 518,000 civilians were killed in the 20th century by nonstate groups of which genuine terrorists (e.g., as opposed to guerilla fighters) are only a part (Rummel, 1996).

Nonetheless, terrorism could be inherently appealing to minorities because it may appear to represent a particularly effective, in some circumstances, the only effective means for achieving their objectives. As the political scientist James DeNardo (1985, Chapters 9–11) noted, small organizations resort to violence to compensate for what they lack in numbers. Indeed, terrorism has been generally considered "the great equalizer," and a source of considerable power. Precisely this logic is articulated in a 1998 speech by the Tamil Tiger's leader, Velupillai Prabhakaran. As he put it, "In terms of manpower, firepower and resources, the enemy was strong and the balance of military power was in his favor. Yet we had an extraordinary weapon which was not in the arsenal of the enemy. The courage and commitment of our fighters was our most powerful weapon in the battle."[†]

To be sure, technology considerably boosts the equalizing potential available to terrorists. By the 19th century, the invention of dynamite was already thought by revolutionaries and anarchists to equalize the relationship between them and the governments they were aiming to topple, a point that was explicitly argued in an 1885 pamphlet written by Johann Most, titled, *Revolutionary War Science* (Goldman, 2003). Of course, the more advanced the technology the greater its equalizing potential. The specter of nuclear, biological, or chemical weapons of mass destruction falling into terrorist hands is the great incubus of our times that fuels the current war in Iraq and has repercussions around the globe. The events of 9/11 have demonstrated the considerable costs in life and property that determined terrorists can

---

[†] LTTE (Liberation Tigers of Tamil Eelam) leader on Sri Lanka's Military Campaign, speech released by International Secretariat of LTTE, London, U.K., May 13, 1998. Available at www.eelamweb.com.

inflict using relatively conventional, albeit highly creative, means (e.g., flying aircraft into buildings). The acquisition by terrorists of weapons of mass destruction raises the stakes of horror a thousandfold. Thibaut and Kelley (1959) defined social power as the ability of one party to move another party over a range of outcomes defined subjectively in terms of their "goodness" or "badness." In these terms, the terrorists wield considerable power indeed, because at one end of the range of outcomes that terrorism can potentially effectuate is the horrific prospect of mass annihilation.

Terrorism as a Form of Innovation

An important, nearly definitional, feature of minority influence is its *innovativeness*. As Moscovici (1980, 1985) characterized it, minority influence consists of a break with extant social realities, including the accepted norms and conventions. In that sense, terrorist activity fits the mold of a minority influence very well.

The *means* whereby terrorists have been inflicting their violence have been characterized by considerable innovation. By now, early into the 21st century, terrorism boasts a rich inventory of tactical techniques honed by decades of terrorist experience, which are recorded in terrorist manuals, available on the Internet, and caught-up with cutting-edge technologies. Whereas the 19th-century anarchists aimed to induce terror through the gunning down of public figures, subsequent terrorist movements enlarged the repertory of violent moves to include plane hijackings, kidnapping and/ or hostage beheading, suicide bombings, car bombings, and poison gas.

Indeed, suicide attacks, one of the latest terrorist "inventions," have become a particularly deadly form of terrorism. Suicide attacks amounted to just 3% of all terrorist incidents from 1980 through 2003, but they accounted for 48% of all fatalities, making the average suicide terrorist attack 12 times deadlier than other forms of terrorism – even if the immense losses of 9/11 are not counted (if they are counted, suicide attacks account for 73% of total deaths). If a terrorist group does get its hands on a nuclear weapon, suicide attack is the best way to ensure that the bomb will go off, depicting the most troublesome scenario for its use. (Pape, 2005, p. 6)

Terrorist attackers have been innovative in their choice of targets, which have ranged from military bases to government buildings to public transportation systems, including the metro, trains, airplanes, and automobiles, to schools, hotels, theaters, discotheques, and restaurants. Terrorist attackers have also shown innovation in their choice of human targets, in the sense that they have ignored the strictest societal taboos: No longer are women, children, the aged, teenagers at a discotheque, tourists, athletes, or ordinary citizens at their places of work protected from harm. Such innovations in weapons, tactics, and targets have instilled in the public a pervasive feeling of danger that can bring disaster to anyone at anytime and anywhere. In the words of the journalist Thomas Friedman (2005), they create a sense that "the world is flat," that the playing field has been leveled and that no political, economic or military might, no geographical distance nor lack of personal involvement suffices to protect oneself and one's loved ones from potential violence that terrorists can unleash. That pervasive sense, fueling the global "war on terrorism" that many western states are currently waging, attests to the considerable power that terrorist minorities can wield through their recourse to unrestrained violence.

Resembling alternative forms of minority influence, wherein departures from accepted means and ways of social influence inspire majority resistance, so also does the normative break that terrorist activities represent evoke considerable resistance, loathing, and revulsion on part of the targeted majority. The combination of violence and the breech of taboos engenders a particularly strong repudiation of terrorism as a tactic and can empower a vehement resistance to terrorism. We revisit this point at a later juncture.

Conflict

A major element of minority influence is that it creates a cognitive conflict for the majority. Terrorist tactics also create considerable conflict having to do with the opposing possibilities of acceding to terrorists on the one hand and resisting them forcefully on the other hand. Acceding to the terrorist demands is appealing in the short run, for it promises to remove the proximal threat and to save lives, for example, in a hostage-taking accident. Not surprisingly, such option is particularly appealing to those most likely to be affected by the specific crisis and most likely interested in these short-term benefits, e.g. the hostages' families and friends. But from a long-term perspective, acceding to terrorist demands has been viewed as an unacceptable option for it may encourage further blackmail and involve humiliation and a loss of face to the acceding party. Thus, governmental officials entrusted with safeguarding their country's image and deterrent power are more likely to take the long view and opt for resisting the terrorists' demands. One might say that the beliefs that a terrorist crisis has been eliminated and that terrorism has been defeated represent two desired closures that are often in conflict with each other.

Terrorism's Conditions of Efficacy

Further insights into the nature of terrorism as a form of minority influence may be gained by close attention to the conditions for its efficacy. According to minority influence theory, minority influence is likely to be effective to the extent that it exhibits behavioral consistency, persistence, and internal coherence (Moscovici & Lage, 1976), and it is also more effective if it is congruent with the Zeitgeist than if it runs against it (Pérez, Papastamou, & Mugny, 1995). Similar features may contribute to the efficacy of terrorism.

PERSISTENCE AND TENACITY. Behavioral consistency, persistence, and internal coherence convey the image that the minority is committed, undeterred, unwavering, and resolute. These features are part and parcel of the terrorist strategy. For instance, the repeated suicide-bombing attempts by Palestinian terrorists or by the Tigers of Tamil in Sri Lanka, despite the attempts at suppression by the Israeli and the Sri Lankan armed forces, are meant to convey the undeterred, tenacious nature of the terrorists' commitment to the cause. Such commitment is vividly expressed in the 1995 statement by Nandini, a female LTTE (Liberation Tigers of Tamil Eelam) fighter: "As Black Tigers, they are a physical embodiment of self-determination and liberation. They employ their lives as missiles armed with the kind of determination and purpose that is unmatched by any conventional weapon that the Sinhala forces may deploy. There lies the strength and honor of our Black Tigers."‡

The very extremity of terrorist's actions and their willingness to die convey this message convincingly. Indeed, "talk is cheap", actions speak louder than words, and extreme, self-sacrificial, actions speak louder than do mild actions. In that sense, terrorism is functionally similar to other forms of minority influence with which social psychologists have been familiar.

CONFORMANCE TO ZEITGEIST. Social psychological analyses of minority influence that followed up on and extended Moscovici's work stress that the success of minority influence depends to some extent on its congruency with the prevailing Zeitgeist, that is, with the values, norms, and goals salient for the majority. How does terrorism fare in this regard? Terrorism seems to be diametrically opposite to the Zeitgest, in that majorities typically object to wanton violence and the killing of innocents. But things are more complex than that. Specifically, whether one considers terrorism as contrary to the Zeitgeist depends on *whose* Zeitgest one has in mind.

Where a terrorist minority serves the goals of an oppressed majority it may acquire an aura of legitimacy following the notion that the "end justifies

‡Quoted in Rohan Gunaratna, "The LTTE and Suicide Terrorism," *Frontline* (India), vol. 17, no. 3 (February 5–8, 2000).

the means". Thus, terrorism is often euphemized as a "fight for freedom" by those who share in the terrorist goals, hence, partake in the same Zeitgeist. For instance, through much of the second Palestinian *intifada*, approximately 80% of Palestinians supported the use of terrorism against Israel (Public Opinion Research of Israel, September 2003). On the other hand, those who do not share in a particular Zeitgeist, or who in fact embrace the opposite Zeitgeist, such as the group targeted by the terrorists (e.g., Israelis targeted by Palestinian terrorists or Americans targeted by global jihadists) are particularly likely to view terrorists' activities as illegitimate and despicable, labeling them as terrorism, a term that today carries a universally pejorative connotation.

In other words, terrorism as an influence tactic is particularly likely to be condoned by a group whose Zeigeist (and the goals and values it represents) the terrorism is assumed to be serving, and it is unlikely to be condoned by a group whose Zeitgeist it opposes. Even though we may regard terrorism as atrocious, the terrorists and their supporters may feel morally justified in their activities if they deem the ends advanced by terrorism superior to the ends forestalled.

Two Sources of Terrorists' Shared Reality: "Bottom-up" and "Top-down" Influences

The issue of zeitgeist is closely related to the phenomenon of the group's shared reality (Hardin & Higgins, 1996). Social psychological theory (e.g., see Jones & Gerard, 1967) suggests that such reality can be fashioned by two major sources. These are (a) majority opinions and (b) charismatic leaders. The former constitutes a "bottom-up" influence on the terrorists' world view, and the latter a "top-down" influence. We consider these in turn.

Terrorist groups can constitute what Crano (2001) recently referred to as "ingroup minorities." These are groups whose ends as well as means are generally approved of by the general communities in which they are embedded. The Zeitgeist of such groups is similar to that of their broader communities. And the terrorist group is thus dependent on the broader community morally and ideologically.

Bottom-up Effects: The Pyramid Model
Mccauley's (2004, p. 51) *Pyramid Model*, which has a social psychological parallel in Simon and Klandermans' model (2001), highlights the broad base of support that terrorist activists often require. The base of the pyramid consists of sympathizers with the terrorist cause who themselves may

not be prepared to launch terrorist attacks. This is the *sentiment pool* on whose support terrorists may count. "In Northern Ireland, for instance, the base of the pyramid is all who agree with 'Brits out'. In the Islamic world, the base of the pyramid is all those who agree that the U.S. has been hurting and humiliating Muslims for fifty years. The pyramid is essential to the terrorists for cover and for recruits." Beyond the provision of moral support, broad community approval also implies the likelihood of material assistance that the majority may extend to the terrorist minority, including escape routes, safe houses, training grounds, and the potential to recruit new members.

In this vein too, Gurr (1998, p. 100) wrote that the "erosion of political support is not an immediate cause of decline in terrorist campaigns but an underlying one." For instance, the decline in the 1970s of the Front de Libération du Québec (Quebec Liberation Front; FLQ) has been attributed to the decline of political support for its activities by the separatist Parti Québécois. Similarly, the decline in the United States of the Weather Underground and the Symbionese Liberation Army (SLA) has been attributed to a withdrawal of public support for the deadly violence these groups perpetrated. As Gurr (1998, p. 97) explained: "The general public's reaction to the rhetoric, disorder, and violence of this era crystallized in ... widespread opposition to the advocacy of radical social change and sharp resentment against groups making extreme demands or using disruptive or violent tactics."

Compare and contrast, for example, the urban European terrorists of the 1970s, such as the Red Army Faction in Germany (the Baader-Meinhof group) or the Brigate Rosse (Red Brigades) in Italy, with the current Islamic terrorist groups: the Hamas (the Islamic Resistance Movement), the Hezbollah, or the Al-Qaeda network. The urban terrorists were largely divorced from the Zeitgeist of the majority population in whose midst they were operating. Indeed, their existence was fraught with considerable hardship, and they were ultimately apprehended and/or defeated. By contrast, the Islamic terrorists, who profess to serve goals shared by the community at large, are doing rather well. In the Israeli-Palestinian context, Hamas was the winner of the 2006 elections; Hezbollah did well in the Lebanese 2005 elections, and it is currently exerting a push to enhance its political influence; and the support for Al-Qaeda in countries like Pakistan and Afghanistan has been considerable.

Top-down Effects
An alternative source of shared reality, of particular importance for terrorist groups that are ideologically estranged from the broader community,

is charismatic leadership. Indeed, charismatic leaders are often found in deviant groups of various kinds (examples include Jim Jones, the late leader of the Peoples Temple, Reverend Sun Myung Moon of the Holy Spirit Association for the Unification of World Christianity [the Unification Church] and many others) and terrorist groups are no exception. Osama Bin Laden, Sheikh AhmadYassin of the Hamas, and Sayid Hassan Nasralla of Hezbollah exemplify the kind of confident leadership that is capable of inspiring thousands of followers and instilling in them the sense that theirs is the correct way and world view.

It is also of interest that, where the group's primary source of epistemic authority (Kruglanski et al., 2005) rests with the charismatic leader, removal of this person may bring the group's activity to a standstill. The rapid and steady decline of Peru's Shining Path, was linked closely to the capture of its founder and supreme leader, Abimael Guzmán, in 1992. Similarly, the capture by Turkish forces of Abdullah Öcalan in 1999 set adrift the Kurdistan Workers' Party that he had led, and it subsequently failed to maintain any sense of its former military or political cohesion (Radu, 2000).

Subjective Rationality of Terrorism

Being in a minority isn't easy, nor is it easy being a terrorist. The considerable sacrifices that participating in a terrorist group demand (including the everpresent possibility, if not certainty, of losing one's life) typically require more than just the assurance that one's actions are consistent with the Zeitgeist or in agreement with the views of a charismatic leader. It is necessary to believe in terrorism and, in particular, that it is an efficient means to achieving important goals to which one subscribes, and that it is not at variance with other goals or moral imperatives.

Evidence for the *efficacy* of terrorism, for instance, the withdrawal of the Americans, the French, and the Italians from Lebanon following the terrorist attacks by Hezbollah in 1983, and of the Israeli forces in 2000 may increase the readiness to embrace terrorism as a tactic. In this vein, the Palestinian Islamic Jihad leader Ramadan Shallah argued in November 2001: "The shameful defeat that Israel suffered in southern Lebanon and which caused its army to flee it in terror was not made on the negotiations table but on the battlefield and through jihad and martyrdom, which achieved a great victory for the Islamic resistance and Lebanese people ... We would not exaggerate if we said that the chances of achieving victory in Palestine are greater than in Lebanon ... If the enemy could not bear the losses of the war on the border strip with Lebanon, will it be able to withstand a long war of attrition in the heart of its security dimension and major cities?"[§]

Even if terrorism is perceived as effective, the question may arise whether there do not exist less costly and/or more effective means to the same ends. Often the answer might depend on matters of time and place. On occasion, a terrorist organization may possess alternative goals whose pursuit may require the relinquishment or the temporary suspension of terrorism. For instance, Hezbollah markedly reduced its attacks against Israel following the Israeli withdrawal from Southern Lebanon. Such attacks, which were likely to prompt costly Israeli reprisals, were at odds with Hezbollah's political goals and those of the Shia Muslim population that constitute Hezbollah's main supporters. In the aftermath of its surprising electoral successes in 2006, Hamas has suspended its terrorist activities against Israel, presumably because they might introduce the kind of instability and disruption that would undermine the task of governance with which Hamas has been entrusted. Based on similar logic, Jibril Rajoub, the PA's (Palestinian Authority) national security advisor and a leader of the second generation of Fatah, expressed his determined objection to the launching of missiles from the Gaza Strip on an Al-Arabiya TV talk show on November 4, 2005, following Israel's disengagement from this territory, on grounds that: "the residents of the Gaza Strip have a right to live in peace." (2005)

Rationales for Terrorism's Efficacy

"Unfreezing" (Kruglanski, 2004)
In classic minority influence theory (Moscovici, 1980), a major effect of minority activity is *epistemic*. The innovative, dissenting views expressed by the minority crack the "smooth surface" of extant social realities and prompt an "unfreezing" of received conventions and accepted world views. At least some terrorist ideologues have been explicitly aiming for such an effect. As the Russian revolutionary Vera Figner described it in 1930, terrorism is "a means of agitation to draw people from their torpor".[¶] Forty-three years later, Fatah's leader Abu Iyad made a similar point in stating, "We are planting the seed. Others will harvest it ..." George Habash of the PFLP (Popular Front for the Liberation of Palestine) noted in 1970 "We force people to ask what is going on" (cited in Crenshaw, 1998, p. 18). And Gudrun Ensslin, Andreas

---

[§] Ramadan Shallah interview, BBC Summary of World Broadcasts, November 3, 2001.
[¶] Vera Figner, Memoires d'une revolutionnaire (Paris: Gallimard, 1930), p. 206.

Baader's lover stated, "As for the state of the future, the time after victory, that is not our concern. We build the revolution, not the socialist model ..." (cited in Crenshaw, 1998, p. 57). Such statements demonstrate that terrorist ideologues are aware of their potential for upsetting the status quo and, hence, for preparing the ground for subsequent developments.

Provocation

A psychologically sophisticated aspect of the terrorist rationale, and one that clearly belongs in the arsenal of "powerless" minorities, is that it anticipates the majority's reactions to terrorism and counts on them. As Crenshaw (1998, p. 19) put it, "Terrorists often think that by provoking indiscriminate repression against the population, terrorism will heighten popular disaffection, demonstrate the justice of terrorist claims, and enhance the attractiveness of the political alternative the terrorists represent. In this vein, the Red Army Faction sought to make fascism visible in Germany. In Brasil, Carlos Marighela aimed to "transform the country's political situation into a military one. Then discontent will spread to all social groups and the military will be held exclusively responsible for failures" (Carlos Marighela, For the Liberation of Brasil. Harmondsworth: Penguin, 1971, p. 113). More recently, Osama Bin Laden (2003) has expressed similar sentiments in hoping that Al-Qaeda activities will transform the United States into a police state and unite the Muslims of the world against America.

Defeating the Majority

The unfreezing and provocation effects are relatively modest in their claims, hence terrorist movements are particularly likely to aim for them in the incipient stages of their efforts. However, after terrorists have been able to claim important material successes – they may become bold enough to hope to attain the desired end states on their own. For instance, according to analysts (www.haaretz.com), some Islamic terrorists (Sayeed Hassan Naserallah, for instance) subscribe to the spider web theory of Western power, which holds that even though states like Israel or the United States appear powerful from the outside – they are internally weak and will retreat and crumble when confronted with resolute force, just like a spider web that can be readily swept away despite its solid, constructed appearance. This view holds that the Western powers are "soft" and "spoiled" rather than "tough," and that they are "unduly" sensitive to the loss of lives and to public opinion. According to this theory, such sensibilities constrain the ability of Western states to carry out a sustained struggle and reduce their willingness and resolve to carry it out.

In this vein, Bin Laden, in a 2003 speech, has described America as a paper tiger that can be coerced into surrender by inflicting relatively modest costs on its society. In his own words "America is a great power possessed of tremendous military might and a wide-ranging economy, but all this is built upon an unstable foundation which can be targeted, with special attention to its obvious weak spots. If America is hit in one hundredth of those spots, God willing, it will stumble, wither away and relinquish world leadership and its oppression. A small group of young Islamic fighters managed ... to provide people with proof of the fact that it is possible to wage war upon and fight against a so-called 'great power' ... because they used Jihad ... any means which brings victory is worthwhile."

The Morality of Terrorism

A major question confronting the practitioners of terrorism is its moral justifiability in reference to such universal values as fairness, justice, or the protection of innocents. Haidt and Graham (2006) recently distinguished between several types of morality, namely, morality of the *ingroup*, morality of *harm* and *reciprocity*, morality of *hierarchy* (obeying the "powers that be"), and morality of *purity (or divinity)*. All of these themes frequently appear in justifications that terrorist ideologues offer to terrorist practitioners and their supporters. Specifically, justifications for terrorism have typically invoked moral arguments having to do with justice to one's people, freedom from oppression, or retribution for crimes against one's nation, representing Haidt and Graham's morality of the ingroup.

The moralities of harm and reciprocity seem apparent in the following justification for terrorism offered by Osama Bin Laden (in a 1997 CNN interview): "We declared jihad against the United States because the U.S. government is unjust, criminal and tyrannical. The mention of the United States reminds us before everything else of those innocent children who were dismembered, their heads and arms cut off ..."

Finally, the morality of purity or divinity is often used to justify terrorism. Abu Musab Al Zarqawi, the architect of the jihadist insurgence in Iraq said this in a 2005 address about the justification of suicide operations: "There is no doubt that Allah has ordered us to target the infidels, to kill them and fight them, by any means that can achieve this." As Pape (2005) noted, any cultural difference between rivals can be manipulated by resistance leaders, and religious difference is ready-made for the purpose of demonization of the enemy and justification of indiscriminate killing because it goes to the heart of the moral code attributed to the opponent. That is so because "most religions claim to possess superior insight into ultimate truths, from which it follows that devotees of any other religion must be misguided, amoral, immoral, or even actively evil" (Pape, 2005, p. 90).

To couch their justifications for terrorism in terms of the morality of purity, Islamic terrorist movements, such as Hezbollah, Hamas, and Al-Qaeda, often look to Islamic clerics for direction and guidance. Muhammad Hussein Fadlallah, the spiritual leader of the Shia Hezbollah issued, in 1996, a statement legitimizing terrorism.[a] The Sunni extremists who bombed New York City's World Trade Center the first time around, that is, in 1993, specifically obtained a *fatwa* from Sheikh Omar Abdel-Rahman, and the founder and spiritual leader of the Hamas movement and a major legitimizer of its campaign of suicide terrorism was the Imam Sheikh Ahmad Ibrahim Yassin.

In summary, as with all forms of minority influence, terrorist activity, too, is anything but "business as usual". For that reason, and for the considerable sacrifices it demands from its practitioners, terrorism requires not only a strong commitment to the shared reality of one's group (whether derived from popular community support or based on charismatic leadership) but also considerable subjective rationality based on arguments for its efficacy given the group's objectives, as well as its morality given the group's values.

HOW EFFICIENT IS TERRORISM AS A FORM OF MINORITY INFLUENCE?

In assessing terrorism's efficacy as a form of minority influence, it may be well to distinguish between its *proximal* and *distal* effects. Terrorism certainly has a profound proximal impact. According to the comprehensive database created by Robert Pape (2005), which includes every known global suicide attack from 1980 until 2003, 7 of the 13 suicide terrorist campaigns completed from 1980 to 2003 were positively correlated with significant policy changes by the target state toward the terrorists' major political goals. In one case, the terrorists' territorial goals were fully achieved (Hezbollah versus U.S./F, 1983); in three cases, the terrorists' territorial aims were partly achieved (Hezbollah versus Israel, 1983–85, Hamas versus Israel, 1994, and Hamas versus Israel, 1994–95); in one case, the target government entered into sovereignty negotiations with the terrorists (LTTE versus Sri Lanka,

---

[a] Quoted in Laura Marlowe, "A Fiery Cleric's Defense of Jihad", Time (New York), January 15, 1996.

1993–94 and 2001); and in one case, the terrorist organization's top leader was released from prison (Hamas versus Israel, 1997) (Pape, 2005, p. 64).

Loss of innocent human lives arouses widespread emotions, inspires considerable fear, and disrupts the normal course of things, causing a major unfreezing and prompting intense cognitive efforts to solve the problems that terrorists bring up. The 9/11 events inflicted damage in the billions of dollars, against an "investment" of less than a hundred thousand dollars, and terrorism in Israel virtually killed tourism to this country, a major source of revenue. A tremendous amount of resources is being spent on various security measures, and the terrorist activities receive ample attention in the media. Proximally then, terrorism can be quite effective.

Up to a point, too, terrorism may be able to accomplish its distal political ends by conveying the resolve and desperation of minorities who resort to this tactic and by drawing attention to the possible legitimacy of its claims. Several countries, including Israel, Kenya, Cyprus, and Algeria, "owe their independence at least in part to nationalist political movements that employed terrorism against colonial powers" (Hoffman, 1998, p. 26). In those cases, the conflict between the opponent forces of yielding versus fighting the terrorism-employing minority is typically resolved when terrorism is replaced by statesmanship and diplomacy, occasionally carried out by the very same people that formerly resorted to terrorist tactics, as exemplified by Yassir Arafat, Menachem Begin, or Itzhak Shamir.

The shift of tactics from terrorism to diplomacy allows the majority to reject terrorism, to uphold its resolve to "never negotiate with terrorists" and hence to save face, while at the same time recognizing the legitimacy of minority claims and making the appropriate compromises to meet those claims. In this case too, the relevance of minority influence theory to understanding terrorism is striking, for this theory has long recognized the duality of overt rejection of minority claims and tactics, coupled with a covert readiness to accept the terrorist arguments and demands (Wood, 2000).

From this perspective, it is of interest to consider the limits to the efficacy of terrorist tactics. Specifically, terrorism may fail in two distinct ways: (a) If its claims are excessive, that is, if they involve goals that the majority feels it cannot grant. For instance, the global shifts in American foreign policy that Al-Qaeda leaders have been hoping for may be simply unacceptable to American administrations. Similarly, allowing millions of Palestinians the right of return to Israel is seen by most Israelis as spelling a demographic disaster and the end of the Jewish state; hence, it is viewed as unacceptable by a majority of Israel's population; (b) where at a crucial point the minority fails to make the switch from the illegitimate use of violence (that terrorism represents for the targeted majority) to more legitimate forms of negotiation. The confluence of these two characteristics: excessiveness of demands and the unwillingness to relinquish violence may in fact harden the resolve of the majority to resist the minority. The toughening of the Israeli public opinion and the election of a "tough guy" like Ariel Sharon in reaction to what was perceived as a return to violence after a series of Israeli concessions by the Israeli governments of Itzhak Rabin, Shimon Peres, and Ehud Barak, reflects that kind of backlash. So does the war on terrorism and the American resolve to demonstrate its toughness by launching campaigns in Afghanistan and Iraq. In those latter instances, the terrorist tactics appeared to have boomeranged to produce the opposite consequences to what the users of terrorism intended.

Of course, it could be argued that these reactions merely help the terrorists in the final analysis in that they represent the succumbing to terrorist provocation by the targeted majorities, which may ultimately bring about their defeat. The negative public opinion (in Europe, Asia, and the Middle East) that greeted the U.S.- and British-led assault on Iraq, could be seen as a case of perceived overreaction to terrorism undermining public support for the reactive majority. Yet, if an excessive response to provocation is effective in eliminating the support for terrorism, the provocation, like the proverbial "surgical operation" might succeed, yet the "patient" (the terrorists, in this instance) may be dead.

Epilogue

In course of the 20th century and beyond, terrorism has been often used by relatively powerless minorities as an influence tactic against powerful majorities. In several regards, the process whereby terrorism exerts its effects is closely akin to the way other forms of minority influence may work. In this sense then, minority influence theory represents a powerful conceptual vehicle for understanding terrorism. And, reciprocally, the observation of the real-world effects of terrorism, reactions to terrorism, successes and failures of terrorism, and the limits of terrorism as an influence tactic may teach us a thing or two about minority influence more generally. Considering minority influence in the context of terrorism research highlights the importance of the distinction between ingroup and outgroup minorities (Crano, 2001). An ingroup minority of a group in conflict with another may be considered an apex of a pyramid which base is constituted by majority of that group. Such minority may be supported by the ingroup majority in carrying out the struggle against the common enemy. In that sense, the minority, far from being a conflict with the majority, is actually venerated and admired by the ingroup majority. Furthermore, withdrawal of the majority support from the minority may bring about its collapse (as attested by the downfall of the Weatherman Underground in the United States in the early 1970s after the American New Left stopped supporting its violent activities; or the decline of the FLQ following the withdrawal of support of its activities by the separatist Parti Québécois (Sprinzak, 1990). In short, whereas ingroup minorities are in a cognitive or behavioral conflict with the ingroup majority, outgroup minorities may present a fighting avant garde representing the broader interests of its own majority. All of which suggests that we, as social psychologists, may benefit from paying close attention to terrorism as a phenomenon and engaging in cross disciplinary discussions and research with other social scientists interested in this topic.

REFERENCES

Crano, W. D. (2001). Social influence, social identity, and ingroup leniency. In C. K. W. De Dreu & N. K. De Vries (Eds.), *Group consensus and minority influence: Implications for innovation* (pp. 122–143). Oxford, UK: Blackwell.

Crenshaw, M. (1978). *Revolutionary Terrorism: The FLN in Algeria 1945–1962*. Stanford, CA: Hoover Institution.

(1990/1998). Questions to be answered, research to be done, knowledge to be applied. In W. Reich (Ed.), *Origins of terrorism: Psychologies, ideologies, theologies, states of mind* (pp. 247–260). Washington, DC: Woodrow Wilson Center Press.

De Nardo, J. (1985). *Power in numbers: The political strategy of protest and rebellion*. Princeton, NJ: Princeton University Press.

Fields, R. M. (1979). Child terror victims and adult terrorists. *Journal of Psychohistory, 1*, 71–75.

Friedman, T. L. (2005). *The world is flat, a brief history of the 21st century*. New York: Farrar, Straus and Giroux.

Ganor, B. (2005). *The counter-terrorism puzzle: A guide for decision makers*. New Brunswick, NJ: Transaction Publishers.

Goldman, E. (2003). *A documentary history of the American years 1890–1901*. Berkeley, CA: University of California Press.

Gurr, T. R. (1990/1998). Terrorism in democracies: Its social and political bases. In W. Reich (Ed.), *Origins of terrorism: Psychologies, ideologies, theologies, states of mind* (p. 94). Washington, DC: Woodrow Wilson Center Press.

Haidt, J., & Graham, J. (2006). When morality opposes justice: Conservatives have moral intuitions that liberals may not recognize. Second draft of invited submission to special issue of *Social Justice Research* on emotions and justice.

Hardin, C. D., & Higgins, E. T. (1996). Shared reality: How social verification makes the subjective objective. In E. T. Higgins & R. M. Sorrentino (Eds.), *Handbook of motivation and cognition: The interpersonal context* (Vol. 3, pp. 28–77). New York: Guilford.

Hoffman, B. (1998). *Inside Terrorism*. New York: Columbia University Press.

Hutchinson, Martha C. (1972). The concept of revolutionary terrorism. *Journal of Conflict Resolution, 16,* 383–396.

Jones, E. E., & Gerard, H. B. (1967). *Foundations of social psychology.* New York: John Wiley.

Kruglanski, A. W., & Fishman, S. (2006). Terrorism between "syndrome" and "tool." *Current Directions in Psychological Science, 15,* 45.

Kruglanski, A. W., Raviv, A., Bar-Tal, D., Raviv, A., Ellis, S., Bar, R., Mannetti, L., et al. (2005) Says who?: Epistemic authority effects in social judgment. In M. P. Zanna (Ed.), *Advances in Experimental Social Psychology, 36,* 345–418.

Kruglanski, A. W. (2004). *The psychology of closed mindedness.* New York: Psychology Press.

Marighela, C. (1971). *For the liberation of Brasil* (p. 113). Harmondsworth: Penguin.

McCauley, C. (2004). Psychological issues in understanding terrorism and the response to terrorism. In C. Stout (Ed.), *The psychology of terrorism* (pp. 36–37). Danbury, CT: Greenwood Publishing.

Moscovici, S. (1980). Toward a theory of conversion behavior. In L. Berkowitz (Ed.), *Advances in experimental social psychology* (Vol. 13, pp. 209–239). New York: Academic Press.

   (1985). Social influence and conformity. In G. Lindzey & E. Aronson (Eds.), *Handbook of social psychology* (3rd ed., Vol. 2, pp. 347–412) New York: Random House.

Moscovici, S., & Lage, E. (1976). Studies in social influence III: Majority versus minority influence in a group, *European Journal of Social Psychology, 6,* 149–174.

Most, J. (1885, July 25). Action as propaganda. *Freiheit.* Retrieved from: http://dwardmac.pitzer.edu/Anarchist_Archives//bright/most/actionprop.html

Osama Bin Laden. (2003). Bin Laden's Sermon for the Feast of the Sacrifice. Middle East Media Research Institute (MEMRI). Retrieved from http://www.memri.org/bin/articles.cgi?Area=jihad&ID=SP47603#

Pape, R. A. (2005). *Dying to win, the strategic logic of suicide terrorism.* New York: Random House.

Perez, J. A., Papastamou, S., & Mugny, G. (1995). Where is the causality: A comment on Clark. (1990). *European Journal of Social Psychology, 25,* 703–710.

Prabhakaran, V. (1998, May 13). LTTE leader on Sri Lanka's Military Campaign. Speech released by International Secretariat of LTTE, London, U.K. Retrieved from www.eelamweb.com

Radu, M. (2000, September 28). Is the PKK in Turkey on the ropes? E-Notes. Retrieved from http://www.fpri.org/enotes/balkansturkey.19990928.radu.pkkontheropes.htm

Rajoub, J. (2005, November 4). Al-Arabiya TV talk show. Translation retrieved from http://www.intelligence.org.il/eng/eng_n/pa_e.htm

Rummel, R. J. (1996). *Death by Government.* New Brunswick, NJ: Transaction Publishers.

Schmid, A. P., & Jongman, A. J. (1988). *Political terrorism: A guide to actors, authors, concepts, data basis, theories and literature.* Amsterdam: Transaction Books.

Shallah, R. (2001, November 3). Ramadan Shallah Interview. *BBC Summary of World Broadcasts.*

Simon, B., & Klandermans, B. (2001). Politicized collective identity: A social psychological analysis. *American Psychologist, 56,* 319–331.

Speckhard, A. (2005). Understanding suicide terrorism: Countering human bombs and their senders. In J. S. Purcell & J. D. Weintraub (Eds.), *Topics in terrorism: Toward a transatlantic consensus on the nature of the threat* (Vol. I, pp. 1–23). Washington, DC: Atlantic Council Publication.

Speckhard, A., & Akhmedova, K. (2006). Black widows: The Chechen female suicide terrorists. In Y. Schweitzer (Eds.), *Female suicide terrorists 2006* (pp. 63–80). Tel Aviv: Jaffe Center Publication.

Sprinzak, E. (1990). The psychopolitical formation of extreme left terrorism in a democracy: The case of the Weathermen. In W. Reich (Ed.), *Origins of terrorism: Psychologies, ideologies, theologies, states of mind* (pp. 65–85). Cambridge: Cambridge University Press.

Thibaut, J. W., & Kelley, H. H. (1959). *The social psychology of groups.* New York: John Wiley.

Wood, W. (2000). Persuasion and social influence. *Annual Review of Psychology, 51,* 539–570.

10

The Stigma of Racist Activism

KATHLEEN M. BLEE

Erving Goffman's (1963, p. 3) description of a stigmatized person as one who is "reduced in our minds from a whole and usual person to a tainted discounted one" captures the stigma that attaches to those involved in the modern racist movement in the United States, a loosely connected confederation of White supremacist, Ku Klux Klan, White separatist, neo-Nazi, and White-power skinhead groups.[1] Media depictions of racist activists typically portray them in caricature as poorly educated, ignorant, pathological, irrational, gullible, and marginal persons who try to compensate for their social and psychological failings by scapegoating other groups. This representation of racists as exhibiting what Mitch Berbrier (1999, p. 411) summarizes as "hatred, boorish irrationality, and violence or violent intent," is widely accepted, notwithstanding studies that find that most racist activists have rather average backgrounds, personalities, and ways of thinking before joining racist groups. Moreover, negative characterizations of racists tend to become explanatory. The personality problems and social isolation of racist activists are accepted as the reason for their distorted ideas, although evidence suggests that such characteristics are likely to be the outcome of being in racist groups, rather than a cause (Blee, 2002).

Unlike many other stigmatized groups, racist activists are stigmatized on the basis of a set of beliefs and practices they have chosen to adopt. In this sense, the stigma of racism is voluntary and under the control of the person who is stigmatized (Klandermans & Linden, 2006), rather than assigned on the basis of an ascribed characteristic like disability, age, or race. However, there are practical limits to the extent to which the stigma of racism, once attached, can be eliminated. Not only can it be dangerous for activists to

I appreciate useful suggestions on an earlier version of this draft from Linda Morrison and the editors.

defect from groups that are engaged in planning or acts of committing violence and terrorism, but, even when exit is possible, it may be difficult to overcome the suspicion that a defector has not entirely renounced allegiance to organized racism.

Little is known about how U.S. racist activists perceive and cope with stigma, in part because few studies focus on activists themselves. Most scholarship on organized racism in the United States relies for data on the public propaganda of racist groups or the pronouncements of those who proclaim themselves to be their leaders or spokesmen.[2] Research based on racist propaganda and public statements identifies two common responses to stigma: *reverse victimization* and *disidentification*. Building on James Holstein and Gale Miller's (1990) idea that claims of victimization are rhetorical practices used to deflect responsibility for problematic action, Berbrier (2000) describes the widespread insistence among racists that Whites are the true victims of discrimination, an impression-management strategy meant to justify their actions as reasonable and necessary in the face of the erosion of White rights. Another response, what Berbrier (1999) terms disidentification, is exemplified by "Wilmot Robertson,[3]" the pseudonym for a White-supremacist author and magazine editor who attempted to evade negative evaluation by presenting himself as a nonviolent intellectual, different from and better than the ordinary racist activists to which stigma is rightfully assigned. Such a response is not confined to the self-proclaimed intellectuals of the racist movement, according to Berbrier (2002), but is found in a number of racist groups that attempt to distance themselves from negative connotations of the label "racist." Unlike the strategy of reverse victimization, disidentification does not challenge the validity of the negative stigmatization of racism but only one's assignment to the stigmatized category.[4] A third response to racist stigma is *normalization*, discussed by Betty Dobratz and Stephanie Shanks-Meile (1997) in their analysis of the discourse and structure of the White-separatist segment of the racist movement. Normalization is a strategy meant to evade stigma by presenting oneself as ordinary rather than extreme. This is evident in the effort of White supremacists and separatists to be seen by the general public as belonging to the mainstream by running for electoral office, as David Duke – long associated with various Klans, neo-Nazis, and other White-supremacist groups – has done repeatedly in the state of Louisiana.

These studies provide a useful view of how racist groups handle stigma, but they are limited to the public face of organized racism; that is, what is available in the propaganda of racist media and the pronouncements of its spokesmen. Such data provide insight into how the racist *movement* deals with its stigmatization, but they give little information about how racist *activists* do so. Indeed, there is reason to suspect that there may be a signifi-cant gap between the public and private sides of contemporary organized racism. A number of works (Aho, 1990; Billig, 1978; Blee, 2002; Ezekiel, 1995; Fielding, 1981) find a disjuncture between the ideas and attitudes dis-played in the public and private spheres of racist or right-wing extremist groups, especially that activists' private views can deviate from the public tenets of their groups. Are there similar differences in how racist individu-als and groups manage stigma in the United States? Research on extremist right-wing party members in the Netherlands finds that, unlike the univer-sal responses portrayed in the public face of extremism, the responses of individual activists to their negative stigmatization as xenophobes, Nazis, fascists, fanatics, troublemakers, and opportunists differ according to how they entered the extreme right (Klandermans & Linden, 2006). Some adopted the stigma as a matter of pride; others denied it or tried to ignore it. The extent to which this finding is generalizable to racists in the United States, however, is questionable. Although Bert Klandermans and Annette Linden argue that negative stigmatization is an "almost inevitable conse-quence of activism of the extreme right," there are likely to be significant differences in how members of official (if extremist) political parties in the Netherlands and the more marginalized and less politically insitutionalized racist groups in the United States are stigmatized and how they respond to stigma.

A STUDY OF ORGANIZED RACISTS

To understand how U.S. racist activists cope with stigma, I examine data from a study of female grassroots activists in a variety of U.S. racist groups in the 1990s. I focus on women for two reasons. First, in contrast to ear-lier periods in which organized racism was predominantly male, the racial movement today is actively, and successfully, recruiting female members. The reasons for this shift are complex, involving competition among groups for increased membership and perceptions by some racist leaders that women are less likely than men to attract police attention and more likely to bring partners and spouses into the movement. In any case, the outcome of this recruiting effort is clear. Most racist groups have an increasing number of women members – although not leaders – and in some groups women are becoming a majority of members (Blee, 2002). Thus, attention to the grassroots level of organized racism – racist activists, rather than leaders – requires attention to its female base. Second, I have found women racists to be more willing than are racist men to discuss how they manage the complexities of life in organized racism. This stems in part from my position as a female interviewer, but also is the result of women's exclusion from roles as leaders or spokespersons in almost all racist groups, which makes them less concerned about the effects of expressing personal opinions that might not fit the official positions of their group.

The narratives presented below are taken from extensive life-history interviews that I conducted in the mid-1990s with 34 women racist activists (Blee, 2002).[5] These women were selected from a purposive sample of racist groups based on a sampling frame of all then-active racist groups that I constructed in a year-long compilation of racist publications, events, postings, and other activities. The groups were selected to create variability in type of group (Klan, neo-Nazi, etc.) and geographical area. Once groups were identified, I solicited from target groups women who varied by age and position (general member, semileader, etc.). This resulted in a sample of respondents who ranged in age from 16 to 90, with a median age of 24. Fourteen were in neo-Nazi (non-skinhead) groups, six were in Ku Klux Klans, eight were White-power skinheads, and six were in other White-supremacist groups.

I identified possible interviewees and convinced them to participate through a variety of methods tailored to individual groups, including using contacts I had with other racists, media, researchers, and even police. I began by asking each woman to describe in detail her life story – how she became a racist activist. From that point, the interviews were very unstructured, allowing the interviewee to define the importance of issues by leading our discussion toward what she regarded as salient concerns (Holstein & Gubrium, 1995). Through these techniques, I sought to record the meaning- and sense-making actions of racist women – how they understood themselves and the racist groups of which they were a part.

RACIST GROUPS AND THEIR ENEMIES

How racist activists perceive and react to the stigma of racial activism is influenced by two interrelated group-level factors: the structure of the contemporary racist movement and racist ideologies about the nature of the larger society. The structure of the racist movement in the United States today increasingly resembles a terrorist network, with small and loosely connected groups, many (although not all) of which are focused on provoking cataclysmic violence[6] to foment "race war" and restore the eroding privileges of White Aryans.

Compared to earlier times, the modern racist movement has few declared, visible members. Although it is difficult to estimate membership in a highly secretive movement in which many adherents guard their involvement carefully and what constitutes membership is difficult to define, it is clear that contemporary racist groups have only a tiny fraction of the number involved in previous waves of organized racism. The Ku Klux Klan of the 1920s had between 3 million and 5 million men and women working for White, native-born, Protestant rights against what they saw as the encroachment of African-Americans, Jews, Catholics, and immigrants (Blee, 1991). In contrast, the modern racist movement may have as few as 10,000 members and five times that number who are associated in some way.

The contemporary U.S. racist movement is not only small; it is also highly fragmented. With hundreds of White supremacist, neo-Nazi, Ku Klux Klan, and White- power skinhead groups, organized racism is a network of loosely linked groups, small cells, and individuals. Indeed, this loose structure – known in the racist movement as the strategy of *leaderless resistance* – is a deliberate effort by several racist leaders to minimize their group's chance of detection and infiltration by government authorities while providing a means by which the ideas of racial hate can be cultivated and plans for ensuring White privilege hatched. Many racist groups, cells, and individuals are now connected with each other primarily through encrypted and coded Internet postings. At the same time, they use the internet as a means by which to spread their views to a broad public that could not be reached through traditional means of propaganda like newsletters and flyers.

In spite of its organizational fragmentation, the racist movement is increasingly integrated by a widespread emphasis on anti-Semitism and conspiratorial ideas, especially the notion that politics, the economy, and even daily life are under Jewish control. The historian George Mosse (1985, p. 134) argues that racism is a "scavenger ideology," a characterization that fits U.S. organized racism. Although U.S. racist movements have consistently regarded African-Americans as their collective enemies, modern racist groups also target a number of other groups, including immigrants from Africa and Asia, gay men and lesbians, federal government workers, and, most pointedly, Jews. Indeed, in recent years, most racist groups have increasingly portrayed Jews as their primary enemy. The focus on Jews reflects the increasing integration of U.S. racist groups into global networks of racism that seek to create an international "pan-Aryan movement" to combat what they regard as the insidious control of Jews in many nations of the world. It also reflects the widespread acceptance of the tenets of Christian Identity across many segments of the racist movement (Barkun,

1994; Gardell, 2003). Christian Identity is a racist theology that argues that peoples of color are descendants of creatures that existed before Adam and Eve were created in the Garden of Eden (thus are "pre-Adamic" and pre-human) and that Jews are the literal descendants of the devil. Traditional anti-Semitic ideologies have portrayed Jews as doing the bidding of Satan, but the ideas of Christian Identity move in a more dangerous direction. If Jews are embodiments of Satan, they must be eradicated, an idea that has fueled fantasies and occasionally practices of extreme anti-Semitic violence.

The centrality of Jews to organized racists today has created unusual alliances and divisions. Earlier racist movements in the United States tended to be fervently nationalistic; the 1920s Klan, for example, characterized itself as "100% American" (Blee, 1991). In contrast, many racists today view the U.S. government – especially at the federal level – as deeply compromised by Jewish values, resulting in what they call a Zionist Occupation Government (ZOG). For this reason, many racists now regard African-Americans as the puppets of Jewish overlords; some even suggest allying with Black anti-Semitic groups to combat their mutual enemy. Some racists have even suggested developing limited alliances with fundamentalist Arab Muslims, a group they generally regard as people of color and therefore an obstacle to White supremacy, as a means of broadening the attack on Jews across the world. In addition to changing its targets, the obsession of organized racists with Jews has been accompanied by heightened conspiratorial thinking (Barkun, 1998). Jews, they claim, control the world, but do so invisibly. Jewish power is insidious because it is difficult to detect; in fact, the very lack of evidence of a world ruling class of Jews is touted as proof of its effectiveness.

The tiny and fragmented nature of the modern racist movement, with its focus on identifying the enemies of White supremacy and its intense belief in conspiracies, nurtures a sense among its adherents that the outside world unfairly victimizes those who support White-supremacist agendas. Racist groups instruct activists to expect negative reactions from those outside their world; indeed, such reactions are commonly presented as evidence that the world is controlled by Jews and others intent on dismantling the rights of White Aryans.

INDIVIDUAL PERCEPTIONS OF STIGMA

In my interviews, racist women spoke often and without prompting about how they perceived themselves as stigmatized as racial activists. They related that people view them – inaccurately – as threatening, naive, and the pawns of husbands and boyfriends (although few actually entered racist groups through male intimates). Particularly offensive to them was the stigma of ignorance. One neo-Nazi confided that "everybody, I don't care who, wonders why. 'Why would she be so stupid as to join something like that?' Or, 'why would she be in that?'"

In their stories, women implied that other people saw their racist activism as what John Lofland (1969, p. 124) terms a "pivotal category," that is, one that "is singled out and treated as the most important and significant feature of the person or persons being dealt with." Some women resented the implication that they should be seen only in terms of their racism. This was particularly problematic for new recruits into organized racism, for whom social relations and status in the nonracist world were important. One young woman complained that since she became involved publicly with the Klan, she has not been able to

> state my opinion where I feel it's needed. Like, I went to church with my grandmother … and a lot of people were whispering. … I don't get up in church and say, 'yeah, I'd like to announce that I'm in the Klan or anything like that.' But I believe that if you go to church then you are putting out your opinion that you're very open-minded and you shouldn't be whispering, talking behind people's back. There was lots of people behind us talking. I heard them mention the Klan and I turned around and I told them [that] I'm not going to get into a discussion. If they would like to discuss it, there's a right time and a proper place, and if they wanted to discuss it outside the church, after church, I'd be more than happy to talk to them. But they left before we did and they naturally did not stay to discuss it.

Other racist women considered the singular focus of outsiders on their racial activism to be less problematic. Indeed, some regarded this as a "badge of honor" (Berbrier, 1999; Klandermans & Linden, 2006). Racist activists who sought to distance themselves from the outside world – generally those who had been in racist groups for some time and were active participants – were proud when strangers saw them firstly and essentially as racial activists. When I asked a Klanswoman why she wore a highly visible Klan insignia on her blouse, even after she had received hostile reactions when doing so, she replied "It's mine … It was the first, you'd say, article of the Klan that I ever had and I wear it a lot 'cause I'm proud of what I'm in, and if people want to watch me wear it, that's fine; if they want to back off, that's fine too." A Nazi similarly commented that she isn't concerned about how others regard her racism activism because in the movement "you're proud of who you are and what you are. It doesn't bother me a bit." When others respond to you as a racist activist, it confirms that you are a true racial warrior. Describing a group that she had been affiliated with, a middle-aged woman recalls their pride in being identified as Nazis:

> It's just a group of people who are not afraid to stand in what they believe in. They [would] be glad to talk to anybody who has any questions. They believe you have a right to believe in what you believe in.

Being open about one's racial beliefs was, for these women, evidence of their strength and commitment, as was evident in how one Klanswoman contrasted those who were willing to be public about their racism and those who were not

> We have some people that are what we call "in the closet," you know, that won't talk, they talk about it [racist beliefs], but low profile, just through the mail. Then we've got some that are real strong about it and will go out on the street and defend on what they think.

The ability of racist women to transform negative stigmas into a matter of pride reflects their absorption into a normative order that is very different than that of mainstream (what they term "alien") society. Goffman (1963, p. 6) recognized that if stigmatized persons hold beliefs about identity that are sufficiently at odds with the rest of society, these insulate them from the negative effects of stigma. Yet, Goffman argued that in the United States, the stigmatized and nonstigmatized tended to hold similar beliefs, a conclusion argued in other studies of stigma (Link & Phelan, 2001; but see Kusow, 2004). Where stigmatized persons substantially share a normative order with the larger society, this allows both the infliction of stigma by society and reactions of shame at being unable to conform to norms among some stigmatized persons. Yet, racist activists are an exception to the presumptive shared normative order. They are dedicated to undermining social norms that they regard as racially biased and corrupted by ZOG. For racist activists, the beliefs held by mainstream society are, by definition, distorted. They feel anger, rather than shame, toward a society that they view as founded in deception.

Although most racist women were not concerned that "aliens" regarded their racial identity as primary, they objected to what they saw as the unfair consequences of how they are perceived. Just as the stigma of HIV-positive status acts as "a shared characteristic of a category of people that becomes consensually regarded as a basis for dissociating from (that is, avoiding, excluding, ostracizing, or otherwise minimizing interaction with) individuals who are perceived to be members of that category" (Leary & Schreindorfer, 1998, p. 15), so, too, racist activism, according to these women, prompts others to avoid interacting with them. A young woman, recently recruited into a West Coast White-supremacist group, recounted how people in her town began to treat her differently after her allegiance became known, a situation that eventually led her to move to a new location: "I could no longer go to certain stores downtown without people [saying] 'Oh, Nazi, redneck, get out of here. You're a Nazi, we don't want you in here.' An older woman, when I asked whether she had been worried about how people might react to her after she started working with the Klan, responded, "No, I wasn't and I was very much surprised when one of my friends stopped calling."

A number of women told of employment problems they attributed to their racial activism. A skinhead said that "I keep it [racial activism] quiet as I have been fired from other jobs because of my pro-White beliefs and activism." Another, a recent recruit to a small White-supremacist group, told me that she was considering leaving the racist movement because of how others treated her:

> Ironically, I can not remain in the "pro-White" movement because my career would be exposed and I would be blacklisted from any professional positions that I would desire. In a land where freedom of speech and religion should be guaranteed, I have found that one only has these freedoms if he/she puts his/her blinders on and keeps his/her mouth shut.

Stigmatization of racists involves dynamics of power and threat that are different from those more commonly found in stigmatizing interactions. In a study of the stigma attached to homeless children, Anne Roschelle and Peter Kaufman (2004, p. 25) conclude that being stigmatized is an outcome of social hierarchies of power, such that, in general, "stigmatized individuals lack power." Indeed, it is common to view stigma as the product of unequal relationships of social power that give one group the ability to differentiate and negatively categorize those in another group (see also Link & Phelan, 2001), but it does not fit the stigmatization of racists. Racist groups carry a stigma in the larger society precisely because they threaten to wield power through threats and acts of violence. Although individual racists and racial groups are socially and politically marginalized, they work hard to engender a sense of fear and vulnerability among those who thwart their agendas.

In so doing, they command an implicit but salient form of power over others (Blee, 2005). Despite parallels in their stigmatization, for example, HIV-positive persons and racist activists differ dramatically in their response to the negative consequences of stigmatization. Whereas organized groups of HIV-positive persons have been vigorous in defending their rights (Gould, 2002), racist activists saw their mission in much more apocalyptic terms: to attack, disable, and/or destroy those they regard as enemies of White supremacism.

Claiming to be stigmatized requires racist women to develop a complicated set of narratives that both embraces and denies the validity of their stigmatized behaviors. One example of such convoluted logic was the statement of a young White-power skinhead who sidestepped her group's reputation for seemingly random acts of ferocious street violence when she complained that, "A lot of people have such preconceived ideas that we're gonna walk up and beat 'em up, when that's by far the last thing we're going to do." Another woman, an ardent Nazi who spoke with admiration of Hitler's accomplishments, told me that she was upset that "people look at us as though we are evil, as though *we* are the problem of society." One member deplored how outsiders regard a White supremacist as someone "who hates Black people or hates Jews or something." And a Klanwoman claimed an astonishing level of ignorance when she told me that "the average person has an idea that the Klan is very military and they're afraid. I wasn't aware of it until just recently" (Blee, 2002).

STIGMATIZING AGENTS

Racist women perceived a variety of stigmatizing agents. Drawing from the propaganda of racist groups, they regarded the media as a primary source of their negative treatment in society:

A NEO-NAZI: The media makes it like we're all a bunch of hardened criminals, that we should be shot and stuff, and it makes it really difficult for anybody trying to do anything positive for their people to even be listened to.

KLANSWOMAN: I had always believed the media's lies about racism being a bad thing and a belief espoused by idiots with no education or intelligence.

The Klan hasn't really been in the spotlight, which is good. I mean because [when] the news is covering it, no matter what the Klan does, they gotta make us look bad.

The government is similarly biased against racist activists, they claimed:

A WHITE SUPREMACIST: Federal agents and local officers called and met with my parents on several occasions to try and scare them about my beliefs. They told several lies such as [that] my friends were child molesters, I am a drug dealer, I am forced to have sex with any man who desires me, etc. and my parents became terrified. They even told my father that the best thing he could do for me was to take everything that I owned from me and throw me out on the street.

A SKINHEAD: Look at Waco and the Weavers[7] and stuff. I mean they choose to move away from society and then all of a sudden are getting their house burned down or getting shot or something over something ridiculous. I mean if we could make our own government and stuff, that would be better, but I wouldn't just want to move to an Aryan Nations[8] or something right now because I think that you would be a prime target for the government.

Racist women also claim that family, friends, and antiracist groups – sources of the stigmatization of extremist right-wing activists in the Netherlands, according to Klandermans and Linden (2006) – are negatively and unfairly arrayed against them.

A WHITE-POWER SKINHEAD: How much I've changed in the last couple of years. I've completely turned my whole life around. I did a lot for myself on my own without, I mean, I had no help from, my parents [who] kind of gave up on me and so they said if I wanted to go back to school and I wanted to do all that, I had to do it on my own.

AN ELDERLY SKINHEAD: They [her grown children] are politically correct yuppies. They don't belong [to my group]. They won't join; they are too interested in BMWs, nine-room houses, pets, children, careers, etc.

A SKINGIRL: I lost a lot of friends at first because, you know, a lot of my friends were antiracist and when I decided that I was going to be a skinhead then I lost pretty much all my friends.

A White supremacist described her encounter with an antiracist group, which, ironically, forced her to seek protection from the police:

All of a sudden, whoom, all these people were running here and there, from behind me. People running here, people running here and just gobs of people, like a herd of elephants. I'm like, "Oh shit, they're gonna kill me if they get ahold of me." They're yelling, "Kill the Nazi, kill the Nazi, kill the bitch, kill the Nazi, kill the bitch" ... the guy that was driving the van got scared to death and took off up the hill. I was left on the street ... I remember police, there was a police officer, a lady officer standing over there just standin' there. I kept tellin' her, "Call some more police. They're gonna kill me."

RESPONSES TO STIGMA

To racist women, the perception that they are stigmatized by the larger society is further evidence of the ruthlessness and widespread influence of ZOG, the very factors that necessitate White racial activism. Stigma, in this sense, fuels their activist resolve. Research finds that stigmatized persons are particularly alert to possible discrimination and tend to overperceive negative behaviors (Crocker, Major, & Steel, 1998; Hebl & Dovidio, 2005). Among racist activists, this psychological dynamic is reinforced by the conspiratorial beliefs of organized racism. Racist groups teach their members that the power of ZOG is absolute, extending from the government, media, and schools to the most mundane aspects of daily life. In racist groups, members learn that Jews will exert influence to debilitate the racist movement and cause problems for its adherents. As an elderly Nazi told me, "There's a certain group of people that have the [rest of the] people in their own control [and] they use it. That is used against [group name] and [so] their following was not as it would have been if they had control of the media which they didn't." To racist women, the power of ZOG not only explains situations in the larger world, but also in their own lives, making the range of possible evidence of Jewish power quite wide. Losing a job is evidence of ZOG power: Since Jews control the economy, they bar White Aryans from employment. Incidents as varied as failing an exam, finding that a boyfriend is unfaithful, even being hit by a car also are taken as indications of Jewish conspiratorial control.

The manner in which racist activists react to stigma is similar to the responses identified among other stigmatized groups, but with particularities that stem from the nature of racist groups. One common response is disengagement from those they see as hostile to the goals of White supremacism. By limiting their social contacts as much as possible to other racists, they seek to limit the effects of stigma (Kusow, 2004; Miller & Kaiser, 2001) and keep their zeal for White power intact. "I have lost some old friends who are politically correct," one Klanswoman related, "but gained many new ones who believe as I do and whom are very important to me. [They are] my best friends ever." Another said that "I spend very little time socializing. Most of my closest friends are in the movement, my [fellow racist] correspondents, and leaders." The desire to be insulated from the rest of society is consistent with White-supremacist belief that the outside world is polluting, although it hampers the ability of racist groups to recruit members from mainstream society.

Some racist women try to blend into mainstream society, both as a response to stigma (Hebl & Dovidio, 2005) and as a strategy to target new recruits. In racist groups, this is the strategy of normalization, presenting organized racism as part of the mainstream. For individual racists, however, this strategy is problematic because their zealous belief in the tenets of organized racism make it difficult for racial activists to want to "pass" as nonracist members of mainstream society. But some assert the need to disguise their racial commitments in particular settings in order to avoid making trouble for themselves:

> [T]he [Klan] hood, you forget it. It's never gonna be attractive. It's just a dunce cap. I hate it. I really do. To me it's a bad image. But you have to have some sort of mask in a lot of things … at least, coverage. Because if you don't, you'll get pulled over by the cops around here because they saw your face on TV [news] and they know you're a racist. And they'll write you a ticket just for the heck of it.

Even as they talked of the toll of being stigmatized, racist women told of flaunting their racist commitments in public situations (Cochrane & Billig, 1984; Crocker, Major, & Steele, 1998), a strategy opposite to those of passing or normalization. For many, this took the form of revealing their membership in a well-known racist group to strangers, sometimes as an attempt to see if that person might be a good target for recruitment. One waitress discussed her customers: "Well, some of them will come in and I'll be wearing one of my Klan shirts or you know, they'll see something on the news and ask me about it and we get in discussions." But others flaunted their racial stances simply to be provocative or awe-inspiring, as a skinhead who spoke of her insignia: "I wear it a lot cause I'm proud of what I'm in, and if people want to watch me wear it, that's fine, if they want to back off, that's fine too." One middle-aged woman spoke similarly, if disingenuously, about what happens when she wears her Klan uniform in public:

> I was in Special Foods in [city] one time and I had it on. It's got the hooded knight and in back it's got a knight on a horse holding a burning cross, and naturally it says the bit about the Knights of the Ku Klux Klan, and people were just kind of backing off from me and looking like "Oh my God," like it's the plague or something … I don't know if they fear it … I don't know why they steer clear.

All racist women engaged in some form of impression management to legitimate participating in a highly stigmatized movement. Some, particularly middle-aged and older respondents and those who had previously held middle-class positions in "alien" society, used disidentification, asserting their distance from the stigmatized stereotype of a racist (Blee, 2003/04). They claim that society misunderstands the racist movement, as a Klanswoman who complained about people who "go back to the 1800s when, oh my gosh, they [Klan] hung people and they burnt crosses in yards." This practice can lead to peculiar outcomes, such as the insistence that the ideas of White supremacism are no different that those of Black power. A Klanswoman's story underscored this perception:

> I had a Black guy in K-Mart one time walk right up to me and he goes, "That's a cool shirt." And he had a Malcolm X t-shirt on. And I said "Well, you know, I wear my thing, you wear yours." And he's, like, "You don't have an attitude about it?" and I said, "What's the point of having an attitude? It's just like the church you go to or the store you shop at. You're faithful to something and you're not ashamed. It's the same as you wearing a Malcolm X shirt." I said, "He's basically your Black [Klan leader]" and he said "Well, you got a point." And we probably talked an hour in K-Mart before we even went shopping. And there was no sign of an attitude on either half.

More commonly, racist women drew distinctions among different kinds of racist activists. They acknowledged that some racists fit the stereotype of racists as "sick, diseased, or violent people" (Berbrier, 2002, p. 561), and thereby deserved to be stigmatized, but insisted that their group did not fit this designation. A White supremacist dissociated herself from groups in "the White movement [which] I think had too much hate ... and that's the reason why they're not getting anywhere. At least I don't think they are." A more confusing rendition was given by a woman who wanted to separate herself from White supremacism while admitting her link to the virulently anti-Semitic and racist ideas of Christian Identity:

> I'm not really part of the [group name]. I don't think [name] has a group anyways. I've met other people who were simply what we call White supremacists and not Christian Identity too much. But I've basically been involved in Christian Identity, not White supremacism.

A more insidious form of impression management is the insistence that racists should not be stigmatized because they express views that are widespread among Whites but that only they have the courage to proclaim publicly. An example of such logic came in an interview with a neo-Nazi who insisted that many Whites secretly were pleased with the 1995 bombing of the federal office building in Oklahoma City by Timothy

McVeigh, who was widely believed to have been involved with right-wing extremists:

> I think there's a certain macho image that people do like. You always hear people speaking with a sense of awe and respect for the Mafia. You even hear people bragging that they have relatives in the Mafia. I don't believe they do, but they do brag about it. So I think there's a certain segment, part of society that sits there and watches the news and applauds these acts, regardless of who does it. They might be, they're not putting it on the news, I don't think, but they would be shocked to find out how many people on the street – who will not say on television – [but] I've even heard it across the board, they were happy about what happened in Oklahoma. There's a lot of anger out there. The people, they felt sorry for the children [who died in the bombing], but the rest of them got what they deserved, the government deserved [it] and the government provoked this.

This strategy is also reflected in claims that Blacks as well as Whites desire racial separation, an assertion that rests on the unspoken understanding that Jews are a common enemy of both races. From a White supremacist:

> We've been together – White power and Black power – on TV programs, etc. We've gotten along just fine, because they believe the same way we believe. They want to take care of their own, their own culture. And that's what we want, too.

A final, and nearly universal, form of impression management employs strategies of victimization to claim that the true victims of racial inequities are White Aryans, the practice identified in the propaganda and public statements of racist group as "reverse discrimination." Such rhetorical practices, as James Holstein and Gail Miller (1990, p. 105) argue, are not simply inaccurate representations of the reality of racial hierarchies. The assignment of victim status also functions to *constitute* a different racial world in which Whites are threatened by, discriminated against, and powerless relative to Jews, African-Americans, and peoples of color across the world. It provides an impetus to and justifies action – even violence – by the victimized to preserve themselves and guarantee a place for their children. Racist activists frequently repeat as racial motto the "14 words" written by David Lane, a member of a racist terrorist organization who was imprisoned for his part in the murder of Denver talk radio host Alan Berg: "We must secure the existence of our people and a future for White children." A Klanswoman put it this way:

> If this is really a democracy, and White Christians are the majority, which is supposedly the case, then they would be the ones promoted in

the government bureaucracy and everything. Instead of which, you have no prayer allowed in school, affirmative action and a whole bunch of other [programs] just trying to exalt the minorities over the majority at the expense of the majority. And it just doesn't go at all with democracy.

Racist women claim that Whites are victimized by a general program of discrimination. The same woman went on to say:

White Christians are treated unjustly in that, first of all, the world wants to blame us for just about everything. You name it, we're blamed for it. We're blamed for the fact that we brought the Black people to America and we're blamed, we're being persecuted still now for the fact that even though they weren't my ancestors, some people who lived here had them as slaves. The Black people were better treated as slaves then than they are now, than they treat themselves or others now. We're persecuted: the Christian, White Christian people are persecuted for being White, they're persecuted for believing in God, persecuted for believing that God created them different, created them superior, we're persecuted for believing that, for making statements, or for wanting to teach about our children about things that George Washington or John Adams, John Quincy Adams, any of the first presidents of the United States, any of the men who wrote the constitution, the declaration of independence, Thomas Jefferson, any of those men who were White did (laughs).

Presenting Whites as racial victims is connected to what James Holstein and Jaber Miller (1990, p. 109) term the "designation of a victim's *complementary opposition*," in other words, a victimizer. Racists use victimization to implicate a wide range of victimizers who act under the control of ZOG. The media is a favorite example of how ZOG victimizes racists and other Whites. A Klan leader told me of media efforts to make a woman in his group appear foolish and illogical when he recounted how an interviewer "tripped her up on the show because she didn't hear the question. He asked her if a White person mugged you, would you hate all White people?, and she said, Yes. And he let it go at that." A neo-Nazi insisted that media will always distort the ideas of Whites: "On TV or [in] the paper, they misquote, they splice together to make it look like you said something you didn't." The assertion of victim status works to shift responsibility from themselves to their victimizers, as in the words of a young skinhead:

A lot of people will start trouble with us, it's just the way they are, but ... we don't go looking for trouble. I don't care what the media says, what an opinionated person says. We do not go looking for trouble. They can say what they want, they can do what they want. If trouble provokes us, we're going to jump back but that's just the human resource in you.

Why racist activists adopt one coping strategy or another can be better explained by the structure of racist groups and the way that members adopt racist ideologies in their personal narratives than by whether they are in Klan, neo-Nazi, skinhead, White-separatist, or White-Klanwoman supremacist groups. Whether an activist uses strategies of insularity or normalization depends on the structure of their group as well as their commitment. Activists are most likely to use coping strategies of insularity when they are in groups that provide the trappings of community life, where members live in close proximity, make money from racist activities like hawking racist literature or teaching in White-separatist schools, and are able to select their friends and romantic partners from among other racists or, conversely, when they are in small and highly focused groups intent on violent or terroristic activities which they want to shield from scrutiny. Activists are most likely to use strategies of normalization when they are in racist groups in which members have substantial interaction with people who are outside the world of racism or when they want to maintain social relations and economic or employment opportunities in the larger society (Blee, 2002). If strategies of insularity and normalization are rooted in the particularities of group structure and individual commitment, strategies of impression management show the absorption of racist propaganda into the interactional and narrative styles of activists. When racist group members declare themselves to have been victimized by anti-White forces or assert that their views differ little from those secretly held by mainstream Whites (or even non-Whites), they are reiterating broad themes of racist ideology as personal belief and experience. Impression management is a means of coping with the stigma of racial activism, but it is also a means by which activists affirm their racist ideas.

CONCLUSION

Racist women perceive themselves to be stigmatized by the larger society and respond to that perception in ways that fit the mission of their particular racist groups. Many of their responses echo the strategies employed in racist group propaganda and by leaders, but the range of their responses is broader than has been identified in research based on those sources. Racist activists employ strategies of victimization/reverse discrimination; disidentification/distancing; and normalization, but they also use tactics of disengagement and assertions that their beliefs are secretly shared by other Whites.

John Manzo (2004) notes that a principal criterion for a stigmatizing condition is that it must be knowable to others, at least in principle. Despite the effort of some members and groups to conceal their racism, racist activists become visible – and thereby able to be stigmatized – when they seek to recruit new members from the general public. Whether this pattern will persist in organized racism in the future, however, is difficult to predict. If the U.S. racist movement continues its trend toward a structure of fragmented groups focused on racial terrorism, racist activists may be increasingly concerned with concealing their identities from outsiders and less likely to interact with persons or groups by whom they would be stigmatized. This is also likely if there is a marked increase in legal scrutiny of the racist movement, as tends to occur in the wake of the discovery of dramatic acts or plans of violence. In these scenarios, the social stigma of racist activism would remain, probably intensify, but the targets of such stigmatization would be difficult to identify. There is a very different scenario that is also possible. Some segments of organized racism may attempt to make themselves appear respectable in mainstream society as a means of acquiring additional members and perhaps even electoral successes. Under these conditions, strategies of distancing and normalization would be more widespread and racist activism might encounter less social stigma. Which of these routes is more likely depends not only on the internal strategies and actions of U.S. racist groups, but also on transnational ties among racist groups, the broader climate toward racial terrorism, and national and domestic politics and ideologies that are impossible to foresee.

NOTES

1. White supremacists in the U.S. believe that the White race is superior to all other races, genetically and/or culturally. The Ku Klux Klan (KKK) consists of small and fragmented groups, each of which claims to be heir to the gangs of White men who violently fought to restore White supremacy in the southern states after the Civil War. U.S. Neo-Nazis display the insignia and proclaim the vicious anti-Semitism (but rarely the nationalism) of German World War II-era Nazis. White separatists favor strict racial separation, including, for some, division of the U.S. into separate racial territories; some White separatists claim they do not support White supremacist ideas, although their agendas are often quite similar to those of White supremacists. White power skinheads are violent gangs of youths who declare themselves to be adherents of White supremacism or neo-Nazism, in distinction to violent antiracist skinheads.

2. Those who declare themselves to be leaders or spokesmen of organized racism are not necessarily those who exert leadership within racist groups or the
   racist movement. Indeed, some of the most prominent public racist figures
   have few followers.

3. Despite his effort to present himself as different from ordinary racists, "Wilmot
   Robertson's" racialist magazine, *Instauration* and book, *The Dispossessed
   Majority* (which traced most social problems to what he termed "unassimi-
   lable minorities") earned him a canonical place among U.S. racists and neo-
   Nazis.

4 These sentiments correspond with a larger strategy of some racist groups to
   portray themselves as respectable and mainstream by contrast with less repu-
   table racists (Berbrier 1999). Such disidentification is evident in David Duke's
   ironically titled "National Association for the Advancement of White People"
   (NAAWP) and so-called "business suit Klans" like Thom Robb's Knights of the
   Ku Klux Klan which distinguish their "positive, family oriented movement"
   from "the tarnished image of the robe" projected by less sophisticated Klans
   (Knights of the Ku Klux Klan 2005).

5. Identifying information has been suppressed or altered to maintain confiden-
   tiality. The narratives have been edited slightly to remove meaningless expressions such as "you know."

6. Such violence generally takes the form of elaborate plans to destroy government installations or Jewish institutions or to disable civic infrastructures;
   thus far, most are foiled by the police or thwarted by the ineptitude or betrayal
   of the conspirators.

7. She is referring to two events that the White supremacist movement uses as
   examples of unwarranted state repression of citizens. Waco is a city in Texas,
   near the site of a 1993 assault by federal agents on the compound of a religious
   sect known as Branch Davidians which ended in the deaths of eighty of the
   church's members. The reference to Weavers is to an incident in which the
   wife and son of White supremacist Randy Weaver were killed in a battle with
   federal agents in 1992 at their house in Ruby Ridge, Idaho.

8. A racist compound, then located in Idaho.

REFERENCES

Aho, J. A. (1990). *The politics of righteousness: Idaho Christian patriotism*. Seattle:
    University of Washington Press.
Barkun, M. (1994). *Religion and the racist right: The origins of the Christian Identity
    Movement*. Chapel Hill, NC: University of North Carolina Press.
    (1998). Conspiracy theories as stigmatized knowledge: The basis for a new age
    racism? In J. Kaplan & T. Bjørgo (Eds.), *Nation and race: the developing Euro-
    American racist subculture* (pp. 58–72). Boston: Northeastern University Press.
Berbrier, M. (1999). Impression management for the thinking racist: A case study of
    intellectualization as stigma transformation in contemporary white suprema-
    cist discourse. *The Sociological Quarterly, 40*(3), 411–433.
    (2000). The victim ideology of white supremacists and white separatists in the
    United States. *Sociological Focus, 33*(2), 175–191.

(2002). Making minorities: cultural space, stigma transformation frames, and the categorical status claims of deaf, gay, and white supremacist activists in late twentieth century America. *Sociological Forum*, 17(4), 553–591.

Billig, M. (1978). *Fascists: A social psychological view of the National Front*. London: Academic Press.

Blee, K. M. (1991). *Women of the Klan: Racism and gender in the 1920s*. Berkeley: University of California Press.

(2002). *Inside organized racism: Women in the hate movement*. Berkeley: University of California Press.

(2003/2004). Positioning hate. *Journal of Hate Studies*, 3, 95–206.

2005. Racial violence in the United States. *Ethnic and Racial Studies*, 28, 599–619.

Cochrane, R., & Billig, M. (1984). I'm not in the National Front Myself, But … *New Society*, 17 (May), 255–258.

Crocker, J., Major, B., & Steele, C. (1998). *The handbook of social psychology* (4th ed.). Boston: McGraw-Hill.

Dobratz, B. A., & Shanks-Meile, S. L. (1997). *White power, white pride! : The white separatist movement in the United States*. New York: Twayne Publishers.

Ezekiel, R. S. (1995). *The racist mind: Portraits of neo-Nazis and Klansmen*. New York: Viking.

Fielding, N. (1981). *The National Front*. London: Routledge and Kegan Paul.

Gardell, M. (2003). *Gods of the blood: The Pagan revival and White separatism*. Durham: Duke University Press.

Goffman, E. (1963). *Stigma*. Englewood Cliffs, NJ: Prentice-Hall.

Gould, D. (2002). Life during wartime: Emotions and the development of ACT UP. *Mobilization*, 7, 177–200.

Hebl, M. R., & Dovidio, J. F. (2005). Promoting the 'social' in the examination of social stigma. *Personality and Social Psychology Review*, 9, 156–182.

Holstein, J., & Miller, G. (1990). Rethinking victimization: An international approach to victimology. *Symbolic Interaction*, 13, 103–122.

Holstein, J. A., & Gubrium, J. F. (1995). *The active interview*. Thousand Oaks: Sage.

Klandermans, B., & Linden, A. (2006). Stigmatization and Repression of Extreme-Right Activism in the Netherlands. *Mobilization: An International Journal*, 11, 213–228.

Knights of the Ku Klux Klan. (2005). Website at http://www.kkk.bz/. Accessed December 11, 2005.

Kusow, A. M. (2004). Contesting stigma: On Goffman's assumptions of normative order. *Symbolic Interaction*, 27, 179–197.

Leary, M., & Schreindorfer, L. (1998). The stigmatization of HIV and AIDS: Rubbing salt in the wound. In V. J. Derlega & A. P. Barbee (Eds.), *HIV and social interaction* (pp. 12–29). Thousand Oaks, CA: Sage.

Link, B. G., & Phelan, Jo. C. (2001). Conceptualizing stigma. *Annual Review of Sociology*, 27, 363–385.

Lofland, J. (1969). *Deviance and identity*. Englewood Cliffs, NJ: Prentice-Hall.

Manzo, J. F. (2004). On the sociology and social organization of stigma: Some methodological insights. *Human Studies*, 27, 401–416.

Miller, C. T., & Kaiser, C. R. (2001). A theoretical perspective on coping with stigma. *Journal of Social Issues, 57,* 73–92.

Mosse, G. L. (1985). *Nationalism and sexuality: Middle-class morality and sexual norms in modern Europe.* Madison: University of Wisconsin Press.

Roschelle, A. R., & Kaufman, P. (2004). Fitting in and fighting back: Stigma management strategies among homeless kids. *Symbolic Interaction, 27,* 23–46.

11

Why Groups Fall Apart: A Social Psychological
Model of the Schismatic Process

FABIO SANI

For decades, social psychologists have explored the processes that lead social groups to achieve oneness and uniformity. For instance, some researchers have investigated the way in which social groups transmit and maintain shared norms and standards (Crandall, 1988; Sherif, 1936). Others have studied the pressures to conform to majority views (Abrams et al., 1990; Asch, 1956) or to obey leaders and authorities (Milgram, 1974). With regard to the field of group decision-making, a substantial body of work has addressed the processes leading group members either to polarize their opinions (Brauer & Judd, 1996; Moscovici & Zavalloni, 1969) or to overlook alternative courses of action because of striving for unanimity (Janis, 1972). Finally, social psychologists have also explored the way in which groups achieve cohesiveness (Hogg, 1992; Lott & Lott, 1965) and people's tendency to loose their sense of individual identity when acting in group situations (Diener, 1979; Zimbardo, 1970).

Undoubtedly, these processes are of central importance for group life and deserve to be studied in depth. However, despite a clear tendency to cohere and to seek consensus, most social groups are internally divided into subgroups (Hornsey & Hogg, 2000). What is more, in some situations the members of a subgroup may decide to undergo a schism; that is, they may leave the parent group either to form a breakaway group or to join a different group.

Schisms can take countless forms. They can have only a local impact, or they can cause social turnabout on a large scale, heavily affecting the equilibrium of social forces. They can give birth to stable breakaway groups or to groups that enter a spiral of further schisms, and also to groups whose life is extremely precarious and short. Schisms can occur in a relatively stable framework or be a part of a context that functions as a hotbed for schisms. They can be either peaceful or characterized by brutality and violence. Nonetheless, from a social psychological point-of-view, at least, schisms seem to share some core characteristics. My aim in this chapter is to present a social psychological model of schism, which results from more than a decade of empirical work. In doing so, I will adopt a chronological approach. That is, I will describe the main studies that I have conducted over the years in chronological order, showing how a general model has gradually emerged out of these studies. I will conclude with a discussion of the implications of this research for current social psychological theorizing on groups.

EXPLAINING THE SCHISM IN THE ITALIAN COMMUNIST PARTY

The first study I conducted, in collaboration with Steve Reicher, was concerned with the schism that took place within the "Partito Comunista Italiano" (Italian Communist Party; PCI) in 1991 (Sani & Reicher, 1998).

Background

The PCI was a very important political and cultural subject in the Italian history of the 20th century (Gundle, 2000). For several decades, this party was in charge of many regions, provinces, and cities, and, while it was never in government, it was the second biggest party of the country, after the Democrazia Cristiana (Christian Democracy). However, in the second half of the 1980s the party began to decline not only in support but also in consensus, and this led the leadership to conclude that survival depended on making some important changes. In November 1989, the general secretary of the party, Achille Occhetto, proposed to create a new political formation that would be free of ideological constraints and would look for a new location in the international scenario. Later on, in October 1990, Occhetto presented a formal proposal for a new program, name, and symbol for the party. The name was "Partito Democratico della Sinistra" (Democratic Party of the Left; PDS) and the symbol was an oak tree with the old symbol, that is, the hammer and sickle, retained in a little circle at the base of the oak tree. At the Party Congress of February 1991 this proposal was upheld, and the PDS was officially born. However, just after the voting a group of seven members led by Armando Cossutta – who had always been in favor of reconstructing a communist party – announced that they would not join the PDS and that they would form a new communist party. The new party was subsequently called "Partito per la Rifondazione Comunista" (Party for

Communist Refoundation; PRC), and it retained the symbol of the former PCI, after a harsh polemic with the PDS.

Methods and Analytic Procedure

This study was conducted retrospectively, approximately one year after the actual schism occurred. Its overall aim was to explore the schismatic process and to come out with some firm conclusions about the core social-psychological factors at play. A sample of active members and leaders of the two breakaway parties (14 members of the PDS and 10 members of the PRC), who had been previously members of the PCI, were interviewed. With regard to their status either in the PDS or in the PRC at the time of the interviews, some of participants were ordinary members whose activity was limited either to part-time administrative duties or simple participation in the life of small local units of the party, while others were officers of either regional units or the national leadership. The interviews, whose average length was one hour, were unstructured. At the beginning of each interview, interviewees were asked to give a brief account of their personal experience of the schism and to explain the reasons for their specific choice. We conducted the interviews in September 1992, that is, 16 months after the final Congress of the PCI, where the schism occurred, and tape recorded them in their entirety. We also made use of two interviews, one of which was given by a leading figure of the PDS and the other by a leader of the PRC, to the newspaper "*L'Unità*" in March 1991. Including these, this made a total of 26 interviews (15 members of the PDS and 11 of the PRC).

The analysis was based upon a mixed procedure involving both qualitative and quantitative techniques, which is called structural analysis of group arguments (SAGA) (Reicher & Sani, 2000). This is a rather complex procedure that, in very broad terms, allows the researcher to extract the arguments that are used to construe the preschism group and the two post-schism groups (the PCI, the PDS and the PRC, in this specific context) and to investigate the conceptual and structural links among these arguments to understand the dynamics of the schism.

Findings

Unsurprisingly, the analysis showed that members of the different breakaway parties construed the PCI, the ingroup, and the outgroup, in very different ways. The members of the PDS argued that the PCI played a very important role in the postwar period in terms of the defence of the

Italian Constitution and the rights of the workers. The party was a power-ful left-wing force that counterbalanced the reactionary tendencies of the Right, thus contributing to the maintenance of democracy in the country. Concerning their own party, the members of the PDS argued that with its new program and organization, this was the only force that could challenge the hegemony of the Right and shift Italy towards a more egalitarian and democratic society. At the same time, members of the PDS also argued that the PRC was a totally utopian party, both because of its unrealistic notion of society and because its pretensions were out of all proportion to its tiny size. For them, the PRC was a sectarian party that served to fragment the left and thereby ensured the continued dominance of the right. As a consequence, it acted against democracy and the interests of the subordinate classes.

Concerning the members of the PRC, they argued that the PCI had always fought for a new society based on the interests of the workers and was used by the working class to defend and advance its rights. In doing so, the PCI was, at least during the first 50 years of its history, inspired by Marxism and by the values of the October Revolution. With regards to their own party, the PRC members contended that it was above all a communist party, still inspired by the ideals of the October Revolution, and aware that the only way to achieve social justice and human solidarity was to oppose the forces representing and supporting the capitalist system, without com-promise. On the contrary, the view of the PDS was that it was a "liberal-democrat" rather than left-wing party, a party practically integrated into the status quo that, therefore, could not serve as an effective force to bring about fundamental changes in the social system.

Clearly, the arguments that members of the two breakaway groups (the PDS and the PRC) gave concerning the ingroup and outgroup were directly related to their arguments concerning the parent group (the PCI). More specifically, the interviewees presented the positions and characteristics of the ingroup as being consistent with the positions of the PCI, and they pre-sented the views and features of the outgroup as being inconsistent with those of the PCI. In other words, the interviewees used the arguments about the PCI and the arguments about the ingroup to affirm that ingroup identity was consonant with the true nature of the PCI.

In the light of these findings, we speculated that the schismatic process within the PCI was set in motion because one faction perceived the changes (new name, symbol, and program), which had been promoted and obtained by another faction, as contradicting and denying the essence of the party, as not being in line with its core values, traditions, and history. However, the members of the faction endorsing the changes did not admit that these contradicted the original identity of the PCI. On the contrary, they contended that the changes were consonant with its identity. Furthermore, they argued that the changes were a way to preserve and strenghten the ideals that were originally at the basis of the PCI. The faction that saw the changes as inconsistent with the PCI identity eventually left the parent group and formed a new breakaway group whose identity, so they claimed, was consistent with that of the PCI.

Discussion

The nature of the PCI identity was clearly at the core of the schism. More precisely, although all members subscribed the implicit theory that a change should be enforced only if it is consonant with the group identity and, if possible, reinforces it, the different factions disagreed over the implications of the change for the party identity. For the members of the faction that eventually seceded and founded the PRC, the change was not consonant with the group identity, and therefore was unacceptable while, for the members of the faction that stayed and gave rise to the PDS, the change was consonant with the group identity, enriched it, and was therefore a necessary step.

Despite their clarity, these data had at least two important limitations. First, and most obvious, findings might have had more to do with the specificities of the Italian Left than about schisms in general. Consequently, it was necessary to conduct further research in different cultural and ideological contexts. Second, the analysis was entirely retrospective. Therefore, findings could have represented people's attempt to reconstrue things so as to claim the legacy of the parent group for their own rather than the rival faction. Hence it was important to demonstrate that arguments about identity are crucial within the schismatic process itself.

APPLYING THE MODEL TO THE CHURCH OF ENGLAND'S SCHISM

This study, also conducted in collaboration with Steve Reicher (Sani & Reicher, 1999; Study 1), was concerned with the schism that occurred in the Church of England over the issue of the ordination of women to the priesthood. Our aim was to address the two limitations of the PCI study discussed in the previous sections. The topic itself addressed the issue of generalizability of findings to different ideological and cultural contexts because this time we were investigating a schism taking place in a group that was English rather than Italian, and religious rather than political. In response to the second concern – that the PCI study was retrospective – this time the data was longitudinal and was gathered during the development of the split.

Background

The Church of England is the officially established Christian church on the English soil and the principal branch of the Anglican Communion. Although the spiritual head of the Church of England is the Archbishop of Canterbury, its supreme governor is actually the British monarch, currently Elizabeth II. The Church of England is a reformed church, having been influenced in various ways by Protestantism, and it does not accept the authority of the Pope, the head of the Roman Catholic Church. However, like both the Roman Catholic Church and the Eastern Orthox Church (a communion including a number of separate churches, and whose highest-ranking representative is the Patriarch of Costantinople), the Church of England sees itself as the continuation of the church established by Christ and the twelve apostles and, therefore, considers itself as part of the "universal church," that is, as being catholic (though, obviously, not Roman Catholic).

The Church of England's debate on the ordination of women to the priesthood began in the early 20th century. However, it was only in 1984 that the General Synod of the Church of England (a kind of parliament including both clergy and lay members) agreed to bring forward legislation to permit ordination of women to the priesthood. Subsequently, at the General Synod of November 11, 1992, the legislation was voted in favor by a two-thirds majority, and in March 1994 the first 32 women were ordained priests at Bristol Cathedral by Bishop Barry Rogerson. The following morning the Revd Glenys Mills, at the Christ Church of Clifton, became the first woman celebrating communion in the history of the Church of England. Over the following decade, hundreds of clergymen and thousands of lay people left the Church of England because of women priests. Many moved to the Roman Catholic Church, which established procedural rules for those who wished to convert, while a relatively small group of leavers either converted to the Orthodox Church or joined very small breakaway churches that were created all around Great Britain.

Methods and Analytic Procedure

This was a longitudinal study where participants were interviewed twice. The first wave of interviews took place in the period from January 1993 to

October 1993, which was after the Synod had agreed in principle to ordain women but before the measure had become law. The second wave took place between June 1994 and August 1994, shortly after the first ordinations. All the interviews, which were unstructured and lasted for approximately 45 minutes, were tape recorded. They focused on the issues surrounding ordination of women to the priesthood. For both the first and the second wave of interviews, the starting question concerned the participant's general opinion and feelings about the issue at stake. Participants were 9 clergymen and 6 lay people. The clergymen were members of either the House of Clergy or the House of Bishops of the General Synod. The lay people were either members of the House of Laity in the General Synod or leading members of organizations concerned with the issue of women priests. Nine of these interviewes were against women's ordination and 6 were in favor of it. At the time of the follow up interview, 2 of the Antis had already left the Church of England.

The first-wave and the follow-up interviews were analysed separately using, again, the SAGA procedure. In this study, SAGA involved the extraction of the arguments that the Pros and the Antis used (a) to define and construe the Church of England and (b) to define the meaning of the ordination of women to the priesthood; this was followed by the investigation of the conceptual and structural interrelations among the arguments. As in the previous study, the aim of this procedure was to reconstrue the dynamics of the schism.

Findings

First Wave of Interviews (Preordination)
Concerning the ways in which the Church of England was depicted, the two subgroups shared some arguments in common. For instance, for both Pros and Antis, the Church of England is faithful to God and His will. However, most arguments were totally opposed. To start with, the Pros stressed the independence of the Church of England from the Catholic Church in terms of making doctrinal decisions, while the Antis claimed that central aspects of Christian doctrine and practice should be adjusted only on an ecumenical basis. Second, the Pros contended that the Church of England has a developing tradition, while the Antis insisted that tradition should not change in accordance to the secular world. Finally, the Pros saw genders as "equal," while the Antis argued that men and women are "complementary."

Concerning portrayals of women priests, Pros and Antis had totally different views. With regards to whether women had been called by God to exercise the ministry in His Church, the Pros saw clear signals that this was the case, while the Antis stressed that the legislation on women priests was against the will of God. The view of the Pros that the legislation on women priests did not undermine ecumenical unity because it had been put forward by an independent church, was countered by the view of the Antis that the legislation on women priests, being a unilateral decision, undermined unity with Rome and the Eastern Orthodox Church. Concerning the relationship between the legislation and culture, the Pros argued that the legislation on women priests was consistent with cultural change because we live in a time when gender equality has been widely recognized, while for the Antis the legislation on women priests was a capitulation to cultural fashion in the secular. Finally, the Pros claimed that the legislation on women priests fully acknowledges that all creatures are equal in Christ, whereas the Antis argued that the legislation on women priest denies the fact that women and men should be involved in the life of the Church in a complementary, not interchangeable, manner.

If we consider carefully the relationship between the Church of England and women priests that is implied in these constructions we see that, for both the Pros and the Antis, arguments that are used to characterize the ordination of women relate to arguments that are used to characterize the Church of England. More precisely, the arguments about the ordination of women to the priesthood put forward by the Pros are consonant with the arguments they use to characterize the Church of England. Conversely, the arguments about women's ordination endorsed by the Antis are in contradiction with aspects of the identity of the Church of England as they characterize it. What is more, for the Pros the ordination of women was not only consonant with the identity of the Church of England, but it also allowed the Church more fully to accomplish its true essence. To quote, women's ordination is "a logical exposition of the position which should exist." Instead, for the Antis the legislation was not just dissonant with the identity of the Church of England but would fundamentally subvert its nature. As one interviewee put it, by ordaining women priests the Church of England had "chucked up scripture, overcome authority, kicked tradition in the teeth, and decided it's a Protestant sect."

Second Wave of Interviews (PostOrdination)
In the follow-up interviews the participants did not produce new arguments that had not been used in the first round interviews. On the other hand, some arguments that had been previously used were no longer found in the follow-ups. However, and importantly, the arguments used by the

Pros were again meant to indicate that the ordination of women confirmed the identity of the Church while the arguments produced by the Antis indicated that the ordination of women had subverted the group identity. In sum, in the postordination-interview respondents maintained the same overall relationship between arguments. Nonetheless, there was an important shift for the Antis in the way they talked about the relationship. In the first wave of interviews the Antis used to say that women priests *would* change the nature of the Church, whereas in the second wave they claimed that women priests *had* changed the nature of the Church. This contrast is well illustrated in the following two quotations from one of the Antis. Before ordination he stated that: "at the moment the first woman is ordained in the Church of England it will cease to be part of the Catholic Church, it will become a Protestant sect." Afterwards he declared that "the Church which I was ordained in has ceased to be; I haven't left the Church, they have left people like myself." In sum, before ordinations became a reality, respondents anticipated that, had women to be made priests, the group identity would have been subverted and, therefore, they would have left, whereas after ordinations, the notion that the group identity had actually been subverted was given as a self-evident reason for leaving the group.

Discussion

These findings were strikingly consistent with the findings from the study of the schism in the PCI. Once again, the secessionist faction decided to leave because of a change that was seen as subverting the true nature of the group. Also consistent with the results of the previous study, the faction that endorsed the change claimed that this change was reinforcing and extending the group identity, rather than denying it. Despite this strong convergence between the studies, the evidence provided by the second study was more compelling. Rather than being retrospective, the data collected in the second study were contemporaneous with the process of division and schism. What is more, rather than having only one interview, the data were longitudinal and covered the period from before to after women were actually ordained. This made us more confident that the arguments were illustrating the schismatic process rather than being retrospective rationalizations.

Obviously, this study retained some limitations. First, as in the PCI study, the cost of an intensive analysis of long interviews was that the sample was inevitably small. Because such a small sample could be potentially unrepresentative, it was necessary to replicate these findings using a much larger sample. Second, our interviewees were the leaders in the debate and were therefore atypical. Leaders may argue over identity and may claim that identity is changed. But they might do so to move group members to action. Therefore, it was important to ascertain that the same perceptions and constructions would be found in ordinary group members.

PROVIDING FURTHER EVIDENCE FOR THE MODEL

In this study (Sani & Reicher, 1999; Study 2), we sought convergent evidence for the findings that emerged from the previous study, while trying to overcome its main limitations. So, we drew a large sample of participants from more ordinary group members. Also, we used a different methodological approach, which this time involved the analysis of purely quantitative data.

Methods and Analytic Procedure

Because our central aim was to investigate the members' developing perception of the essence of the Church of England, we decided to explore the way in which both the Pros and the Antis constructed the relationships between the various groups involved in the debate. We chose this strategy because our interviewees tended to conceptualize the change of essence of the Church of England in terms of its changing relationships with other Christian groupings. Moreover, because the Antis claimed that the identity of the Church of England would "officially" change the moment the first women were ordained, we decided to assess the construction of the relationships both before and after the first women were actually ordained.

The study involved 185 participants (138 Pros and 47 Antis). This sample included lay people, who were members of either the Synod or organizations concerned with the issue of the ordination of women, and clergymen, who were either deacons or priests but not high-ranking members such as bishops and archdeacons. They completed the first questionnaire approximately three months before the first ordinations (end of December 1993 / beginning of January 1994) and the second questionnaire approximately three months after the first ordinations (June 1994). The questionnaire took into consideration 9 groups, which were those that our interviewees had characterized as significant to the debate. These included the Church of England (taken as a whole), the House of Bishops (which was seen as the leadership of the Church of England), the Roman Catholic Church, the Orthodox Church, the two main pro ordination organizations, that is, the Movement for the Ordination of Women (MOW) and Priests for

Women's Ordination (PWO), and the three main antiordination organizations, that is, Forward in Faith (FiF), Women Against the Ordination of Women (WAOW), and Cost of Conscience (CofCON). More specifically, respondents were presented with each possible pairing of the 9 groupings, and asked to rate the similarity of the pair on a 5-point scale ranging from "very similar" to "very different." We then submitted the scores to multidimensional scaling (MDS).

Findings

The output of the results of the MDS was in the form of four two-dimensional figures. Figures 11.1A and B show how the Antis constructed the relationships between the groups both before and after the first ordinations.

Let us focus on Figure 11.1A first. The horizontal dimension has the antiordination organizations and the conservative churches at one extreme and the proordination organizations and the Bishops at the other, with the Church of England in between – although closer to the proordination pole. This was interpreted as an "ideological" dimension. Its poles could be understood in the terms used by antiordination interviewees as, respectively, "tradition" and "liberalism." It is notable that, on this dimension, the Church of England is seen as rather distanced from its own leadership – the bishops. This makes sense insofar as the leading archbishops strongly supported the new measure and, in voting at the Synod, the bishops as a whole supported it by a stronger majority than the other constituent houses – the clergy and laity. On the vertical dimension, all the churches – Church of England, Roman Catholic Church, and Orthodox Church – are grouped towards the top pole while all the groupings within churches are grouped together towards the bottom pole. We interpreted this dimension in terms of structure, with institutions at the top and sectional groupings at the bottom. It should also be observed that the bishops were once again far from the Church of England as a whole, suggesting that they were not seen as representing it but rather as a partial interest within it.

The analysis of the postordination questionnaires is shown in Figure 11.1B. By comparison with the preordination analysis, the horizontal dimension shows no change: the Orthodox and Catholic churches along with the antiordination groupings remain at the traditional pole; the proordination groupings along with the bishops remain at the liberal pole; the Church of England stays between but nearer the liberals. The fact that, from an ideological point of view, the ordination of women was not seen as implying

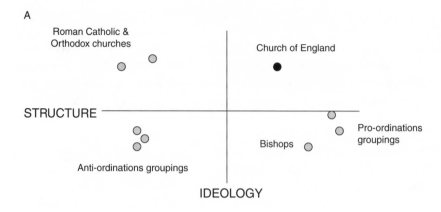

A

Roman Catholic &
Orthodox churches

Church of England

STRUCTURE

Pro-ordinations
groupings

Bishops

Anti-ordinations groupings

IDEOLOGY

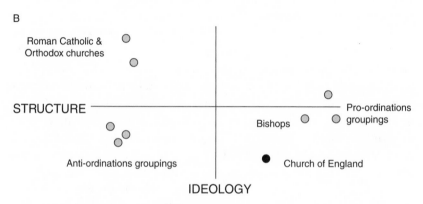

B

Roman Catholic &
Orthodox churches

STRUCTURE

Pro-ordinations
groupings

Bishops

Anti-ordinations groupings

Church of England

IDEOLOGY

FIGURE 11.1. A: Antis' construction of categories *before* the first ordinations (January 1994). B: Antis' construction of categories *after* the first ordinations (July 1994).

Source: Adapted from Sani & Reicher, 1999.

a change is explicable in historical terms. The Church of England was founded on a compromise between radical Protestantism and Catholic tradition, and conservative groupings have always accepted that the Church was more liberal than they would have liked on a series of issues, including the position of women. Moving now to the vertical dimension, it can be observed that the Orthodox and Catholic churches, and all the groupings within the Church of England, maintain more or less the same position that they had in the preordination survey. However, the Church of England itself shifts from being virtually the highest to being the lowest category.

In short, the Church of England has moved from the company of the historical churches to the company of pressure groups. This can be explained by the conviction of the Antis that the Church of England is no longer an established institution, but is rather a "local Protestant church," or even a "sect," concerned with pursuing its own narrow, "liberal" agenda. In sum, the Church of England's identity has been subverted; it is now a different thing, with a different essence.

Lack of space prevents me from providing a detailed analysis of the constructions of the Pros. However, it will suffice to say that their constructions, both before and after ordinations, were very similar to that made by the Antis before ordinations, and that such constructions did not change over tests. In other words, the Pros did not perceive any structural change in the Church of England as a consequence of the ordination of women priests. For them, there was no subversion of identity.

Discussion

Findings provided quantitative corroboration for the model derived from the first two studies, showing that such model applied to the broad mass of those actively involved in the debate, not just the leadership. That is, these results confirmed that debates giving rise to schisms concern the group identity. The faction that ends up seceding from the parent group sees the group as having departed from its true values and beliefs and as having become a different type of group. In sum, members of a schismatic faction construe the difference between them and members of the other faction as a difference between preserving and destroying identity.

Of course, at this stage of research the model did not constitute a full model of schism. Most obviously, not all the Antis intended to leave the Church of England. It was therefore important to investigate other factors that might mediate the relationship between perceptions of identity subversion and schismatic intentions. This is what it was done in the studies that follows.

EXTENDING THE MODEL THROUGH A FURTHER CHURCH OF ENGLAND STUDY

The preliminary model produced by the previous studies postulated that groups, which are engaged in an ongoing debate over the content of their identity, may face disagreements between factions over the consistency of a new norm with the core principles forming the group identity. When members of one faction believe that a new norm is subverting the group identity, they *may* decide to leave the parent group and join a schism. But in which cases does the perception of identity subversion actually lead to schism? What are the variables that mediate the effects of perceived identity subversion on schismatic intentions? The study summarized in this section was conceived to answer this question by testing a new, extended model of the schismatic process (Sani, 2005).

The Extended Model

The model that I tested started with the hypothesis that the perception of identity subversion has important cognitive and affective consequences. First, it has a negative effect on group identification. Basically, those who see the group as changed beyond recognition find it harder to feel part of it and to derive a sense of pride and honour from being part of it.

Second, based on ethnographic evidence from the interviewees in studies 1 and 2, those who perceive identity subversion experience a mixture of both dejection-related emotions (e.g., disappointment, sadness) and agitation-related emotions (e.g., apprehension, uneasiness). This is because they see the essence of the new, actual group (i.e., the group resulting from subversion of identity) as dissonant with both what they wish the group to become (the ideal group), and what the group has the obligation to be (the ought group). This idea is based on applications of Higgins' (1987) self-discrepancy theory to the collective self by Bizman & Yinon (2002). These authors studied Israeli's representations of their own national group and found that a discrepancy between actual and ideal group produced group-based, dejection-related emotions while a discrepancy between actual and ought group prompted agitation-related emotions.

The third important consequence of perceived identity subversion was that it leads to lowered *perceived group entitativity*, a term coined by Campbell (1958) to refer to the degree to which a group is subjectively perceived as a singularity, constituting a unified whole. This is because those who perceive identity subversion are acutely aware of the presence of two ideologically incompatible factions in the group. This specific hypothesis is consistent with research that I have conducted in collaboration with John Todman and Judith Lunn. This research showed that a group whose members are divided on principles that are perceived to be fundamental for the group identity is seen as less entitative than a group whose members are divided on principles that are considered only peripheral to the group identity (Sani, Todman, & Lunn, 2005).

A further prediction of the extended model was that perceived group entitativity has a positive effect on group identification. This prediction was based on research by Yzerbyt and his colleagues demonstrating that people prefer to be members of entitative, rather than nonentitative groups (Yzerbyt, Castano, Paladino, & Leyens, 2000).

Concerning the factors that are directly linked to schismatic intentions, I predicted that the less group members identify with the group, and the more they experience dejection/agitation increases, the higher their schismatic intentions. Lower identification leads to higher schismatic intentions because, consistent with social identity theory (Tajfel & Turner, 1986), leaving their group to join a more positively judged group helps people to achieve a more positive identity. A greater degree of dejection/agitation leads to stronger intention to leave the group because the group is inevitably seen as the cause of emotional distress.

Finally, according to this model, both the negative effects of group identification and the positive effects of dejection/agitation on schismatic intentions are moderated by the level of perceived voice held by those members who are against the change. More precisely, the perception that those who oppose the change will not be marginalized and discriminated against within the group should reduce both the negative effects of group identification and the positive effects of dejection/agitation on schismatic intentions. This idea is consistent with Tyler and Smith's (1999) argument that people who are allowed to participate actively in the life of the group, and therefore feel valued and accepted, are more willing to act on behalf of the group, even when the group is not a source of pride.

Method

A random sample of 1,080 priests in the Church of England (1,012 were men, 60 were women, and 8 failed to specify) completed a questionnaire including items aimed at measuring the 6 variables in the model. These variables were as follows: Identity subversion (4 items; $\alpha = .92$; "The ordination of women has subverted the true nature of the Church of England"); Group identification (10 items; $\alpha = .90$; "I identify with other members of the Church of England"); Dejection/agitation (6 items; $\alpha = .96$; "When I think about the fact that the Church of England ordains women I feel sad"); Entitativity (5 items; $\alpha = .84$; "The Church of England is a unified whole"); Schismatic intentions (4 items; $\alpha = .93$; "I will move to another church because of the ordination of women"); Voice (5 items; $\alpha = .86$; "Those opposing women's ordinations are discriminated against within the Church of England"). All items were rated on a 7-point scale, with higher numbers indicating greater agreement with the item.

In this study I also wanted to test the hypothesis that those who are in favor of women priests will see the ordination of women as strengthening and enhancing the group identity. Therefore, I included items measuring perceived identity-enhancement (3 items; $\alpha = .86$; "The ordination of women strengthens the identity of the Church of England") resulting from women's ordinations; as with the items concerning the model variables, participants had to indicate agreement on 7-point scales.

Analytic Procedures and Findings

To test the predicted model I followed a structural equation modelling (SEM) approach. The outcome of the analysis is shown in Figure 11.2.

All paths coefficient were statistically significant, and, importantly, the amount of variance explained by the model as a whole was more than one half of the overall variance ($R^2 = .56$). Concerning goodness-of-fit indexes, the following values were obtained for our model: NFI $= .98$; CFI $= .99$; RMSEA $= .05$, indicating a good fit of the data.

Subsequently, I performed moderation analysis to test the prediction that both the negative effects of group identification and the positive effects of dejection/agitation on schismatic intentions are moderated by the degree of perceived voice held by those members who are against women priests. It was found that Voice had a significant moderating effect on both the path linking Group identification to Schismatic intentions [F change $(1, 1016) = 224.23$, $p < .001$] and the path linking Dejection/agitation to Schismatic intentions [F change $(1, 1026) = 143.22$, $p < .001$]. Therefore, the nature of the effect of Voice on both paths was as predicted.

Concerning the items measuring the possibility that women's ordinations enhanced the group identity, I compared the scores of both the Pros and the Antis with the midpoint in the scale. (Whether participants were Pros or Antis had been determined through an item included in the questionnaire asking for their opinion on the legislation.) It emerged that the Pros were generally in agreement with this proposition; their scores ($M = 5.29$; $SD = 1.14$) were significantly higher than 4 (i.e., the midpoint in the scale): t $(825) = 32.53$; $p < .001$. On the contrary, the Antis disagreed with this proposition; their scores ($M = 1.94$; $SD = 0.90$) were significantly lower than the midpoint of the scale: t $(204) = 32.83$; $p < .001$. Clearly, the scores of the Pros were significantly higher than the scores of the Antis: t $(1029) = 39.14$; $p < .001$.

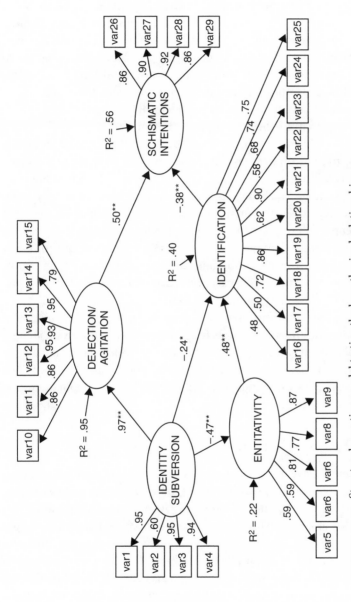

FIGURE 11.2: Structural equation model testing the hypothesized relationships.
source: This figure originally appeared in Personality & Social Psychology Bulletin, Vol. 31 (2005), p. 1080, published by Sage Publications.

Discussion

This study led to a model that was more comprehensive and articulated than the preliminary one. However, in the future it might be useful to conduct further research on the emotional reactions to perceived identity subversion. For instance, those who perceive identity subversion will presumably believe that other group members have done something bad to the group. This, in turn, might prompt anger, not just dejection and agitation. Therefore, in further studies it might be useful to include a measure of anger to assess the extent to which the model will gain from that.

Having said that, I believe that anger was not a widespread emotional reaction in the Church of England's schism. To start with, anger is typical when a negative outcome comes as a surprise but not when it had been seen as a true possibility (Roseman, 1991). Concerning the Church of England, it is well documented that the voting in favor of the ordination of women was not unexpected. Furthermore, anthropologists have demonstrated that whether people will respond to negative outcomes with dejection or anger will be entirely dependent on cultural norms concerning what is or is not appropriate (Barr-Zisowitz, 2000). It is unlikely that members of an important Christian institution will consider intensive anger toward other group members as an appropriate emotional reaction.

This study also confirmed that, according to the Pros, the ordination of women to the priesthood is not only fully consistent with the group identity but also enhances it. That is, the Pros agreed with the legislation not simply because they saw it as not causing a subversion of the group identity, but also because they saw it as implying *continuity* with a developing tradition rather than discontinuity and rupture.

GENERAL DISCUSSION

In this chapter I have described the process that has led me to the creation of a general model of schisms in social groups. This model is based on a general theoretical postulate, according to which a collection of individuals who share the same group (or "social") identity, assume that (a) they should adopt *norms* – beliefs, practices, values, and behavior – that are consistent with the nature of the group identity and that (b) there should be common agreement on the content of these norms (Turner, Oakes, Haslam, & McGarty, 1994). Because of this assumption, group members are engaged in an ongoing process of argumentation aimed at reaching agreement on what norms are consistent with the group identity and should therefore be adopted. My model shows that in the course of this process of "consensualization" (Haslam, Turner, Oakes, McGarty, & Reynolds, 1998) there may be circumstances in which members of a faction perceive a given norm that is endorsed by another faction representing the group as a whole, as subverting the essence of the group identity. In other words, the members of a faction may accuse members of the other faction of having transformed the group into something that is totally different from what it used to be and what it is meant to be. Importantly, however, the members of the faction endorsing the change do not consider the change as subverting the group identity. On the contrary, they see the change as a development that is fully consonant with the group identity. These contrasting perceptions may constitute the first step of a schismatic process, ending up with the secession of the faction that considers the group identity as subverted.

A core idea of this model is, therefore, that "the group identity is the referent against which decisions about changes in the group norms are made, and debates about possible changes revolve around the implications of a proposed change for the group identity" (Sani, 2005, p. 1083). That means that members of ideological groups hold a more or less implicit "theory" according to which a change can be enforced *only* if it is consistent with the group identity and, if possible, reinforces it. In sum, underlying a schism there is a disagreement over the nature of the relationship between a proposed new norm (which represents a change in the group's ideological and doctrinal corpus) and the group identity.

Although the causal link between perceived identity subversion and schismatic intentions is at the heart of the model, the role played by several important mediating variables is also considered. The model shows, for instance, that perceptions of identity subversion have effects on the level of identification with the group and on the group-based emotions that may be experienced and that, in turn, low group identification and the experience of aversive emotions tend to increase schismatic intentions. Finally, the model takes into account an important moderator, that is, the degree to which those who oppose the change are seen as having the ability to voice their dissent, showing that the more the perceived voice of the opponents, the less the effects of the mediating variables on schismatic intentions.

Although the current model appears satisfactory and seems to account for a good deal of variance, there is a lot more work to be done. In this final section I will briefly mention some of the issues that I believe should be part of the agenda for future research in this domain.

The first important issue is concerned with the generalizability of the model. Basically, would this extended model be applicable to other types of groups? Because schisms are the consequence of disagreement over the implications that a given change may have for the group identity, the model should, then, be applicable to groups that are based on beliefs, values, and worldviews forming the basis of the group identity, around which the members tend to cohere. Typical examples of this type of groups – that have been defined as *"common-identity"* groups by Prentice, Miller, and Lightdale (1994) – are political parties, religious institutions, and social movements. Clearly, to investigate this possibility, future research should test the model in various types of common-identity groups, including social movements, ethnic-national groups, identity-based organizations, and, of course, other political parties and religious institutions. However, the model might be unable to account for schism in groups such as small, face-to-face groups based on task (e.g., a scientific expedition) or on interpersonal relationships (e.g., a group of friends), which Prentice, Miller, and Lightdale have defined as *"common-bond"* groups. This is because these groups tend to put little emphasis on ideology and identity-related issues. Future research should also test the ability of the model to explain schisms in these types of group.

The second issue stems from the striking conceptual consistency of this model of schismatic processes with social psychological accounts of mergers in groups and organizations (e.g., Terry, Carey, & Callan, 2001). More specifically, research by van Knippenberg, van Knippenberg, Monden, and de Lima (2002) has revealed that the extent to which group members can experience a sense of continuity between the premerger and the postmerger group will determine whether the merger is happily endorsed or not. When the postmerger group looks very different from the premerger group, group members may conclude that the postmerger group is no longer their group and, as a consequence, may not identify with it. These findings are totally consistent with my schismatic model, according to which group members who perceive a given change as creating a fundamental discontinuity between past and present group identity will not identify with the group any longer, and consider leaving it. In sum, perceived continuity/discontinuity of the group identity following a change appears to be a central process in both mergers and schisms. I therefore believe that, in the future, researchers of schism and merger should capitalize on each other's insights. This might lead to a more integrated understanding of the different phenomena that are somehow concerned with the constant de-composition and recomposition of social groups that is so entrenched in our contemporary world.

The third issue to be addressed in future research is concerned with the fact that the current model is derived from the secession of a faction that is against a change endorsed by the group majority. Clearly, factions may also secede because they advocate a change that is *impeded* by the group majority. To what extent can this model explain schisms caused by the secession of a "radical," rather than "conservative" faction? Future research should address this issue, by testing an adapted model to schisms determined by radical factions.

I would anticipate, however, that the nature of the group identity is what prompts all schisms occurring within common-identity groups, regardless of the nature of the faction (conservative or radical) initiating the schism. Arguably, the "only" difference will be that, while for conservative factions the first step toward secession is the perception that the group identity has been subverted, for radical factions the first step is the perception that the group is blocking the development of the group identity, by impeding the realization of the group values and beliefs in accordance with everchanging historical contingencies. Put it differently, while conservative factions advocate strict adherence to the group norms, and blame the majority of endorsing changes that imply the subversion of identity, radical factions are motivated to renew and revitalize the group identity, and accuse the majority of dogmatism, stagnation, and rigidity. Concerning the other steps into the schismatic process, it is possible that the path followed by radical factions matches the model. Basically, members of a radical faction that considers the current identity as stagnant may become especially aware of group disunity, feel less proud of their group, and experience aversive emotions. These perceptions and feelings might, in turn, increase their schismatic intentions.

However, the schismatic intentions of a radical, innovative faction would be crucially moderated by its perceived ability to voice dissent. As emphasized in the classic literature on minority influence (Moscovici, 1976; Mugny, 1982), to convert a majority it is necessary to instill a cognitive conflict in the mind of its members by confronting them with a plausible alternative position on the issue at stake. However, this presupposes that the position of the radical faction is heard by the majority. Therefore, if the members of the radical faction perceive themselves as having voice, they would probably decide to stay in the group. This would allow working toward the creation of psychological conflict in the majority members thereby producing the necessary conditions for their conversion. On the other hand, if the members of the radical factions believe that their voice is unheard, they will likely think that they have no hopes to create a conflict in the majority members and eventually convert them, and will therefore opt for a schism.

Arguably, if the legislation on the ordination of women had been impeded for too long, those who were in favor of women priests could have become a radical secessionist faction. After all, although these group members never claimed that they wanted to turn the Church of England into a totally different thing, they thought that the preordination of women Church of England should have renewed its values and beliefs to survive in a time of fast and overwhelming social transformations. Therefore, lack of innovation and reform might have decreased these members' group identification and produced negative emotions. This might have led them to leave the group, especially if they had felt excluded and voiceless.

Finally, it is necessary to consider the issue of the size of the secessionist faction. Is faction size a relevant variable? Are small factions more or less likely to pursue a schism than large ones? Would the model discussed in this chapter apply equally well to both small and large factions? Perhaps, members of a tiny faction may have to work harder to maintain a sense that their view of group identity is valid and legitimate. However, as long as the faction members remain convinced that the current group identity is unacceptable, I suspect that the schismatic process would be put into motion regardless of the faction size. It is possible, though, that the size of the faction will affect the perceived group entitativity. Presumably, a very small faction that is facing a very large majority would be unlikely to see the group as being strongly divided and fragmented, and therefore as having low entitativity. How this might affect the overall schismatic process is an open question, which future research should certainly address. Also, a small faction might have more problems to make its voice heard by other group members and, therefore, it might be more prone to secede than a large one. Again, it would be interesting to conduct research aimed at exploring this possibility.

In conclusion, although social psychological research on schism is still in its infancy, it has moved a first important step. I hope that this will stimulate researchers to investigate this fascinating topic further, thereby enriching and extending our social psychological understanding of group processes.

REFERENCES

Abrams, D., Wetherell, M., Cochrane, S., Hogg, M.A., & Turner, J.C. (1990). Knowing what to think by knowing who you are: Self-categorization and the nature of norm formation, conformity and group polarization. *British Journal of Social Psychology*, 29, 97–119.

Asch, S. (1956). Studies of independence and conformity: I. A minority of one against a unanimous majority. *Psychological Monographs: General and Applied*, 70, 1–70.

Barr-Zisowitz, C. (2000). "Sadness" – Is there such a thing? In M. Lewis & J.M. Haviland-Jones (Eds.), *Handbook of emotions* (2nd ed., pp. 607–622). New York and London: The Guilford Press.

Bizman, A.,& Yinon, Y. (2002). Social self-discrepancies and group-based emotional distress. In D.M. Mackie & E.R. Smith (Eds.), *From prejudice to intergroup emotions: Differentiated reactions to social groups.* (pp. 13–30) New York and Hove: Psychology Press.

Brauer, M., & Judd, M. (1996). Group polarization and repeated attitude expressions: A new take on an old topic. *European Review of Social Psychology, 7,* 173–207.

Campbell, D.T. (1958). Common fate, similarity, and other indices of the status of aggregates of persons as social entities. *Behavioral Science, 3,* 14–25.

Crandall, C.S. (1988). Social contagion of binge eating. *Journal of Personality and Social Psychology, 55,* 588–98.

Diener, E. (1979). Deindividuation, self-awareness, and dishinibition. *Journal of Personality and Social Psychology, 37,* 1160–71.

Gundle, S. (2000). *Between Hollywood and Moscow: The Italian Communist Party and the challenge of mass culture, 1943–1991.* Durham, NC: Duke University Press.

Milgram, S. (1974). *Obedience to authority: An experimental view.* New York: Harper & Row.

Moscovici, S. (1976). *Social influence and social change.* London: Academic Press.

Haslam, S.A., Turner, J.C., Oakes, P.J., McGarty, C., & Reynolds, K.J. (1998). The group as a basis for emergent stereotype consensus. In W. Stroebe & M. Hewstone (Eds.), *European Review of Social Psychology* (Vol. 9, pp. 203–239). Chichester: John Wiley.

Higgins, E.T. (1987). Self-discrepancy: A theory relating self and affect. *Psychological Review, 94,* 319–340.

Hogg, M.A. (1992). *The social psychology of group cohesiveness: From attraction to social identity.* London: Harvester Wheatsheaf.

Hornsey, M.J., & Hogg, M.A. (2000). Assimilation and diversity: An integrative model of subgroup relations. *Personality and Social Psychology Review, 4,* 143–156.

Janis, I. (1972). *Victims of groupthink: A psychological study of foreign-policy decisions and fiascos.* Boston: Houghton Mifflin.

Lott, A.J., & Lott, B.E. (1965). Group cohesiveness as interpersonal attraction: A review of relationships with antecedent and consequent variables. *Psychological Bulletin, 64,* 259–309.

Moscovici, S., & Zavalloni, M. (1969). The Group as a polarizer of attitudes. *Journal of Personality and Social Psychology, 12,* 125–135.

Mugny, G. (1982). *The power of minorities.* London: Academic Press.

Prentice, D.A., Miller, D.T., & Lightdale, J.R. (1994). Asymmetries in attachments to groups and to their members: Distinguishing between common-identity and common-bond groups. *Personality and Social Psychology Bulletin, 20,* 484–493.

Roseman, I.J. (1991). Appraisal determinants of discrete emotions. *Cognition and Emotion, 5,* 161–200.

Sani, F. (2005). When subgroups secede: Extending and refining the social psychological model of schisms in groups. *Personality and Social Psychology Bulletin, 31,* 1074–1086.

Sani, F., & Reicher, S. (1998). When consensus fails: An analysis of the schism within the Italian Communist Party (1991). *European Journal of Social Psychology, 28,* 623–645.

(1999). Identity, argument and schism: Two longitudinal studies of the split in the Church of England over the ordination of women to the priesthood. *Group Processes & Intergroup Relations, 2,* 279–300.

(2000). Contested Identities and Schisms in Groups: Opposing the ordination of women as priests in the Church of England. *British Journal of Social Psychology, 39,* 95–112.

Sani, F., Todman, J. & Lunn, J. (2005). The fundamentality of group principles, and perceived group entitativity. *Journal of Experimental Social Psychology, 41,* 567–573.

Sherif, M. (1936). *The social psychology of social norms.* New York and London: Harper & Brothers Publishers.

Tajfel, H., & Turner, J.C. (1986). The social identity theory of intergroup behaviour. In S. Worchel & W.G. Austin (Eds.), *Psychology of intergroup relation (pp. 7–24).* Chicago: Nelson-Hall.

Terry, D.J., Carey, C.J., & Callan, V.J. (2001). Employee adjustment to an organizational merger: An intergroup perspective. *Personality and Social Psychology Bulletin, 27,* 267–280.

Turner, J.C., Oakes, P.J., Haslam, S.A., & McGarty, C. (1994). Self and collective: Cognition and social context. *Personality and Social Psychology Bulletin, 20,* 454–463.

Tyler, T.R., & Smith, H.J. (1999). Justice, social identity, and group processes. In T.R. Tyler, R.M. Kramer, & O. John (Eds.), *The psychology of the social self* (pp. 223–264). Mahwah, NJ: Lawrence Erlbaum.

van Knippenberg, D., van Knippenberg, B., Monden, L., & de Lima, F. (2002). Organizational identification after a merger: A social identity perspective. *British Journal of Social Psychology, 41,* 233–252.

Yzerbyt, V., Castano, E., Leyens, J.-P., & Paladino, M.-P. (2000). The primacy of the ingroup: The interplay of entitativity and identification. In W. Stroebe & M. Hewstone (Eds.), *European review of social psychology* (Vol. 11, pp. 257–295). Chichester: Wiley & Sons.

Zimbardo, P.G. (1970). The human choice: Individuation, reason, and order versus deindividuation, impulse, and chaos. In W.J. Arnold & D. Levine (Eds.), Nebraska Symposium on Motivation, 1969 (Vol. 17, pp. 237–307). Lincoln: University of Nebraska Press.

PART 3

COPING WITH INCLUSION

12

Multiple Identities and the Paradox of Social Inclusion

MANUELA BARRETO AND NAOMI ELLEMERS

INTRODUCTION

Modern societies, and organizations within these societies, are characterized by increasing diversity and the coexistence of multiple groups. How to successfully manage this diversity has been the focus of much political debate and scientific research. One of the core goals of diversity-management strategies is to avoid schisms and conflict between groups. This will enable the achievement of a socially cohesive society in which members of all groups are included. Two opposing strategies to achieve social inclusion are commonly proposed: assimilation and multiculturalism (or pluralism; see Fredrickson, 1999 for an overview). Proponents of assimilation strategies argue that social cohesion can only be achieved when subgroup identities are relinquished (e.g., Barry, 2001; Schlesinger, 1992). However, in line with the multiculturalism ideology, we propose that the maintenance of subgroup identities is essential for the development of healthy identities and positive relationships with other groups (e.g., Berry, 2001; Lambert & Taylor, 1990). In this chapter, we provide an analysis of the consequences of assimilationist pressures for the individual, for the group, and for society at large. We review social psychological evidence bearing on this issue and conclude that far from promoting *social inclusion*, assimilationist pressures have the paradoxical effect of actually contributing to the *social exclusion* of minority group members.

THE IDENTITY THREATS OF ASSIMILATION

According to Berry and Kim (1988), minority-group members can adopt one of four different acculturation strategies when they enter a host society: they can choose to maintain their native cultural identity and develop new relationships with the groups that are part of the host society (*integration*), they can choose to give up their native cultural identity and develop a new identity based on their membership in the host society (*assimilation*); they can choose to maintain their native cultural identity alone, without developing ties with the host group (*separation*); or they can give up their native identity without developing a new identity based on their membership in the host society (*marginalization*). Despite the variety of strategies preferred by minority group members, diverse societies often tend to promote one of these as the "best" for minority group members and for society as a whole. Societies that support multicuralism are those where minority group members are welcomed to endorse an integrative acculturation strategy, while assimilationist societies are those that require minorities to endorse an assimilation strategy.

One of the arguments surrounding the assimilationist ideology is thus that migrants can only be fully included in the host society if they relinquish their native culture and substitute it by the host culture. The idea is that the more minority group members endorse the values and norms of the host society, the better they will function within and serve this society. However, assimilationist ideologies also defend that the adequate endorsement of norms and values of the host society can only be achieved if minority group members distance themselves from their native culture. This is expected to result in greater similarity between minority group members and majority group members, which will presumably lead to smooth relationships between these groups, as well as to the inclusion of all groups within society at large.

However, besides the fact that this idea is based on the questionable assumption that greater intergroup similarity leads to smoother and less conflicting subgroup relations (see Jetten, Spears, & Manstead, 1997 for evidence of the opposite effect), social psychological research suggests that this strategy presents several threats to the identity of minority group members. These identity threats occur because people are simultaneously members of multiple groups and thus hold multiple identities (e.g., Deaux, 1996; Tajfel, 1981; Turner, Hogg, Oakes, Reicher, & Wetherell, 1987). This creates the potential for the occurrence of identity discrepancies because the identities that are salient to perceivers, or that perceivers wish to impose on targets, are not necessarily the same identities that are salient to targets themselves or that targets wish to emphasize in a particular context (Branscombe, Ellemers, Spears, & Doosje, 1999; Breakwell, 1983). For example, gender is a readily available categorization cue, leading perceivers to categorize targets according to their gender in a variety of contexts. However, targets do not necessarily see themselves primarily according to their gender. This is largely due to the fact that, although social categorizations are heavily based on the characteristics of the stimuli present in a given social context, motivational factors also play a role in determining how people are categorized, and these motivational factors may lead to different categorizations for targets and for perceivers (Oakes, Haslam, & Turner, 1994; Turner et al., 1987). As a consequence, the same context may lead perceivers to categorize targets in one way, while it may lead targets to see themselves in quite a different way. So, following our example, while gender may be a salient categorization cue for perceivers, a given target may instead wish to stress his or her professional identity during a meeting with a client.

One important consequence of motivational processes in situations of identity discrepancy is that the way people describe themselves or express their identity may be quite strategic, instead of simply reflecting people's cognitive representations of their social group memberships (Deaux & Ethier, 1998). That is, in line with theories of impression management (Baumeister, 1982; Leary & Kowalski, 1990; Schlenker, 1980), statements of identification may be seen as communicative tools through which people express how they wish to be seen by a particular audience (Barreto, Spears, Ellemers, & Shahinper, 2003; Ellemers, Barreto, & Spears, 1999). This is particularly likely to be the case when the target in question is confronted with an audience that represents some form of threat to their identity (see also Klein & Azzi, 2001; Reicher & Levine, 1994; Reicher, Spears, & Postmes, 1995).

A study we carried out among members of ethnic minority groups in the Netherlands serves to illustrate this point (Barreto et al., 2005). We compared how people described themselves in relation to different social groups and toward different audiences. Specifically, we asked participants to indicate the extent to which they identified with their ethnic minority group and the extent to which they identified with the host group (the Dutch). We examined how respondents communicated their identity to a native or host audience by varying the way the research group was presented (e.g., as Portuguese – we indicated the first author of this chapter as the responsible researcher – or as Dutch – we indicated the second author of this chapter as the responsible researcher), as well as by varying the language in which the questionnaire was written (native versus host/Dutch language). We approached members of a group that tends to be seen as separate and is continuously pressured to assimilate in Dutch society (Turkish migrants), as well as members of a group that is perceived as relatively integrated and is much less a target of assimilative pressures in this context (Portuguese migrants) (e.g., Van Oudenhoven et al., 1998). We reasoned that since prior work in this same context has shown that migrants tend to endorse a dual identity, identifying with both the native and the host group (e.g., Van Oudenhoven et al., 1998), those migrant groups who are seen as separate and who are pressured to assimilate by the host society should experience a stronger identity threat than those who are seen as integrated. As a consequence, we expected Turkish migrants to experience more of a threat to their preferred dual identity than Portuguese migrants when confronted with a Dutch audience, and we expected this to be reflected in a (strategic) greater endorsement of both native and host identities by our Turkish respondents when addressing a Dutch audience.

The Portuguese migrants in our sample (who experienced relatively little identity threat) smoothly adapted their identity to the relevant social context. That is, they indicated identifying more strongly with the native group when communicating with a native audience, but reported identifying more strongly with the Dutch when addressing a Dutch audience (cf. the alternate cultural model; LaFromboise, Coleman, & Gerton, 1993). However, a different response pattern was revealed by the minority group that experiences the greatest identity threat in this context. Indeed, when Turkish migrants faced an audience that represented a threat to their identity (i.e., when addressing a Dutch audience) they claimed their preferred (dual) identity – that is, they indicated identifying more strongly with *both* native and host groups to the host audience than they did to the Turkish audience. That is, when addressing the audience that pressures them to assimilate and give up their minority identity, Turkish respondents made it clear that they are indeed very Turkish, but that this does not get in the way of also endorsing a Dutch identity. We think these results demonstrate that assimilative pressures are threatening to the identity of minority groups and that pressuring minority groups to assimilate can have the paradoxical result of causing them to strategically emphasize their minority identity, or a dual identity. Importantly, these results also show that minority group members are much less likely to place such a strong emphasis on their dual identity in contexts where they do not experience such an identity threat (as did our Turkish participants in the Turkish context).

In sum, our central concern is that minority group members who are targets of assimilative pressures are confronted with an imposed superordinate categorization at the level of the nation, while they may see themselves primarily on the basis of their ethnic identity, or (more often) as holders of a dual identity (e.g., Berry, 1990; Van Oudenhoven, Prins, & Buunk, 1998). This introduces an identity discrepancy that can be experienced as a threat. In particular, assimilative pressures present a threat to the *distinctiveness* of the subgroup's identity (Hornsey & Hogg, 2000b) because they prevent or undermine the distinctiveness of the subgroup (Branscombe, Ellemers, Spears, & Doosje, 1999; Breakwell, 1983). In addition, assimilation policies threaten feelings of *subgroup respect* because they communicate a disregard for the value of the subgroup's identity (Huo & Molina, 2006). Finally, assimilation pressures threaten minority group member's *self-definition* (categorization threat) because they impose external definitions of the self while disregarding people's preferred identities (Barreto & Ellemers, 2003; Branscombe et al., 1999; Breakwell, 1983; Ellemers, Spears, & Doosje, 2002).

In this chapter, we review evidence suggesting that assimilative pressures lead to the identity threats outlined earlier, which, in turn, have a negative impact on social cohesion and on the inclusion of all groups in a superordinate category. Specifically, we argue that this is the case for three reasons:

1) Because assimilation pressures promote conflict between minority and majority group members, they *weaken the ties between minority group members and the host society.*
2) Because assimilation pressures are disrespectful of minority group members' identity, they have *negative psychological consequences for minority group members.*
3) Because assimilation implies inclusion in a superordinate category that is not representative of minority group members, the identity-management strategies such members have to use to succeed (e.g., "passing" as a member of the majority group) *accentuate their disadvantage.*

ASSIMILATION PRESSURES LEAD TO INTERGROUP CONFLICT AND WEAKEN TIES WITH THE SUPERORDINATE CATEGORY

Past research has emphasized the importance of defining a common, superordinate identity as a means of avoiding intergroup conflict (Gaertner & Dovidio, 2000; Gaertner, Mann, Murrell, & Dovidio, 1989) and to enhance cooperation between members of different subgroups (Kramer & Brewer, 1984; Wit & Kerr, 2002). However, other research has revealed that full assimilation into a single superordinate category is not necessarily the best strategy. Instead, in support of the multiculturalism view, research has shown that the most positive subgroup relationships are achieved when emphasis is placed both on subgroup identities and on the superordinate identity (Gaertner, Rust, Dovidion, Bachman, & Anastasio, 1994; Haunschild, Moreland, & Murrell, 1994; Hornsey & Hogg, 2000a; Terry, Carey, & Callan, 2001). That is, defining people's relationships to each other both in terms of the common superordinate category and in terms of their different subgroup identities leads to better subgroup relationships than a sole emphasis on the superordinate identity (or a sole emphasis on the subgroup identity). In fact, some of this research suggests that a sole focus on the superordinate identity can actually lead to enhanced subgroup identification, which can be seen as an important precursor of ingroup bias and intergroup conflict (Hornsey & Hogg, 2000a).

Such enhanced intergroup conflict and subgroup identification are seen as the result of the *distinctiveness threat* created by the erosion of subgroup boundaries (Hewstone & Brown, 1986; Hornsey & Hogg, 2000b). According to Branscombe et al., (1999) a distinctiveness threat occurs when a group's distinctiveness is prevented or undermined in a particular context (see also Breakwell, 1983; Brewer, 1991). People seek group distinctiveness because it clarifies group boundaries and provides unambiguous cues as to where they belong and what norms they should follow (Tajfel, 1974; Turner et al., 1987). This need for group distinctiveness can be so strong that it is even more important than establishing a positive identity (Mlicki & Ellemers, 1996). Accordingly, past research has demonstrated that the erosion of group boundaries (implied by a comparison with a similar outgroup) leads group members to actively differentiate their group from the other group, for example by expressing greater ingroup bias or enhanced group identification (e.g., Jetten et al., 1997; Roccas & Schwartz, 1993; Van Rijswijk, Haslam, & Ellemers, 2006). This is in line with optimal distinctiveness theory, which clearly states that people seek to differentiate themselves or their group *only to the extent that does not threaten inclusion* in a higher-order category (Brewer, 1991). In fact, this is what is achieved when both superordinate and subordinate identities are emphasized in a multiculturalism approach.

Research on the effects of *subgroup respect* also suggests that the identity threats introduced by assimilation strategies can hurt subgroup relationships (Huo & Molina, 2006). Subgroup respect is a mechanism parallel to intragroup respect but at a higher level of analysis (as defined by Tyler, Degoey, & Smith, 1996; Tyler & Lind, 1992) in that it refers to the perception that one's subgroup is respected by the people or institutions that represent a higher-order category, such as the nation. As had also been revealed in research on the effects of intragroup respect, the perception that one's subgroup is respected is a precondition for the acceptance of the superordinate category, as well as for the norms it upholds (e.g., Huo, 2003; Huo, Smith, Tyler, & Lind, 1996). By contrast, a lack of respect is associated with cognitive dis-engagement and withdrawal (Sleebos, Ellemers, & De Gilder, 2006).

Huo and Molina (2006) observed that ethnic minorities who perceive that their subgroup is respected in American society also reported more positive evaluations of other ethnic groups and evaluated America as a whole more positively. By contrast, those who perceived a threat to subgroup respect reported more negative evaluation of other ethnic subgroups. This research on subgroup respect suggests that respect is a two-way road: Only by receiving respect can group members, in turn, respect members of other groups as well as the (norms of the) inclusive category as a whole (see also Tyler & Lind, 1992).

Further evidence for the harmful effect of assimilation (versus the beneficial effect of multiculturalism) on the relationship with the superordinate group stems from an examination of the effects of *categorization threat*. Categorization threat has been defined as the threat that results from being categorized against one's will (Branscombe et al., 1999; Breakwell, 1983). This includes situations where one is categorized in a given group when one would prefer individualized treatment or when one would prefer to be categorized in another group (*unwanted categorization*). Past research showed that under these circumstances people do their best to communicate their disagreement with the categorization. For example, people who are categorized against their will try to undermine the usefulness of the categorization by pointing out within-group differences and identifying similarities between groups (Doosje, Ellemers, & Spears, 1995; Yzerbyt, Castano, Leyens, & Paladino, 2000). Additionally, they will try to demonstrate the inappropriateness of the categorization by stressing the extent to which they differ from other ingroup members (Spears, Doosje, & Ellemers, 1997). Indeed, people only endorse the (behavioral) norms of a group in which they are (externally) categorized when they also (internally) identify with that group (Barreto & Ellemers, 2000; Ouwerkerk, de Gilder, & de Vries, 2000). That is, belonging to a social category according to some objective or external criteria like birth place is not enough or even necessary for people to accept and follow the norms of this social category. Instead, research shows that people accept and follow the norms of social categories with which they subjectively identify, irrespective of whether they fulfill such objective or external membership criteria.

Researchers focusing on the acculturation attitudes of minority and majority group members have suggested that this type of identity threat can create a problematic or conflictual relationship with the host society

(Bourhis, Moise, Perreault, & Senecal, 1997). Specifically, in their model of interactive acculturation, Bourhis and colleagues indicate that the quality of the relationship between migrant groups and the host society will depend on whether the acculturation attitude of the minority group is in line with the acculturation orientation of the host society (as defined by state policies). Problematic or conflictual relationships emerge when these acculturation attitudes are discrepant, for example, when the minority group endorses integration (i.e., the maintenance of the native culture and the development of ties with the host culture), but the host society promotes assimilation (which involves relinquishing the native identity and focusing exclusively on ties with the host society).

A specific consequence of categorization threat is that it often implies that people are not categorized in a group where they would prefer to be categorized (*identity neglect*; Barreto & Ellemers, 2002; 2003; Barreto, Ellemers, Scholten, & Smith, in press). Central to this approach is the consideration that people strive to have their preferred self-views respected by others (akin to a self-verification process at the collective level of self-definition, Swann & Read, 1981; Chen, Chen, & Shaw, 2004). That is, people will not only do their best to communicate their disagreement with unwanted categorizations (e.g., by distancing themselves from the imposed category), but they will also go to great lengths to affirm their preferred identities (e.g., by affirming their identification with the group or showing bias in favor of their preferred group; Finchilescu, 1986). As a consequence, imposing an unwanted identity while neglecting a preferred one is likely to backfire because it simultaneously elicits rejection of the imposed identity and affirmation of the neglected identity.

To empirically address this issue, we examined people's identification with and loyalty to an imposed category membership (such as the superordinate national category) as a function of the neglect or respect of an important identity (such as the minority identity; Barreto & Ellemers, 2002). The results of this study show that neglecting self-important identities weakens ties with externally imposed identities. In particular, participants whose preferred identity was neglected in favor of an externally ascribed identity expressed low identification and low wish to cooperate with the ascribed identity. Moreover, participants whose preferred identity was neglected showed identity affirmation, by enhancing their identification with the preferred group and displaying behavior in favor of this group.

Importantly, our results also showed that acceptance of an externally imposed identity (e.g., a national identity that encompasses all minority and majority groups) can be promoted by respect for self-important identities (e.g., minority identities). In fact, in this study participants whose preferred identity was respected, not only showed less identity affirmation, but also reported higher identification with and loyalty to the externally ascribed group. That is, participants were willing to accept and internalize an imposed identity when they experienced respect for their self-preferred identity.

These results have clear implications for the issues we examine in this paper because they suggest that social policies that pressure minority group members to adopt the host identity and relinquish their native identity (and thereby disrespect preexisting ethnic identities) will tend to be ineffective. That is, such assimilative policies have the paradoxical effect of promoting affirmation of the neglected identity and inviting rejection of the imposed identity, thereby fostering separation instead of integration. By contrast, social policies which acknowledge the importance of multiple identities and promote their coexistence (as multiculturalism) actually motivate minority group members to consider alternative bases for self-definition, and facilitate acceptance of and identification with the superordinate category.

ASSIMILATION PRESSURES HAVE NEGATIVE PSYCHOLOGICAL CONSEQUENCES FOR MINORITY GROUP MEMBERS

In this section, we examine the impact of categorization threats on the self and thereby consider evidence demonstrating that assimilative pressures are damaging for individual psychological well-being. Given that these pressures are felt by minority group members but not by majority group members, the psychological distress they create, which can undermine performance and social integration, is specifically experienced by minorities. We thus propose that this constitutes another important way in which assimilation pressures promote inequality and social exclusion.

Researchers focusing on the influence of acculturation on individual well-being have dedicated great attention to what is designated as *acculturation stress* or *culture shock* (e.g., Ward, Bochner, & Furnham, 2001). For a long time, the dominant idea in this field was that migrants would experience a great deal of stress not only because of the concrete changes that they underwent through the migration process but also because of the fact that many of them would be "living between two cultures" (Watson, 1977). However, empirical research in this domain reveals that it is those migrants who actually do manage to live between two cultures (i.e., those who endorse biculturalism) that reveal the best mental health on various indexes (e.g., Berry & Kim, 1988; Phinney, 1990). In fact, bicultural individuals are those who hold multiple cultural identities, by striving to maintain their ethnic identity while developing strong ties with the host group. In doing so, these individuals reap both the health benefits of a strong ethnic identity (Gurin & Epps, 1974) and the benefits of functional adaptation to the norms of the host society (see also LaFromboise et al., 1993).

Thus, the endorsement of biculturalism in itself does not seem to lead to psychological distress. However, when bicultural individuals are exposed to assimilative pressures, they may, nevertheless, experience psychological distress. In other words, besides the acculturation strategy endorsed by specific individuals, the acculturation ideology prevalent in a given society will tend to influence the mental health of any migrants living in that society. Specifically, it has been argued that individual mental health would be best in migrants who acculturate in multicultural societies than in migrants who acculturate in societies governed by assimilative ideologies (Berry & Kim, 1988; Murphy, 1965). This would, presumably, be due to the reduced identity discrepancies experienced in multicultural societies, especially given that the majority of migrants appear to endorse acculturation strategies that are consistent with multiculturalism and not with assimilation (e.g., Berry, 1990). However, while existing data at a macrolevel of analysis suggests this may be the case, empirical evidence directly examining the claim that identity discrepancies are damaging to psychological well-being is, so far, very scarce.

In our own research we therefore addressed the possibility that categorization threat may actually constitute at least part of the process through which assimilative pressures yield negative psychological outcomes (Barreto et al., in press). We predicted categorization threats to result in psychological distress because they constitute a form of disrespectful treatment. This is in line with prior research showing that people take the way they are treated by others as a sign of how much they are valued as individuals or as group members (Brockner, 1988; Tyler & Lind, 1992). As a consequence, whether people feel they are treated with respect has an impact on the emotions they express and on their self-esteem (e.g., Krehbiel & Cropanzano, 2000; Tyler et al., 1996; Vermunt, Wit, van den Bos, & Lind, 1996). It thus follows that categorization threats should also have an impact on individual emotional well-being.

To offer an empirical examination of these ideas, we investigated the effect of the type of categorization threat that results from the imposition of unwanted categorizations on individual psychological well-being (Barreto et al., in press). In doing this, we compared the impact of categorization threat depending on whether the unwanted categorical treatment is imposed in an implicit or an explicit way. We examined this issue because, so far, the examination of identity threats has mainly focused on threats that are quite explicitly imposed (e.g., when people are explicitly allocated to a group with which they do not identify). However, explicit identity threats are not the only – and, arguably, not even the most common – identity threats people are confronted with in modern societies. In fact, most modern societies, and individuals and organizations within these societies, only pay lip service to the importance of diversity and multiculturalism while endorsing discriminatory practices; exerting implicit pressures toward assimilation (e.g., Benokraitis & Feagin, 1995; Devine, Plant, & Blair, 2001; Dovidio, 2001) and defining the norms and values of the host society as inherently superior (Mummendey & Wenzel, 1999).

When we think of the characteristics of implicit and explicit categorization threat, it becomes clear that the impact of these two types of threat on the self is likely to be quite different. Generally, explicit identity threats focus one's attention on the source of threat and direct coping efforts toward changing or eliminating the threat. In particular, explicit categorization threats constitute clear, unambiguous treatment that is inconsistent with one's wishes or beliefs. When the source of threat is clear, explicit categorization threats are likely to elicit expressions of hostility toward the source of the treatment and attempts at restoring respectful treatment (such as protest). This, in fact, corresponds to people's usual responses to disrespectful or unfair treatment, as documented in prior research (Krehbiel & Cropanzano, 2000; Tyler et al., 1996; Vermunt et al., 1996). For these reasons, we expected to find this type of response to explicit categorization threat.

By contrast, the source of an implicit identity threat is by definition unclear and so also less easy to recognize. People submitted to an implicit threat of any kind, and so also to an implicit identity threat, are likely to feel uncertain about what is happening to them, and also about the cause of the stress they experience. As a result, those who are exposed to an implicit identity threat are less likely to cope with this threat by expressing negative other-directed emotions (such as hostility) and responses aimed at changing the source of stress (such as protest). Alternatively, they may attribute the threat experienced to causes that are solely internal to themselves and express negative affect that is directed at themselves rather than at the source. For this reason, we expected targets of implicit identity threats to report more emotions that signal negative, self-directed affects (such as insecurity and low self-esteem) than targets of explicit identity threat.

This is what we found when we examined how people respond to implicit versus explicit categorization threat (Barreto et al., in press; see also Barreto & Ellemers, 2005 for an examination of a similar process as a result of exposure to subtle versus blatant prejudice). Participants in three studies were informed that one team member would allocate a set of tasks among the group members and asked to indicate what their two preferred tasks would be. The various tasks to be performed had been carefully piloted to be equally attractive to our female participants while differing in the degree to which they were stereotypically associated with the female stereotype. In fact, some of the tasks to be performed corresponded to stereotypically male tasks, while others were stereotypically female, and the remaining were stereotypically neutral tasks. Although participants had expressed their own preference, they were only asked to perform female stereotypical tasks. As a consequence, even though gender categorization was inappropriate in the task context, our female participants were all treated on the basis of their gender identity. Participants who were implicitly categorized received no other information regarding the reasons underlying this task allocation, whereas participants who were explicitly categorized were told that they were assigned those particular tasks because of their gender.

Our results across the three studies were consistent with the argument we described in previous sections. Participants who were explicitly categorized expressed more disagreement with the task allocation, more anger, and more wish to protest than participants who were implicitly categorized. That is, participants who were explicitly categorized reported more negative emotions directed at the appropriate target (i.e., the source of disrespectful treatment) and directed their effort at changing the source of stress. By contrast, participants who were implicitly categorized reported greater insecurity and lower personal self-esteem than participants who were explicitly categorized. This is consistent with the idea that targets of implicit identity threats are less able to cope appropriately with the stress to which they are exposed and, therefore, reveal the negative impact of this stress on the self.

Taken together, these results demonstrate the negative psychological impact of categorization threat on its targets. It is important to note that although these results indicate that there are important differences in the way people experience explicit and implicit identity threats, they also clearly demonstrate that categorization threats lead to negative emotional experiences irrespective of the way they are imposed. In fact, people whose contextual choice of identity was neglected in favor of a categorization that was externally imposed (as is characteristic of assimilative treatment) expressed negative emotions, irrespective of whether the identity threat was implicit or explicit.

If we keep in mind that assimilative pressures imply categorization threat (by neglecting alternative bases of categorization, other than the superordinate category), it is clear that minority group members are more likely to be targets of these types of threat and hence to suffer the negative psychological consequences we described than are majority group members. This is another mechanism through which assimilation ideologies may contribute to inequality between minority group and majority group members and foster social exclusion instead of achieving integration.

ASSIMILATION PRESSURES LEAD TO THE USE OF IDENTITY-MANAGEMENT STRATEGIES THAT ACCENTUATE DISADVANTAGE

A final reason that assimilation ideologies may result in social exclusion is because they refer to the goal of inclusion in a superordinate category that is defined solely by reference to the values, norms, and traditions of the majority group (Mummendey & Wenzel, 1999). In this sense, assimilation is a one-way acculturation strategy, which implies that minority group members must adapt to a preexisting national category. That is, the reverse process of changing the definition of the national category because of the inclusion of different subgroups is not contemplated. Since the norms and values of the superordinate category serve as a template against which individuals are judged as worthy, minority group members in assimilationist societies are subjected to more negative expectations and evaluations than majority group members. In this way, the assimilationist ideology intellectually and morally justifies the superiority of the dominant culture (Fredrickson, 1999; Verkuyten, 2005). Indeed, it has been observed that those majority group members who endorse the assimilationist ideology evaluate members of other groups relatively negatively (Verkuyten, 2005).

As a result, the only chance that minority group members have to be positively evaluated in assimilative contexts is to adopt strategies that increase their similarity to the prototype of the superordinate category. That is, to seek inclusion in assimilative societies, minority group members must downplay the characteristics that make them deviate from the prototype of the superordinate category, and endorse characteristics that increase their match to that prototype. Since even small deviations from the prototype can

lead to exclusion (as demonstrated within research on the ingroup overexclusion effect, Yzerbyt, Leyens, & Bellour, 1995), to secure social inclusion,
minority group members often need to actually try to *pass as* members of
the majority group. However, we argue that employment of this strategy
is costly in important ways. Passing leads to negative psychological outcomes, even if the true identity of those who try to pass is left undiscovered.
In turn, these negative psychological outcomes are likely to accentuate the
disadvantage of minority group members, and thereby contribute to their
social exclusion instead of resolving it.

Passing is an identity-management strategy that is often used by minority group members who wish to counteract the negative stereotypes and
expectations that are commonly associated with their category membership
(Croteau, 1996; Goffman, 1963; Jones et al., 1984; Katz, 1981; Tajfel, 1981).
People may choose to pass because they have internalized an assimilationist ideology according to which they should try to resemble majority group
members as much as possible. Indeed, it has often been found that the more
minority group members internalize the assimilation ideology, the less they
identify with their minority group (Verkuyten, 2005). However, disidentification with the native category is not a necessary condition or motivation
for the endorsement of this strategy. In fact, people may also choose to pass
simply because they realize that their devalued identity makes them vulnerable to discrimination, and they expect that passing will reduce this vulnerability (Clair, Beatty, & MacLean, 2005; Croteau, 1996; Ostfield & Jehn, 1999
for reviews of motives to pass).

Despite the expectation that passing will constitute a beneficial strategy,
empirical research indicates that this strategy is also associated with important costs. Because passing implies both covering the devalued identity and
actively adopting a new identity, it involves both an act of deceit and an act
of positive self-presentation (see also Griffin, 1992). While the act of positive self-presentation may lead to the benefit of protecting the individual
from negative expectations and stereotypes, the act of deceit is associated
with important costs.

Specifically, people who pass report worse physical health (Cole,
Kemeny, Taylor, & Visscher, 1996; Pennebaker, Kiecolt-Glaser, & Glaser,
1988) and more negative emotions (such as shame and guilt) than people
who choose to reveal a devalued identity (Harris, 2001; Major & Gramzow,
1999; Paxton, 2002). Those who pass also experience apprehension about the
possibility of being exposed as impostors and, as a consequence, carefully
and painstakingly monitor their thoughts and behaviors to avoid revealing their true identity (Frable, 1993; Smart & Wegner, 1999). This increased

self-monitoring can actually lead to thought intrusion, which is in itself disturbing and also leads to the increased salience of the devalued identity (Smart & Wegner, 1999). Finally, those who pass in the work context report lower work satisfaction, lower productivity, and lower loyalty to the organization. In fact, the costs of hiding are so high that people often prefer to project an authentic but negative view of themselves than to present themselves positively (e.g., Swann, 1990).

Most previous research on the effects of passing follows a correlational methodology, with the consequence that causal relations between variables cannot be clearly established. Recently, researchers have begun to uncover these effects with resort to experimental methods. For instance, the negative cognitive consequences of passing have been thoroughly and experimentally examined by Smart and Wegner (1999). However, the emotional and performance-related consequences of passing have still not been subject to sufficient experimental scrutiny. The causal questions this raises, such as the questions of whether passing has negative emotional consequences or whether those who are emotionally distressed are the ones who most often choose to pass, are quite important.

To address this issue, we conducted a series of studies in which we experimentally examined the effects of passing on emotional well-being. For instance, we approached a sample of lesbian, gay, and bisexual individuals (Barreto, Ellemers, & Tiemersma, 2005) and randomly asked them either to reflect on their experiences with revealing their homosexuality at work or to describe their experiences with passing as heterosexual in the work context. Results of this study confirmed the emotional costs of passing: Those who described an experience with passing reported feeling less positive and more negative affect, as well as more anxiety and depression. Additionally, when passing, people felt less accepted and more isolated than participants who revealed their homosexuality. Finally, passing had negative work-related consequences: Participants who passed reported lower work satisfaction, as well as lower organizational and team commitment than participants who revealed their homosexual identity.

In another set of studies we specifically focused on feelings about the self as a consequence of passing (Barreto, Ellemers, & Banal, 2006). Based on past research showing that the operation of self-fulfilling prophecies leads members of devalued groups to report low self-confidence (e.g., Biernat, Crandall, Young, Kobrynowicz, & Halpin, 1998; Cadinu, Maass, Frigerio, Impagliazzo, & Latinotti, 2003; Stangor, Carr, & Kiang, 1998), we explored the possibility that, when an individual passes as a member of a positively evaluated group, similar self-fulfilling prophecies might result in an increase in self-confidence (cf., Shih, Pittinsky, & Ambady, 1999). Our expectation in these studies was that passing as a member of a more-valued group would not lead to this benefit for self-confidence. The basic argument was that although passing can present the self more positively to others, it presents the self less positively "to oneself" because of the act of deceit it implies (Goffman, 1963; Leary, 1999). As a consequence, passing was expected to be accompanied by negative self-directed affect, such as guilt and shame (Harris, 2001; Major & Gramzow, 1999; Paxton, 2002), which should undermine the self-confidence of those who passed.

This is, in fact, what we found in a series of two studies. In line with our manipulations, participants who were induced to pass indeed thought that passing would improve the expectations their partner had of them. Nevertheless, participants who passed reported lower (performance-related) self-confidence than participants who revealed the devalued identity. In addition, participants who passed reported feeling more guilt and shame than participants who revealed, and these emotions actually mediated the effect of passing on self-confidence. Furthermore, no performance benefits of passing could be observed; task performance turned out to be associated with self-confidence – not with partner's expectations.

Taken together, these findings indicate that members of devalued groups find themselves in a no-win situation. If they reveal the devalued identity they are vulnerable to negative stereotypes and social exclusion. However, if they try to pass as members of a more-valued group (such as the majority group) they suffer psychological costs, such as negative self-directed affect (e.g., guilt and shame), and loss of self-confidence. This is likely to have important, negative implications for individual work and social performance, which promote social inequality and perpetuate the disadvantages of minority group members.

DOES ASSIMILATION FOSTER SOCIAL INCLUSION?

In this chapter we reviewed evidence to show that attempts to enhance social inclusion by advocating assimilation are likely to achieve the opposite effect. That is, because they imply various types of identity threat, assimilation pressures induce intergroup conflict and undermine social cohesion. Furthermore, we have argued that minority group members tend to suffer important psychological costs as a result of assimilation pressures, which drive them to engage in strategies that increase rather than alleviate these psychological costs. Thus, the paradox of social inclusion is that measures which seemingly ensure individualized, meritocratic treatment result in systematic inequality and disadvantage for members of minority groups. Indeed, assimilative pressures may often be well-intended to reduce group-based differences and ensure the meritocratic treatment of newcomers and of other minorities. However, as we demonstrated in this chapter, such pressures are inappropriate tools with which to reach the goal of social equality.

As an alternative to assimilation, we have proposed that multiculturalism – the recognition of multiple identities – is a more fruitful strategy for achieving true integration and the social inclusion of minority group members. In reviewing the empirical evidence relevant to this issue, we have come to the conclusion that for minority group members in particular, the endorsement of a dual identity (i.e., as a minority group member and as a member of the more inclusive national category) may be seen as perfectly compatible. Indeed, when this dual identity is acknowledged by others, it can actually help alleviate stress instead of contributing to it, as it is often thought to do. The achievement of social inclusion thus requires a consideration of differences between groups within society that must be respected and embraced. This does not necessarily imply that minority group members will prefer to be treated on the basis of their minority identity but that their preference – whether to define themselves in terms of this identity – must be respected by others.

In a society that is characterized by assimilationist beliefs, minority group members are put at a disadvantage. Importantly, this is not only the case for minority group members who do not wish to relinquish their native identity. That is, even those who go along with the view that the majority identity is superior and try to pass as majority group members suffer psychological costs due to their passing attempts, which make it less likely that they are successful. Again, this indicates that societal norms and beliefs that (implicitly) present the majority identity as superior or normative, actually enhance the disadvantage and exclusion encountered by minority group members, even when they give in to assimilation pressures or try to pass as majority group members. Additionally, those who aim for assimilation not only may face rejection by the majority group despite their attempts to assimilate (cf. LaFramboise et al., 1993), but they also run the risk of being rejected by other ingroup members because they have relinquished ingroup norms and values (Branscombe & Ellemers, 1998; Postmes & Branscombe, 2002). Ultimately, they may come up empty-handed when they are not fully accepted by the majority and then discover that they cannot turn back to the minority group for support. Again, this illustrates the costs associated with pressures toward assimilation for minority group members, in particular.

In considering our proposition, some may counterargue that many events currently hitting the news media dispute the effectiveness of multiculturalism in ensuring social cohesion. Indeed, ethnic tensions in societies that are commonly seen as true models of multiculturalism, such as the Netherlands, may be seen as demonstrating that multiculturalism has failed. However, in our opinion, the problem is not that multiculturalism has failed but that ideologies and practices that are de facto promoting assimilation are so often ill-defined as multiculturalism. That is, very often the success of multiculturalism is gauged by the extent to which migrants are seen to have relinquished their native culture in the (mistaken) belief that only by doing so can they truly adopt the values and norms that characterize the host society. First, this assessment demonstrates a fundamental misunderstanding of what multiculturalism and integration are all about. Indeed, it must be noted that the assumption that native and host norms and values are incompatible is one that underlies assimilationist ideologies, not multiculturalism. Second, as we demonstrated in this chapter, it is important to stress that the endorsement of the norms and values of the host society is not endangered by the maintenance of native values. In fact, quite the contrary situation occurs: Experiencing respect for native values actually promotes the endorsement of the norms and values of the host society (see also Derks, Van Laar, & Ellemers, 2006). Thus, what is often seen as the failure of multiculturalism is no more than a clear demonstration of the negative effects of assimilationist pressures.

Although in our present reasoning we mainly focused on ethnic minorities and problems of social integration, in principle, similar processes apply to other cases in which members of different groups interact with each other in a context that is characterized by multiple identities. A case in point is that of professional women in organizations, who may prefer to simultaneously define themselves in terms of their gender identity *and* in terms of their professional identity. Due to the different mechanisms we have examined in this chapter, when these women are treated by others in terms of one of these identities only (i.e., only as women or only as professionals) they will suffer psychological disadvantage that is likely to undermine work commitment and work performance. By contrast, when the dual identities they represent and the multiple roles they fulfill are acknowledged by others, these women tend to be happier and to function better both at work and at home (Ellemers & Rink, 2005; Van Steenbergen & Ellemers, 2007).

In this chapter, we argued that the achievement of social inclusion requires a bilateral process through which minority group members, on the one hand, endorse and follow the norms and values of the host society but, on the other hand, are treated as full members of society who are respected for their distinct identity. Consistent with pluralist ideologies, this implies that *mutual respect* for the similarities and differences that characterize various groups in society provides a solid basis for social equality and integration (Glazer, 1997; Huo & Molina, 2006).

REFERENCES

Barreto, M., & Ellemers, N. (2000). You can't always do what you want: Social identity and self-presentational determinants of the choice to work for a low status group. *Personality and Social Psychology Bulletin, 26,* 891–906.

Barreto, M., & Ellemers, N. (2002). The impact of self-identities and treatment by others on the expression of loyalty to a low status group. *Personality and Social Psychology Bulletin, 28,* 493–503.

Barreto, M., & Ellemers, N. (2003). The effects of being categorised: The interplay between internal and external social identities. In W. Stroebe & M. Hewstone (Eds.), *European review of social psychology (Vol. 14,* pp. 139–170). Chichester: Wiley.

Barreto, M., & Ellemers, N. (2005). The perils of political correctness: Responses of men and women to old-fashioned and modern sexist views. *Social Psychology Quarterly, 68,* 75–88.

Barreto, M., Ellemers, N., & Banal, S. (2006). Working under cover: Negative expectations and performance-related self-confidence among members of contextually devalued groups who try to pass. *European Journal of Social Psychology, 36,* 337–352.

Barreto, M., Ellemers, N., Scholten, W., & Smith H. (in press). To be or not to be: The impact of implicit versus explicit identity dis-respect on the self. *British Journal of Social Psychology.*

Barreto, M., Ellemers, N., & Tiemersma, J. (2005). The effects of passing on emotional well-being and work-related outcomes. Manuscript in preparation.

Barreto, M., Spears, R., Ellemers, N., & Shahinper, K. (2003). The influence of linguistic context on the expression of social identity among minority group members: Evidence for strategic self-presentation. *British Journal of Social Psychology, 42,* 299–318.

Barry, B. (2001). *Culture and equality.* Cambridge, UK: Polity Press.

Baumeister, R. (1982). A self-presentational view of social phenomena. *Psychological Bulletin, 91,* 3–26.

Benokraitis, N. V., & Feagin, J. R. (1995). *Modern sexism (2nd ed.).* Englewood Cliffs, NJ: Prentice-Hall.

Berry, J. W. (2001). A psychology of immigration. *Journal of Social Issues, 57,* 615–631.

Berry, J. W., & Kim, U. (1988). *Acculturation and mental health.* In P. Dasen, J. W. Berry, & N. Sartorius (Eds.), *Health and cross-cultural psychology: Towards applications (pp. 207–236).* London: Sage.

Biernat, M., Crandall, C. S., Young, L. V., Kobrynowicz, D., & Halpin, S. M. (1998). All that you can be: Stereotyping of self and others in a military context. *Journal of Personality and Social Psychology, 75,* 301–317.

Bourhis, R. Y., Moise, L. C., Perreault, S., & Senecal, S. (1997). Towards an interactive acculturation model: A social psychological approach. *International Journal of Psychology, 32*, 369–386.

Branscombe, B., & Ellemers, N. (1998). Use of individualistic and group strategies in response to perceived group-based discrimination. In J. Swim & C. Stangor (Eds.), *Prejudice: The target's perspective* (pp. 243–266). New York: Academic Press.

Branscombe, N., Ellemers, N., Spears, R., & Doosje, B. (1999). The context and content of social identity threat. In N. Ellemers, R. Spears, & B. Doosje (Eds.) *Social identity: Context, commitment, content* (pp. 35–58). Oxford: Blackwell.

Breakwell, M. (1983). *Coping with threatened identities.* New York: Methuen

Brewer, M. B. (1991). The social self: On being the same and different at the same time. *Personality and Social Psychology Bulletin, 17*, 475–482.

Brockner, J. (1988). *Self-esteem at work: Theory, research, and practice.* Lexington, MA: Lexington Books.

Cadinu, M., Maass, A., Frigerio, S., Impagliazzo, L., & Latinotti, S. (2003). Stereotype threat: The effect of expectancy on performance. *European Journal of Social Psychology, 33*, 267–285.

Chen, S., Chen, K. Y., & Shaw, L. (2004). Self-verification motives at the collective level of self-definition. *Journal of Personality and Social Psychology, 86*, 77–94.

Clair, J., A., Beatty, J. E., & MacLean, T. L. (2005). Out of sight but not out of mind: Managing invisible social identities in the workplace. *Academy of Management Review, 30*, 78–95.

Cole, S. W., Kemeny, M. E., Taylor, S. E., & Visscher, B. R. (1996). Elevated physical health risk among gay men who conceal their homosexual identity. *Health Psychology, 15*, 243–251.

Croteau, J. M. (1996). Research on the work experiences of lesbian, gay, and bisexual people: An integrative review of methodology and findings. *Journal of Vocational Behavior, 48*, 119–124.

Deaux, K. (1996). Social identification. In. E. T. Higgins & A. Kruglanski (Eds.), *Social psychology: Handbook of basic principles* (pp. 777–798). New York: The Guilford Press.

Deaux, K., & Ethier, K. A. (1998). Negotiating social identity. In J. K. Swim & C. Stangor (Eds.), *Prejudice: The target's perspective* (pp. 302–323). San Diego, CA: Academic Press.

Derks, B., Van Laar, C., & Ellemers, N. (2006). Striving for success in outgroup settings: Effects of contextually emphasizing ingroup dimensions on stigmatized group members' social identity and performance styles. *Personality and Social Psychology Bulletin, 32*, 576–588.

Devine, P. G., Plant, E. A., & Blair, I. V. (2001). Classic and contemporary analyses of racial prejudice. In R. Brown & S. Gaertner (Eds.), *Blackwell handbook of social psychology: Intergroup processes* (pp. 198–217). Oxford, UK: Blackwell.

Doosje, B., Ellemers, N., & Spears, R. (1995). Perceived intragroup variability as a function of group status and identification. *Journal of Experimental Social Psychology, 31*, 410–436.

Dovidio, J. F. (2001). On the nature of contemporary prejudice: The third wave. *Journal of Social Issues, 57*, 829–49.

Ellemers, N., Barreto, M., & Spears, R. (1999). Commitment and strategic responses to social context. In N. Ellemers, R. Spears, & B. Doosje (Eds.), *Social identity: Context, commitment, content* (pp. 157–146). Oxford: Basil Blackwell.

Ellemers, N., & Rink, F. (2005). Identity in work groups: The beneficial and detrimental consequences of multiple identities and group norms for collaboration and group performance. *Advances in Group Processes, 22,* 1–41.

Ellemers, N., Spears, R., & Doosje, B. (2002). Self and social identity. *Annual Review of Psychology, 53,* 161–186.

Finchilescu, G. (1986). Effect of incompatibility between internal and external group membership criteria on intergroup behavior. *European Journal of Social Psychology, 16,* 83–87.

Frable, D. E. S. (1993). Being and feeling unique: Statistical deviance and psychological marginality. *Journal of Personality, 61,* 85–110.

Fredrickson, G. M. (1999). Models of American ethnic relations: A historical perspective. In D. A. Prentice & D. T. Miller (Eds.), *Cultural divides: Understanding and overcoming group conflict* (pp. 23–34). New York: Russell Sage Foundation.

Gaertner, S. L., & Dovidio, J. F. (2000). *Reducing intergroup bias: The common ingroup identity model.* Philadelphia, PA: Psychology Press.

Gaertner, S. L., Mann, J., Murrell, A., & Dovidio, J. F. (1989). Reducing intergroup bias: The benefits of recategorization. *Journal of Personality and Social Psychology, 57,* 239–249.

Gaertner, S. L., Rust, M. C., Dovidio, J. F., Bachman, B. A., & Anastasio, P. A. (1994). The contact hypothesis: The role of a common ingroup identity on reducing intergroup bias. *Small Group Research, 22,* 267–277.

Glazer, N. (1997). *We are all multiculturalists now.* Cambridge, MA: Harvard University Press.

Goffman, E. (1963). *Stigma: Notes on the management of spoiled identity.* Englewood Cliffs, NJ: Prentice-Hall.

Griffin, P. (1992). From hiding out to coming out: Empowering lesbian and gay educators. In K. M. Harbeck (Ed.), *Coming out of the classroom closet* (pp. 167–196). Binghamton, NY: Harrington Park Press.

Gurin, P., & Epps, E. (1974). *Black consciousness, identity, and achievement.* NY: John Wiley and Sons.

Harris, C. (2001). Cardiovascular responses of embarrassment and effects of emotional suppression in a social setting. *Journal of Personality and Social Psychology, 81,* 886–897.

Haunschild, P. R., Moreland, R. L., & Murrell, A. J. (1994). Sources of resistance to mergers between groups. *Journal of Applied Social Psychology, 24,* 1150–1178.

Hewstone, M., & Brown, R. J. (1986). Contact is not enough: An intergroup perspective on the "contact hypothesis." In M. Hewstone & R. J. Brown (Eds.), *Contact and conflict in intergroup encounters* (pp. 1–44). Oxford, UK: Blackwell.

Hornsey, M. J., & Hogg, M. A. (2000a). Assimilation and diversity: An integrative model of subgroup relations. *Personality and Social Psychology Review, 4,* 143–156.

Hornsey, M. J., & Hogg, M. A. (2000b). Subgroup relations: A comparison of mutual intergroup differentiation and common ingroup identity models of prejudice reduction. *Personality and Social Psychology Bulletin, 26,* 242–256.

Huo, Y. J. (2003). Procedural justice and social regulation across group boundaries: Does subgroup identity undermine relationship-based governance? *Personality and Social Psychology Bulletin, 29*, 336–348.

Huo, Y. J., & Molina, L. E. (2006). Is pluralism a viable model of diversity? The benefits and limits of subgroup respect. *Group Processes and Intergroup Relations, 9*, 359–376.

Huo, Y. J., Smith, H. J., Tyler, T. R., & Lind, E. A. (1996). Superordinate identification, subgroup identification, and justice concerns: Is separatism the problem, is assimilation the answer? *Psychological Science, 7*, 40–45.

Jetten, J., Spears, R., & Manstead, A. S. R. (1997). Strength of identification and intergroup differentiation: The influence of group norms. *European Journal of Social Psychology, 27*, 816.1–7.

Jones, E. E., Farina, A., Hastorf, A. H., Markus, H., Miller, D. T., & Scott, R. A. (1984). *Social stigma: The psychology of marked relationships*. New York: Freeman.

Katz, I. (1981). *Stigma: A social psychological analysis*. Hillsdale, NJ: Lawrence Erlbaum.

Klein, O., & Azzi, A. (2001). The selective confirmation of meta-stereotypes: How group members attempt to tailor an outgroup's representation of themselves. *British Journal of Social Psychology, 40*, 279–293.

Kramer, R. M., & Brewer, M. B. (1984). Effects of group identity on resource use in a simulated commons dilemma. *Journal of Personality and Social Psychology, 46*, 1044–1057.

Krehbiel, P. J., & Cropanzano, R. (2000). Procedural justice, outcome favourability, and emotion. *Social Justice Research, 13*, 339–360.

LaFromboise, T., Coleman, L. K. H., & Gerton, J. (1993). Psychological impact of biculturalism: Evidence and theory. *Psychological Bulletin, 114*, 395–412.

Lambert, W. E., & Taylor, D. M. (1990). *Coping with cultural and racial diversity in urban America*. New York: Praeger.

Leary, K. (1999). Passing, posing, and "keeping it real." *Constellations, 6*, 85–96.

Leary, M. R., & Kowalski, R. M. (1990). Impression management: A literature review and two-component model. *Journal of Personality and Social Psychology, 107*, 34–47.

Major, B., & Gramzow, R. H. (1999). Abortion as stigma: Cognitive and emotional implications of concealment. *Journal of Personality and Social Psychology, 77*, 735–745.

Mlicki, P., & Ellemers, N. (1996). Being different or being better? National stereotypes and identifications of Polish and Dutch students. *European Journal of Social Psychology, 26*, 97–114.

Mummendey, A., & Wenzel, M. (1999). Social discrimination and tolerance in intergroup relations: Reactions to intergroup difference. *Personality and Social Psychology Review, 3*, 158–174.

Murphy, H. B. M. (1965). Migration and the major mental disorders: A reappraisal. In M. B. Kantor (Ed.), *Mobility and mental health* (pp. 5–29). Springfield: Thomas.

Oakes, P. J., Haslam, S. A., & Turner, J. C. (1994). *Stereotyping and social reality*. Oxford: Blackwell.

Ostfield, M. L., & Jehn, K. A. (1999). Personal revelation and conflict in organizational settings: The gay individual as social perceiver of power and safety. *Research on Negotiation in Organizations, 7*, 179–202.

Ouwerkerk, J. W., de Gilder, D., & de Vries, N. K. (2000). When the going gets tough, the tough get going: Social identification and individual effort in inter-group competition. *Personality and Social Psychology Bulletin, 26,* 1550–1559.

Paxton, S. (2002). The paradox of public HIV disclosure. *AIDS-Care, 14,* 559–567.

Pennebaker, J. W., Kiecolt-Glaser, J. K., & Glaser, R. (1988). Disclosure of traumas and immune function: Health implications for psychotherapy. *Journal of Consulting and Clinical Psychology, 56,* 239–245.

Phinney, J. S. (1990). Ethnic identity in adolescence and adults: Review of research. *Psychological Bulletin, 108,* 499–514.

Postmes, T., & Branscombe, N. R. (2002). Influence of long-term racial environ-mental composition on subjective well-being in African Americans. *Journal of Personality and Social Psychology, 83,* 735–751.

Reicher, S., & Levine, M. (1994). On the consequences of deindividuation manipu-lations for the strategic considerations of self: Identifiability and the presenta-tion of social identity. *European Journal of Social Psychology, 24,* 511–524.

Reicher, S. D., Spears, R., & Postmes, T. (1995). A social identity model of deindi-viduation phenomena. *European Review of Social Psychology, 6,* 161–198.

Roccas, S., & Schwartz, S. H. (1993). Effects of intergroup similarity on intergroup relations. *European Journal of Social Psychology, 23,* 581–595.

Schlenker, B. (1980). *Impression management: The self-concept, social identity and interpersonal relations.* Monterey, CA: Brooks/Cole.

Schlesinger, A. M. (1992). *The disuniting of America.* New York: Norton.

Shih, M., Pittinsky, T. L., & Ambady, N. (1999). Stereotype susceptibility: Identity salience and shifts in quantitative performance. *Psychological Science, 10,* 80–83.

Sleebos, E., Ellemers, N., & De Gilder, D. (2006). The paradox of the disrespected: Disrespected group members' engagement in group-serving effort. *Journal of Experimental Social Psychology, 42,* 413–427.

Smart, L., & Wegner, D. M. (1999). Covering up what can't be seen: Concealable stigma and mental control. *Journal of Personality and Social Psychology, 77,* 474–486.

Spears, R., Doosje, B., & Ellemers, N. (1997). Self-stereotyping in the face of threats to group status and distinctiveness: The role of group identification. *Personality and Social Psychology Bulletin, 23*(5), 538–553.

Stangor, C., Carr, C., & Kiang, L. (1998). Activating stereotypes undermines task performance expectations. *Journal of Personality and Social Psychology, 52,* 613–629.

Swann, W. B. (1990). To be adored or to be known: The interplay of self-enhancement and self-verification. In R. M. Sorrentino & E. T. Higgins (Eds.), *Handbook of motivation and cognition* (Vol 2., pp. 408–448). New York: Guilford Press.

Swann, W. B., & Read, S. J. (1981). Self-verification: How we sustain our self-concep-tion. *Journal of Experimental Social Psychology, 17,* 351–372.

Tajfel, H. (1981). The social psychology of minorities. In H. Tajfel (Ed.) *Human groups and social categories: Studies in social psychology* (pp. 309–343). Cambridge: Cambridge University Press.

Terry, D. J., Carey, C. J., & Callan, V. J. (2001). Employee adjustment to an organi-zational merger: An intergroup perspective. *Personality and Social Psychology Bulletin, 27,* 267–280.

Turner, J. C., Hogg, M. A., Oakes, P. J., Reicher, S., & Wetherell, M. S. (1978/1987). *Rediscovering the social group: A self-categorization theory.* Oxford: Blackwell.

Tajfel, H. (Ed.) (1974). Social identity and intergroup behaviour. *Social Science Information,* 13, 65–93.

Tyler, T., Degoey, P., & Smith, H. (1996). Understanding why the justice of group procedure matters: A test of the psychological dynamics of the group-value model. *Journal of Personality and Social Psychology,* 70, 913–930.

Tyler, T. R., & Lind, E. A. (1992). A relational model of authority in groups. In M. Zanna (Ed.), *Advances in Experimental Social Psychology* (Vol. 25, pp. 115–191). New York: Academic Press.

Van Oudenhoven, J.-P., Prins, K., & Buunk, B. (1998). Attitudes of minority and majority members towards adaptation of immigrants. *European Journal of Social Psychology,* 28, 995–1013.

Van Rijswijk, W. Haslam, S. A., & Ellemers, N. (2006). Who do we think we are: The effects of social context and social identification on ingroup stereotyping. *Biritsh Journal of Social Psychology,* 45, 161–174.

Van Steenbergen, E., & Ellemers, N. (2007). *The work-family alliance: Distinct types of work-family facilitation and outcomes for women and men.* Manuscript under review.

Verkuyten, M. (2005). Ethnic group identification and group evaluation among minority and majority groups: Testing the multiculturalism hypothesis. *Journal of Personality and Social Psychology,* 88, 121–138.

Vermunt, R., Wit. A., Van den Bos, K., & Lind, E. A. (1996/1997). The effects of unfair procedure on negative affect and protest. *Social Justice Research,* 9, 109–118.

Ward, C., Bochner, S., & Furnham, A. (2001). *The psychology of culture shock.* London: Routledge.

Watson, J. L. (1977). *Between two cultures: Migrants and minorities in Britain.* Oxford: Blackwell.

Wit, A. P., & Kerr, N. L. (2002). "Me vs. just us. vs. us all" categorization and cooperation in nested social dilemmas. *Journal of Personality and Social Psychology,* 83, 616–637.

Yzerbyt, V., Castano, E., Leyens, J.-P., & Paladino, M.-P. (2000). The primacy of the ingroup: The interplay of entitativity and identification. *European Review of Social Psychology,* 11, 257–295.

Yzerbyt, V., Leyens, J.-P., & Bellour, F. (1995). The ingroup overexclusion effect: Identity concerns in decision about group membership. *European Journal of Social Psychology,* 25, 1–16.

13

Prominority Policies and Cultural Change: A Dilemma for Minorities

ANGELICA MUCCHI-FAINA

According to the minority influence theory (Moscovici 1976, 1980), determined and persistent minorities can start social change. To reach this goal, minorities have to obtain visibility and be capable of conflict with the majority, consistently affirming their rights, opinions, and diversity. Differentiation and opposition allow the minority to achieve both external visibility and internal cohesion. At this stage, minorities need to display courage and determination, denouncing status disadvantage that was previously hidden or considered normal. By means of a consistent behavioral style, minorities obtain respect and acknowledgment, produce the defreezing of previous beliefs and social representations, and start a new way of thinking, which, in turn, leads to cultural and social change. Evidence supporting this theory has been obtained not only in the laboratory (for a review, Moscovici, Mucchi-Faina, & Maass, 1994) but also through the observation of successful social movements (e.g., Mucchi-Faina, 1987). In the 1960s and 1970s, for example, many social and ethnic minorities consistently challenged their traditional marginal role and protested against their condition of social segregation. Minorities, in those years, not only demanded equal treatment and opportunities, but also affirmed the importance of diversity. These conflicts led to a new and widespread consideration of the needs of underprivileged groups and categories and induced the authorities to formulate social policies, norms, and recommendations aimed at reducing the unfair treatment of minorities. In addition, they activated a cultural change and a process of social transformation. In this manner, these minorities confirmed that powerless groups can, through conflict and differentiation, exert social influence.

After the initial, "heroic" period of conflict, minorities begin a new phase in which acquired acknowledgment and rights must be institutionalized and put into daily practice. According to Moscovici (1976), in this stage, minorities should be prepared to negotiate their space by compromising with the majority and creating alliances with other groups. By adopting a more supple and fair behavioral style, they can expand their sphere of influence even to the majority factions that have been the most hostile and ideologically distant.

In contrast to this analysis – and notwithstanding the wide range of behavioral options that are available to minorities in everyday settings (Levine & Kaarbo, 2001) – research on social influence says very little about minority strategies during the second phase. In line with Moscovici, I suggest in this chapter – using two empirical examples – that when their right to equal treatment has been recognized and when initiatives have been activated to remedy past injustices, minorities must rethink and reformulate their strategy because demanding redress for unfairness is often no longer the best approach. Claiming special treatment can in the long run have high psychological costs for minority members, help maintain negative stereotypes about them, and hinder their communication with other segments of society. On the contrary, focusing on equality may well be more effective.

SOCIAL MINORITIES IN THE SECOND PHASE: IS DIFFERENTIATION STILL THE WINNING STRATEGY?

According to its ideological position, a minority may be more or less motivated to eliminate barriers and asymmetries between itself and the majority. Minority strategies can also differ depending on whether their *focus* is on difference or equality. Consequently, by crossing motivation and focus, four main strategies can be identified (see Table 13.1). Strategy A (no motivation for change and focus on difference) assumes that, since the barriers between the minority cultures and majority cultures and tasks are impossible to overcome, keeping the two groups definitively separated is the best solution. This approach – supported by very radical or orthodox minorities, such as some feminist or religious fundamentalist groups – leaves status inequality unchanged because power and social responsibility are completely delegated to the dominant group. On the contrary, strategy B (no motivation for change and focus on equality) maintains complete equality, disregarding the barriers between the two groups' cultures and tasks. Minority members who take this position search for individual acknowledgment by strictly adapting themselves to the majority behaviors and roles and by renouncing minority values and diversity. Referring to Tajfel's (1978) distinction, the first strategy is totally determined by group membership, whereas the second strategy is totally determined by interpersonal relations.

TABLE 13.1. *Minority strategies according to motivation for social change by focus*

		Motivation for social change	
		No	Yes
Focus	Difference	A	C
	Equality	B	D

Whereas strategy A is adopted by people who believe that eliminating asymmetries between the majority and the minority is *impossible*, strategy B is adopted by people who believe that it is *unnecessary*. Thus – although for opposing reasons – both kinds of people are unmotivated to act for social change. More important in the present perspective are the strategies preferred by people who think that social change is both *possible* and *necessary* and who believe that dealing proactively with the problems related to prejudice, discrimination, and underrepresentation can lead to equal opportunities for minorities. Such people strongly believe in diversity's social value but differ on the way to reach acknowledgment by the majority. People who favor strategy C (motivation for change and focus on difference) start from an analysis of societal asymmetries and minority disadvantages. They claim that, to obtain equal opportunity, it is first necessary to redistribute social power – directly modifying the composition of political and social institutions – and even resorting to forced interventions or forms of constraint. They maintain that to make visible and salient the difference between the majority and minority is still the best way to obtain equality. On the contrary, people supporting strategy D (motivation for change and focus on equality) believe that minority members have to obtain recognition based on their individual accomplishments. They think that only by showing merit can minority members cause their culture and diversity to be appreciated and respected; corrective actions are considered an *extrema ratio* – used only in cases of evident and strong underrepresentation and discrimination and, even in these situations, limited in scope and time.

I suggest that, while C is the most effective strategy in the first phase, at the second step, strategy D is more effective than strategy C, although neither is totally without risks and problems. This contention is supported by data concerning two social policies that have been implemented to reduce social – specifically gender – asymmetries: affirmative action programs and language reforms.

"HARD" VERSUS "SOFT" AFFIRMATIVE
ACTION (AA) PROGRAMS

American affirmative action (AA) programs (and the equivalent European "positive action" programs) are advocated and inspired by social minorities, including Blacks and women, with the ultimate goal of eliminating prejudice and discrimination related to certain demographic factors (e.g., ethnicity, gender).* These programs involve preferential treatment in recruiting, training, or promoting minority group members (Crosby, 1994). In general, policies based on equal opportunity call for remedial actions only when there is a strong indication of discrimination, and they presuppose that without overt discrimination all individuals are given the same treatment. In contrast, AA programs assume that the obstacles to equality do not always take the form of overt discrimination and, for that reason, they actively check on whether equal opportunity actually exists (Crosby, Iyer, Clayton, & Downing, 2003).

It is important to distinguish between two different categories of AA, referred as *hard* and *soft* (Taylor-Carter, Doverspike, & Cook, 1995).† Hard AA stipulates that a woman should be favored and granted an opportunity (in employment, education, or other fields) on the basis of gender as long as she meets the minimum requested qualifications. Therefore, emphasis is given to membership in a minority group, and decisions are based primarily on demographic status. The main aim of this kind of AA is to correct and compensate for past injustice (*compensatory justice*). Soft AA refers to selection for jobs and education as well – meaning that as long as a woman and a man are *equally* qualified, the woman is chosen – and also to special training or simply to the removal of employment barriers. In the second approach, merit is seen as the critical factor, and the action mainly aims to adequately recognize or reinforce competence and skills (*procedural justice*). Therefore, hard and soft AA refer to two different strategies, both of which aim to obtain equal opportunities: the first is focused on difference (demography) and the second on equality (merit).

A few decades after the AA programs started, a number of studies evaluated their impact (Crosby et al., 2003; Kravitz et al., 1997). Preferential treatment has undoubtedly increased the number of women in male-dominated

---

* We use the term social minority to refer to disadvantaged societal groups, recognizing that some of these groups, for example, women, are not necessarily numerical minorities.
† Because our data concern women, our discussion of AA focuses on women, rather than members of other minorities.

professions and educational fields. But have AA programs produced a real change in social representations, prejudice, and stereotypes? Have they facilitated equitable relationships between women and men in jobs and education? In sum, have they been rewarding for women as a whole?

In this chapter, I examine the efficacy of hard and soft AA as a minority strategy based on the literature on the topic. On the whole, research shows that soft AA is generally more successful than hard AA regarding three important outcomes: (a) psychological costs for beneficiaries, (b) attitudes toward individual beneficiaries, and (c) attitudes toward the minority group as a whole.

1. Effects of AA on Psychological Costs for Direct Beneficiaries

Many researchers have pointed out that AA undermines the self-esteem and motivation of individuals who are intended to benefit from the programs. This contention is supported by strong evidence but only when difference alone (i.e., gender) is the criterion of the choice. Heilman and colleagues have conducted many experimental studies concerning the undesirable consequences to the beneficiary of non-work-related preferential selection. Specifically they have compared the effect of gender-based selection with that of merit-based selection. In their first study (Heilman, Simon, & Repper, 1987), participants of both genders succeeded or failed on a task involving working as a leader. Results indicated that when they were selected on the basis of gender (versus merit), women (but not men) devalued their performance, accepted less acknowledgment for success, considered themselves less competent as leaders, and were less interested in maintaining the leadership position (see also Heilman, Lucas, & Kaplow, 1990). In another study (Heilman, Battle, Keller, & Lee, 1998), participants were exposed to selection policies that differed in the degree to which merit and gender membership were considered. Women who believed they were selected on the basis of gender rather than merit evaluated their performance as lower. The target women's negative self-perceptions and self-evaluations were reduced when it was clear that merit was central in the decision. Additionally, in the absence of information about merit, participants supposed that merit was unimportant in the decisions.

In a survey concerning the task motivation of women in managerial roles (Chacko, 1982; cit. by Kravitz et al., 1997), women who believed they had been the target of a gender-based preferential selection reported lower job satisfaction than women who did not believe gender played an important role in their hiring. Nevertheless, these results are controversial (for contrasting results see, Heilman et al., 1987; Turner, Pratkanis, & Hardaway 1991; Turner & Pratkanis, 1993).

Gender-based preferential treatment can also have negative repercussions on a target's subsequent performance and behavior. In research focused on academic performance (Brown, Charnsangavej, Keough, Newman, & Rentfrow, 2000, Study 1), women who believed that they had been selected because of gender alone performed significantly worse on a subsequent problem-solving task than women who believed they had been selected at random or because of both their gender and merit (but this finding was not replicated when a brainstorming task was used, see Nacoste, 1989; Turner & Pratkanis, 1993). Another study (Heilman, Kaplow, Amato, & Stathatos, 1993) indicated that women who were selected preferentially on the basis of gender (versus merit) gave more negative evaluations to female (but not male) applicants for a position and recommended hiring women less often and less keenly.

Researchers have also examined how selection affects task and job choice. Heilman, Rivero, and Bretto (1991) reported that women selected because of gender subsequently chose a less difficult task than did women selected because of merit. More importantly, a subsequent study showed that only women selected on the basis of gender *rather than* merit chose the less difficult task. Women who were selected because of both gender *and* merit, like women who were selected only because of merit, were more likely to choose the more challenging task. Finally, women who thought that others viewed them as having been preferentially selected because of gender (versus merit) experienced negative emotions, viewed themselves as less competent, and chose less demanding tasks (Heilman & Alcott, 2001).

To sum up, hard AA (focused on gender difference) can produce harmful effects in areas such as evaluation of one's own competence, performance, self-efficacy, motivation, job choice, and subsequent behavior. In contrast, practices that provide clear evidence of qualification (focusing also on merit, that is, soft AA) do not produce negative results. In fact, receiving preferential treatment as member of a discriminated group can make salient for the person the negative stereotypes linked to membership, with the related adverse consequences pointed out by studies on stereotype threat (Steele & Aronson, 1995). Short-term consequences could also translate into long-term negative consequences of (learned) helplessness and dependence when the recipient perceives a low level of personal control to change the situation (a hypothesis advanced by Turner & Pratkanis, 1994). Hard AA can also induce attributional ambiguity on the part of recipients (Major, Feinstein, & Crocker, 1994). Beneficiaries may experience uncertainty about the causes of their outcomes because these outcomes may be attributed to group membership rather than to any personal characteristics, qualifications, or behaviors. When beneficiaries are informed that their outcomes are based on individual merit *as well as* group membership (that is, soft preferential treatment), attributional ambiguity about personal capacity is reduced and negative reactions are attenuated. An experiment has supported this idea (Major et al., 1994): Women participants who believed they had been selected for a leadership position on the basis of gender reported more negative affect – and attributed their selection less to their personal merit and more to their gender – than did women who believed they had been selected solely on the basis of merit. More importantly, women selected because of both gender and merit did not differ from those selected only because of merit in reported affect or in their attributions to personal merit.

2. Effects of AA on Attitudes of Others toward Individual Beneficiaries

People who have taken advantage of hard preferential treatment are often perceived as less competent than those who have not. In one of the first studies in the area (Jacobson and Koch, 1977, cited by Kravitz et al., 1997), male participants were paired and asked to perform a communication task with female confederates who – according to condition – were assigned to a leadership position on the basis of gender, chance, or merit (performance on a test). After performing the task, participants were told that the group had either succeeded or failed. Results showed that women who were selected based on gender were held responsible for the group's poor performance but were not given credit for the group's good performance. This latter phenomenon has been interpreted in terms of the discounting principle (Kelley, 1973): People often discount the qualifications of individuals whose success can be attributed at least partially to an AA program (Crosby et al., 2003).

Heilman and colleagues have carried out many studies concerning the effects of preferential treatment, not only on the target woman, but also on the attitudes and feelings of nontargets. In a study reported above (Heilman et al., 1998), it was found that the less merit was central in a selection decision, the less others perceived the woman target as competent. In another study (Heilman, Block, & Lucas, 1992), the stigma of incompetence was related to benefiting from AA. Women said to have been recently hired for a job were negatively evaluated on competence – by both women and men – when they were associated with an AA program, regardless of the kind of job they received (highly or moderately male gender typed). Participation in AA was also negatively associated with evaluations of activity and potency, assessments of interpersonal skills, and predictions of career progress. Additionally, the stigma of incompetence related to participation in AA is not easily overcome by information about successful performance: To disconfirm the stigma, such information has to be unequivocal. Indeed, two further studies have shown that the stigma of incompetence remains unchanged when information is either imprecise and ambiguous about the degree of success or unclear about the source of that success (Heilman, Block, & Stathatos, 1997). Moreover, gender-based preferential selection provokes negative feelings, attitudes, and behaviors (i.e., refusal to provide future help to a researcher) in male nontargets, not only when they are informed of their superior capability, but also when no information about comparative ability is provided (Heilman, McCullough, & Gilbert, 1996).

Finally, the effect of the perceived fairness of AA on female and male students' evaluation of a female university applicant has been studied (Dietz-Uhler & Murrell, 1998). The investigators manipulated the admission procedure that was ostensibly used for the applicant. In the quota condition, places were set aside to admit women who were underrepresented in certain areas. In the standard selection condition, it was simply mentioned that the university did not discriminate on the basis of sex, race, and so on. Results showed that the standard selection policy was perceived as more just than the quota policy. Moreover, findings pointed out the central role of the selection procedure's perceived fairness. First, participants who perceived the selection policy to be fair (versus unfair) tended to evaluate the applicant more favorably. Second, women evaluated the (ingroup) applicant more positively than men evaluated the (outgroup) applicant when the procedure was perceived as fair. In contrast, when the procedure was perceived as unfair, women evaluated the applicant more negatively than men did. These findings were interpreted on the basis of social identity theory (Tajfel & Turner, 1986): Because individuals are motivated to promote their own group, they favor the ingroup member who increases, but derogate the member who threatens ingroup reputation (about this issue, cf. also the literature about the black sheep effect; Marques, Yzerbyt, & Leyens, 1988; and the subjective group dynamics model, e.g., Abrams, Marques, Bown, & Henson, 2000; Marques, Abrams, & Serôdio, 2001).

3. Effects of AA on the Attitudes of Others toward
the Minority Group as a Whole

Can the effects of AA on the beneficiary be extended to the minority as a whole? It is crucial to distinguish between the individual level and group level of analysis, as perception of a group does not necessarily coincide with perception of individuals who are group members (Esses & Seligman, 1996). Stereotypes of and prejudices against the minority group could persist even if they are not applied to the individual, and vice versa.

Certain social minorities have questioned the utility of AA because they think that this intervention is detrimental for their groups (e.g., S. Steele, 1991, cited by Truax, Cordova, Wood, Wright, & Crosby, 1998). Their idea is that the mere presence of AA programs can support the perception that the minority is inferior and incapable of succeeding without special help. Therefore, if AA emphasizes the inferiority of a recipient and the need for remediation and help, it may threaten the image of the whole group. Few studies have been done on this important topic, and, unfortunately, none of them refers to gender categories. A potentially relevant experiment was run in Canada with the aim of examining whether the presence of AA programs reinforces unfavorable attitudes toward an immigrant group (Maio & Esses, 1998). Participants were asked to read a fictitious editorial containing a positive description of a little-known ethnic minority. In the experimental condition, the editorial stated that the group members would benefit from AA programs, whereas, in the control condition, it did not include this information. Participants were then asked about their perceptions of and attitudes toward the group. Results indicated that when AA was mentioned, the participants evaluated the group less positively and felt less favorable to the group's immigration.

Although there is evidence in this study that AA participation adversely effects the minority group as a whole, it is not advisable to apply these results to gender groups. The effects of AA programs on women could differ from the effects of these programs on other less-known minorities. Indeed, differences in the content and processing of stereotypes could have different effects on perceptions of AA policies targeted to those groups. Because gender stereotypes are complex and have many context-sensitive subtypes (e.g., the feminist, the career woman, the housewife), the effects of AA are not attributed to the category as a whole, but rather to the subtype that is thought to benefit from it (Eberhardt & Fiske, 1994), that is, women applying for male gender-typed jobs or education. Moreover, research has shown that when discrimination is indisputable, even nontarget people with a strong preference for the merit principle tend to reduce their opposition to preferential-treatment programs (Son Hing, Bobocel, & Zanna, 2002). Therefore, it could be supposed that when the perception of group discrimination is strong, the adverse effects of AA on attitudes toward the group should be reduced, too.

Although some issues are still unexplored and some results controversial, research shows that receiving special treatment merely because of difference (hard AA) can produce negative effects, not only on the direct recipient, but also on attitudes of nontarget people toward the recipient and members of the recipient's group. Different findings have been obtained when selection was based on both merit and gender (soft AA). When clear and compelling evidence of their qualifications is provided, the women involved in the program are not damaged, and they report more positive personal evaluations (pleasure, relaxation, satisfaction, etc.) than the women who were selected because of gender (Major, Feinstein, & Crocker, 1994). In addition, nontarget people are also less opposed to AA and see beneficiaries in a more favorable way. Therefore, self-perception and others' perceptions drastically change when AA underlines equality and merit, pursuing procedural justice, rather than difference and status, pursuing compensatory justice.

LANGUAGE REFORMS: VISIBILITY OR INCLUSION?

The feminist writer Iris Young has termed the minority disadvantage that is due – not to the conscious determination of a dominant group – but to the everyday practices of a well-intentioned liberal society, "structural oppression" (Young, 1990). The notion indicates that the process of devaluation is often activated because of widespread prejudices, stereotypes, and social representations that are more or less consciously shared by minority members themselves. Among the initiatives that have tried to deal with this kind of oppression are those concerning language.

In the last 20 years, several countries have made a great effort to discourage sexist language, that is, the use of expressions that are derogatory toward women or that underline and support their marginality. The conversion from sexist to nonsexist language can be done in two primary ways (Mucchi-Faina, 2005): (a) by *inclusion*, that is, trying to highlight the common denominator among individuals and making gender irrelevant (e.g., using plural nouns and epicenes, that is, nouns that have only one form for both sexes, like *person*) and (b) by *visibility*, that is, making gender salient and constantly recalling that women are present in a specific field (e.g., using paired pronouns or nouns, like *she/he*, alternating feminine and masculine, or even creating neologisms if the feminine version of words does not exist). The choice between the two options is partly dependent on the ideological approach (e.g., whether gender is considered relevant or irrelevant in a certain area) and partly related to specific features of a language (e.g., some languages have grammatical gender categories, whereas others do not). A linguistic practice that is considered sexist almost everywhere is the use of the generic (or false) masculine form (e.g., chairman) to refer to women as well as men. In gender-marked (e.g., neo-Latin) languages most guidelines recommend feminization of the lexicon and professional titles. The generic masculine form is considered particularly unfair in reference to professions and titles associated with prestigious positions when the feminine form exists and is used only for lower-status jobs traditionally delegated to women.

Would referring to a woman using a gender-marked title facilitate or reduce her credibility and persuasive impact? A study on this topic has been conducted in Italy (Mucchi-Faina & Barro, 2006). In Italian, it is possible to refer to professors in two different ways: (a) by placing the addressing title before the name or (b) by mentioning the professional position after the name. For a male professor, the term used is always the same, "professore", e.g., Professore Giovanni Bianchi or Giovanni Bianchi, professore di.... For a woman, the usual title is "professoressa" (Professoressa Anna Bianchi), whereas the generic masculine term "professore" (Anna Bianchi , professore di...) can be used for the professional position. Although the suffix "-essa" is normally considered derogatory, changing the traditional title professoressa has been never been proposed in the official nonsexist language guide (Sabatini, 1986), suggesting that it is considered acceptable. The study was aimed at ascertaining whether a woman would be considered more persuasive when she was referred to by the generic masculine professional position than by the traditional gender-marked title. Participants read a passage from a letter addressed to a newspaper. According to condition, the letter was ascribed to "Professoressa Giovanna Grossi who teaches History in Bologna," to "Giovanna Grossi who is professor of History in Bologna," to "Professore Giovanni Grossi who teaches History in Bologna," or to "Giovanni Grossi who is professore of History in Bologna." Participants' agreement with the professor's opinion and their impression about her/him were then measured. Findings showed that participants agreed less with the woman referred to by the feminine title "professoressa" than with the man referred to by the corresponding title and the woman referred to by the generic masculine term. Therefore, the feminine title acted as an unfavorable cue (Petty & Cacioppo, 1986), reducing the woman's persuasive impact.

These findings question linguistic reform that aims at changing generic masculine terms (Ministro, Avvocato) into gender-specific terms (Ministra, Avvocata). Even in language, stressing equality seems to be more useful than stressing difference. Is this forced change in language, then, really suitable for women? A gender-marked title underlined the minority status rather than the competence and, as a consequence, activated traditional, stereotyped representations that made the speaker less persuasive and credible to others. Visibility, favoring a more gender-balanced perception (Prentice, 1994; Stahlberg, Sczesny, & Braun, 2001; Wilson & Ng, 1988), should be, undeniably, the first choice. However, visibility can not only make traditional gender-related representations more accessible but can also sometimes trigger sarcasm and irony, as in the case of odd neologisms. Using the standard qualification, on the contrary, gender passes into the background and evaluation is made, above all, on the basis of personal competence (man or woman). Considering the avoidance of women's derogation as a priority, it could be then preferable to employ the generic masculine-role definition instead of maintaining the traditional feminine form or proposing new words destined to be derided or refused. Moreover, the increase of women working in male, gender-typed jobs creates de facto neutralization because the term, though grammatically masculine, no longer provides information about the gender of the target person. In fact, in gender-marked languages, there is no automatic agreement between grammatical and natural gender assignment; for instance, the Italian term "persona" and the French "personne" are feminine in grammar but neutral in sex. With reference to professional roles, we can then posit that, even were the masculine form retained, the terms could become not *false* but *true* generic terms over time.

CAVEAT

From the analysis of both AA and language reforms, it seems that the most profitable strategies for women are those stressing equality. However, even this choice is not without problems and risks.

The first problem is that standards of competence are not the same for women and men. Research has shown that women are evaluated with a lower minimum-competency standard and a higher ability standard than men (Biernat & Kobrynowicz, 1997). On one hand, because people expect limited competence from women, the standard level of minimal performance is lower for women than it is for men. On the other hand, a woman must do more than a man to prove her capabilities, and she has to provide more examples of her skills: Women's successful performance seems more unexpected, and unexpected results elicit a stricter standard (Jones, Davis, & Gergen 1961). Therefore, paradoxically, it is more difficult for a highly competent woman than it is for a less competent one to be appreciated.

A second problem, strongly linked to the first, is that even an equality strategy is not without psychological costs, especially for those who aim at recognition of a high level of competence. Specifically, it requires strong energy and investment. To be equal, as we have seen before, women must be better, especially in reaching high standards (Foschi, Lai, & Sigerson, 1994). Moreover, as Eagly (2002) has shown, it is more difficult for women than for men to become leaders and to achieve success in leadership roles. In fact a) women are perceived less favorably than men as potential occupants of leadership roles and b) behavior that fulfills the prescriptions of a leader's role is evaluated less favorably when enacted by a woman instead of a man. Therefore, to compete in equality could be very demanding for women.

Finally, it is necessary to mention two risks. First, the temporary acceptance of majority standards and practices may induce, over time, a real assent by minority members (Bem, 1972), inducing, in turn, a loss of motivation and interest in social change. In this case, a woman might personally shift from the "equality and social change" strategy (cell D in Table 13.1) to the "equality and no change" strategy (cell B), an individual option that delays collective achievements (Tajfel, 1981). The second risk is linked to the use of language unmarked for gender. To be presented by a generic masculine title (like professor) favors a woman's impact but, at the same time, tends to evoke male imagery and is associated with masculine characteristics (McConnell & Gavinski, 1994; McConnell & Fazio, 1996). This ambivalent outcome illustrates very clearly the dilemma faced by women: choosing between obtaining less social visibility and more benefits or affirming and making their diversity salient, thus losing social influence.

CONCLUSION

Despite the above-mentioned problems and risks, the literature supports the idea that, at the second step, a strategy focused on equality is more profitable for women than one based on collective differentiation. However, some critical aspects of the influence process need to be more carefully investigated. Specifically, I would like highlight two important questions.

The first question concerns *how* and *when* the transition from the first to the second phase of the process takes place. Because research on minority influence has been mainly conducted using paper-and-pencil methods or ad hoc groups, temporal changes, which are typical of natural groups, have been generally neglected (among the few exceptions is the work by Levine & colleagues, e.g., Levine & Moreland, 1985; Levine & Kaarbo, 2001; see also Worchel, Grossman, & Coutant, 1994). However, many historical examples could be found showing that successful minorities eventually change their strategy from collective protest and differentiation to individual or small-group efforts. For example, in a study on the Italian feminist movement during the 1960s and 1970s (Crespi & Mucchi-Faina, 1988; Mucchi-Faina, 1987), the researchers observed a new stage after the initial period of collective claim. This stage was called *femminismo diffuso* ("pervasive feminism"; Calabrò & Grasso, 1983) because it was marked by the widespread propagation of actions – undertaken by individual or small groups – aimed at changing intergender relations in different contexts and situations (e.g., in families, at work, in institutions). The new phase started when (a) the social relevance of the movement was recognized by majority leaders and the media; (b) the more specific and concrete aim of the conflict (namely, depenalization of abortion) was reached; and (c) the internal conflict between different subgroups decreased. Unfortunately, the study of a single minority does not permit us to establish what kind of relationship – independency, correlation, or causation – exists between the observed circumstances. More empirical investigations are thus necessary to explore the topic. An archive research, collecting data on different natural minority groups or movements, could be very useful to start with.

A second point concerns the possibility of generalizing the above analysis of women strategies to other active minorities. Years ago an article by Susan Fiske and Laura Stevens (1993) identified several differences between women and other social minorities. The title of the article was, "What's so special about gender?" Now let's consider the opposite question, namely, "What's not so special about gender?" Minorities exert influence and obtain social acknowledgment by consistently and persistently stressing their diversity. In the following phase, however, when their right to equal treatment has been recognized and many initiatives have been activated to redress the situation, stressing their difference may no longer be the best strategy. Pointing out, again and again, their peculiarity and claiming special treatment as a minority group can, in the long run, have high psychological costs for minority members, help maintain negative stereotypes, and hinder constructive communication and relationships between minority and majority members. Adopting a fair behavioral style and searching for equality, even in the face of risks and problems, may be more effective in the long run. The value of diversity will appear in practice. The strong presence of minority culture and perspective can transform jobs and traditional roles, introducing different modalities of work and interaction. But this can only happen when the minority position is considered legitimate.

REFERENCES

Abrams, D., Marques, J. M., Bown, N. J., & Henson, M. (2000). Pro-norm and anti-norm deviance. *Journal of Personality and Social Psychology, 78*, 906–912.

Bem, D. J. (1972). Self-perception theory. In L. Berkowitz (Eds.), *Advances in Experimental Social Psychology, 6*, 1–62. New York: Academic Press.

Biernat, M., & Kobrynowicz, D. (1997). Gender and race-based standards of competence: Lower minimum standards but higher standards for devaluated groups. *Journal of Personality and Social Psychology, 72*, 544–557.

Brown, R. P., Charnsangavej, T., Keough, K. A., Newman, M. L., & Rentfrow, P. J. (2000). Putting the "affirms" into affirmative action: Preferential selection and academic performance. *Journal of Personality and Social Psychology, 79*, 736–747.

Calabrò, A. R., & Grasso, L. (1983). *Dal movimento femminista al femminismo diffuso*. Milano: Angeli.

Crespi, F., & Mucchi-Faina, A. (Eds.). (1988). *Le strategie delle minoranze attive*. Napoli: Liguori.

Crosby, F. J. (1994). Understanding affirmative actions. *Basic and Applied Social Psychology, 15*, 13–41.

Crosby, F. J., Iyer, A., Clayton, S., & Downing, R. A. (2003). Affirmative action: Psychological data and the policy debates. *American Psychologist, 58*, 93–115.

Dietz-Uhler, B., & Murrell A. J. (1998). Evaluation of affirmative action applicants: Perceived fairness, human capital or social identity? *Gender Roles, 38*, 933–951.

Eagly, A. H., & Karau, S. (2002). Role congruity theory of prejudice towards female leaders. *Psychological Review, 109*, 573–598.

Eberhardt, J. L., & Fiske, S. T. (1994). Affirmative action in theory and practice: Issues of power, ambiguity and gender versus race. *Basic and Applied Social Psychology, 15*, 201–220.

Esses, M. V., & Seligman, C. (1996). The individual-group distinction in assessments of strategies to reduce prejudice and discrimination. The case of affirmative action. In R. M. Sorrentino & E. T. Higgins (Eds.), *Handbook of motivation and cognition: The interpersonal context*, Vol. 3. New York: Guilford.

Fiske, S. T., & Stevens, L. E. (1993). What's so special about sex? Gender stereotyping and discrimination. In S. Oskamp & M. Costanzo (Eds.), *Gender issues in contemporary society*. Newbury Park, CA: Sage.

Foschi, M., Lai, L., & Sigerson, K. (1994). Gender and double standards in the assessment of job applicants. *Social Psychology Quarterly, 57*, 326–339.

Heilman, M. E., & Alcott, V. B. (2001). What I think you think of me: Women's reactions to being viewed as beneficiaries of preferential selection. *Journal of Applied Psychology, 86,* 574–582.

Heilman, M. E., Battle, W. S., Keller, C. E., & Lee, R. A. (1998). Type of affirmative action policy: A determinant of reactions to sex-based preferential selection? *Journal of Applied Psychology, 83,* 190–205.

Heilman, M. E., Block, C. J., & Lucas, J. A.(1992). Presumed incompetent? Stigmatization and affirmative actions efforts. *Journal of Applied Psychology, 77,* 536–544.

Heilman, M. E., Block, C. J., & Stathatos, P. (1997). The affirmative action stigma of incompetence: Effects of performance information ambiguity. *Academy of Management Journal, 40,* 603–625.

Heilman, M. E., Kaplow, S. R., Amato, M. G., & Stathatos, P. (1993). When similarity is a liability: Effects of sex-based preferential selection on reactions to like-sex and different-sex others. *Journal of Applied Psychology, 78,* 917–927.

Heilman, M. E., Lucas, J. A., & Kaplow, S. R. (1990). Self-derogating consequences of sex-based preferential selection: The moderating role of initial self-confidence. *Organizational Behavior and Human Decision Processes, 46,* 202–216.

Heilman, M. E., McCullough, W. F., & Gilbert, D.(1996). The other side of affirmative action: Reactions of nonbeneficiaries to sex-based preferential selection. *Journal of Applied Psychology, 81,* 346–357.

Heilman, M. E., Rivero, J. C., & Brett, J. F. (1991). Skirting the competence issue: Effects of sex-based preferential selection on task choices of women and men. *Journal of Applied Psychology, 76,* 99–105.

Heilman, M. E., Simon, M. C., & Repper, D. P.(1987). Intentionally favored, unintentionally harmed?: Impact of sex-based selection on self-perceptions and self-evaluations. *Journal of Applied Psychology, 72,* 62–68.

Jones, E. E., Davis, K. E., & Gergen, K. J.(1961). Role playing variations and their informational value for person perception. *Journal of Abnormal and Social Psychology, 63,* 302–310.

Kelley, H. H. (1973). The processes of causal attribution. *American Psychologist, 28,* 107–128.

Kravitz, D. A., Harrison, D. A., Turner, M. E., Levine, E. L., Chaves, W., Brannick, M. T., et al. (1997). Society for Industrial & Organizational Psychology, Retrieved December 12, 2000, from http://www.siop.org/AfirmAct/siopsaartoc.html

Levine, J. M., & Kaarbo, J. (2001). Minority influence in political decision-making groups. In C. K. W. De Dreu & N. K. De Vries (Eds.), *Group consensus and minority influence: Implications for innovation.* Oxford: Blackwell Publishers.

Levine, J. M., & Moreland, R. L. (1985). Innovation and socialization in small groups. In S. Moscovici, G. Mugny, & E. Van Avermaet (Eds.), *Perspectives on minority influence.* Cambridge: Cambridge University Press.

Marques, J. M., Abrams, D., & Serôdio, R. G. (2001). Being better by being right: Subjective group dynamics and derogation of in-group deviants when generic norms are undermined. *Journal of Personality and Social Psychology, 81,* 436–447.

Marques, J. M., Yzerbyt, V. Y., & Leyens, J.-P. (1988). The black sheep effect: Judgmental extremity towards ingroup members as a function of group identification. *European Journal of Social Psychology*, *18*, 1–16.

McConnell, A., & Fazio R. H. (1996). Women as men and people: Effects of gender-marked language, *Personality and Social Psychology Bulletin*, *22*, 1004–1013.

McConnell, A. R., & Gavanski, I. (1994). *Women as men and people: Occupation titles suffixes as primes*. Paper presented at the 66th annual meeting of the Midwestern Psychological Association, Chicago, IL.

Maio, G. R., & Esses, V. M. (1998). The social consequences of affirmative actions: Deleterious effects on perceptions of groups. *Personality and Social Psychology Bulletin*, *24*(1), 65–74.

Major, B., Feinstein, J., & Crocker, J. (1994). Attributional ambiguity of affirmative action. *Basic and Applied Social Psychology*, *15*, 113–141.

Moscovici, S. (1976). *Social Influence and social change*. London: Academic Press.

Moscovici, S. (1980). Toward a theory of conversion behavior. In L. Berkowitz (Ed.), *Advances in Experimental Social Psychology*, *13*, 209–239.

Moscovici, S., Mucchi-Faina, A., & Maass, A. (Eds.). (1994). *Minority influence*. Chicago: Nelson-Hall.

Mucchi-Faina, A. (1987). Mouvements sociales et conversion. In S. Moscovici & G. Mugny (Eds.), *Psychologie de la conversion*. Cousset: Delval.

Mucchi-Faina, A., & Barro, M. (2006). Il caso di "professoressa": Espressioni marcate per genere e persuasione. *Psicologia sociale*, *3*, 517–530.

Mucchi-Faina, A. (2005). Visible or influential? Language reforms and gender (in) equality. *Social Science Information*, *44*, 189–215.

Nacoste, R. W. (1989). Affirmative action and self-evaluation. In F. A. Blanchard & F. J. Crosby (Eds.), *Affirmative action in perspective*. New York: Springer-Verlag.

Petty, R. E., & Cacioppo, J. T. (1986) *Communication and Persuasion*. New York: Springer.

Prentice, D. A. (1994) Do language reforms change our way of thinking? *Journal of Language and Social Psychology* *13*, 3–19.

Sabatini, A. (1986). *Raccomandazioni per un uso non sessista della lingua italiana*. Roma: Commissione nazionale per la realizzazione della parità tra uomo e donna, Presidenza del Consiglio dei Ministri.

Son Hing, L. S., Bobocel, D. R., & Zanna, M. P. (2002). Meritocracy and opposition to affirmative action: Making concessions in the face of discrimination. *Journal of Personality and Social Psychology*, *83*, 493–509.

Stahlberg, D., Sczesny, S., & Braun, F. (2001) Name your favorite musician: Effects of masculine generics and their alternatives in German. *Journal of Language and Social Psychology* *20*, 464–469.

Steele, C. M., & Aronson, J. (1995). Stereotype threat and the intellectual test performance of African Americans. *Journal of Personality and Social Psychology*, *69*, 797–811.

Tajfel, H. (Ed.). (1978). *Differentiation between social groups: Studies in the social psychology of intergroup relations*. London: Academic Press.

Tajfel, H. (1981). *Human groups and social categories*. Cambridge, UK: Cambridge University Press.

Tajfel, H. E., & Turner, J. C. (1986). The social identity theory of intergroup behaviour. In S. Worchel & W. G. Austin (Eds.), *Psychology of intergroup relations* (2nd ed., pp. 7–24). Chicago: Nelson.

Taylor-Carter, M. A., Doverspike, D., & Cook, K. (1995). Understanding resistance to gender and race-based affirmative-action: A review of research findings. *Human Resource Management Review, 5,* 129–157.

Truax, K., Cordova, D. I., Wood, A., Wright, E., & Crosby, F. (1998). Undermined? Affirmative action from the targets' point of view. In J. K. Swim & C. Stangor (Eds.), *Prejudice: The target's perspective* (pp. 172–185). New York: Academic Press.

Turner, M. E., & Pratkanis, A. R. (1993). Effects of preferential and meritorious selection on performance: An examination of intuitive and self-handicapping perspectives. *Personality and Social Psychology Bulletin, 19,* 47–58.

Turner, M. E., & Pratkanis, A. R. (1994). Affirmative action as help: A review of recipient reactions to preferential selection and affirmative action. *Basic and Applied Social Psychology, 15,* 43–69.

Turner, M. E., Pratkanis, A. R., & Hardaway, T. (1991). Gender differences in reactions to preferential selection: Towards a model of preferential selection as help. *Journal of Social Behavior and Personality, 6,* 797–814.

Worchel, S., Grossman, M., & Coutant, D. (1994). Minority influence in the group context: How group factors affect when the minority will be influential. In S. Moscovici, A. Mucchi-Faina, & A. Maass (Eds.), *Minority influence* (pp. 97–114). Chicago: Nelson-Hall.

Wilson, E., & Ng, S. H. (1988) Sex bias in visual images evoked by generics: A New Zealand study. *Sex Roles, 18,* 159–68.

Young, I. M. (1990). *Justice and the politics of difference.* Princeton, NJ: Princeton University Press.

14

Influence without Credit: How Successful Minorities Respond to Social Cryptomnesia

FABRIZIO BUTERA, JOHN M. LEVINE,
AND JEAN-PIERRE VERNET

In October 2007, the Nobel Committee awarded its Peace Prize jointly to the Intergovernmental Panel on Climate Change (IPCC) and the American politician Al Gore "for their efforts to build up and disseminate greater knowledge about man-made climate change, and to lay the foundations for the measures that are needed to counteract such change" (Nobel Foundation, 2008). This award represented the first unambiguous statement by the Committee of the importance of defending the environment. True, the 2004 Peace Prize given to Wangari Maathai mentioned her contributions to sustainable development, but the primary criterion for the award was her work on behalf of "democracy, human rights and women's rights in particular" (Nobel Foundation, 2008). Thus, the 2007 award can be considered a milestone in the decades-old struggle to bring attention to the harmful effects of human activities on the environment, a recognition that environmentalists have been waiting for a long time.

Or can it? Are the ecology activists who have fought for the preservation of the environment for decades – by joining the words "green" and "peace", by demonstrating in the streets, by chaining themselves to gates, by spending time in jail – pleased with the 2007 award? Do they feel happy with this highly visible recognition of the cause for which they have so long fought? Or do they feel bitter disappointment that the prize was awarded, not to one or more of their organizations, but instead to two relative newcomers to the cause – an intergovernmental panel and a professional politician? More generally, what are the reactions of minority groups that have succeeded in inducing social influence and have not received credit for it? This question is at the heart of the issues we address in this chapter.

MINORITY INFLUENCE AND SOCIAL CREDIT

Many of our widely shared and strongly held beliefs were initially proposed by small groups of "true believers" who were punished for their audacity in challenging the status quo. As Moscovici noted, "Stir the ashes of most of our now widely accepted maxims … and at the bottom you will rediscover the flame of a revolutionary creation for which a handful of men suffered martyrdom" (1985a, p. 48). There are many notable historical examples of small minorities that turned science upside down, created revolutions in art or music, produced profound changes in religion, and so on. Although some of these innovators are well-known (e.g., the Vienna Circle, the French Impressionists, the early Christians), in many cases their identities have been long forgotten. We simply accept their ideas as part of the intellectual landscape, without acknowledging their contribution.

Take for instance the case of feminist movements. Two waves of such movements, the first starting in the 19th century with the action of the suffragettes and the second developing widely during the 20th century, have stimulated enormous progress in women's rights in such areas as politics, employment, education, and health care, at least in Western societies (Michel, 1979; Vernet & Butera, 2005). Nowadays, these rights are taken for granted and their history is often forgotten. Consider, for example, the responses that one of us (Butera) recently received to a question about when the right to vote was granted to women. A large majority of French university students (mostly women) answered, "during the French revolution, in 1789, with the Declaration of the Rights of Man (sic!) and the Citizen." Consistent with this anecdote, a large body of evidence indicates that women's rights are widely acknowledged in today's society; suggestions that women are inferior to men are no longer acceptable in public discourse (e.g., Glick & Fiske, 1996; Swim, Mallett, & Stangor, 2004); and people are convinced that "discrimination against women is no longer a problem" (Swim, Aikin, Hall, & Hunter, 1995).

Can we say, however, that feminist groups are generally seen in positive terms, in the sense that people (particularly women) view them as having played a critical role in improving human welfare? Evidence obtained by sociologists (e.g., Marx-Ferree & Tripp, 2006), social psychologists (e.g., Vernet & Butera, 2003; in press) and historians (e.g., Rochefort, 1999) indicates quite the opposite. In general, feminists are seen as extremists; most women do not identify with them, and they are targets of negative stereotypes and derogatory behaviors (Twenge & Zucker, 1999), even from women (Tougas, Brown, Beaton, & St-Pierre, 1999).

As this example shows, even when a minority induces major social change, it may not be credited for its influence. This state of affairs raises an interesting question – how do successful but uncredited minorities respond to their fate? Do such minorities consider that they have no more need to proselytize or to maintain their group identity because their position has gained majority acceptance? Do they feel satisfaction in knowing that they prevailed, or do they feel resentment at not receiving the credit they deserve? Do they dissolve as a social group because there is nothing left to fight for, or do they maintain their group identity, perhaps adopting an even more extreme position?

MINORITIES AS SOURCES OF INNOVATION

According to Moscovici (1976), the primary social function of minorities is to produce innovation. When this idea was first proposed, it was in sharp contradiction to the dominant view in social psychology that minorities are troublesome deviates whose fate is to either conform to the majority or suffer rejection (see Levine, 1989; Levine & Kerr, 2007). Instead, Moscovici proposed that, under some conditions, minorities can be sources of influence in groups. He argued that the primary factor underlying minority influence is behavioral style, in particular the minority's consistency in advocating its position. According to his analysis, consistent minorities create conflict, which forces majority members to pay attention to their message and stimulates movement toward their position (see also Mugny & Pérez, 1991; Pérez & Mugny, 1996). Moscovici's analysis was revolutionary because it suggested that minorities, rather than simply being troublemakers, were potentially valuable group members.

Research on minority influence has evolved since the seminal experiment by Moscovici, Lage, and Naffechoux (1969), and an extensive literature now exists (for recent reviews, see De Dreu & De Vries, 2001; Martin & Hewstone, 2001, 2008; Quiamzade, Mugny, Falomir-Pichastor, & Butera, in press). Not surprisingly, in light of Moscovici's emphasis on minorities as sources of innovation, relevant research has focused on changes that minorities induce in majorities. This research has also emphasized intraindividual (cognitive), rather than interindividual (social), mediators of such influence (Levine & Kaarbo, 2001). For instance, it has been shown that minorities induce profound cognitive changes, which include improving cognitive performance (Butera, Mugny, Legrenzi, & Pérez, 1996; Nemeth, 1986), enhancing creativity (Nemeth, 1994), and motivating people to engage in deep cognitive processing (Martin & Hewstone, 2003).

Moreover, in cases in which minority influence has been analyzed at the group rather than the individual level, how minorities change as a function of interacting with majorities has rarely been investigated. One exception involves historical analyses of the evolution of minority movements as they struggle with majorities (e.g., Crespi & Mucchi Faina, 1988; Mucchi-Faina, 1987; Petrillo, 1994). However, these analyses have not examined how minorities respond to the outcomes (e.g., successful or unsuccessful, credited or uncredited) of these struggles. A second exception is experimental research by Prislin and her colleagues (see Prislin & Christensen, 2005, this volume) investigating how members of initial minority and majority factions respond to social change produced by the minority gaining sufficient members to become the majority or the majority losing sufficient members to become the minority. However, this research has not examined how members of minority factions respond when they influence others to adopt their position but do not receive credit for the change they produce. In attempting to understand these responses, it is useful to consider Moscovici's analysis of minority influence in more detail.

FOUR STAGES OF MINORITY INFLUENCE ... AND A FIFTH

Moscovici (1985a) suggested that minority influence involves four stages and is mediated by the production and reduction of conflict – the "essential tension" responsible for social change. The first stage is *revelation*, during which the minority reveals its strongly held opposition to the majority (its antinomic position) and tries to attract attention. At this stage, the majority's reaction typically involves distrust, disdain, and rejection of the minority's ideas. To the extent that the minority is consistent and does not give up the fight, however, it induces social and cognitive conflict that forces majority members to consider its position seriously. During the second stage, *incubation,* majority members engage in careful processing of the minority's message, which often reveals strengths in its logic. This processing leads to the third stage, *conversion*, during which the majority internalizes the minority's arguments and moves toward the minority's position at the private, or covert, level. Finally, after realizing that others have also changed toward the minority's position, majority members reveal their new opinion publicly during the fourth, or *innovation*, stage. The outcome of this four-stage process is that, "What was against the norms becomes a norm" (Moscovici, 1985a, p. 51).

It is interesting that, according to Moscovici's four-stage model, the minority disappears after the innovation stage. Because the minority's deviant position has become the majority's normative position, the distinction between the minority and the majority evaporates – they merge into an undifferentiated whole. However, we know from research on social movements and from observation of historical minorities that this does not always occur. For example, work on social movements (Klandermans, 1997) shows that the dissolution of a movement is a complex process that depends on several factors besides its level of success, including the generality of its goals (Zald & Ash, 1966) and the degree of its organization and structure (Gerber, 1991). It is worth noting that social psychology has mainly addressed the question of the emergence of social movements (e.g., Simon & Klandermans, 2001), leaving the question of their development to sociology and political science (e.g., Snow, Soule, & Kriesi, 2004). The present chapter represents a social-psychological contribution to the study of the development of active minorities. The fact that minority groups often continue to exist after they prevail against the majority suggests that Moscovici's model should be extended by adding a fifth stage, namely *social cryptomnesia*.

SOCIAL CRYPTOMNESIA AND MESSAGE-SOURCE DISSOCIATION

The term "cryptomnesia" refers to an individual pathology that involves forgetting the origin of an idea. Within social psychology, Mugny and Pérez (1989a, 1989b) have used the term "social crytomnesia " to refer to a social pathology that involves forgetting that a majority idea was once a minority idea. In explaining the origin of social cryptomnesia, Pérez and Mugny (1990) argued that people do not want to be identified by others (and probably also by themselves) as deviants (see also Mugny, Kaiser, Papastamou, & Pérez, 1984), because they know that deviants typically face denigration, rejection, and punishment (cf. Levine, 1989; Levine & Kerr, 2007), especially from their own group (Marques, Abrams, Paez, & Hogg, 2001). Because publicly espousing a minority point of view increases one's risk of being seen as sympathetic to the minority, people sometimes adopt such a position while simultaneously denying the minority's espousal of it. In this way, people dissociate the message from its source and deny the minority the credit it deserves. Because this dissociation takes place during the incubation stage of minority influence, by the innovation stage the minority's role is long forgotten. In minority influence research, this dissociation process is seen as an important factor explaining why active minorities induce social influence involving "conversion", that is attitude change that occurs

on delayed, unconscious, private, or indirect measures, but not on immediate, conscious, public, or direct measures (Crano & Prislin, 2006; Maass,
West, & Cialdini, 1987; Moscovici, 1980). The irony, of course, is that social
influence targets, in adopting minority arguments, "forget" the source of
these arguments (Pérez & Mugny, 1990).

In persuasion research, a similar phenomenon has been described,
namely, the "sleeper effect." Hovland, Lumsdaine, and Sheffield (1949)
discovered this effect while studying the effect of propaganda films on
American soldiers during World War II. They observed that when a persuasive message was accompanied by a discounting cue, i.e., an element
questioning the credibility of the message, attitude change did not appear
immediately, but after some time. This effect is relevant to the foregoing
discussion of minority influence, since low credibility of the source (e.g., its
minority status) can be considered a discounting cue. Even more relevant,
Hovland and Weiss (1951) explicitly hypothesized that the sleeper effect is
due to a dissociation process: If the discounting cue inhibits immediate attitude change, over time the cue and the message lose their association in
memory, which allows delayed attitude change (see Kumkale & Albarracín,
2004, for a recent discussion of the various explanations proposed for this
effect). And, indeed, a parallel between minority influence and the sleeper
effect was suggested by Moscovici, Mugny, and Papastamou in 1981. In sum,
it is plausible that the influence of minority, low-credibility sources is due to
dissociation between their message and their identity.

The fact that minorities are often not perceived as the authors of their
ideas has two related consequences. The first is that they are not given the
credit they deserve for promoting social change. The second is that, because
they do not receive this credit, they continue to be perceived (and treated)
negatively. For instance, as pointed out earlier, although a large majority
of people favor equal rights for men and women, many continue to view
feminists – who initially fought for this equality – as a deviant group. An
experiment by Mugny and Pérez (1989a; see also 1989b) illustrates this
phenomenon. One group of participants was asked to express its attitudes
toward five values: liberty, equality between the sexes, equality among ethnic groups, respect for the environment, and peace. A second group was
asked to express its attitudes toward the same five values, but this time
the values were paired with the minorities that traditionally fought for
them – liberty/anarchists, equality between the sexes/feminists, equality
among ethnic groups/antiracists, respect for the environment/ecologists,
and peace/pacifists. Finally, a third group was asked to express its attitudes
toward the five minorities with no mention of the values. Results showed

that participants rating the minorities alone expressed negative attitudes toward them. Moreover, participants who rated the five values in the context of their associated minority group approved of them significantly less than did participants who rated the values alone. Apparently, one can approve of a value and yet respond negatively to the minority group that promoted it.

MINORITY REACTIONS TO SOCIAL CRYPTOMNESIA

How does being the victim of social cryptomnesia affect a successful minority? First of all, let us specify which types of minorities are affected, and which are not, by social cryptomnesia. This question does not arise for what Moscovici (1976) calls *anomic* minorities, minorities that do not advocate strong alternatives – counternorms – to the majority viewpoint, such as delinquents or homeless people. In fact, some groups, for instance youth gangs, take pride in living at the margins of society and, although they reject the majority's norms, do not intervene in the public arena with a specific claim for their way of life (e.g., Emler & Reicher, 2005; also Emler, this volume). Thus, such groups do not produce social influence and do not experience success in the first place. The above question also does not arise for what Moscovici and Pérez (2007) call *victim* minorities, such as gypsies, which ask for compensation for their suffering (see also Moscovici & Pérez, this volume). As we indicated above, active minorities typically produce indirect influence, because the fear of being associated with a deviant group inhibits direct influence. Victim minorities, however, act upon the majority's guilt feelings and therefore produce direct influence (e.g., compensation) by closely associating their identity with their message. In a way, we could say that through their particular behavioral style – recrimination instead of conflict – they are "immune" to social cryptomnesia. Finally, this question does not arise for *normalized* minorities, that is, groups that occupy a subordinate position within society, but do not offer a particular claim for change because their members consider the social system as fair, justify it (Jost & Major, 2001), and believe in a just world (Hafer & Bègue, 2005). In fact, research in the area of system justification has shown that the majority of individuals who belong to an underprivileged group, e.g., Blacks in the United States or women, have internalized system-justifying ideologies, such as individualism or meritocracy (Jost & Hunyady, 2005), that lead them to think that anyone can succeed in society and that the solution to their underprivileged status is individual mobility (e.g., Ellemers, Spears, & Doosje, 1997; Wright, 2001). Thus, although a number of social movements have their origin in these groups, many members of these groups do not perceive injustice, do not fight for a cause, and thereby do not constitute a source of influence (Simon & Klandermans, 2001).

The situation is quite different for *nomic* minorities, such as highly committed political factions, which do put forward alternative positions of their own. If they succeed in producing social influence but fail to receive credit for doing so, they are likely to experience social cryptomnesia. Because of the effort they put into persuading the majority and the obstacles they overcame in winning acceptance for their ideas, they should be upset by their failure to obtain the credit they deserve. This feeling, combined with the strong social bonds they probably developed during their struggle (Gerard, 1985; Gerard & Hoyt, 1974), should cause them to maintain group cohesion and continue to assert their distinctiveness. This reasoning is consistent with research indicating that people whose social identity is threatened often seek to reaffirm this identity (e.g., Branscombe, Ellemers, Spears, & Doosje, 1999; Jetten, Branscombe, Schmitt, & Spears, 2001; Jetten & Branscombe, this volume). The research reported in this chapter tests the hypothesis that, in the case of nomic minorities, social cryptomnesia is a threatening event that stimulates efforts to "keep up the fight."

AN INITIAL STUDY OF MINORITY REACTION TO SOCIAL CRYPTOMNESIA

Several methodologies might be used to investigate group members' responses to social cryptomnesia. These include analyses of archival records of minority members' responses to being denied credit for their influence, interviews with members of contemporary minorities experiencing cryptomnesia, and observations of these members' interactions with one another and/or people who refuse to acknowledge their influence. Although each of these approaches has advantages (see Levine & Moreland, 2006), none allows unambiguous causal statements about relations between independent and dependent variables. For this reason, we developed an experimental paradigm for studying responses to social cryptomnesia. This paradigm, which is described in the next sections, was used to compare a crytomnesia condition, in which a two-person minority ostensibly convinced a four-person majority to adopt its position but did not receive credit for its influence from a third party, with two theoretically relevant control conditions – (1) credited influence, in which the minority was influential and did receive credit, and (2) no influence, in which the minority failed to change the majority's position.

In an initial study using this paradigm, we sought to test the general hypothesis that minorities in the cryptomnesia condition would behave more like active minorities (Moscovici, 1976) than would those in the credited-influence and the no-influence conditions. More specifically, we predicted that minorities exposed to cryptomnesia would display more attitudinal homogeneity and more resistance to majority influence than would those in the remaining two conditions. These hypotheses were based on the following reasoning: Because attitudinal homogeneity increases the likelihood that a minority will be able to influence a majority, minorities with high motivation to exert influence (those in the cryptomnesia condition) should display more homogeneity than minorities with lower motivation (those in the credited-influence and no-influence conditions) (cf. Gerard, 1985). In addition, because behavioral consistency increases the likelihood that a minority will be influential (Moscovici, 1985b; Wood, Lundgren, Ouellette, Busceme, & Blackstone, 1994), minorities in the cryptomnesia condition should be more resistant to majority influence (i.e., less likely to change their views when they are exposed to a majority of dissenting confederates) than minorities in the other two conditions (cf. Mugny, 1982; Simon & Klandermans, 2001).

Selection of Discussion Topic and Majority Arguments

Prior to the main experiment, pilot testing was used to select the topic of the group discussion and to develop arguments that the majority could use during this discussion. Euthanasia was chosen as the discussion topic for three reasons. First, members of the participant population (undergraduates at a French university) indicated that they were familiar with the topic. Second, they held a consensual opinion about it (88 percent favored euthanasia). Finally, participants did not believe that students at their university held a uniform position regarding euthanasia. This last finding was important, because it reduced the likelihood that discussion participants would be suspicious when a majority of their peers disagreed with their opinion.

When asked what arguments might be made against euthanasia, pilot participants listed the following: hope, possible abuse, difficult moral responsibility for doctors and family, right-to-life, and diverse moral, ethical, and religious problems. These were used to construct the confederates' arguments during group discussions.

Experimental Procedures

Thirty undergraduates took part in the experiment, and five pairs of participants were randomly assigned to each of the three conditions. When they arrived at the laboratory, the two participants met four other alleged participants, who were actually confederates of the experimenter. After being seated around a table, the six group members were asked to complete a questionnaire containing demographic items and a question assessing their attitude toward euthanasia. All naive participants expressed a favorable attitude toward euthanasia. Next, participants were asked to publicly express their personal positions regarding euthanasia. The two naive participants responded first in order to avoid immediate majority influence (Asch, 1951). Again, naive participants expressed a favorable attitude toward euthanasia. As a result of this procedure, participants learned that they held a minority position that was opposed by the majority of group members.

Participants were then given an opportunity to "get acquainted." During this period, the four confederates talked among themselves (e.g., "where do you come from?" "do you like skiing?") without addressing the two participants. When a participant addressed a comment to a confederate (which always happened), the confederate paused and then asked in a serious voice, "Do you really think that one can be in favor of euthanasia?" At this point, the experimenter intervened by saying that there would be time to discuss the topic later. The confederates then continued their conversation, always ignoring the two participants. Thus, minority members were ostracized (Williams, 2001, Williams & Carter-Sowell, this volume) by the majority because of their opinions.

The experimenter stopped the conversation after a few minutes and explained that research has shown that preparing arguments before a discussion increases the likelihood of interesting arguments and animated discussions. He went on to say that, because the current group seemed to be composed of two factions, a pro-euthanasia minority and an anti-euthanasia majority, it would be useful if each faction prepared its arguments separately. Each faction was then taken to a different room and asked to write down arguments that it could use during the subsequent discussion. Next, participants completed individual questionnaires assessing their current attitude toward euthanasia.

The two factions were then brought together, seated on opposite sides of a table, and asked to discuss euthanasia. Participants and confederates took turns speaking for two rounds. During this discussion, confederates offered the arguments against euthanasia that were obtained in the pilot testing. A public vote concluded the discussion. During this vote, majority members either unanimously changed their position to favor euthanasia or continued to oppose it.

In "summarizing" the discussion, the experimenter induced the three experimental conditions. When the minority was unsuccessful in converting the majority (no-influence condition), the experimenter stated that the two factions did not agree and briefly described each faction's position while looking at the relevant faction. When the minority was successful in converting the majority, the experimenter acted in one of two ways. In the credited-influence condition, the experimenter stated that the majority and the minority now agreed, acknowledged that the majority adopted the minority's ideas, and briefly described the final group position while looking at the *minority* and praising it ("you convinced the other faction to change its position"). In the cryptomnesia condition, the experimenter stated that the majority and the minority now agreed, that they were now one big group with the same ideas, and briefly described the final group position while looking at the *majority* and praising it ("you made some very good points"). Finally, group members completed individual questionnaires assessing their perceptions of other members and their current attitude toward euthanasia.

Results

Manipulation-check data indicated that participants accurately perceived the attitudinal positions of other members of the minority and majority factions.[*] In addition, they viewed their minority partner more positively (e.g., as nicer and less aggressive) than majority members. Finally, they correctly perceived that majority members moved closer to their position at the end of the discussion in the credited-influence and cryptomnesia conditions than the no-influence condition.

Attitudinal Homogeneity

We predicted that, because attitudinal homogeneity increases the likelihood that a minority can influence a majority, minorities with high motivation to exert influence (those in the cryptomnesia condition) would display more homogeneity than would minorities with lower motivation (those in the credited-influence and no-influence conditions). To test this prediction, we calculated the difference between the two members of each minority in the third (and final) attitude reports regarding euthanasia (1 = strongly against, 13 = strongly in favor; low difference scores indicate high homogeneity). As

---

[*] In this experiment, participants interacted and therefore had the potential to influence one another's responses. To determine whether this was the case, we calculated the intraclass correlation for all our measures. Because these correlations were not significant, we used the individual participant as the unit of analysis (Kashy & Kenny, 2000).

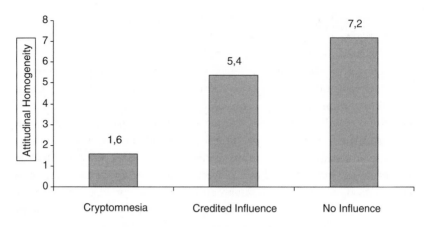

FIGURE 14.1. Minority members' attitudinal homogeneity.
Note: Low numbers reflect high homogeneity.

Figure 14.1 indicates, minorities in the cryptomnesia condition had the most homogeneous attitudes, followed by minorities in the credited-influence condition, which in turn were more homogeneous than minorities in the no-influence condition. Mann-Whitney U tests indicated that the cryptomnesia condition differed significantly from the other two conditions (ps < .01), which did not differ significantly from one another.

Resistance to Majority Influence
We also predicted that, because behavioral consistency increases the likelihood that a minority will be influential, minorities in the cryptomnesia condition would be more resistant to majority influence than would those in the other two conditions. One way to test this hypothesis is to examine the consistency of minority members' private attitudes toward euthanasia across the three measurements (at the beginning of the experiment – Time 1; after the factions met to develop arguments – Time 2; at the end of the experiment – Time 3). Table 14.1 presents correlations between minority members' attitudes toward euthanasia at Time 1 and Time 2 and at Time 2 and Time 3 in the three experimental conditions. These correlations indicate high attitudinal consistency from Time 1 to Time 2 in all three conditions, which is not surprising given that the experimental manipulations were not introduced until after Time 2. Of greater interest are the correlations between Time 2 and Time 3. Here the correlations revealed high attitudinal consistency in the cryptomnesia condition, but *not* in the remaining two

TABLE 14.1. *Minority Members' Attitudinal Consistency*

Correlations	Cryptomnesia	Credited Influence	No Influence
Between Time 1 & 2	0,7906**	0,8227**	0,8568**
Between Time 2 & 3	0,9004**	−0,1751	0,2489

*p < .05 ; **p < .01*

conditions (credited-influence and no-influence). These findings suggest, consistent with our hypothesis, that participants in the cryptomnesia condition were particularly resistant to majority influence.

This interpretation may or may not be correct, however. Whether the attitudinal *consistency* between Time 2 and Time 3 in the cryptomnesia condition reflects resistance to majority influence depends on the nature of the attitudinal *inconsistency* in the other two conditions. This inconsistency might reflect movement toward the majority, but it also might reflect movement away from the majority (anticonformity) or simply random movement. Only if it reflects movement toward the majority can we feel confident that the absence of movement in the cryptomnesia condition indicates resistance to majority influence. To address this question, we examined minority members' attitudes toward euthanasia across the three measurements in the three experimental conditions (see Figure 14.2). As would be expected on the basis of the foregoing correlations, participants' attitudes were quite similar at Time 1 and Time 2 in all three conditions. Moreover, *t* tests indicated that these attitudes did not differ significantly between conditions at either time point. However, at Time 3, minority members' attitudes toward euthanasia were significantly more positive in the cryptomnesia condition than in the credited-influence and no-influence conditions (*t* tests, *p*s < .05), which did not differ significantly from one another. Thus, whereas minority members in the cryptomnesia condition remained steadfast in their positive attitude toward euthanasia after the experimental manipulations were introduced, those in the other two conditions shifted their views in the direction of the majority (i.e., conformed to the majority). This pattern of results was confirmed by analyses of attitude change scores from Time 1 to Time 3 in the three conditions. Participants in the cryptomnesia condition (*M* = .03) yielded significantly less to the majority than did those in the credited-influence (*M* = −1.2) and no-influence (*M* = −1.8) conditions (*t* tests, *p*s < .05), which did not differ significantly from one another. So, we can feel relatively confident that cryptomnesia did indeed cause minority members to resist majority influence.

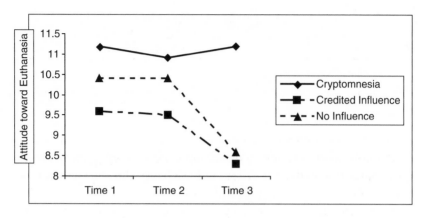

FIGURE 14.2. Minority members' attitude toward euthanasia.

Conclusion

This study had two aims. One was to develop an experimental paradigm for investigating how minority factions respond to social cryptomnesia with the goal of facilitating research on this topic by other investigators. The second was to obtain initial information about two such responses, namely; attitudinal homogeneity and resistance to majority influence. The paradigm worked well and yielded interesting data regarding the impact of social cryptomnesia. As predicted, minorities that exerted influence but did not receive credit for this influence displayed behaviors typical of active minorities, whereas those that exerted influence and did receive credit displayed behaviors typical of passive minorities (i.e., they capitulated to the majority to the same degree as did failing minorities). These findings provide evidence that how minorities respond to success depends on how success is defined. Although one might suppose that prevailing against a majority would always be highly reinforcing and cause the successful minority to "relax," perhaps to the point of renouncing its unique identity, this was not the case. In the present study, prevailing without credit had just the opposite effect.

CYNICAL USE OF SOCIAL CRYPTOMNESIA

In this and the following section, we go beyond the data reported above and venture into more speculative territory regarding the causes and consequences of social cryptomnesia and its relationships to related phenomena. We begin by discussing how dominant groups (majorities) can cynically use cryptomnesia to reinforce their power and reduce that of subordinate groups (minorities). As noted earlier, minority influence is facilitated by the cognitive dissociation of the minority group from the minority claim, which allows the target of influence to accept this claim without feeling threatened by identity similarity with the minority. It would not be surprising, therefore, if some majorities purposely used social cryptomnesia for their own ends by publicly downplaying the minority's critical role in stimulating an innovation and taking credit for that innovation themselves. In other words, when it is impossible to stop minority change, majorities can deny recognition to the real authors of that change and enhance their own status and power by claiming credit for it.

These ideas are relevant to both social dominance theory (e.g., Pratto, Sidanius, & Levin, 2006; Sidanius & Pratto, 1999) and system justification theory (e.g., Jost & Hunyady, 2005). Social dominance theory contends that hierarchical relationships between groups in society are maintained in part by legitimizing ideologies, such as meritocracy, which reinforce existing power relations between dominant and subordinate groups (Sidanius, Levin, Federico, & Pratto, 2001). Social cryptomnesia is relevant to this process because, by minimizing the minority's role and exaggerating the majority's role in stimulating innovation, it reinforces and justifies the majority's right to play the dominant role in society. System justification theory seeks to explain how dominant groups justify the existing social system, and social cryptomnesia contributes to explaining how they can do it even in the face of social conflict and minority claims for more power and resources. In this contentious environment, social cryptomnesia allows dominant groups to claim that they are the origin of change and that subordinate groups' claims to the contrary are false, which in turn justifies the existing system and legitimizes dominant groups' continuing power. In sum, through dissociation of minority claims from minority groups, social cryptomnesia renders the status quo legitimate and the voices of dominated groups illegitimate (Kaiser & Miller, 2001).

IRONIC CONSEQUENCES OF SOCIAL CRYPTOMNESIA

It has been argued for some time (Freud, 1915), and empirically demonstrated more recently (Wegner, Schneider, Carter, & White, 1987), that when a person tries to avoid thinking about a specific object or idea, the relevant thought comes to mind at a later time. This ironic process is stimulated by what Freud called "repression" and by what Wegner and colleagues called "thought suppression." The common theme is that when a person tries to remove a thought from consciousness, because it is painful or because an experimenter asks him or her to do so, the thought reappears later. Social cryptomnesia can be considered a form of *historical thought suppression*, which involves suppressing the social origin of an idea. Such suppression can have ironic consequences of a different kind than that described by Freud and Wegner. As the study reported above demonstrated, a minority's resentment at failing to obtain credit for introducing an idea may cause it to become even more committed to this idea and more likely to press for its adoption. Thus, social cryptomnesia can have the ironic effect of causing a minority to become even more active in pursuing its goals.

Clearly, however, cryptomnesia does not always have this effect. In some cases, minorities that fail to gain recognition for their contributions become disheartened and give up their struggle. Therefore, it is important to understand the factors that motivate "victims" of social cryptomnesia to maintain (or increase) their commitment to their position and their efforts to gain wider support for it. Several such factors, which have not received systematic theoretical and empirical attention, are plausible candidates for future investigation.

One factor is the minority's dominant goal in initially espousing its views. Among these goals are the minority's desire to (a) feel more confident about the validity (correctness) of its position (cf. Levine & Higgins, 2001); (b) maintain or increase its distinctiveness (Jetten, Spears, & Postmes, 2004); (c) obtain social acceptance and equal rights; (d) gain resources and power (cf. Levine & Kaarbo, 2001); and (e) enhance the welfare of the wider social system (Dovidio, Piliavin, Schroeder, & Penner, 2006). Social cryptomnesia may have different consequences, depending on which of these goals is thwarted. For example, a minority that lacks confidence in its position may lose cohesion and dissolve when it fails to get credit for its views, whereas a minority that seeks distinctiveness may adopt a more extreme position and work harder to gain converts to that position.

Another factor that may influence how a minority responds to social cryptomnesia is the difference between the amount of credit it receives for espousing its position and the amount of credit it believes it deserves. For example, if a minority believes that it deserves 100 percent credit for espousing a position that was eventually adopted (e.g., because it alone initially espoused that position), then receiving 50 percent credit will elicit a relatively negative response. In contrast, if a minority believes that it deserves only 50 percent credit (e.g., because other groups held similar positions), then receiving 50 percent credit will elicit a relatively positive response. One cannot discount the possibility, of course, that minorities often make the self-serving attribution that, no matter how many others shared their position, their own advocacy of the position was solely responsible for its adoption; hence, they deserve 100 percent credit for it. Our examples so far refer to varying levels of "positive" credit for espousing a position. However, "negative" credit is also possible, as when a minority is accused of espousing a position that they do not really hold. In this case as well, we would predict that a minority's response to cryptomnesia will depend on the difference between the amount of credit it receives and the amount it believes it deserves (e.g., a minority that feels it deserves +100 percent credit and gets -50 percent credit will be more distressed than a minority that feels it deserves +100 percent credit and gets -25 percent credit).

Finally, the source of the credit may be important. It is likely that failing to receive positive credit (or receiving negative credit) for espousing a position will be more aversive if the source of the credit claims "ownership" of that position than if it does not. In the experiment reported above, a third party (the experimenter) denied credit to the deserving minority and awarded it to the nondeserving majority instead. It is plausible that the minority would have responded even more strongly if the majority had publicly claimed ownership of the minority's position. Moreover, in cases in which the source of credit is a third party, various characteristics of that party may influence how victims of social cryptomnesia respond to their plight. For example, cryptomnesia may elicit more negative responses when a third-party source is seen as biased (rather than unbiased) against the victim and knowledgeable (rather than ignorant) about the history of the issue under consideration.

These factors are not meant to be an exhaustive list of the determinants of responses to social cryptomnesia. Rather, they are examples that we hope will stimulate increased theoretical and empirical attention to the important question of how nomic minorities respond when they are denied the credit they deserve for producing social influence.

REFERENCES

Asch, S. E. (1951). Effects of group pressure upon the modification and distortion of judgment. In H. Guetzkow (Ed.), *Groups, leadership and men* (pp. 177–190). Pittsburgh: Carnegie Press.

Branscombe, N. R., Ellemers, N., Spears, R., & Doosje, B. (1999). The context and content of social identity threat. In N. Ellemers, R. Spears, & B. Doosje (Eds.), *Social identity: Context, commitment, content* (pp. 35–58). Oxford: Blackwell.

Butera, F., Mugny, G., Legrenzi, P., & Pérez, J. A. (1996). Majority and minority influence, task representation and inductive reasoning. *British Journal of Social Psychology, 35*, 123–136.

Crano, W. D., & Prislin R. (2006). Attitudes and persuasion. *Annual Review of Psychology, 57*, 345–374.

Crespi, F., & Mucchi-Faina, A. (1988). *Le strategie delle minoranze attive. [Strategies of active minorities].* Napoli: Liguori.

De Dreu, C. K. W., & De Vries, N. K. (Eds.). (2001). *Group consensus and minority influence: Implications for innovation.* Oxford: Blackwell.

Dovidio, J. F., Piliavin, J. A., Schroeder, D. A., & Penner, L. A. (2006). *The social psychology of prosocial behavior.* Mahwah, NJ: Lawrence Erlbaum.

Ellemers, N., Spears, R., & Doosje, B. (1997). Sticking together or falling apart: Group identification as a psychological determinant of group commitment versus individual mobility. *Journal of Personality and Social Psychology, 72*, 123–140.

Emler, N., & Reicher, S. (2005). Delinquency: Cause or consequence of social exclusion? In D. Abrams, J. Marques, & M. Hogg (Eds.), *The social psychology of inclusion and exclusion* (pp. 211–241). Philadelphia: Psychology Press.

Freud, S. (1915). *Repression. In the standard edition of the complete psychological works of Sigmund Freud, Volume XIV (1914–1916).* London: Hogarth Press.

Gerard, H. B. (1985). When and how the minority prevails. In S. Moscovici, G. Mugny, & E. Van Avermaet (Eds.), *Perspectives on minority influence* (pp. 171–186). Cambridge: Cambridge University Press.

Gerard, H. B., & Hoyt, M. F. (1974). Distinctiveness of social categorization and attitude towards ingroup members. *Journal of Personality and Social Psychology, 29*, 836–842.

Gerber, J. (1991). From bottles to bombs: The role of success and occupying a unique niche in organizational transformation. *Sociological Focus, 24*, 225–243.

Glick P., & Fiske S. T. (1996). The ambivalent sexism inventory: Differentiating hostile and benevolent sexism. *Journal of Personality and Social Psychology, 70*, 491–512.

Hafer, C. L., & Bègue, L. (2005). Experimental research on just-world theory: Problems, developments, and future challenges. *Psychological Bulletin, 131*, 128–167.

Hovland, C. I., Lumsdaine, A. A., & Sheffield, F. D. (1949). *Experiments on mass communication.* Princeton, NJ: Princeton University Press.

Hovland, C. I., & Weiss, W. (1951). The influence of source credibility on communication effectiveness. *Public Opinion Quarterly, 15*, 635–650.

Jetten, J., Branscombe, N. R., Schmitt, M. T., & Spears, R. (2001). Rebels with a cause: Group identification as a response to perceived discrimination from the mainstream. *Personality and Social Psychology Bulletin, 27*, 1204–1213.

Jetten, J., Spears, R., & Postmes, T. (2004). Intergroup distinctiveness and differentiation: A meta-analytical investigation. *Journal of Personality and Social Psychology, 86*, 862–879.

Jost, J. T., & Hunyady, O. (2005). Antecedents and consequences of system-justifying ideologies. *Current Directions in Psychological Science, 14*, 260–265.

Jost, J. T., & Major, B. (Eds.). (2001). *The psychology of legitimacy: Emerging perspectives on ideology, justice, and intergroup relations.* New York: Cambridge University Press.

Kaiser, C. R., & Miller, C. T. (2001). Stop complaining! The social costs of making attributions to discrimination. *Personality and Social Psychology Bulletin, 27,* 254–263.

Kashy, D. A., & Kenny, D. A. (2000). *The analysis of data from dyads and groups.* In H. T. Reis & C. M. Judd (Eds.), *Handbook of research methods in social and personality psychology.* (pp. 451–477). New York: Cambridge University Press

Klandermans, B. (1997). *The social psychology of protest.* Oxford: Blackwell.

Kumkale, G. T., & Albarracín, D. (2004). The sleeper effect in persuasion: A meta-analytic review. *Psychological Bulletin, 130,* 143–172.

Levine, J. M. (1989). Reaction to opinion deviance in small groups. In P. Paulus (Ed.), *Psychology of group influence* (2nd ed., pp. 187–231). Hillsdale, NJ: Lawrence Erlbaum.

Levine, J. M., & Higgins, E. T. (2001). Shared reality and social influence in groups and organizations. In F. Butera & G. Mugny (Eds.), *Social influence in social reality: Promoting individual and social change* (pp. 33–52). Bern, Switzerland: Hogrefe & Huber Publishers.

Levine, J. M., & Kaarbo, J. (2001). Minority influence in political decision-making groups. In C. K. W. De Dreu & N. K. De Vries (Eds.), *Group consensus and minority influence: Implications for innovation* (pp. 229–257). Malden, MA: Blackwell Publishers.

Levine, J. M., & Kerr, N. L. (2007). Inclusion and exclusion: Implications for group processes. In A. E. Kruglanski & E. T. Higgins (Eds.), *Social psychology: Handbook of basic principles* (2nd ed., pp. 759–784). New York: Guilford.

Levine, J. M, & Moreland, R. L. (2006). Small groups: An overview. In J. M. Levine & R. L. Moreland (Eds.), *Small groups* (pp. 1–10). New York: Psychology Press.

Maass, A., West, S., & Cialdini, R. B. (1987). Minority influence and conversion. In C. Hendrick (Ed.), *Group processes: Review of personality and social psychology* (Vol. 8, pp. 55–79). Newbury Park, CA: Sage.

Marques, J. M., Abrams, D., Paez, D., & Hogg, M. A. (2001). Social categorization, social identification, and rejection of deviant group members. In M. A. Hogg, & R. S. Tindale (Ed.), *Blackwell handbook of social psychology: Group processes* (pp. 400–424) Oxford, UK: Blackwell.

Martin, R., & Hewstone, M. (2001). Conformity and independence in groups: Majorities and minorities. In M. A. Hogg & R. S. Tindale (Eds.), *Blackwell handbook of social psychology: Group processes* (pp. 209–234). Oxford, UK: Blackwell.

(2003). Majority versus minority influence: When, not whether, source status instigates heuristic or systematic processing. *European Journal of Social Psychology, 33,* 313–330.

(2008). Majority versus minority influence, message processing and attitude change: The source-context-elaboration model. In M. P. Zanna (Ed.), *Advances in experimental social psychology* (Vol. 40, pp. 237–326). New York: Academic Press.

Marx-Ferree, M., & Tripp, A. M. (2006). *Global Feminism: Women's Transnational Activism, Organizations and Human Rights.* New York: New York University Press.

Michel, A. (1979). *Le féminisme*. [Feminism]. Paris: Presses Universitaires de France.

Moscovici, S. (1976). *Social influence and social change*. London: Academic Press.

(1980). Toward a theory of conversion behaviour. In L. Berkowitz (Ed.), *Advances in experimental social psychology* (Vol. 13, pp. 209–239). New York: Academic Press.

(1985a). Innovation and minority influence. In S. Moscovici, G. Mugny, & E. Van Avermaet (Eds.), *Perspectives on minority influence* (pp. 9–51). Cambridge: Cambridge University Press.

(1985b). Social influence and conformity. In G. Lindzey & E. Aronson (Eds.), *The handbook of social psychology* (Vol. 2, pp. 347–412). New York: Random House.

Moscovici, S., Lage, E., & Naffrechoux, M. (1969). Influence of a consistent minority on the responses of a majority in a color perception task. *Sociometry, 32*, 365–380.

Moscovici, S., Mugny, G., & Papastamou, S. (1981). "Sleeper effect" et/ou effet minoritaire? Etude théorique et expérimentale de l'influence sociale à retardement [Sleeper effect and/or minority effect?]. *Cahiers de Psychologie Cognitive, 1*, 199–221.

Moscovici, S., & Pérez, J. A. (2007). A study of minorities as victims. *European Journal of Social Psychology, 37*, 725–746.

Mucchi-Faina, A. (1987). Mouvement social et conversion. [Social movements and conversion]. In S. Moscovici & G. Mugny (Eds.), *Psychologie de la conversion* (pp. 181–196). Cousset: Delval.

Mugny, G. (1982). *The power of minorities*. London: Academic Press.

Mugny, G., Kaiser, C., Papastamou, S., & Perez, J. (1984). Intergroup relations, identification and social influence. *British Journal of Social Psychology, 23*, 317–322.

Mugny, G., & Pérez, J. A. (1989a). L'effet de cryptomnésie sociale. [The social cryptomnesia effect]. *Bulletin Suisse des Psychologues, 7*, 3–6.

(1989b). L'influence sociale comme processus de changement. [Social influence as a change process]. *Hermès, 5–6*, 227–236.

(1991). *The social psychology of minority influence*. Cambridge: Cambridge University Press.

Nemeth, C. J. (1986). The differential contributions of majority and minority influence. *Psychological Review, 93*, 23–32.

(1994). The value of minority dissent. In S. Moscovici, A. Mucchi-Faina, & A. Maass (Ed.), *Minority influence* (pp. 3–15). Chicago: Nelson-Hall.

Nobel Foundation (2008). *Nobel peace prize*. Retrieved July 16, 2008, from http://nobelprize.org/

Pérez, J. A., & Mugny, G. (1990). Minority influence, manifest discrimination and latent influence. In D. Abrams & M. Hogg (Eds.), *Social identity theory*. Hertfordshire: Harvester Wheatsheaf.

(1996). The conflict elaboration theory of social influence. In E. Witte & J. Davis (Eds.), *Understanding group behavior* (Vol. 2, Small group processes and interpersonal relations, pp. 191–210). Mahwah, NJ: Lawrence Erlbaum.

Petrillo, G. (1994). Collective movements and minority influence: The processes of social influence beyond the confines of experimental groups. In S. Moscovici, A.

Mucchi Faina, & A. Maass (Eds.), *Minority influence* (pp. 209–230). Chicago, IL: Nelson Hall:

Pratto, F., Sidanius, J., & Levin, S. (2006). Social dominance theory and the dynamics of intergroup relations: Taking stock and looking forward. *European Review of Social Psychology, 17*, 271–320.

Prislin, R., & Christensen, P. N. (2005). Social change in the aftermath of successful minority influence. *European Review of Social Psychology, 16*, 43–73.

Quiamzade, A., Mugny, G., Falomir-Pichastor, J. M., & Butera, F. (in press). The complexity of majority versus minority influence processes. In R. Martin & M. Hewstone (Eds.), *Minority influence and innovation: Antecedents, processes and consequences*. Hove, UK: Psychology Press.

Rochefort, F. (1999) L'antifeminisme à la belle époque: une réthorique réactionnaire. [The "belle époque" antifeminism: a reactionary rhetoric]. In C. Bard (Ed.), *Un siècle d'antiféminisme* (pp. 133–147). Paris: Fayard.

Sidanius, J., Levin, S., Federico, C., & Pratto, F. (2001). Legitimizing ideologies: The social dominance approach. In J. Jost & B. Major (Eds.), *The psychology of legitimacy: Emerging perspectives on ideology, justice, and intergroup relations* (pp. 307–331). New York: Cambridge University Press.

Sidanius, J., & Pratto, F. (1999). *Social dominance: An intergroup theory of social hierarchy and oppression*. New York: Cambridge University Press.

Simon, B., & Klandermans, B. (2001). Politicized collective identity: A social psychological analysis. *American Psychologist, 56*, 319–331.

Snow, D. A., Soule, S. A., & Kriesi, H. (2004). *The Blackwell companion to social movements*. Oxford: Blackwell.

Swim, J. K., Aikin, K. J., Hall, W. S., & Hunter, B. A. (1995). Sexism and racism: Old-fashioned and modern prejudices. *Journal of Personality and Social Psychology, 68*, 199–214.

Swim, J. K., Mallett, R., & Stangor, C. (2004). Understanding subtle sexism: Detection and use of sexist language. *Sex Roles, 51*, 117–128.

Tougas, F., Brown, R., Beaton, A. M., & St-Pierre, L. (1999). Neosexism among women: The role of personally experienced social mobility attempts. *Personality and Social Psychology Bulletin, 25*, 1487–1497.

Twenge, J. M., & Zucker, A. L. (1999). What is a feminist? Evaluations and stereotypes in closed and open-ended responses. *Psychology of Women Quarterly, 23*, 591–605.

Vernet, J. P., & Butera, F. (2003). Guilt for cryptomnesia moderates attitudes towards feminists. *New Review of Social Psychology, 2*, 16–20.

(2005). Women, women rights and feminist movements. *Social Science Information, 44*, 175–188.

Vernet, J. P., Vala, J., Amâncio, L., & Butera, F. (in press). Conscientization of Social Cryptomnesia Reduces Hostile Sexism and Rejection of Feminists. *Social Psychology*.

Wegner, D. M., Schneider, D. J., Carter, S., & White, T. (1987). Paradoxical effects of thought suppression. *Journal of Personality and Social Psychology, 53*, 5–13.

Williams, K. D. (2001). *Ostracism: The power of silence*. New York: Guilford Publications.

Wood, W., Lundgren, S., Ouellette, J., Busceme, S., & Blackstone, T. (1994). Minority influence: A meta-analytic review of social influence processes. *Psychological Bulletin, 115,* 323–345.

Wright, S. C. (2001). Restricted intergroup boundaries: Tokenism, ambiguity and the tolerance of injustice. In J. Jost & B. Major (Eds.), *The Psychology of legitimacy: Emerging perspectives on ideology, justice, and intergroup relations* (pp. 223–254). New York: Cambridge University Press.

Zald, M., & Ash, R. (1966). Social movement organizations: Growth, decay and change. *Social Forces, 44,* 327–341.

15

Influence and Its Aftermath: Motives for Agreement Among Minorities and Majorities

RADMILA PRISLIN AND P. NIELS CHRISTENSEN

For most minorities, *nomen est omen*. Derived from the Latin term minor (lesser), minority denotes inferiority. Defined in terms of inferior size, inferior importance, or both, almost all minorities are disadvantaged. They are on the receiving side of many social ills as is evident in their disproportionably higher unemployment rates (Evers & van der Flier, 1998) and incarceration rates (Barrett & William, 2005), but lower earnings (U. S. Census Bureau, 2004) and access to health care (National Center for Health Statistics, 2004). These tangible costs of being in a minority are compounded by psychological tolls, including feelings of marginalization (Brewer & Pickett, 1999; Frable, Blackstone, & Scherbaum, 1990) and social stigmatization (Crocker, Major, & Steele, 1998; Moscovici, 1994). Minorities often need active coping strategies to develop a positive social identity, and a sense of correctness, which are the default for members of the majority (for review, see Prislin & Christensen, 2005a). The heavy burdens of minorities led Moscovici (1976) to conclude that although there is nothing wrong with being a minority, "it is tragic to remain one" (p. 74). The looming "tragedy" of a permanent minority position motivates minorities to seek change. This motivation is at the heart of the social influence process.

As obvious as minorities' *motivation* for change may be, their *ability* to effect change was not recognized until Moscovici's (1976) seminal reconceptualization of social influence as bidirectional and rooted in social conflict. The ability of minorities to convert others to their position, though constrained by many factors, is axiomatic within contemporary theorizing about social influence (Prislin & Wood, 2005). Importantly, contemporary research on minority influence is limited to the persuasive effects of minorities on individual targets (Crano & Prislin, 2006). As this volume documents, we now know that minorities can effect processing and acceptance of their advocacy by individual members of a majority. Effecting change at the level of an individual, however, is not a minorities' ultimate goal. After all, many members of the majority have their "best friends" among members of the minority. Yet, in spite of making the "best friends" list of individual members of the majority, minority groups continue to be disadvantaged.* Thus, when minorities exert social influence, it is for the purpose of social change (Prislin, in press). Often, this translates into the goal of becoming a new majority.

If the goal of minority influence is to become a majority, then theorizing and research in this domain should necessarily move beyond the individual level of analysis to address the dynamics of groups in which minorities become majorities, and vice versa. As a step toward understanding the dynamics of groups undergoing social change, we developed a model that explains how a switch in minority and majority positions *within* a group represents a change *of* the group. In this chapter, we briefly describe the model and present summary results of the first several studies testing its postulates. Next, we provide initial evidence that the dynamics of groups in the aftermath of social change may be affected by specific motives for this change. Finally, we conclude by discussing how a motivational approach may advance our understanding of both minority influence and the dynamics of groups with active minorities.

SUCCESSFUL MINORITY INFLUENCE: THE GAIN-LOSS ASYMMETRY MODEL OF CHANGE IN MINORITY AND MAJORITY POSITIONS

To guide our thought and research on social change, we recently proposed the gain-loss asymmetry model of change in minority and majority position (Prislin & Christensen, 2005a; Prislin, Limbert, & Bauer, 2000). The basic propositions of the model address the differential valuation of minority and majority positions, the subjective experience and reactions to change in these positions, and the resultant dynamics of the group undergoing change. The first postulate about *more positive valuation of the majority position than the minority position* is derived from the well-documented advantages associated with being in the majority and disadvantages associated with being in the minority. Elites notwithstanding, the minority position is substantially less conducive to the satisfaction of primary and secondary needs than the majority position. This discrepancy makes the

---

* In terms of social identity theory (Tajfel, 1981), social mobility of individual members of a minority cannot improve the minority group's position. Only social change can.

majority position desirable and preferred to the minority position (Brendl & Higgins, 1996).

Given that the two numerical positions represent two different reference points, changes away from the minority and majority positions should be experienced differently. Specifically, change away from the majority position should be experienced as a loss, whereas change away from the minority position should be experienced as a gain. Because losses loom larger than the corresponding gains (Kahneman & Tversky, 1979), *any movement away from the majority position should be experienced more intensely than the corresponding movement toward the majority position.* This prediction resonates with social identity and self-categorization theories (Tajfel, 1981; Turner, Hogg, Oakes, Reicher, & Wetherell, 1987). According to these theories, perceived similarity with others provides the basis for a shared social category and, in turn, should make members of a majority more likely to assimilate with and positively value the group. Because people expect to agree with and be supported by ingroup members (Turner & Oakes, 1989), they should react intensely negatively to loss of support within the group. By the same token, members of a minority whose opinions (or other characteristics) are initially rejected by others should be less likely to self-categorize and positively value the group. The subsequent support by other members of the group should therefore be considered of little consequence and met with only mildly positive reactions. Taken together, the presumed intensely negative reactions to loss of the majority positions, accompanied by measured positive reactions to gain of the majority position, should lower the overall attachment to the group. Thus, change in minority and majority positions should represent more than mechanical reversals in which factions within a group switch positions but the overall group situation remains the same. Rather, *immediately in the aftermath of social change, the group is expected to be weaker than prior to change in that its overall value to the group members should decrease.*

The hypothesized weakening of the group was examined in several studies that assessed identification with a group whose minority and majority factions either remained stable or switched their positions as a result of successful minority influence. All studies involved experimentally created interacting groups whose members exchanged opinions on important social issues (e.g., assisted suicide, death penalty, immigration, foreign aid). Across studies, groups varied in size from four to eight members. Only one of the group members was a participant; others were confederates. During the course of group interactions, confederates provided scripted responses to the participant's opinions on the social issues. Initially, most of the

confederates expressed either supporting opinions in order to effectively
place the participant in the majority position, or they expressed opposing
opinions to effectively place the participant in the minority position. The
initially established majority and minority positions either remained stable
throughout the group interaction, or were altered when some of the confederates switched from supporting (opposing) to opposing (supporting) the
participant halfway through the interaction. An important aspect of this
procedure is that participants actively experienced their social positions in
direct interaction with the alleged members of their groups.

Consistent with Tajfel's (1982) multidimensional conceptualization of
social identification, positive evaluation of the group and self-categorization
in the group were assessed as separate but correlated aspects of group identification. Across five studies (Prislin & Christensen, 2002; 2005b, Study 1;
Prislin, Brewer, & Wilson, 2002; Prislin et al., 2000, Study 1 & Study 2),
group evaluation was operationalized as attraction to the group and self-
categorization was operationalized as group-self similarity. In addition to
these uniformly assessed indicators of group identification, several studies
assessed the quality of anticipated interactions with the group in the future
(Prislin & Christensen, 2002; Prislin et al., 2000).

Supporting the postulate that change away from the majority position
(loss) should be experienced more intensely than change toward the majority position (gain), combined results across the studies revealed a strong
asymmetry in reactions to loss and gain of the majority position (Figure
15.1). In comparison to stable majorities, those whose initial majority position was turned into minority dramatically decreased their attraction to the
group and perceived group-self similarity. By contrast, minorities-turned-
majority, in comparison to stable minorities, showed only a mild increase in
their attraction to the group and perceived group-self similarity. In none of
the studies did this increase reach statistical significance. A similar asymmetry was observed in expectations for future interactions with the group. A
significant decrease in expectations for positive interactions in response to
loss of the majority position was met with only a minimal increase for positive expectations in response to gain of the majority position. At the same
time, expectations for negative interactions increased significantly with loss
of the majority position but barely changed with gain of the majority position (Prislin & Christensen, 2002; Prislin et al., 2000).

These findings clearly demonstrate that detachment from the group
in response to loss of the majority position is not counterbalanced with
a comparable increase in attachment to the group in response to gain of
the majority position. As a result, the overall level of identification with

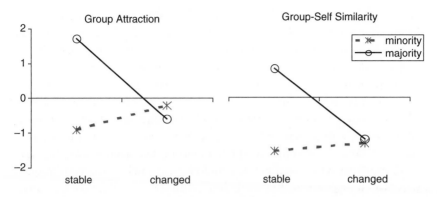

FIGURE 15.1. Group attraction and group-self similarity as a function of gain and loss of the majority position (aggregate results across five studies).

the group in the aftermath of social change is low. New majorities, just like new minorities, perceive similarly low levels of group-self similarity and group attraction (Figure 15.1). In none of the studies reviewed here did new majorities and new minorities differ significantly in their (low) identification with the group. This stands in contrast to groups with stable factions in which identification with the group was consistently and significantly higher in majorities than minorities. Thus, in contrast to the stable group whose majority elevates the overall level of identification, a group that has undergone social change has majority and minority factions equally unenthusiastic about common group identity.

Clearly, a group whose active minority attracts a sufficient following to transform itself into a majority is not a mirror image of the group with stable minority and majority factions. The overall decrease in identification with the group in the aftermath of change renders the group weak and therefore vulnerable to external threats. Equally troubling, relations within the group are likely to deteriorate. The new majority's (former minority's) detachment from the group suggests likely intolerance for dissent that may turn into hostility toward a new minority (former majority). This possibility is additionally suggested by our findings that new majorities, though unwavering in their detachment from the group, significantly strengthened their attitudes upon gaining the majority position. This was documented in two studies that assessed several indicators of attitude strength (certainty, importance, and involvement) in addition to identification with the group (Prislin, Boyle, Farley, Jacobs, & Zandian, 2007; Prislin et al., 2000). Attitude certainty was assessed via self-reported confidence about one's opinions on the issue under discussion, attitude importance was assessed via self-reported personal importance of the issue under discussion (both in absolute terms and relative to other issues), and attitude involvement was assessed via one's latitude of rejection or the number of attitudinal positions that were found unacceptable. The effect of changes in majority-minority position on attitude strength were comparable regardless of the particular operationalization. Attitude strengthening was evident in the new majorities' increased certainty about successfully disseminated attitudes (Prislin, et al., 2007), importance accorded to such attitudes, and in a broadened scope of unacceptable attitudinal positions (Prislin et al., 2000). The new majorities' increased certainty about their own attitudes, coupled with their rejection of a large scope of dissenting attitudes on an issue of increased importance is likely to make new majorities hostile to new minorities. While potentially clashing with new minorities on attitudinal issues, new majorities join new minorities in the refusal of a common group identity. In doing so, both factions tear apart the foundation that makes majorities lenient toward dissent (Crano, 2001), and minorities constructive in their dissent (Wenzel, 2002).

THE COMPLEX WORLD OF MINORITY DESIRES: MOTIVES FOR BECOMING MAJORITY

There is no small paradox in former minorities' reactions to becoming majorities: While expressing preference for the majority position (Krueger, 1998; Krueger & Clement, 1997), and carefully crafting their influence strategies to realize their preference (Prislin et al., 2007), former minorities remain detached from the group that elevates them to the desired position. What might account for the finding that active minorities seek social change but show little identification with the group once they effect the change? We propose that understanding this paradox requires closer scrutiny of the minorities' goals. To what extent do minorities achieve their goals once they successfully convert a sufficient number of their opponents to transform themselves to the majority? The results presented so far suggest that there might be more to minorities' goals than getting others to nod to their position.

What motivates minorities to become majorities? Surprisingly, this question has not received much attention in the minority influence research.[†] Lack of attention to motivational issues is surprising because even a cursory

---

[†] Sigall (1970) and Dutton (1973) provided early evidence for the moderating effect of motives on reactions of a source of influence to the yielding target in the dyadic context.

analysis of real-life minorities suggests a variety of motives. For example, few would argue that the early advocates of evolutionary theory, civil rights movement, and the current Republicans in the state of California – all exemplars of active minorities – share the same motive for becoming majority. Although preference for the majority position may be universal (Ellemers, Doosje, van Knippenberg, & Wilke, 1992; Erb & Bohner, 2001; Kruegger, 1998; Simon & Hamilton, 1994), reasons for the preference likely vary. To desire what is widely desired is not to desire it for the same reason.

Multiple motives for becoming a majority are suggested by the multiple advantages of the majority position (Prislin & Christensen, 2005a; Prislin & Wood, 2005). Some advantages are intangible in the form of desirable psychological states; others, however, are tangible in the form of desirable resources. Among the former, the sense of validation (correctness) and belonging (acceptance) stand most prominently, though intangible benefits of being in the majority may also include self-enhancement (Cialdini & Trost, 1998; Festinger, 1950; Moscovici, 1976), and social status (Tajfel & Turner, 1986)

Social Validation (Correctness)
Being in the majority by virtue of sharing consensus within a group provides a sense of correctness (Festinger, 1954). The power of consensus to provide orientation by conferring accuracy and objectivity to an otherwise chaotic world (Sherif, 1935) may well be the reason for its presumably universal appeal (Erb & Bohner, 2001). Yet, in spite of the absence of consensual support, minorities must have an initial sense of correctness in order to exert social influence. Their initial sense of correctness may be derived from their ability to link what they advocate to a consensually accepted value. For example, the suffragette movement's sense of correctness, at a time when a woman's ability to make sound political decisions was widely questioned, likely originated from linking a woman's right to vote to the consensually accepted value of equality. Alternatively, the minority's sense of correctness may originate from factors that are only remotely social, as it is often the case among innovators in science and art. For example, Galileo's sense of correctness likely originated from congruence of his theory and remotely social scientific criteria. This initial sense of correctness, though essential in creating minority dissent, can survive only through broader social support. By obtaining consensual support for their position, minorities transform what initially is construed as their subjective opinion into consensually accepted fact. The function of additional support, therefore, is to transform minorities' "subjectively" correct dissent into a

consensual, "objectively" correct position synonymous with reality (Hardin & Higgins, 1996) .

Social Acceptance (Belonging)

Another motive that may fuel a minority's attempts to become a majority is acceptance or belonging to the group. The pervasiveness of the motive to belong (Baumeister & Leary, 1995; Brewer, 1991) presumably reflects the survival value of alignment with others that emerged through evolution (Barchas, 1986; Bugental, 2000; Caporael & Baron, 1997; Moreland, 1987). Social influence research has traditionally assumed that the need to belong motivates yielding to social influence (Deutsch and Gerard, 1955), not exerting it. Yet, to the extent that belonging is experienced as a state of cognitive merging within a group (Baumeister & Leary, 1995), it cannot be satisfied through acquiesce. Yielding to others may satisfy the need for affiliation but not the need for integration. The latter presumes assimilation with others into the same category, not giving in to others to join their category (Baumeister & Leary, 1995; Brewer, 1991). Thus, if minorities are to satisfy their need for integration within a group, they should proselytize within the group. "A minority which neither proselytizes nor convinces becomes isolated or disappears" (Moscovici, 1985, p. 47). The looming peril of social isolation and ultimately disappearance may motivate minorities to engage others, seeking to influence them, and not only yielding to their influence. The latter may not even be a viable option for some minorities that, as in the case of gays and lesbians, seek to satisfy (among others) their need to belong by advocating acceptance in a society-at-large.

Social Control (Instrumentality)

In addition to the intangible value of validation and belonging, the majority position typically carries substantial tangible benefits. As discussed earlier, majority members typically enjoy preferential treatment in the distribution of resources. In comparison to minorities, majority members receive more in the distribution of positive outcomes (e.g., salary) and less in the distribution of negative outcomes (e.g., unemployment) than minorities. The worth of these tangible benefits may be a potent motivator of social behavior (Fiske, 2002). Surprisingly, however, the motivational power of tangible rewards has been largely neglected in the social influence literature. Yet, the palpable value of privileges associated with the majority position may well be the most prominent reason for advocacy by socially, politically, and economically disadvantaged minorities. Their influence strategies and, ultimately, their reactions to successful transformation into majorities may differ from those observed in validation-motivated and belonging-motivated minorities. Indeed, recent analyses of political minorities illustrate how the presumed dominance of the instrumental motive in these groups may shape their interactions with political majorities to produce influence strategies not examined in the contemporary minority influence research (Levine & Karbo, 2001; Smith & Diven, 2002).

The motivational foundation of minority advocacy may not be exhausted in the three mentioned motives; however, these motives represent constitutional elements of many motivational systems, including those more comprehensive (Fiske, 2002). An important dimension along which these motives differ is the underlying, motive-implied meaning of the majority position. Under the validation and belonging motives, the majority position represents a goal in and of itself. In contrast, under the instrumentality motive, the majority position represents an intermediary step toward a more distant, delayed goal. The motives therefore cast the majority position as an end in itself versus a means toward an end. The end-versus-means distinction further implies that the criteria for valuing the majority position should differ. If the majority position is to effect an end result of a desired psychological state (correctness, belonging), it must convey not only the presence of a sizeable support for the advocated position but also the quality of support for the position. The support must be perceived as authentic in that it stems from genuine rather than strategic reasons for yielding to influence.[‡] By contrast, if the majority position is a means for obtaining desired tangible benefits, all it needs to satisfy is the criterion of critical size. That is, support must reach just the sufficient size that delivers the benefits. The quality of support, though welcome, is secondary.

A MOTIVATIONAL ANALYSIS OF THE MINORITY INFLUENCE PARADOX

Motives for becoming a majority may explain the minority influence paradox evident in successful minorities' unenthusiastic response to the group in which they gained support for their position. Studies that established the paradox likely activated the belonging motivation, validation motivation, or a combination of the two motives for seeking the majority position. At

---

[‡] The social influence literature has considered strategic reasons for yielding to majority but not minority influence (Prislin & Wood, 2005). Though possibly more likely in response to majority influence, strategic yielding to minority influence is not uncommon. It may be inspired by the Zeigeist, inherent instability of specific targets of minority influence, or both.

minimum, belonging and validation motives were stronger than the instrumentality motive as no tangible rewards were associated with the majority
position in any but one of these studies (Prislin et al., 2000, Study 2). Under
belonging and validation motives, gaining support is necessary but not sufficient for motives satisfaction. Additionally, newly won supporters must
be perceived as authentic, trustworthy followers. Authenticity, however,
presumes reliability, which, by definition, is questionable in converts. The
instability inherent in conversion inevitably casts doubt on the reliability of
converts. Thus, the very same condition necessary to satisfy the criterion of
(majority) size is an obstacle to satisfying the criterion of (majority) reliability. Unless resolved, this contradiction may leave new majorities (former
minorities) apprehensive and therefore reluctant to embrace not only their
newly won supporters but also the entire group in which they prevailed.

Resolution of the conversion contradiction requires that converts to the
minority position document the authenticity of their support. To the extent
that they present their movement to the minority position as informed by
minority advocacy rather than extraneous factors unrelated to the advocacy, they should assuage the presumed concerns about their reliability.
Assured about the quality of support for their position, former minorities
should embrace their newly won supporters and the group in which they
were elevated to the majority position.

These hypotheses were tested in a study in which supporters for a
minority faction, which either remained stable or was changed to majority, expressed either genuine, superficial, or no reasons for siding with the
minority (Prislin, Levine, & Christensen, 2006). In the context of a mock
political campaign, a naive participant who played the role of a political candidate, and five confederates acting as voters exchanged opinions on a controversial social issue. In the initial stages of the "campaign," the participant
was opposed by four confederates and supported by a single confederate.
This 2:4 ratio that effectively placed the participant in the minority position
either remained stable throughout the entire course of the "campaign" (stable minority), or it was reversed half-way through the "campaign," when
two of the initial opponents of the participant converted to supporters.
The latter effectively changed the participant's initial minority position to
majority (4:2 ratio of support and opposition). The confederates cast their
ballots in line with their final support (opposition) for the participant.
Those who voted for the participant were asked to explain their support
so that researchers "can better understand what gets a candidate elected."
Reasons for support, selected in a separate study, conveyed either a genuine
adoption of the participant's position (e.g., "the candidate made me rethink

my position"), or a superficial switch to the participant's position (e.g., "just want to get over with it"). Confederates in the control condition offered no reasons for their endorsement of the candidate. Following the campaign, the participant's identification with the faction of supporters and with the group as a whole was assessed by measuring supporter (group) attraction as an indicator of valuation and perceptions of supporter- (group-) self similarity as an indicator of self-categorization.

Corroborating the hypotheses, the quality of support moderated the former minorities' (new majorities') identification with the faction of supporters and the group as a whole. Genuine support made the faction of supporters, as well as the group, significantly more attractive than either superficial or unexplained support, which did not differ from each other (Figure 15.2). Similarly, genuine support generated stronger self-categorization with the faction of supporters and with the entire group than either superficial or unexplained support. Almost identical reactions of new majorities to superficial and unexplained support suggest that in the absence of explicitly stated reasons for change, conversion was suspected to be inauthentic. Apparently, when in doubt, former minorities "err" on the side of caution, treating converts to their position, as well as the entire group, as unreliable until proven authentic.

The apparent attributional skepticism of former minorities indicates that newly gained numerical prevalence within a group does not automatically generate a phenomenological experience of majority. Translation of a numerical into a phenomenological majority may take time, especially when

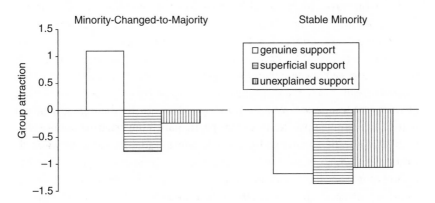

FIGURE 15.2. Group attraction as a function of gain of the majority position and quality of support.

Source: Prislin, Levine, & Christensen, 2006.

former minorities are not offered explicit arguments about the authenticity of conversion to their position. Former minorities, therefore, may need more than one-time support for their position in order to react like majorities. Continual support over a period of time should address former minorities' attributional concerns (Kelley, 1973), eventually transforming them to the phenomenological majority. As a result, they should increasingly accept both their newly won supporters as well as the entire group. This reasoning is consistent with the previously documented high threshold for support needed to consider others members of one's own social category (Leyens & Yzerbyt, 1992).

The effects of continual support for former minorities were examined in a study ostensibly on the longitudinal functioning of debate groups (Prislin & Christensen, 2005b, Study 2). In each session, a naive participant and three confederates exchanged opinions on one of five controversial social issue (environmental protection, human life, health care, education, and taxes). The discussion issue was selected at random for each group and groups that met for multiple sessions discussed a different topic each time. In the initial session, all participants were placed in the minority position by being opposed by all the confederates. This concluded participation for those in the 1-week minority condition. In four additional conditions, participants, who were placed in the minority position in the first session, returned for one to four additional sessions over the period of one to four additional weeks. During the second session, the participant's position was changed to the majority when two of the confederates who opposed him or her in the first session, switched to support. The majority position acquired in the second session was maintained for participants who returned for their third, fourth, and fifth session. Thus, there was a total of five experimental conditions: a one-week minority, a two-week minority that changed to majority during the second session, and three- , four- , and five-week minorities that also changed to majorities during the second session, remaining in the majority position for the duration of their participation. Upon completion of their last discussion session, participants indicated their identification with their supporters as well as identification with the group as a whole.

Multiple indicators converged to indicate a gradual increase in identification with both a faction of supporters and the group as a whole over the period of five weeks. As evident in Figure 15.3, there were significant linear trends in attraction to supporters and to the group as a whole. With each additional week spent in the majority position, former minorities increased their positive valuation of their newly won supporters (converts to their position) and the entire group. Moreover, valuation of supporters mediated

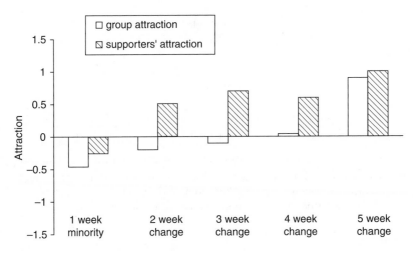

FIGURE 15.3. Group attraction and supporters' attraction as a function of time spent in gained majority position.

Source: Prislin & Christensen, 2005b.

the effect of time spent in the acquired majority position on valuation of the group as a whole, suggesting that the assessment of converts may be crucial for the phenomenological experience of majority (Figure 15.4).[§]

Taken together, the results of these two studies demonstrate that when former minorities are assured about authenticity of their newly won support, either through supporters' explicit pledge of allegiance or consistency over time, they come to accept the group as their own. Reassurances about authenticity apparently resolve the conversion contradiction, eliminating doubts about converts' possible volatility. As a result, former minorities begin to react in accordance with their newly acquired numerical dominance, signaling its transformation to the phenomenological majority. The apparent lag between numerical dominance and phenomenological experience may have important implications for influence strategies within the group. In contrast to the new majorities in our studies that passively waited for converts to establish their reliability, new majorities not constrained by experimental settings may actively seek proofs of allegiance. For example, they may require converts to denounce their original positions, elaborate

[§] Transformation to phenomenological majority is additionally indicated by a significant linear trend in group-self similarity, as well as in the conceptualization of interaction with others as occurring at the level of a single, unitary group (see Prislin & Christensen, 2005b).

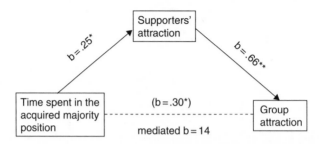

FIGURE 15.4. Supporters' attraction mediates the effect of time spent in gained majority position on group attraction. The *b*s represent unstandardized regression coefficients, * *p* < .05, ** *p* < .01. Reduction in the effect of time spent in gained majority position from *b* = 0.30 to 0.14 was statistically significant (*Z* = 2.22).

arguments for their newly adopted position, or proselytize on behalf of the new majority. This would suggest that minority influence in service of the belonging and validation motives may not end with the attainment of numerical dominance. Rather, it may evolve to incorporate new strategies aimed at firmly establishing the new majority within the group and eventually fully satisfy its motives.

Structural Foundation of the Motivation to Influence

Our previous analysis is based on the assumption that in the absence of tangible rewards, the primary motives for seeking others' support would be belonging and possibly validation. Although not assessed in previous studies, belonging is the strongest self-reported reason for seeking support from other members of a group (Christensen, Prislin, & Jacobs, 2007). This finding was obtained in a relatively context-free survey of college students asked to assess their motives for seeking others' support in a group context. This "baseline" motivational landscape, however, should be altered when motives are assessed in the context of specific group membership (cf. Brewer, 1991; Tajfel, 1981; Turner, Oakes, & Haslam, 1994). We propose that the relative strength of the three motives for influencing others in order to obtain their support (belonging, validation, and instrumentality) should vary as a function of one's structural position within the group (minority vs. majority) and stability of the position. In the context where majority support could potentially satisfy all three motives, only those continually enjoying others' support (stable majorities) should find all three motives equally important. In contrast, those who experience the minority position either presently (stable minorities and new minorities that lost their previous majority position) or in the past (former minorities who gained the majority position) should find the validation motive least important. The hypothesis about comparatively diminished importance of the validation motive in those who have experienced the majority position but comparable importance to other motives in the stable majority is consistent with the postulates of social identity and self-categorization theories (Tajfel, 1981; Turner et al., 1987). Stable majority members assimilate with and positively value the ingroup category significantly more than stable minority members or their changed counterparts (Prislin & Christensen, 2005a). Because correctness presumably is defined by an ingroup standard (Tajfel, 1981), those who identify strongly with the group (stable majority) should be more likely to subscribe to such a standard than those whose identification with the group is weak (stable minority and both changed counterparts). Thus, the experience of being in minority at any point in time should undermine the importance of others' support for the sense of correctness, instead strengthening the importance of others' support for obtaining tangible rewards and acceptance by the group.

As part of a larger study, we manipulated initial position (minority vs. majority) and stability of the initial position (stable vs. changed) in the context where majority size was instrumental for gaining tangible rewards (Christensen, Prislin, & Jacobs, in press). Using the previously described political campaign procedure (see above), participants were initially placed in either the minority position (2:4) or majority position (4:2) that either remained stable or was reversed half way through the political campaign. Participants expected that minority and majority factions created in the political campaign would later engage in group decision-making. The experimenter explained that, just as in real life, the majority faction would be granted power to make decisions about proposals put forward by the minority faction. Before the alleged decision-making part of the experiment, participants responded to a questionnaire assessing the importance of others' support for validation (e.g., "what majority of others think is probably accurate"), belonging (e.g., "others support satisfies a basic human need to belong with others"), and instrumentality (e.g., "others support makes it possible for me to control more things."). Participants indicated their agreement with each item on scales ranging from 1 (*not at all*) to 9 (*very much*).

As anticipated, a 2 (initial position: minority vs. majority) x 2 (stability of the initial position: stable vs. change) x 3 (motive: validation vs. belonging vs. instrumentality) repeated measures ANOVA, with motive as the within-subjects factor, yielded a significant three-way interaction,

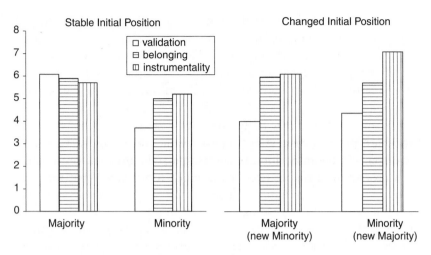

FIGURE 15.5. Motives for gaining majority position as a function of initial position and stability of initial position.

$F(2, 132) = 3.26$, $p < .05$ (see Figure 15.5). This three-way interaction was decomposed by conducting separate 2 x 3 (initial position x motive) mixed model ANOVAs within each level of the stability of initial position variable. The two-way interaction proved significant within the stable initial position conditions, $F(2, 66) = 5.63$, $p < .01$. As hypothesized, simple effect tests revealed no significant difference in the importance of the three motives for stable majorities, all $ts(17) < 0.92$, ns. For stable minorities, however, the validation motive was significantly less important than the belonging motive, $t(16) = 3.91$, $p < .001$, and the instrumentality motive, $t(16) = 3.16$, $p < .001$. Comparisons within each of the motives revealed stable majorities considered the validation motive significantly more important than stable minorities, $t(33) = 4.15$, $p < .001$. Stable majorities and minorities did not differ significantly in the reported importance of the belonging motive and the instrumentality motive, both $ts < 1.69$, ns. A 2 x 3 (initial position x motive) ANOVA within the changed initial position conditions revealed only a significant main effect for motive, $F(2, 66) = 33.09$, $p < .001$. For both changed majority (new minority) and changed minority (new majority), the validation motive was less important than the belonging motive and the instrumentality motive, both $ts(33) > 3.94$, $ps < .001$, which did not differ significantly, $t(33) = 0.89$, ns.

These findings have interesting implications for possible influence dynamics within groups. In groups with stable majorities and minorities, both factions appear similarly highly motivated to seek others' support to feel accepted and tangibly rewarded. Others' support, however, appears more important for the validation of stable majorities than stable minorities. Thus, when it comes to certainty about correctness of their positions, majorities may be more vulnerable to minority dissent than minorities would be to the lack of a widespread support for their position. If so, then stable majorities may be predominantly defensive in their influence strategies, perhaps dismissing, appeasing, or even suppressing minority dissent. Stable minorities, in contrast, may be predominantly offensive, promoting their position not so much to validate it but for more pragmatic reasons of belonging and instrumentality. Interestingly, one consequence of a minority's successful influence appears to be an altogether more pragmatic motivational landscape within a group. In groups that have just undergone change, new majorities and new minorities congruently emphasize the importance of more "pragmatic" motives for instrumentality and belonging over validation. This suggests that in the aftermath of social change, influence attempts may focus on proving who is "might" rather than who is "right." Of course, these speculations need to be tested in future research.

In conclusion, numerical factions in groups may exert influence to validate their positions, satisfy their need for inclusion and belonging, and to gain access to and consume tangible rewards. This trio does not constitute an exhaustive list of possible motivations. Yet, these motives are particularly important because of their previously documented effects on reactions to social influence, their relative accessibility, and likelihood of being openly reported (Christensen et al., in press; Prislin & Wood, 2005). A motivational approach may enhance our understanding of minority influence by guiding hypotheses about influence strategies likely to be implemented by differentially motivated minorities and their reactions to (lack of) success in the influence process. As our research has begun to document, the motivational approach may enhance our understanding of group dynamics in the aftermath of successful minority influence. For belonging- and validation-motivated minorities, gaining numerical dominance within a group likely is necessary but not sufficient for identification with the group. In addition, they appear to need evidence of authenticity of conversion to their position. As a result, their identification with the group is likely to be delayed until such evidence is received. The lingering low identification of former minorities, coupled with an instantly low identification of former majorities, renders the group fragile. However, not all minorities seek the majority position because of its inherent value in creating satisfactory psychological

states of belonging and validation. A powerful additional motive is instrumentality or the value of majority position in creating access to tangible
rewards. In the contexts where numerical dominance is associated with
tangible rewards, minorities may be equally, if not predominantly, instrumentally motivated. To the extent that instrumental motivation prevails,
minorities should consider numerical dominance necessary and sufficient for satisfaction of their goals. If so, they may be more strategic in
their reactions toward the group in which they gain numerical dominance,
increasingly valuing the group but not necessarily self-categorizing with the
group. For instrumentally motivated former minorities, valuation and self-
categorization as two aspects of group identification may not necessarily be
closely related (Prislin, in press). A proposal for the motivational approach
outlined in this chapter is a step toward opening new avenues in research
on minority influence. Recognizing motivational diversity in minorities
holds promise of deepening our understanding of the dynamics and consequences of minority influence.

REFERENCES

Barchas, P. (1986). A sociophysiological orientation to small groups. In E. Lawler
(Ed.), *Advances in group processes* (Vol. 3, pp. 209–246). Greenwich, CT: JAI
Press.
Barrett, K. H., & William, G. (2005). *Race, culture, psychology, and law.* Thousand
Oaks, CA: Sage.
Baumeister, R. F., & Leary, M. R. (1995). The need to belong: Desire for interpersonal
attachments as a fundamental human motivation. *Psychological Bulletin, 117,*
497–529.
Brendl, M. C., & Higgins, T. E. (1996). Principles of judging valence: What makes
events positive or negative. In M. Zanna (Ed.), *Advances in Experimental Social
Psychology,* (Vol. 28, pp. 95–160). San Diego, CA: Academic Press.
Brewer, M. B. (1991). The social self: On being the same and different at the same
time. *Personality and Social Psychology Bulletin, 17,* 475–482.
Brewer, M. B., & Pickett, C. L. (1999). Distinctiveness motives as a source of the
social self. In T. R. Tyler, R. M. Kramer, & O. P. John (Eds.), *The psychology of
the social self* (pp. 71–87). Mahwah, NJ: Lawrence Erlbaum.
Bugental, D. B. (2000). Acquisition of the algorithms of social life: A domain-based
approach. *Psychological Bulletin, 126,* 187–219.
Caporael, L. R, & Baron, R. M. (1997). Groups as the mind's natural environment.
In J. A. Simpson & D. T. Kendrick: *Evolutionary social psychology* (pp. 317–343).
Mahwah, NJ: Lawrence Erlbaum.
Cialdini, R. B., & Trost, M. R. (1998). Social influence: Social norms, conformity,
and compliance. In D. T. Gilbert, S. T. Fiske, & G. Lindzey (Eds.), *The hand-
book of social psychology* (pp. 151–192). Boston, MA: McGraw-Hill.
Christensen, P. N., Prislin, R., & Jacobs, E. (2007). *Motives for seeking agreement in
a group.* Unpublished data. Radford University.

Christensen, P. N., Prislin, R., & Jacobs, E. (in press). Motives for social influence after social change: Are new majorities power hungry? *Social Influence*.

Crano, W. D. (2001). Social influence, social identity, and ingroup leniency. In C. K. W. De Dreu & N. K. De Vries (Eds.), *Group consensus and minority influence: Implications for innovation* (pp. 122–159). Oxford, UK: Blackwell.

Crano, W. D., & Prislin, R. (2006). Attitudes and persuasion. *Annual Review of Psychology*, *57*, 345–374.

Crocker, J., Major, B., & Steele, C. (1998). Social stigma. In D. T. Gilbert, S. T. Fiske, & G. Lindzey (Eds.), *The handbook of social psychology* (pp. 504–595). Boston, MA: McGraw-Hill.

Deutsch, M., & Gerard, H. B. (1955). A study of normative and informational influences upon individual judgment. *Journal of Abnormal and Social Psychology*, *51*, 629–636.

Dutton, D. G. (1973). Attribution of cause for opinion change and liking for audience members. *Journal of Personality and Social Psychology*, *26*, 208–216.

Ellemers, N., Doosje, B. J., Van Knippenberg, A., & Wilke, H. (1992). Status protection in high status minority groups. *European Journal of Social Psychology*, *22*, 123–140.

Erb, H.-P., & Bohner, G. (2001). Mere consensus effects in minority and majority influence. In C. K. W. De Dreu & N. K. De Vries (Eds.), *Group consensus and minority influence: Implications for innovation* (pp. 40–59). Malden, MA: Blackwell.

Evers, A., & van der Flier, A. (1998). Ethnic minorities on the labor market. In P. J. D. Drenth, T. Henk, & C. J. de Wolf (Eds.), *Handbook of work and organizational psycholog* (Vol. 2, pp. 229–259). Howe, UK: Psychology Press.

Festinger, L. (1950). Informal social communication. *Psychological Review*, *57*, 271–282.

Festinger, L. (1954). A theory of social comparison processes. *Human Relations*, *7*, 117–140.

Fiske, S. T. (2002). Five core motives, plus or minus five. In S. J. Spencer, S. Fein, M. P. Zanna, & J. Olson (Eds.), *Motivated social perception: The Ontario Symposium* (pp. 233–246). Mahwah, NJ: Lawrence Erlbaum.

Frable, D. E. S., Blackstone, T., & Scherbaum, C. (1990). Marginal and mindful: Deviants in social interactions. *Journal of Personality and Social Psychology*, *59*, 140–149.

Hardin, C. D., & Higgins, E. T. (1996). Shared reality: How social verification makes the subjective objective. In R. M. Sorentino & E. T. Higgins (Eds.), *Handbook of motivation and cognition* (Vol. 3, pp. 28–84). New York: Guilford.

Kahneman, D., & Tversky, A. (1979). Prospect theory: An analysis of decision under risk. *Econometrica*, *47*, 263–291.

Kelley. H. H. (1973). The process of causal attribution. *American Psychologist*, *28*, 107–128.

Krueger, J. (1998). On the perception of social consensus. In M. Zanna (Ed.), *Advances in experimental social psychology* (Vol. 30, pp. 164–240). San Diego, CA: Academic Press.

Krueger, J., & Clement, R. W. (1997). Estimates of social consensus by majorities and minorities: The case for social projection. *Personality and Social Psychology Review*, *1*, 299–313.

Levine, J. M., & Kaarbo, J. (2001). Minority influence in political decision-making. In C. K. W. De Dreu & N. K. De Vries (Eds.), *Group consensus and minority influence: Implications for innovation* (pp. 229–257). Oxford, UK: Blackwell.

Leyens, J.-P., & Yzerbyt, V. Y. (1992). The ingroup overexclusion effect: Impact of valence and confirmation on stereotypical information search. *European Journal of Social Psychology, 22*, 549–569.

Moreland, R. L. (1987). The formation of small groups. In C. Hendrick (Ed.), *Group processes. Review of personality and social psychology* (Vol. 8, pp. 80–110). Newbury Park, CA: Sage.

Moscovici, S. (1976). *Social influence and social change.* New York: Academic Press.

Moscovici, S. (1985). Innovation and minority influence. In S. Moscovici, G. Mugny, & E. Van Avermaaet (Eds.), *Perspective on minority influence* (pp. 9–51). Cambridge: Cambridge University Press.

Moscovici, S. (1994). Three concepts: Minority, conflict, and behavioral style. In S. Moscovici, A. Mucchi-Faina, & A. Maas (Eds.), *Minority influence* (pp. 233–251). Chicago, IL: Nelson-Hall.

National Center for Health Statistics (2004). *Health, United States.* Hayattsville, MD: National Center for Health Statistics.

Prislin, R. (in press). Dynamics of change: Minority influence makes the world go around. In M. Hewstone & R. Martin (Eds.), *Minority influence and innovation: Antecedents, processes, and consequences.* Howe, UK: Psychology Press

Prislin, R., Boyle, S., Farley, A., Jacobs, E., & Zandian, F. (2007). *The effects of increasing and decreasing support on the intent to persuade and persuasiveness.* Unpublished data. San Diego State University.

Prislin, R., Brewer, M., & Wilson, D. J. (2002). Changing majority and minority positions within a group vs. an aggregate. *Personality and Social Psychology Bulletin, 28*, 640–647.

Prislin, R., & Christensen, P. N. (2002). Group conversion versus group expansion as modes of change in majority and minority positions: All losses hurt but only some gains gratify. *Journal of Personality and Social Psychology, 83*, 1095–1102.

Prislin, R., & Christensen, P. N. (2005a). Social change in the aftermath of successful minority influence. *European Review of Social Psychology, 16*, 43–73.

Prislin, R., & Christensen, P. N. (2005b). The effects of social change within a group on membership preferences: To leave or not to leave. *Personality and Social Psychology Bulletin, 31*, 595–609.

Prislin, R., Levine, J. M., & Christensen, P. N. (2006). When reasons matter: Quality of support affects reactions to increasing and consistent agreement. *Journal of Experimental Social Psychology, 42*, 593–601

Prislin, R., Limbert, W. M., & Bauer, E. (2000). From majority to minority and vice versa: The asymmetrical effects of losing and gaining majority position within a group. *Journal of Personality and Social Psychology, 79*, 385–397.

Prislin, R., & Wood, W. (2005). Social influence: The role of social consensus in attitude and attitude change. In D. Albarracín, B. T. Johnson, & M. P. Zanna (Eds.), *Handbook on attitudes and attitude change* (pp. 671–706). Thousand Oaks, CA: Sage.

Sherif, M. (1935). A study of some social factors in perception. *Archives of Psychology, 27*, 1–60.

Sigall, H. (1970). Effects of competence and consensual validation on a communicator's liking for the audience. *Journal of Personality and Social Psychology, 16,* 251–258.

Simon, B., & Hamilton, D. L. (1994). Self-stereotyping and social context: The effects of relative in-group size and in-group status. *Journal of Personality and Social Psychology, 66,* 699–711.

Smith, C. M., & Diven, P. J. (2002). Minority influence and political interest groups. In V. C. Ottati, R. S. Tindale, J. Edwards, F. B. Bryant, L. Heath, D. C. O'Connel, et al. (Eds.), *The social psychology of politics* (pp. 175–192). New York: Kluwer Academic/Plenum.

Tajfel, H. (1981). *Human groups and social categories: Studies in social psychology.* Cambridge, MA: Cambridge University Press.

Tajfel, H. (1982). *Social identity and intergroup relations.* Cambridge, MA: Cambridge University Press.

Tajfel, H., & Turner, J. C. (1986). The social identity theory of intergroup conflict. In W. Austin & S. Worchel (Eds.), *The social psychology of intergroup relations* (pp. 33–48). Pacific Grove, CA: Brooks/Cole.

Turner, J. C., Hogg, M. A., Oakes, P. J., Reicher, S. D., & Wetherell, M. S. (1987). *Rediscovering the social group: A self-categorization theory.* Oxford and New York: Basil Blackwell.

Turner, J. C., & Oakes, P. J. (1989). Self-categorization theory and social influence. In P. B. Paulus (Ed.), *The psychology of group influence* (2nd ed., pp. 233–275). Hilldale, NJ: Lawrence Erlbaum.

Turner, J. C., Oakes, P. J., & Haslam, S. A. (1994). Self and collective: Cognition and social context. *Personality and Social Psychology Bulletin, 20,* 454–463.

U. S. Census Bureau. (2004). Evidence from Census 2000 about earnings by detailed occupation for men and women.

Wenzel, M. (2002). What is social about justice? Inclusive identity and group values as the basis of the justice motive. *Journal of Experimental Social Psychology, 38,* 205–218.

INDEX